THE ART OF PERMANENCE

MATE SELECTION AND MARRIAGE IN A WORLD OF BROKENNESS

TIM SWICK

WESTBOW
PRESS®
A DIVISION OF THOMAS NELSON
& ZONDERVAN

THE HOLY BIBLE, NEW INTERNATIONAL VERSION®, NIV® Copyright © 1973, 1978, 1984, 2011 by Biblica, Inc.® Used by permission. All rights reserved worldwide.

This book is a work of non-fiction. Unless otherwise noted, the author and the publisher make no explicit guarantees as to the accuracy of the information contained in this book and in some cases, names of people and places have been altered to protect their privacy.

Credits
Cover Design: Shana Mason
Cover Photo: Haylee Ham
Editor: Debbie FitzSimmonds
Photos:
Carved Chain – William Solgerius
Boy with Sign - Katlin and Sean Wedding
Dad and the Bride - Katlin and Sean Wedding

WestBow Press books may be ordered through booksellers or by contacting:

WestBow Press
A Division of Thomas Nelson & Zondervan
1663 Liberty Drive
Bloomington, IN 47403
www.westbowpress.com
1 (866) 928-1240

Because of the dynamic nature of the Internet, any web addresses or links contained in this book may have changed since publication and may no longer be valid. The views expressed in this work are solely those of the author and do not necessarily reflect the views of the publisher, and the publisher hereby disclaims any responsibility for them.

Any people depicted in stock imagery provided by Thinkstock are models, and such images are being used for illustrative purposes only.
Certain stock imagery © Thinkstock.

ISBN: 978-1-5127-9799-2 (sc)
ISBN: 978-1-5127-9798-5 (hc)
ISBN: 978-1-5127-9800-5 (e)

Library of Congress Control Number: 2017912474

Print information available on the last page.

WestBow Press rev. date: 09/19/2017

CONTENTS

PART 4   THE ROLE OF SEX

PART 5   HUMAN BONDING

PART 6   FAITH DYNAMICS

PART 7   MARRIAGE

PREFACE

The research, study and experiences presented in this book can only begin to point us in the direction of understanding mate selection. There is very little if any research that begins to present a comprehensive understanding of how the mate selection choice and decision is made. For all that has ever been written about love, no one can adequately define it or present a sound theory as to how it takes place between two persons. There are no studies to present the validation of a couple's choice to get married. Research is not done over a couple's lifetime and therefore can only be validated in the few years of marital bliss for which a study may last. At best the evidence of the permanence of a marriage is anecdotal in the testimonies presented by the couple themselves.

On the other hand, enough research is being completed to begin to present a limited comprehension of the mate selection process. We are beginning to find some of the key factors which draw persons together to form relationships. There are only a few clues as to what may create permanence in a relationship. However, there is no comprehensive understanding of either mate selection or permanence in relationships. For Christians the best understanding of both mate selection and permanence comes from what is taught in the Bible. The Bible's method of authorship, spread over multiple centuries and multiple authors, provides it with the best historical credence in understanding mate selection, marriage, and permanence. The divine inspiration of the Bible's authorship profoundly qualifies its content and message as being the most trustworthy and definitive measure for evaluating all that we understand of mate selection, marriage, and permanence.

INTRODUCTION

The Need for Permanence

There seems to be an almost universal craving for permanence in relationships among people at any age. I asked a group of boys ages seven through nine if they wanted a permanent relationship with a woman as their wife when they grew up. The hands went up quickly indicating a desire for a permanent marriage in their future. Then I asked them if they knew how to get a really good woman as their future wife. Only a couple of hands went up, and a couple of reasonable suggestions were offered. I then told the boys that if they wanted a really good woman they had to become a really good man. I wonder how many parents are teaching their children that the secret to a permanent relationship, which lasts a lifetime, is to become a high quality person who honors Jesus.

Athletes train for decades to become the best in their area of excellence. They sacrifice many other aspects of life just to excel in one area. I frequently encounter parents who insist on their children getting good grades. Many also spend exorbitant amounts of time and money ensuring that their children have private lessons in sports, music, etc. Those parents who shine the most, in my opinion, are the ones who encourage their children to excel at Bible memorization. Those parents who deserve even more credit are those who teach their children to pray. Children are encouraged to excel in every aspect of life. Parents want their children to excel at being and having friends. They want them to excel at dating. They want their children to excel at marriage and as parents of their grandchildren.

They want their children to excel at occupations and in leadership of their communities. The smart parents want their children to excel at their relationship with Jesus over and above every other aspect of excellence in the children's lives.

Parents frequently convey to their children that the only criteria for success in mate selection and marriage are money and education. Parents convey the message that if their children are good wage earners and sufficiently educated, they will automatically secure high quality mates and live in permanent marriages. The only real training they provide their children is their own example from their own life and marriage. If these parents asked their children if they wanted a marriage that is like the one in which their parents are living, how many children would desire such a marriage? The current divorce rate should serve as a strong clue in answering this question.

The thing that confuses me is that parents want their children to excel in all these ways, but they give their children no specialized training, encouragement, or emphasis on preparing to be the kind of person who can secure a top quality mate and maintain a permanent lasting relationship. Until parents attach the same priority and urgency to providing their children with the skills to become the kind of person who will be a top quality mate, their success as a parent is highly questionable.

I know there are a lot of fine quality young adults. Many of them are my friends, and many of their parents are people whom I am proud to know. These young people make me proud to be associated with them, not because of what they have accomplished, but because of the outstanding character I see in their lives. Then there are the younger adults whom I read about in the newspaper, see on TV, or encounter in other places. Their lives are broken. Their multiple marriages are a bust. Their children are tyrants, and their pain is too great for them to bear. They see life as a series of parties, one night stands, and successive failures. They want no permanence in any relationships because all they have ever seen and encountered is failure and impermanence.

Many young adults today do not believe in permanence. They crave it with their whole hearts but they do not believe in it. To have permanence, you must have absolutes. You also must have a God who is unchanging, exclusive, and intolerant. To have permanence you must have values that do not change with the context. You also must be willing to completely expose yourself in intimacy with another person.

For those raised with a postmodern philosophy, the only God that has relevance to their lives must be totally tolerant. For them only a God who completely loves them without judging them can ever be a true God. They have no concept of justice because justice implies intolerance and moral absolutes. The current generation of young adults has experienced so much brokenness in family relationships and serial monogamy that they cannot believe in any kind of permanence. All they see around them and within their own lives is brokenness. Anyone who implies wholeness and safety has to be a false messiah.

As a result of the brokenness in which they live and through which they perceive society, they do not seek permanence. In their experience, everything breaks. Jobs will end and a new one will be found. They do not need to own a house, because homes break. People get scattered, and failed relationships hurt. The only way to protect oneself from the pain is to live without any expectation of any kind of permanence in any kind of relationship.

As a result of the rejection of permanence, they seek non-permanent relationships. The only safe relationships to them are devoid of emotion and intimacy. Sex is removed from a context of the permanency of marriage and reduced to multiple series of pleasure seeking events. When emotional intimacy is craved they move on to cohabitation or "living together." This is usually done on a trial basis with mostly an expectation of failure. At this point their ability to live in intimacy is destroyed by the constant disloyalty of their serial pleasure seeking events. As a result, emotional intimacy is hindered by both 1) the destruction of their ability to remain loyal and 2) the destruction of their ability to trust their partner's ability to remain loyal. Cohabitation relationships and marital relationships following cohabitation consistently demonstrate significantly higher rates of failure than marital relationships not preceded by cohabitation.

Marriage is based on a covenant between two partners with the expectation of permanence. It can be very difficult for couples to make the transition from the contractual test relationship of cohabitation, with an expectation of failure, to the covenant expectation of permanence and absolute loyalty which are necessary for marriage.

The failure of marriage then reinforces, for the newly broken couple and their peers, any belief in in-permanence and the pain of serial monogamous relationships. Without the examples of permanent marriages, wholeness in lives which are unbroken, and intimacy which trusts a partner enough to risk emotional pain and destruction, society will continue to perpetuate an age of brokenness.

The Church's Response

My question to the church is this: While you are spending all of your time feeding the poor, caring for the needy, ministering to the widows and the fatherless, evangelizing the unsaved, while you seek to clean up the messes in the broken lives that come through your doors, while you seek to counsel and console those with no hope, what are you doing to prevent the same self-destruction in the next generation? I see Christian leaders cry out for apologetics and truth for the next generation. I see churches creating parties and activities to attract youth to their churches. I also see churches who are challenging youth to be exceptional in their faithfulness to Jesus. What I do not see is churches teaching teenagers and young adults to be intimate with each other while maintaining sexual purity. I do not see churches teaching youth how to build the skills that will make them excellent mates and future parents. I do not see churches teaching youth and young adults how to find healing for the pains that are destroying their lives. I see churches teaching that God demands holiness, but I do not see them teaching that holiness is the most enjoyable and beneficial lifestyle – and, indeed, the only lifestyle -- which can and will bring permanence to all of your relationships including marriage.

The Research

Recent studies have clearly demonstrated the need for permanent marriages in our society and the key factors for making marriages more permanent (Wilcox & Cherlin, 2011). When you add a primary relationship with Jesus Christ as the center of the marriage and a faithful participation in spiritual disciplines such as Bible reading and prayer, the divorce rate for these Christian couples starts dropping to almost single digits.

PART 1

The Cave

Entrance to the Cave

Chapter 1
The Parable of the Cave

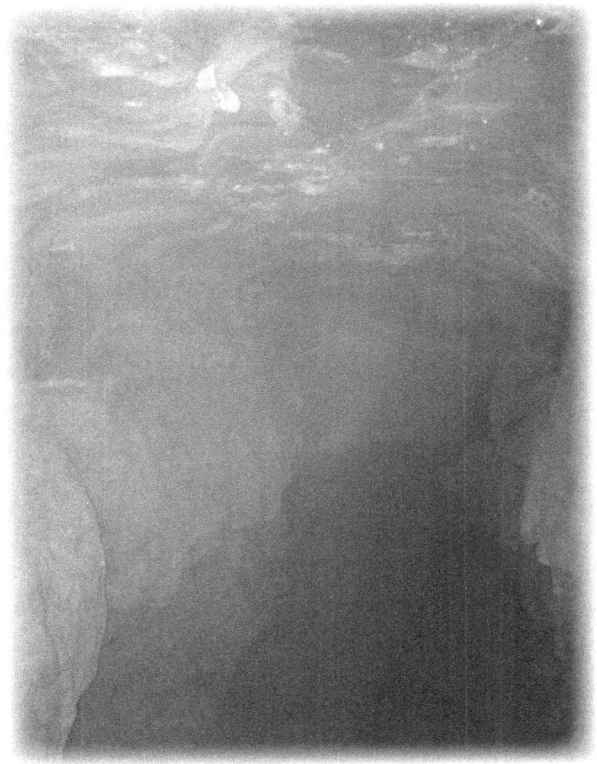

Inside the cave with no lights.

W hat would happen if you were trapped deep underground in a maze of caves and did not know the way out? What if the person leading you was the person with the only light in the cave? The only way out is to follow the voice of the leader and to stay close enough in proximity to see by his or her light. Can you imagine dying deep underground in this maze of caves with no light – lost and starving to death? What if the person leading you was a complete stranger and you did not know if you could trust that person?

When you think about it, the image of being lost in a maze of caves is much like mate selection. You are trying to find a way out of the isolation of your life. You want your life to be a success. You want your life to have meaning, and you want to make contributions which will have an impact on the people of this world. You want someone with whom to share your life, and you may also want the two of you to have children with whom to share your life.

Now think about this: Who in your life can offer you the best guidance and direction in finding a prospective mate, forming a successful relationship, and ultimately sealing the bond between you and your mate in marriage? Of the people you trust the most, how good are you at listening to them and taking their direction? Are you willing to stake your whole future and your choice of a mate on their guidance and instructions? How successful have you been in allowing them to direct and guide you in the past? What have been the results of following their directions? It would be much easier if you had an instruction manual. Do you actually follow directions when they are given to you? How completely do you follow those directions? Do you end up going with your own revised set of instructions instead of following the instructions to the last precise detail? Most of us have learned never to fully trust the instruction manuals or other people for directions and guidance. Frequently they offer beneficial assistance, but sometimes they are wrong. Also, most of us just prefer to do our own thing. Where can you get directions or an instruction manual for mate selection?

Think about it! Mate selection is the second most important decision we make in life. This decision determines whether our life will be blessed and full of joy or if it will be a painful calamity. If it is a calamity then it will bring disastrous effects on us, our mate, our children, our extended family, and our friends. Who is the person who can best guide us through this big decision? Now realize, we only follow directions of people we trust and we only trust people whom we have learned to follow. So, how are you going to listen to this person's guidance and direction if you have not learned to trust and follow this person in the past? Think about it. Jesus is God. He knows everything. He knows the people with whom you will be most compatible as possible mates. He can arrange your opportunities to meet these people. The only catch is that you must have learned to listen to him and to follow his directions. He can only bring you out of the cave if you follow Him. Otherwise, you have to find your own way out of the darkness.

The point is – the best preparation you can make for finding a mate is to learn to listen to and take directions from Jesus Christ. This takes years of practice and trust development.

Chapter 2

The Purpose of the Cave

The cave produces great beauty.

We are not made to be alone. If we look at young adulthood as a time of being lost and alone deep underground in a cave, this analogy provides an excellent insight into the emotions and mindset of the young adult age group.

In the book <u>The Cardinal in the Kremlin</u>, Tom Clancy describes a case where the KGB tortures a woman until she breaks, using sensory deprivation. Part of sensory deprivation is total isolation from all other people. (Clancy, 1988). We are not created to handle a sensory deprivation environment. We are not even created to handle isolation from other people. If we are to live in a cave deep underground with no hope of getting out, it will not take very long before most of us give up and die.

> The purpose of the cave (total isolation) is to teach us that we cannot live alone. This is why the young adult years are so painful.

Young adults know the peer group is no longer an acceptable substitute to provide the intimacy with other people. To magnify this issue, many of them have not learned to be comfortable in intimacy with either sex. They have friends, but they do not know how to get close to them.

They are also struggling with questions of the meaning and significance of their lives, and they do not know how to share their thoughts and questions with other people. When they want to be intimate they are scared to death to share the deepest and most personal questions of their lives, for which they have no answers. On some level they are also acutely aware that their closest friends are also struggling with the same questions and the same lack of answers. This conundrum between intimacy/isolation and one's purpose/significance in life produces a tension that drives young adults to seek solutions to both issues at the same time. The conundrum creates a blockage to pursuing the development of intimacy necessary for resolving the most crucial issues which they face in this period of life.

I believe this double struggle with purpose and intimacy occurs specifically at this point in life for two reasons. First, it drives the young adult to learn that the answer to one's purpose in life only comes with the development of an intimate relationship with God through faith in Jesus Christ. We are not created to live in isolation from either God or people. Second, it highlights and reinforces the understanding that we cannot live in intimacy with other people, and specifically a spouse, until we develop an intimate relationship with Jesus Christ. Only an intimate relationship with God, through the forgiveness of sins and faith in Jesus, enables us to acquire the healing for brokenness which is left by sin (and the psychological trauma induced by sin) in our lives.

Facing and overcoming the conundrum of purpose and isolation is the only solution for finding our way out of the cave. The experience of being lost and isolated in the cave, in the transition to adulthood, forms the environment which bashes the emotions and drives the young adult to develop intimacy with both God and other people.

I believe the current state of most of our academic institutions is the cruelest environment which we can foist upon our people in the young adult stage of life. The humanistic approach of the university says - not only do you have to develop the critical thinking ability to derive your own answers, but there are also no answers. The only answers to the questions you face in life are the answers which you create for yourself. If there are no answers why are students required to use critical thinking to create both the questions and the answers?

This humanism also denies that Jesus Christ even exists, let alone is someone with whom you can have an intimate relationship.

How to get out of the cave

Follow the Light

The primary criterion for determining your ability to listen to and follow the guidance of Jesus Christ in selecting a mate is your answer to the following question.

> *Is your God about your life? Or is*
> *your life about your God?*

In order to answer this question, you need to examine the following issues in your understanding of God. God only wants what is good and excellent for your life. He never desires to bring evil into your life. As long as you follow Him, He will always seek to bring good into your life. When you disobey Him, He will allow you to reap the consequences of your disobedience, because he will not violate your free will.

> *The only person who can correctly guide you to the best possible choice you can make in selecting a mate is Jesus Christ!*

If your God is not Jesus Christ, then you are too broken physically, mentally, socially, and spiritually to be properly prepared for marriage. You may end up making a good choice of a mate, but the odds are against your success. Even more, your ability to live in a long term successful marriage is very unlikely. The reason it is unlikely is because you do not have adequate quality of health, in all aspects of your being, to be capable of giving yourself in adequate intimacy, to develop a healthy and quality long term marriage. If you are a Christian but you are not living a fully surrendered life to Jesus, this statement will also equally apply to you. The primary criterion for mate selection as a Christian is that your life be about your God. When your life is truly focused on your relationship to Jesus Christ, your relationship with Him will, in and of itself, provide you with the preparation you need to be the kind of person who is capable of living in a long term relationship of intimacy with another person. I am not saying your marriage will be without struggle; I am just saying that only when your life is focused on Jesus Christ, are you able to open yourself to the level of personal development and healing, in all aspects of your life, which is necessary to make you into the kind of person capable of being a quality mate. This maturity and healing does not take place overnight. It takes years, and it continues throughout your life. Only as your life is properly focused on a commitment to Jesus Christ, will you be able to live a life that is about your God, and be capable of seeking a mate whose life is focused on his or her God. Only when both your life and your mate's lives are fully focused on Jesus Christ, are you capable of living in the highest quality of long term marriage relationship.

Let me ask you two questions: How are you going to have an intimate relationship with a mate if you cannot develop an intimate relationship with God? How are you going to develop an intimate relationship with God if you cannot develop and live in an intimate relationship with your mate? These two intimate relationships must go together if you are to live in a truly optimal marriage.

PART 2

God's Design

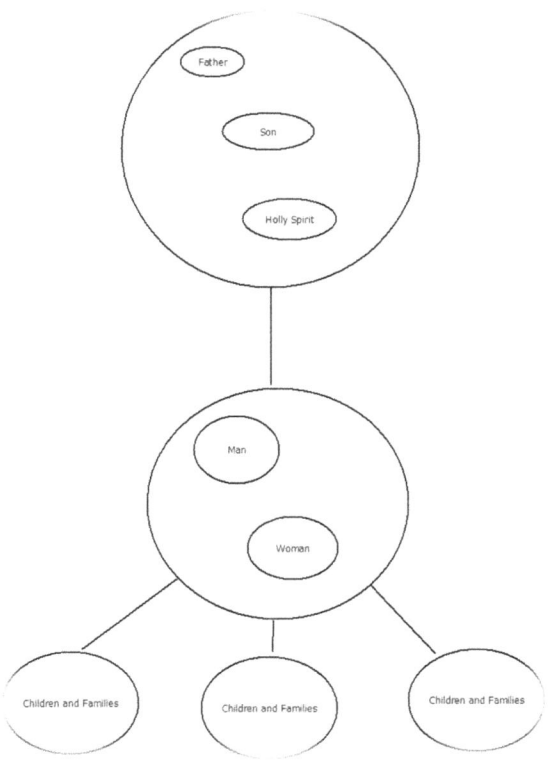

God's Design

Chapter 3

The Purpose of Mate Selection

The purpose of mate selection is to procure a mate with whom we can develop intimacy in a relationship which pushes us to develop a holiness of life which, in turn, prepares us for an eternal intimate relationship with God.

What is your purpose in mate selection? Does it match God's purpose in mate selection? If the purpose of mate selection deals as much with your eternal relationship with God as it does with your life, then your relationship with God and your relationship with your spouse will necessarily intertwine. This manner of intertwining relationships will be so profound that the quality of one relationship is dependent on the quality of the other relationship.

If intimacy with God is the purpose of mate selection, then we need to understand how we develop and come to excel at intimacy.

You can only live in intimacy with your mate to the extent that you have intimacy with God.

You can only live in intimacy with God to the extent you have intimacy with your mate.

Chapter 4

Understanding God's Design in the Stages of Life

Human Development

E very aspect of permanence in our lives starts with and depends on our proficient completion of Erickson's Stages of Life. These eight stages describe the human life cycle and the accomplishments most necessary for mature development of a person's personality and character at each stage.

We cannot begin to understand permanence and its role in our lives without equally understanding the aspects of permanence brought into our lives by each of Erickson's stages. The successful completion of each of these stages of life is critical to our development as human beings. Without the successful completion of each stage we fail to develop the aspects of character necessary to develop as a person and necessary to secure our desirability as a prospective mate.

Any time you find one of these stages insufficiently completed in a person's life, you know approximately at what age the person experienced brokenness and trauma in life. When a stage is incomplete, the person frequently will remain forever locked developmentally at that stage in life. He or she will be unable to complete the accomplishments of later stages until the trauma existing in the earlier stage is healed

The Individual Stages

Erickson's Infancy stage occurs between birth and age two. This stage deals with the need to develop trust. Failure to complete this stage will result in lifelong mistrust of everyone a person encounters in life. It also results in total inability to bond with other people. If trust is developed in this stage, a child gains hope and a positive outlook upon his or her world. The person who completes proper development in this stage will not only have trust toward parents, but will develop hope and expectancy for trust in all relationships.

Without trust the child becomes unrealistic, spoilt, and deluded. As an adult he or she will withdraw and become neurotic, depressed, and bound by fear.

The primary relationship in developing this trust is with the child's mother. If this relationship with the mother is broken, a child will have difficulty establishing trust, bonding, and developing the ability to function in relationships with other people. The only way to overcome this mistrust is to develop bonds with a mother figure that will heal the relationship that was broken in the early years of life. The distrust a child has of his or her mother results in a deep distrust of the church. Trust in a father is equally important as trust in a mother. Without developing trust in a father, it is very difficult for a person to trust men and especially to trust God in later years of life. The only way to overcome this mistrust is to develop bonds with a father figure that will heal the relationship that was broken in the early years of life. This lack of trust ultimately results in the child considering him or herself to be a mistake of creation which creates feelings of being rejected by God as a malformed, worthless mistake. For any person who has trust issues, it is a good assumption that the issues derive from a broken trust in the parental dynamics in the very earliest years of life.

This lack of trust cannot be overcome by marriage and will destroy all relationships including marriage. A person with trust issues in not capable of staying in a long term relationship without healing for the destruction of trust in the early years of life.

The **Early Childhood** stage occurs between two to three years of age. This stage deals with the need to develop autonomy. It is the stage when a child recognizes that he or she is distinct from other persons and from the world around him or her. A proper completion of this stage of life results in the development of will. It is the will to become and to exist autonomously from other individuals. It is the will to make one's own decisions and face one's own consequences rather than have decisions made by others. Also, at this stage the child develops a sense of will and determination that grows into a drive to achieve and accomplish later in life.

Failure to develop autonomy at this stage results in an inability to become responsible and accountable for one's own actions. Instead it results in an overwhelming sense of shame and doubt. The child feels that he or she is a non-person or non-entity. He or she is a mistake in this world. There is no self-value and therefore no value for others.

Without the development of will at this stage, the child always blames failure in his or her life on other people. The child can never accept personal responsibility for personal failure in his or her behavior and never develops a sense of personal achievement. Such a child will be reckless, inconsiderate, thoughtless and impulsive. As an adult the person will become self-limited, afraid of failure, and compulsive.

Without autonomy, a person is unable to come out of the peer group. Marriage may be strongly desired, but will be hampered by successive failures, infidelity, and desire for multiple relationships. This person's inconsideration and thoughtlessness will severely damage any and all relationships. This person will have difficulty maintaining a job and accomplishing adult responsibilities.

The **Play** stage occurs between three and five years of age. This stage deals with the need to develop initiative which will allow the child to accomplish tasks independently. With the accomplishment of this stage, the child begins to understand he or she has purpose in life and can contribute to society.

Failure to develop initiative results in guilt. The child realizes he or she is unable to accomplish what the parents expect and what other children freely demonstrate. Carrying this guilt, the child becomes unable to succeed in the simplest tasks. The child will go through life feeling he or she is a failure. This child will demonstrate behavior that is ruthless, exploitative, uncaring, and dispassionate. Eventually, the child becomes a person who is inhibited, unmotivated, slothful, and a parasite on society. The only way to overcome this guilt is to develop bonds with another family or family figure that will push the child to develop personal initiative and independent functioning in life. Only in the acceptance of personal initiative is the guilt destroyed so that the child goes on to become a self-motivated and fully functioning human being. Because the child has not developed independent initiative, there can be no understanding of a Christian community or family. The child will always consider him or herself as an outsider who is too guilty to be loved and accepted. Perhaps the greatest concern at this point is the overly protective family which encourages independence and then complains when the child takes the risk to become independent.

This person may marry but will lack the ability to fulfill adult spouse and parental roles. The person may have to be prodded and threatened instead of personally motivated to be proactive in caring for spouse and family.

The **School** stage occurs between ages six and twelve. This stage deals with the need to develop industry. At this age, independence ceases to be as much of a developmental concern as the ability to accomplish in groups and with other people. Here the child moves from play as his or her work, to work and accomplishment as his or her play. The child begins to thrive in accomplishment and recognition for accomplishment. This provides the child with a strong sense of competence so that he or she is willing to take on almost any task just to prove to him or herself that the goal can be accomplished.

Without success at developing industry the child develops a strong sense of inferiority. He or she is not able to accomplish what other children accomplish. Even worse he or she is not able to accomplish what adults accomplish. Therefore, he or she will never be able to become an adult. At this point the child may become forever locked in childhood. No matter how much his or her body grows up, he or she remains a person with childish attitudes and child-like behaviors. This stunted development results in an immature adult who cannot grow up. When the child completes the development of industry, the child gains a sense of competence. This sense of competence boosts the child's comfort with trying new things, succeeding at even more difficult accomplishments, and developing a love for work. The only way to overcome the sense of inferiority is to find a mentor or mentoring community that will push the child to complete tasks which build a sense of accomplishment in the child. The biggest issue is for the child to have a few adults who will praise any form of work the child accomplishes and encourage more. Because the child has such a strong sense of inferiority, there is the constant fear of rejection by the community and society. You cannot fit into a Christian community when you feel rejected by your school and society as a whole. The person who fails to develop industry may become a workaholic, obsessed with his or her own narrow minded self-righteousness. These feelings of inferiority may also be expressed as a laziness, apathy and purposelessness.

A marriage relationship with such a person would be consumed in the person's self-loathing. Feelings of inferiority and inability to perform in a manner worthy of love and acceptance as a spouse and parent would cloud and strangle the marital relationship.

The **Adolescence** stage occurs between ages twelve and eighteen. This stage deals with the need to develop identity. Here the child is concerned with the questions, "Who am I?" It is not so much the concern with "Do I matter?" but rather "Am I who I really want to be? Am I who I really think I am?" In the accomplishment of this stage the adolescent develops fidelity. This fidelity is not so much being faithful and loyal to others, as it is being faithful and loyal to one's self-identity.

It is the peer group which functions as an external locus of control for the adolescent. This peer-group function assists the adolescent to progress from dependence on parents and family for identity and morals, to dependence on self for identity and morals. In other words, the adolescent is seeking to gain independence as a functioning adult. In many ways it is the issue of locus of control that determines the adolescent's identity. Parents are an external locus of control. The peer-group is an external locus of control. Without a substitute locus of control for the parental figures, the child is unable to develop the internal locus of control necessary for maturity as an adult. The transition from an external locus of control to an internal locus of control determines who you are as you move from adolescence to adulthood.

The question "Who am I?" is only answered for the adolescent when he or she can finally say, "I control myself." When an adolescent develops the sense of identity derived from an internal locus of control, he or she also develops a sense of fidelity. This is the sense that says, "I like myself. I am happy with myself and I know who I am. Because I like myself, other people will be able to like me. Because I am in control of myself, I can be faithful to myself and to other people. I do not have to be subject to an external locus of control (peer group) that could compromise my fidelity and loyalty. Because I have achieved personal fidelity, I can begin a search for a mate, with whom to share my fidelity." Also with fidelity comes the ability to establish and maintain a relationship with God.

During this period the males will separate from their parents in order to secure autonomy. They measure their maturity by their independence from the parental family. The females will become more greatly connected to their parents and especially their mothers. For women their connectedness may be seen as immaturity, instead of the maturity it really demonstrates. In the midst of this process there is likely to develop a strong antagonism against the parent of the same gender until the process is completed in the early to mid-twenties. Adolescent males base their moral choices on what they perceive as an individual's rights. Adolescent females base their moral choices on what they feel will maintain connected relationships with other people.

The only way to overcome the sense of identity confusion is to find a model or hero that will push the adolescent to build an internal locus of control. Because the adolescent has such a strong sense of confusion, there is the constant fear of rejection by the peer group and leadership models. To be rejected by either of these is to lose all locus of control. You have no internal locus of control and you have no external locus of control. This means that you are out of control. As a result you are a danger to yourself and to others. Perhaps it is for this reason that there is such a high rate of suicide among teenagers.

Adolescence is one of the periods in a person's life when a person is most responsive to God. When an adolescent is grasping to transition his or her locus of control, a relationship with Jesus Christ seems to offer an ultimate locus of control. At this point a relationship with God is one of the most powerful relationships we can ever offer to any adolescent. Also, the most powerful concept we can ever offer to an adolescent is that Jesus Christ is an external locus of control who demands an internal locus of control in a relationship with God.

The failure to develop identity may result in a person feeling he or she is a self-important extremist. This person may become fanatical and confused in prioritizing personal and social values. In the extreme this person may repudiate society and relationships.

Marriage and faith in Jesus are the two relationships where a person finally completes his or her search for identity and fulfills the role of intimacy. For a person who has not achieved an understanding of his or her identity, marriage can be catastrophic. Instead of moving into intimacy, the person will likely demonstrate inappropriate boundaries, become fanatically possessive, and isolate self, spouse, and family from outside social relationships.

> *The most powerful concept we can ever offer to an adolescent is that Jesus Christ is an external locus of control who demands an internal locus of control in a relationship with God.*

The **Young Adult** stage occurs between ages nineteen and thirty-five. This stage deals with the need to develop intimacy. The intimacy accomplished in this stage is essential for lasting relationships with friends, God, self, and one's mate. Intimacy must occur on all of these levels for adequate accomplishment of the goal of this stage.

This is the period of seeking a lifelong mate. Now that the search for identity has been completed, there develops a desire for sharing intimacy with other people, both male and female, who will be lifelong friends and partners. Friendship partners are as important as sexual partners in having someone with whom to share intimacy. The intimacy is just not shared as deeply with non-sexual partners. It is this development of intimacy and respecting proper boundaries in intimacy that allow a person to develop working relationships with coworkers and social relationships with friends. This stage establishes the proper concepts of boundaries and intimacy that enable the relationships which provide the ultimate meaning of a person's life. If intimacy is successfully developed, the young adult is adequately prepared for developing loving relationships. Love cannot exist without intimacy and intimacy cannot exist without love.

Men are more focused on what is external and transcendent about their world and universe. For this reason men focus on their career. The career is the means to purchase what is necessary for the spouse and family to live. They will seek someone to mentor them through their career and other aspects of life. In the late twenties and early thirties, men change their life goals. Men often change careers and frequently also change spouses and mentors.

Women are more focused on what is internal and imminent about their world and universe. Therefore, women seek to develop intimacy with their spouse, family and close friends. The may give up all other goals in their lives to ensure the success of the intimacy they seek to develop. It is through this intimacy that they nurture their spouse and their children. It is these relationships which give meaning to their lives. Women also go through changes in life (usually a couple of years earlier than men), where they begin to focus more on developing themselves.

The only way to overcome the sense of isolation that becomes so prevalent without a life partner is to either find a life partner or to subsume that isolation in a relationship with God. Your church, your family, your friends, your coworkers and work environment all help to overcome any isolation in your life, but a solid and intimate relationship with Jesus is the only relationship which can adequately satisfy the isolation in your life.

The biggest challenge for the young adult is to find the healing for issues in his or her life that will enable him or her to bond with a life partner. Any time a person has not succeeded in bonding with a life partner, you can be confident that he or she is stuck in a prior stage of development that prevents success in the current stage of development. Because the young adult has such a strong sense of isolation, there is the constant fear of rejection by any partner. The more rejection experienced in the search for a life partner, the greater the sense of rejection by God. After all, if no one else likes me why should God like me?

The lack of development of intimacy frequently results in the inability to function in relationships. These people may become sexually needy and promiscuous, demonstrate an unhealthy vulnerability and sensitivity to criticism, and enforce self-isolation on their lives. They feel very isolated and become loners who appear self-contained and alone.

Marriage to these people is very difficult, as they become very self-destructive and susceptible to addictive behaviors. They frequently develop behaviors and practices that become bondages in their lives as they create substitutes for their lack of intimacy and enwrap their lives in self-isolation from friends and society.

> *Adolescence is one of the periods in a person's life when a person is most responsive to God. When an adolescent is grasping to transition his or her locus of control, a relationship with Jesus Christ seems to offer an ultimate locus of control. At this point a relationship with God is one of the most powerful relationships we can ever offer to any adolescent. Also, the most powerful concept we can ever offer to an adolescent is that Jesus Christ is an external locus of control who demands an internal locus of control in a relationship with God.*

The **Adulthood** stage occurs between ages thirty-five and sixty-five. This stage deals with the need to complete accomplishments which are passed on to younger generations. Generativity deals with the issue, "What will I pass on to succeeding generations?" This may be as simple as what a person desires to pass on to his or her children and grandchildren. It may also encompass what a person desires to leave as a legacy to the whole human race. What a person passes on is most frequently skills, knowledge, and wisdom. A generative person wants to know that he or she has taught someone how to be successful in life in at least the ways he or she has been successful. The accomplishments produced by a generative person are not just physical objects and relationships. They also include skills learned, life lessons, and values that a person considers critical for future generations to master.

At this point women move from caring for their families, spouse's and friends' needs to caring for their own needs. Men who have sacrificed family, spouse and friends for their careers now begin to develop the need to spend their time passing on love, care, values, skills, etc. to the people around them. It is this focus on generativity which frequently provides the cure for the so called midlife crisis. This midlife crisis may occur multiple times in the early stages of this generative period in life. During the generativity phase women develop their masculine side and men develop their feminine side.

Failure to complete this stage will result in stagnation. This stagnation is epitomized in a sense that the person is leaving no success and no legacy in life. It creates the feeling that life is passing the person by. He or she is a bystander watching as his or her own life amount to nothing and no one cares. Stagnation ultimately results in deep depression.

The only way to overcome the sense of stagnation is to have a spouse or other partner that will push the person to mentor other people and to find some task which will enable him or her to leave behind a mark of success on this world. Because the adult has such a strong sense of stagnation, there is the constant fear that life has no meaning and that he or she is alone in being the only person who will never leave a positive mark on the world. Ultimately this adult begins to feel rejected by God because there is no sense of accomplishment of anything that can be passed on to successive generations. The adult feels he or she has no worth before God.

The person who fails to properly develop generativity may become a do-gooder or meddling busybody. He or she frequently becomes over extended and stagnated. If the failure to develop generativity is not corrected, these people soon start rejecting society and relationships. They become disinterested and cynical.

The failure to develop generativity may contribute to later age divorces, as these people find themselves stagnated in their marriages, unwelcome in social circles, and self-isolated from social relationships.

The **Old Age** stage begins around age sixty-five. This stage deals with the need to develop integrity. Integrity is more than just integrity of character. It is the satisfaction of knowing that a person's life has had meaning and significance. It is the work of taking each aspect of a person's life and determining what significance is to be assigned to each of those aspects.

The failure to understand and to assign meaning to the aspects and accomplishments of a person's life results in deep despair and an ultimate sense of failure at being a person. The success of assigning meaning to all aspects of life results in great wisdom to be shared with family and friends about what has the greatest meaning and value in life.

At this stage elderly people seek to integrate their life as a whole and determine what has been the purpose of their life. It is this integration that now gives meaning to their life. In this process they prepare themselves and their families for their death. Frequently they will seek someone to assist them in accomplishing the things they consider incomplete in their life. This is the time to check off the things on their bucket list. This period answers the question, "What do I need to do before I die?"

The only way to overcome the sense of despair is to find that your life has meant something to the people around you. At this point wealth, possessions, and reputation mean nothing to the individual. Now, only relationships with other people matter. Only the adult who finally learns that it is his or her relationship with God, self and others which provides true significance in life can truly integrate his or her personality. Because the undeveloped adult has such a strong sense of dis-integration and lack of meaning in life, there is the sense that he or she has failed to be a human being and, subsequently, has failed the creator – God. On the other hand, if the integration is successful there is great joy at the success the person has made of his or her life and for his or her God.

The failure to develop integration may result in a person who is conceited, arrogant and presumptuous. These people frequently suffer from despair and seek a quick end to life or pray to die. They find that their lives have been miserable failures. They feel unfulfilled and blame everyone around them for hindering their pursuit of a life with meaning. These people are the ultimate failures at developing intimacy. Their narcissism destroys everything they have ever desired in life.

Chapter 5

The Critical Stages
for Mate Selection

There are two key stages of life in which most of the world's population make decisions about choosing a mate. These two primary stages are late adolescence and early adulthood. More selections of a mate are made in these periods than any other period of life. Let's begin by looking at these two particular stages of life in regards to mate selection.

The family in which you are raised is always the most critical human relationship in preparing you for mate selection. The peer group is perhaps the second most critical set of human relationships in preparing you for mate selection. In the peer group you begin to examine your identity in relationship to the other people in the world. You also begin your search for the significance of your position in the world and society in relationship to other people. The capability you develop in the peer group to be faithful and trustworthy in your relationships with your friends determines your ability to be faithful to a mate. In the peer group you form the locus of control of your life. You ultimately decide that you will be responsible for your own decisions and actions or that other forces and people outside of yourself will control your life.

As an adolescent, if you are not faithful to your friends then you will be excluded. If you are excluded, you will have no friends and you will be excluded not just by your select group of friends, but by all other groups of friends. You are judged as unworthy of relationships. As a result, all teenagers must prove their loyalty to the peer group in order to make the transition to adulthood.

When you are in the peer group you feel alone. This aloneness derives from the loss of self-individuation in the group. The peer group makes you feel safe, but you still feel alone. You are only defined by your group and not by who you are. Without the separation from the group there can be no intimacy. The group is not intimate because the group is one. There are no individuals in the group; there is only the group.

> *The greatest fear of the adolescent is to be ostracized.*

The peer group allows adolescents to progress out of their fear of being alone. In this process the peer group completes an even greater accomplishment in the life of the individual. The peer group enables the young adult to develop fidelity. Fidelity not only contains the aspect of loyalty; it also contains the aspect of faithfulness, of conformity to the original. This faithfulness is applied to both relationships and to standards of quality as in the duplication of an exact representation of an original.

In a peer group, an adolescent learns to be faithful to the group. This aspect of faithfulness is essential not only to friendships, marriage, and other aspects of human relationships, but is also essential in a person's relationship with God. It is not a stretch of the truth to say that without the peer group a teenager would never be capable of being faithful to a marriage, or to a relationship with God. The peer group is so critical to the development of the teenager that parents should beg their children to form these groups and to be faithful to them.

Fidelity not only implies loyalty, but it also contains the aspect of conformity to the original. High fidelity recordings are copies that strongly resemble original music and/or sounds. Adolescents develop fidelity as copies of their parents. If their parents are godly, they frequently prefer to become godly in their own approach to life.

The godly character and behavior of the peer group is also essential in our children's becoming godly adults. What is modeled for them is what they respond to as being normal.

> *It is not a stretch of the truth to say that without the peer group a teenager would never be capable of being faithful to a marriage or to a relationship with God.*

As adolescents transition into young adulthood, they have difficulty letting go of the peer group because they fear not only the loss of fidelity but also a resulting isolation. Young adults are desperate for relationships not because of the desire for intimacy and a mate, but because of the fear of isolation. They frequently rush into relationships because they cannot stand being alone. The question then becomes - how do adolescents make the transition to young adulthood?

Locus of Control

I believe that this transition to young adulthood is cemented in the formation of a dual locus of control in the person's personality. The main differentiation between adults and children is the development of an internal locus of control for one's life. The most important concept for late adolescents and early young adults in learning to grow out of the peer group is that of a dual locus of control. Our external locus of control is Jesus as our personal Lord and Savior. Jesus, as our external locus of control, demands we develop an internal locus of control. The internal locus of control which we must develop is taking responsibility for our own lives, our relationship with Jesus, and our relationships with other people. Maturing to adulthood puts us in the unique position of having a dual locus of control.

For a child to move through the teenage years, develop an internal locus of control, and become an adult require both a great transformation and a great transition. Both the transformation to adulthood and the transition through the teenage years are brought about through one of God's greatest gifts to the teenager –the peer group. The peer group provides the transitional media by which adolescents move from being controlled by their parents and authority figures to developing their own self-control and responsibility in their transformation to adulthood. If adolescents continue to live under the control of parents and authority figures, they can never become adults because they never develop an internal locus of control.

As adolescents develop they realize that in their early years parents and authority figures were their external locus of control. In their teenage years, they move to the peer group as their external locus of control. Most adolescents find it a slow and difficult process to develop an internal locus of control. For many young adults, their internal locus of control may be totally self-centered. This is easily seen in the focus on the acquisition of things that becomes one of the distinctive aspects of the late teen years and the young adult life.

The peer group, adults and authority figures all fail as an external locus of control. None of them are capable of being an appropriate external standard for guiding a person's life. The reason for this failure is simply that all humans are fallible. Teens have consistently seen that their parents and authority figures fail to consistently model moral, ethical, fair, and, especially, holy behavior. Because of this failure, they move themselves to the peer group as their external locus of control. At this point they soon determine that the peer group is even more fallible as an external locus of control than the adults in their lives. Their dilemma is that they know they cannot go backward to adolescence and they cannot go forward because they do not know who or what to go toward. This being stuck forces them to develop an internal locus of control as a mediator and guide in seeking a new external locus of control.

Those who do not find an adequate external locus of control in their progress to adulthood may remain stuck with an underdeveloped sense of moral values and a stunted growth into young adulthood. They may surround themselves with a new group of peers, both in personal life and in the workplace, who form a new locus of control for their lives instead of developing their own internal locus of control. Soon, this new locus of control becomes so integrated into their lives that they forget about seeking any other alternative. They proceed to live with the new external locus of control and allow their lives to be dictated and guided by this new peer group.

Some young adults who fail to develop an external locus of control develop a rigid legalism of external rules, morals and ethics in place of a person as their external locus of control. There are some who find a fate even worse than an inferior external locus of control. They continue to live with only an internal locus of control. As result, they develop a deep narcissism, where nothing matters except what they themselves desire. They deceive themselves into thinking there is no external locus of control and they seek to answer to no one, except to those forces which restrict their lives in manners which make it impractical to persist in their own narcissism. What actually happens is that by failing to develop an adequate internal locus of control, they allow each external event to become an individual locus of control. As a result they find their lives controlled and shaped by what is outside of themselves and outside of their control. Consequently, many of these people eventually find themselves in prison, or behaving as terrorists, because they are controlled by other events, things, and people who do not bring positive influences into their lives.

An adequate center of control is never found in a system of moral behavior, a set of laws, or in some simple objective answer. An adequate external locus of control can only be found in an intimate relationship with a supreme being.

For those who seek to find an adequate external center of control, the solution is simply a relationship with Jesus Christ. He is the only person and being who is moral, ethical, and holy. He is the only one who is capable of a personal intimate relationship with the person seeking an external center of control for his or her life. Interestingly, Jesus is an external locus of control who also demands the development of an internal locus of control in a person's life.

The danger of this developmental task lies in the failure to find an adequate relationship with the Supreme Being. Failing to develop adequate intimacy in one's relationship with the Supreme Being prevents the formation of a wholesome external center of control for our lives. It also prevents us from achieving proper levels of trust, both with Jesus and with other people (including our mate), which is not only essential to our lives, but also to enabling us to maintain an adequate internal center of control in our lives.

The Great Questions

In the teen years adolescents begin to ask themselves two important questions: "Who am I? What is my purpose in life?" The "who am I?" question is demonstrated in trying on different personas in an attempt to see what fits. It is the determination that nothing fits that enables adolescents to begin to figure out that each and every one of them is unique. The question "what is my purpose in life?" is demonstrated as adolescents begin to explore their talents and interests and seek to find direction towards an occupation in life.

The greatest struggle for teens lies in finding the answer to these two questions. Like everything else in life they believe the answer is simple. They believe the answer is a thing. What they are incapable of discerning is that the answers to these two questions are not things and they are not simple. The answer to these two questions can only be found in an intimate relationship with the only person who can be an adequate external center of control for their lives and who can enable them to be an adequate internal center of control for their lives. Only if they correctly develop both their external and internal centers of control in their lives will they ever achieve the correct answer to these two questions.

Therefore, I believe the most critical task of the adolescent's struggle in Identity vs Identity Confusion resulting in Fidelity is developing this dual locus of control over one's life. The focus of fidelity must be both the internal and external center of control of one's personal life. Only in a dual locus of control can a person develop fidelity to oneself which is necessary for developing fidelity in other relationships.

An inadequate locus of control, both internal and external, results in a performance based life. A performance based life in relationship to God is slightly different from a works-righteousness mentality. Works-righteousness is based on earning one's own salvation. Performance based relationship derives from deep feelings of inferiority and inadequacy. People seek to perform for God in hopes that they will be accepted by him. They hold both a conscious and subconscious hope that they can win God's approval and be of value to Him. They seek for affirmation of their value in all of their relationships based on what other people think of them. They believe that if they perform adequately that God and other people will approve of them. The belief in personal inadequacy usually derives from overly critical parents or guardians and their lack of intimacy with them.

Faithfulness to the Original

Besides loyalty, the other aspect of fidelity which a teenager must learn is faithfulness to the original. This encompasses both parents and God. Adolescents are learning who they are as individuals, while at the same time developing their own identity as faithful copies of their parents. They are taking the positive aspects of their parents' personalities and sometimes also the bad aspects and making those aspects a part of their own personalities. This is why an adolescent with a poor mother image will not trust church and will refuse to attend. This is why an adolescent with a poor father image will refuse to trust God and will have great difficulty in becoming a follower of Jesus Christ. At the same time they are also appropriating the aspects of God's holiness and character into their own being. Fidelity to the original demonstrates the critical importance of a teenager learning about God at this age.

As much as adolescents seek to differentiate themselves from their parents, they desperately desire for their parents and for other adults to approve of them, encourage them, and model for them the patterns of character and of behavior which they seek to develop in their own person. They also desire a relationship with their creator as a model for fidelity in imparting the aspects of God's holiness into their lives. Without the relationships with parents, adults, and Jesus, adolescents are left with inadequate models on which to base their faithfulness in reproducing the originals (character, morals, behaviors, intimacy, etc.) by which they must build their lives.

The greatest thing you can do for any adolescent is to provide an adequate model of fidelity to the original in your personal relationship with God, to which an adolescent can look as a model for reproducing in his or her own life. The easiest way to do this is simply to step into his or her life and to interact with the teenager. If you notice them, they will notice you. If you acknowledge and applaud their efforts, they will seek to emulate your example. It does not take much effort to radically transform a person's life. A simple statement, a simple word of direction or encouragement can set a person on a path that God wants for that person's life.

The difference between a man or woman of God and a rebellious hellion may be the few minutes you spend interacting with that person to create intimacy between you and the adolescent whom you befriend.

> *The difference between a man or woman of God and a rebellious hellion is the few minutes you spend interacting with that person to create intimacy between you and the person whom you befriend.*

The person who had the most far reaching impact on my life encountered me when I was in 8th grade. He was not a person who taught me much or who was capable of making me a disciple. But he was the person who came into my life at the right time and challenged me on the most foundational principles of the Christian life. He became my Sunday school teacher. He confronted me about asking Jesus into my life. He took me to church and led me to Jesus. After I became a Christian, he kept pushing me to read my Bible and to spend time in prayer every day. As a result, I took him up on the challenge. I started reading at least two chapters of the Bible a day. When I went to college, I took that same challenge a step further.

I started reading my Bible for an hour a day and praying for an hour and a half a day. Meeting that challenge built a foundation that over many years has made a radical difference in my life. You may not have a teenager in your family, but how are you challenging the ones whom you encounter in your church?

Fidelity Is a Relationship

Fidelity is learned in relationships. Adolescents learn in relationships. If what they are taught is not relational, it is of no practical use for them. Adolescents have no desire to learn non-relational theology. Theology, properly understood, is not a philosophy or a religion; it is a relationship. It is not that adolescents cannot understand a non-relational presentation of theology or appreciate it, but rather that it is not an effective way of presenting it because theology, when explained in terms which are non-relational, runs counter to the learning style appropriate for the adolescent. Any person who teaches a teenager in a non-relational manner will totally turn the teenager off and push the teenager away from God as he or she enters the pre-adult years of life. Therefore, we cannot expect adolescents to develop fidelity to God, or even to themselves and their friends, through non-relational presentations. Instead, adolescents will learn the most important aspects of fidelity in a relationship to Jesus, in a relationship to self, and in a relationship to other people through their relationship with the presenter of the message. To an adolescent, the relationship is <u>ALL</u> important. To learn fidelity to God, to friends, and to a future mate, adolescents have to be provided with rich relationships from non-parental adults of both sexes.

Adolescents need to learn to pray even more importantly than they need to learn to read their Bibles. God is a relational God and adolescents must learn to approach him on a relational level. Parents are relational beings and they need to approach their adolescent children on a relational level. If we model the right relationships with our adolescents, they will be comfortable in developing a prayer life that provides them with a strong relationship with God. Without prayer, they will not develop intimacy with God and they will be restricted in developing the relationship with the guide (Jesus) who can and will lead them throughout life.

The Role of Parents in Preparing Adolescents for Mate Selection

The most important thing an adolescent desire's is to be listened to, without hearing your opinion, your condemnation, or your criticism. Remember they are relying on the peer group. You must allow them to make this transition. Adolescents need to be informed that the transition to adulthood is very painful. The transition is painful to them because their friends in the peer group will be jealous and seek to wound them. It is painful to us as adults because we still want to protect them. We as parents must allow them to see that we understand how critical it is to them as adolescents to be independent of us and to know that we will support this transition.

Only if we listen to them in this manner will they allow us to still have input into their lives. Yes, they are going to make mistakes. It is critical for us to be there to catch them when they fall, and to help them to clean up their own mess. Do not clean up their mess for them. Just encourage them to clean the mess up for themselves instead of running away from it. Only if we treat adolescents in this manner, can we model a Jesus who will be relational with them for their entire life. Only in this way will they come to understand that God is not about rights and wrongs, but about relationships. He is about being their creator, father, friend, and lord. He wants to assist them in becoming even greater individuals than they themselves believe they can become. If an adolescent is taught to experience a daily relationship with God, through proper modeling by parents and other adults, he or she will learn more theology than a life of classroom talks can teach him or her.

Conveying Fidelity in Modeling for Mate Selection

So, how do we teach adolescents to date and select a mate? Just because adolescents are focused on the peer group for their transition to adulthood and resist adults' opinions and meddling in their lives does not mean that they do not value what you show them as models for them to emulate as they create fidelity in their lives.

First, I believe the most critical place to start is by modeling a relationship with God, one which stresses that intimacy with God is not only desirable but mandatory. A person will never have true intimacy with his or her mate unless they have true intimacy with God. Only a relationship with God and intimacy with him will force them to face themselves and deal with the issues in their own lives before attempting to face the issues in their mate or spouse.

Second, parents must model the fact that only God can heal the dysfunctional brokenness which people experience and feel most intensely in the adolescent years. For adolescents, life is like a bunch of pieces and parts that do not fit together. This stack of disjointed parts produces much pain and hopelessness in their lives. They do not understand that they are supposed to feel this way. It is just the discomfort of the assembly process as God enables them to put their lives together. Remember that it is the peer group which provides the supportive, caring environment in which a bunch of teenagers, whose lives are a bunch of disjoined and misfitting parts, find the relationships which enable them to assemble their own stack of pieces and parts. The parents who can speak comfortably and forthrightly about their own pain in the adolescent years (during those few moments in which their children will listen) provide the best model of assurance that God is making a person of wondrous beauty and value, one whose friendship and support their friends will treasure throughout life.

Third, the way to the greatest permanence in marriage is with a Christian mate. God is the one who brings permanence to relationships. He demands a permanent relationship with us which lasts forever. This is the whole point of the biblical concept of covenant. The parent who demonstrates permanent intimacy and love to an adolescent child models the greatest aspect of permanence in the universe. When you can make that uncomfortable bundle of disjointed pieces and parts feel that he or she is (second to Jesus) the most important and permanent relationship in your life, you build the hope for permanence. Remember an adolescent is a person who does not feel he or she is lovable today, let alone capable of feeling lovable for a permanent relationship in the future.

Fourth, adolescents should be encouraged to date. Dating should first be done in groups. Then, as adolescents age, individual dates should be allowed. In group dates, adolescents will learn fidelity and loyalty to the group and to the date. Parents need to model the feelings and fears they themselves faced and still face in risking relationships and starting new things in life. They need to express their own failures in relationships and the pain that came with those failures. They need to express also the successes and joys that came in some of those early relationships.

Fifth, parents need to model how to deal with the awkwardness and discomfort of talking with the opposite sex. Teenagers need to learn that talking to a boy or girl is no different and no more risky than the awkwardness of making a new friend. Parents need to model acceptance of rejection and the pain of crushes with unrequited love. Teenagers need to know that even adults develop crushes on other adults. It is normal and appropriate to develop crushes. For adults these crushes are normally extremely short lived. What is not appropriate is for either adults or adolescents to allow crushes to develop into inappropriate relationships. As parents properly model relationships with the opposite sex, adolescents will learn to be comfortable in talking with the opposite sex, and they will begin to form intimacy in their relationships. In their later years all of these learning factors will become more focused, and they will begin to discern what they do and do not want in a mate.

Sixth, in preparation for the dating process and during that process, adolescents should have modeled for them the importance of sexual purity as the key factor in maintaining their ability to develop intimacy in relationships. The example of the pain of crushes is a great example to a teenager of the pain of inappropriate aspects of intimacy and sex in a relationship. The development of intimacy, while maintaining sexual purity, is the key item necessary for couples to live in permanence once they enter marriage. When sexual purity is destroyed, the potential for permanence is destroyed. Sexual impurity brings brokenness. It destroys intimacy. It destroys families, relationships and marriages. It is the greatest enemy to everything a teenager seeks in life. Sex inside of marriage is a great blessing. Sex outside of marriage leaves both yourself and your partner broken and destroyed. This destruction impacts not only your present but your distant future. It destroys the potential for intimacy and permanence in the future. It will destroy not only your personal life, but will also profoundly and negatively impact the lives of both your spouse and your children in the future. It will also have strongly negative effects on your sexual partner's spouse and children in the future. The question becomes – how much are you willing to negatively impact the lives of your future family and the lives of your sexual partner's future family for a few minutes of sexual pleasure?

The parent who has always been appropriate in intimacy, sexually pure and permanently faithful provides an excellent model for his or her children. The parent who admits failures in these areas also provides a model for adolescents when they are appropriately presented and explained as models of how not to live.

Seventh, God is the only person who can guide you in mate selection. He is your greatest resource for making a proper and wise choice and not destroying your future with a bad choice. If you sincerely ask God to tell you whom you are to marry, He will tell you! He is not likely to tell you before you actually meet that person, but He will tell you when the time is right for you to know.

The parent who models seeking Jesus' guidance and leadership provides the greatest model of all for an adolescent. This is the model which builds hope and faith in the future and the possibility of permanence in future mate selection and marriage. This is also the model which teaches that there is a God who is assisting him or her in putting together all the pieces and parts to make one into a person of quality and holiness. Jesus can and will enable a person to become not only someone who is comfortable with the fit and assembly of those disjointed pieces and parts, but also someone who is delighted with who he or she has become and the beauty that they are enabled to bring into other people's lives.

The model you as a parent set for your children, more than any other factor, will impact either positively or negatively the permanence your children find in their future relationships and marriages. In the following chapters we will look at some of the key concepts which are necessary for building the fidelity to the original plans and patterns necessary for permanence in the relationships of life and marriage.

Foundations for the Development of Intimacy in Young Adults

The stage of Young Adulthood ranges in age from nineteen to thirty five. Erickson determined that the main accomplishment for persons in this stage of life is the development of intimacy with people of both sexes. Failure to excel at the ability to become intimate with other people leads to isolation throughout the person's life. With the achievement of intimacy comes the ability to love other people, to love God, and especially to love your chosen mate.

The transition from adolescence, with its raging hormones, to young adulthood gives way to a very personal emotional crisis. This crisis involves many aspects, but the strongest aspect revolves around love and acceptance. Can I be loved by another person? Will I be loved by a spouse? Will I have friends that love me and care about me? As teens' transition from the peer group completes, there is still a deep need for friends and colleagues who accept them and stand by them. This need for friends continues for the rest of life. The friends who are in our inner circle change throughout life, but there are always new friends, and it is our responsibility to touch their lives, care for them, and minister to them.

The greatest fear of young adults is isolation!

Validation of Truth:

Due to the young adults maturing out of the peer group, the young adult years begin with an inner desire to know truth and to know how to discern truth. Young adults do not want a philosophical understanding of truth. They want an inner truth detection system that will enable them to distinguish what is real from what is imaginary. They want to know what constitutes truth. Only in knowing what constitutes truth can they begin to deal with the other foundational issues in this period of life. All of the developmental aspects which they face in this stage of life hinge on this one issue. They can only know their success in accomplishing each aspect of this stage of life to the degree that they are able to discern truth. The knowledge and understanding of truth may not be completed in this stage, but the desire and drive to seek and know truth is critical in ascertaining the validity of all the other issues which they seek to resolve at this stage of life. The modern secular persuasion that a person cannot know truth because truth is relative is foundationally destructive in this period of life. If you cannot know truth, then you cannot know God. You cannot know your purpose in life. You cannot know yourself and you cannot know anyone whom you would choose for a spouse. How can you choose a spouse if you cannot know truth about the most critical decisions which you make in your life?

The need to establish the validity of truth has two aspects which strongly influence a young adult's quest for intimacy:

Personal feelings: In the early years of young adulthood, there is an underlying tension in a person's development as he or she seeks to comprehend the validity of personal feelings. One aspect of this issue is attempting to understand the nature of one's true personal feelings. Are these feelings real or are they a delusion? Can I trust my feelings? How much can I rely on my feelings as a guide to truth in in my relationships and my development of intimacy in relationships? What is the balance between my feelings and my reason? Which one, reason or feelings, do I rely on in which situation or circumstance? Can I rely on both feelings and reason? Is this combination a trustworthy guide for me to follow?

Trust in relationships: Who can I trust and how much can I trust this person? Trust is highly dependent on a person's personal feelings and on a person's ability to validate truth. Personal feelings determine how much a person wants to pursue a relationship with another person, and how much a person will allow another person to pursue a relationship with oneself. In answering the questions arising from the need to trust another person in a relationship, the ability to validate the truth of one's own feelings, reason, and desires becomes critical.

Purpose and Place:

Young adults also continue the quest to understand their purpose in life and place in the world. There are two prime aspects of the pursuit of purpose and place that can work against the young adult's proficiency in preparing for marriage: the desire to be productive and the desire to acquire things. Like most things in life, these two desires have both positive and negative aspects; it is just the nature of the stage in life which each person must navigate. Most of us tend to pursue both the negative and positives at the same time. I am not trying to indicate that young adult choices are right or wrong. Instead, I am trying to say that these are common behaviors and choices for the young adult stage of life. As such, we need to expect these behaviors and choices to have both potentially positive and negative impacts on the young adult's life.

As parents and older adults, it is extremely important that we understand the motivations for choices and behaviors. We must respond with compassion and silence that allows the young adult to grow through both bad and good choices at the person's own pace. We can offer guidance and maybe a few words of caution, but we have to allow him or her to make their own mistakes. After all, we did not get to be extremely wise and seasoned adults without encountering our own bruises and scars from the decisions we made in our early adult stage of life.

As stated, there are two key factors in determining one's purpose and place in life:

Productiveness: Young adults are very highly motivated to prove that they can be productive. For this reason they tend to be highly sensitive to criticism. Also, they are not easily mentored. They want to prove that as adults they are proficient at whatever they set out to accomplish. The ability to "proficiently accomplish" is a significant aspect of their quest to find purpose and place in life. This is also one of the reasons that they are resistant to input from other adults about whom they date and/or marry.

Acquisition: Young adults are heavily oriented to acquisition. This flows from the drive to start adult life with the material items considered essential for equipping a home and family. This acquisition phase also tends to prod young adults to seek to acquire "toys and trinkets" which they believe will give them a sense of their place in the world. The problem comes when "toys and trinkets" take priority over the need to acquire and prepare a home for a spouse and family. It is even more difficult for them to be motivated to prepare a home and family when they have not yet acquired a spouse. As a result, they are frequently poorly prepared when the time comes to enter a marriage and start a home together. The choices made in seeking acquisitions are even more critical when they impact the couple's ability to prepare for and care for newly arriving children in the family.

Young adults only find purpose in life as they form intimate relationships with a spouse and the other friends and family around them. Even more critically they only find their personal purpose in life as they develop a relationship with God and learn to seek His guidance in the day to day aspects of their lives. Young adults only find their place in life as they combine the aspects of intimacy formed in marriage, family, friendship, and other relationships with their day to day walk with Jesus. It is Jesus and Jesus alone, who alone pulls together the aspects of our lives which give us His perspective of our place in His world. Out of the understanding of purpose comes Identity.

Chapter 6

Understanding Intimacy

Intimacy: The Foundation to All Relationships

I ntimacy can only occur if we adequately achieve the goals of each of the previous stages of life.

Only if we develop <u>trust</u> can we hold and maintain *hope* for a future. Without hope for a future we are not capable of maintaining intimacy and developing marital purity. Only if we develop <u>autonomy</u> and the freedom from shame that it brings can we develop the *will* to be persistent in our pursuit of intimacy in all our significant relationships. Only if we develop <u>initiative</u> can we be free from failure and gain the *purpose* in life to seek the depth of intimacy that sustains a marriage throughout a lifetime. Only if we develop <u>identity</u> can we develop the *fidelity* to remain faithful to a mate and to protect the intimacy necessary for sustaining a marriage. Only if we develop <u>intimacy</u> can we develop the kind of *love* that maintains the bonds of marriage and relationships forever.

As long as adolescents are in the peer group, they lack a wholesome sense of self. If there is no me (but only the peer group – the Borg, the collective), then I cannot be an individual person. Intimacy requires the differentiation of the self from the collective – peer group. As adolescents come out of the peer group they begin to seek intimacy. The bonds of group fidelity are no longer sufficient as the foundation of relationships. (Borg is a term from *Star Trek: The Next Generation* describing a collective of individuals united into a cybernetic entity.)

Young Adulthood is the stage of life wherein men and women learn relational intimacy. Intimacy is a factor of closeness in a relationship which we experience all through life. As such it is a factor which we must not only learn to receive but also to express. Our intimacy in relationships with other human beings and in our relationship with God is simultaneously intertwined. As we develop intimacy on the human level, we also develop our capability to express and experience intimacy on the divine level. As we develop our intimacy with Jesus on the divine level, we also enhance our capability to express and experience intimacy on the human level. Whether we focus on developing our ability to express and experience intimacy on the human or divine level does not matter. The development of intimacy on one level, human or divine, also develops our ability for intimacy on the other level.

I consider the development of intimacy with Jesus as the most important preparation for mate selection and preparation for intimacy with other persons. When we develop intimacy with Jesus we also develop a trust in Him to protect us. This is not just physical protection, but protection through His divine wisdom and foreknowledge. It is a trust in His ability to know what is best for us, no matter how painful His will is for us at the present time.

When we come to the point where we are willing to accept what God brings into our lives no matter how painful those events and circumstances may be, it enables us to endure the pain of broken relationships, ended dreams, relational rejections, and failed crushes. It enables us to trust Jesus to bring about whatever is best for our lives in the future regardless of the pain of the present. This unfailing trust in Jesus to bring about what is best for our lives builds in us the capacity to trust and develop intimacy to a far greater extent just because we know Jesus will pull us through no matter how much pain we should have to endure if the relationship fails.

If people do not develop the ability to be intimate in relationships, they never become prepared for marriage. As a result, they are also incapable of developing an intimate relationship with God.

> *If the church really did its job, it would teach young adults to maintain sexual purity while at the same time developing intimate relationships with both sexes. For this age group the key to effective evangelism is a pro-relationship message that focuses on developing intimacy with friends, and eventually a mate, while maintaining sexual purity.*
>
> *The most important message for this age group is that the extent of your intimacy with a potential mate is not only correspondent to, but dependent on your intimacy with Jesus. Your greatest capacity for intimacy with other people is an outgrowth of intimacy developed in your personal relationship with God. When is the last time you saw a church that focused their young adult's ministry on developing intimacy in relationships?*
>
> *The greatest ministry a church can have with young adults is to teach them to develop intimacy in their relationships while maintaining sexual purity before marriage. Both the aspect of intimacy in relationships and the aspect of sexual purity outside of marriage have to go together.*
>
> *Here is the reason the church's message on sexual purity has failed. The church has consistently maintained that intimacy and sexual purity can only exist if they are separated before marriage.*
>
> *Until the church proclaims the message that intimacy and sexual purity must exist in unison, the church's message has no relevance to the young adult.*

Definition of Intimacy

In recent research intimacy is portrayed as having multiple themes. The themes of intimacy are commitment, affective intimacy, cognitive intimacy, physical intimacy, and mutuality (Moss & Schwebel, 1993). Other research has compartmentalized intimacy into four different aspects: physical, emotional, cognitive, and experiential (Wikipedia, Intimate Relationship, 2015).

Intimacy is the creation of a shared sacred space between individuals that is built upon mutual respect and care. Intimacy is made when you can share your individual experiences with another who listens and honors your experience. It also comes from having shared experiences in which you give and receive support to each other. Intimacy can be equally founded upon sharing pleasure or sharing adversity (Scherer & Kemp, 2015). Intimacy is the shared depth and closeness of a relationship we hold with another person or group of people. It is expressed in all aspects and levels of the relationship, from spiritual intimacy to physical intimacy.

Intimacy is a most crucial aspect of any relationship. It is that aspect which we most crave and prize in our connections with other people. We know intimacy when we see it. We love it when we experience it. Just do not ask us to define it. The best definitions of intimacy describe a relationship in which there is both revelation and knowledge/understanding shared between two people through both emotive and physical aspects. I believe the most common agreement as to the definition of intimacy would stress that it is the strongest bond expressed between two people when they develop aspects of a relationship which go beyond mutual friendship and they develop an affinity for each other which involves aspects of true love.

Intimacy involves every aspect of our being. God created sex. He knows what He wants it to accomplish in a couple's life together. Sex is not dirty. However, sex in and of itself is not intimacy. Instead sex is meant to be a celebration of holiness and relational integrity. It's purpose is to celebrate the health and wholeness within a relationship, which has been nourished in intimacy. It is an expression of joy and reverence for God as a couple express to each other, the love they have created in their relationship together. The development of intimacy results in an outpouring of love from one partner to the other. That love pours from the couple to all those around them.

Secular Concept of Intimacy

The secular understanding of intimacy expresses the following concepts.

Behavioral Activities Which Promote Intimacy
Self-disclosures
Emotional expressiveness
Unconditional support
Physical contact
Trust
Sexual contact
Sharing activities
(Monsour, 2013)

Recent research indicates that intimacy is expressed and shared in various methods ranging from physical contact to emotional support to expressing trust. In this list we see the most frequently stated methods of sharing intimacy between young adults. Christians would most likely add corporate and private aspects of worship and prayer to the list of methods for sharing intimacy. Intimacy is not limited to relationships between humans. It can also include relationships with pets and with God. (Monsour, 2013).

We need to understand that intimacy cannot be manufactured. Intimacy is not something we can perform or experience on demand. It must be spontaneous.

➢ Setting a goal for intimacy results in a more elusive attainment of intimacy.
➢ The core ingredient for intimacy is trust wrapped in self disclosure.
➢ Intimacy must elicit the response of empathy.
➢ Intimacy flows from relationships which provide caregiving, communication, joint problem solving, and mutuality.

These four factors must emerge in sequence for the strongest impact of intimacy to occur and be maintained. (Wynne & Wynne, 1986).

Another secular presentation of intimacy expresses these five levels of intimacy.

Five levels of Social Intimacy

Safe Communication
Others' Opinions and Beliefs
Personal Opinions and Beliefs
My Feelings and Experiences
My Needs, Emotions and Desires
(Wilson, 2013)

Let's examine these five levels more closely.

1. In the safe communication level we exchange information without emotional commitment and without fear of rejection. This is the level of interaction among strangers whom we encounter in public interaction.
2. At the second level of sharing others' opinions or beliefs, we state opinions expressed by other people which may or may not reflect our own opinions. In this exchange we risk no personal exposure because we do not make known what we ourselves believe.
3. At the next level, that of sharing personal opinions or beliefs, we begin to risk sharing those personal beliefs which we consider to be inconsequential in our relationship with the other person. At this point we can always rescind our opinion if the other person takes objection to our belief.
4. When we get to the point where we begin to share our feelings and experiences, we begin to make ourselves vulnerable to the other person or persons. This is usually a very limited exposure of our selves. At this point we may get hurt if we are rejected, but it is a limited hurt with which we can live.

5. The last level is that of sharing our needs, emotions and desires. At this point we are letting other person(s) see the real us. We are giving of ourselves and trusting the other person(s) not to reject us. If we are rejected at this point, there is nothing we can do but accept the rejection or try to minimize the rejection. This is the level of intimacy we save for family and friends with whom we want to share our lives.

This perspective is severely limited in that it focuses only on self. It does not consider the needs and desires of the other person with whom one becomes intimate. I would like to remind you that regardless of your definition of and perspective on intimacy, a couple's experience of intimacy is dependent on both persons' ability to mutually progress through the stages of intimacy at the same rate. Either person moving at a different rate from the other person will impede the development of the relationship. For this reason *the level of intimacy should always be measured at the weakest point.*

Intimacy as a Developmental Role

As we have seen, according to Erickson, the developmental role of young adults is intimacy. When and if the foundational stages (developing the capacity to become emotionally and psychologically intimate with other people) have been accomplished, then the young adult will form relationships which will naturally build intimacy between friends and prospective mates. If young adults do not develop the ability to be intimate in relationships with other people of both sexes, they never become prepared for marriage, and they are incapable of developing an intimate relationship with God.

The speed at which one is able to become intimate with another person depends on both parties' capacity for intimacy and ability to establish trust with each other. This also depends on the amount of emotional pain and trauma each party has experienced in life.

Ephesians 5:33 is very clear that the key factor for intimacy for males in a marital relationship is respect, and for females it is feeling loved. For this reason, males will experience the greatest intimacy in a relationship when **respect** for their position within society and within the family, along with their personal accomplishments, is demonstrated. Females will thrive in a relationship where a **context of love** is built around them. From this perspective we can see that males and females experience intimacy in relationships in two very distinct and separate manners.

For males the key factor in intimacy is respect. The more a man feels and perceives that he is respected by his peers and mate, the greater his capacity for intimacy in the relationship. When a man feels disrespected, he becomes very emotional. This emotion is seldom demonstrated in tears. Rather it is demonstrated in anger. When conflict arises a woman wants to control her environment and everyone within that environment. This causes a man to feel that his judgement is disrespected. This is one of the greatest pains a man experiences in relational difficulties. It is also probably the most persistent wound which women inflict on their mates. This is especially prevalent in differences of opinion about both major and minor decisions. I am not saying that a woman should not express her opinion or always give in to the man's decision. I am saying that it is critical for a woman to understand his perspective and reasoning before outright rejecting the man's decision or steamrolling over his opinion. Men also like to figure things out for themselves. A man may not have the ability or knowledge to accomplish a specific task, but he wants the opportunity to try regardless of whether he succeeds or fails. This task of figuring things out for himself is frequently displayed in driving without asking for directions. Which is more important, not getting lost or showing respect for his efforts? Which one of these two is going to build your relationship?

Most men also do not need to be reminded about household tasks and projects. They just have different priorities. Men frequently think through the priority of their tasks and they desire to accomplish those tasks in a specific order. Disrupting that order is understood by them as disrespect. They also need time to determine the exact approach to a task which they wish to undertake. They will be doing research without telling anyone. This frequently results in women thinking they are just procrastinating. It is not the size of the job that requires the most research. It is the desire to do the job right the first time. This is especially critical in an area where a man has little or no experience.

Without respect males shut down and close off their emotions in anticipation of wounds and pain to follow. Few women realize how very fragile the male ego is. Much of a woman's power with a man lies in this very fact that he is afraid of losing the respect of the woman he loves. (Feldhahn, 2004, pp 21-52).

For females the key factor in intimacy is feeling loved. Women's psychology differs from males in that women live in a social context of mutual support and caring. Their world is cooperative and supportive as opposed to the competitive world of males. Therefore, in order to feel loved, a female must know that she is supported in whatever she does or decides. She must feel that she is in a mutual and cooperative relationship with her spouse and other people. For this reason the man must always seek to make his mate perceive, feel, and be convinced that they are working together as a couple for common goals and aspirations in the relationship. A woman wants to know that what a man does for her and says to her is an expression of his love for her. She wants a safe, secure environment where she is protected and where warmth and romance are placed before her. She wants to be held and touched in a manner that makes her feel loved and secure. She wants to be provided for, not with extravagance, but with the sense that she is of more worth to the man that anything else in life. She wants to know that she is desired above all other women.

We also need to remember that Intimacy Requires Our Whole Being. Intimacy is expressed in all aspects of our being and personality. These include Personal, Emotional/Psychological, Social, Spiritual, and Physical aspects of the relationship.

Complete intimacy requires the personal integration of personality with no compartmentalization. Compartmentalized personalities separate specific aspects of personality so that they can behave in different manners in different social settings. Because the personality is compartmentalized, the person has no issue with being immoral or unethical in one instance and then presenting himself or herself as possessing high morals and ethics in a different social setting. Only a person who has fully integrated his or her personality can allow another person to see the complete and real personality he or she possesses. Therefore, intimacy begins with the wholly integrated individual. Only a fully integrated person can experience full and complete intimacy with himself or herself, and hence with others.

Intimacy Development and Character Formation

We have both positive and negative character traits. Hopefully we have very few negative character traits. Our negative character traits destroy our intimacy in relationships. Character is frequently defined as the attitudes you express and behaviors you perform when you have no audience other than yourself. In other words our real character is what we display to ourselves. It is our real character which has the most impact on our capacity for intimacy and for healthy relationships with those around us. Negative character traits destroy our capacity for intimacy and may eventually destroy our most precious relationships. Therefore our character is one of the most important aspects of our personality which must be positively developed.

The attempts to adequately define character, in my opinion, have mostly failed. The definitions which have been presented over the centuries are inadequate. (Vessels & Huitt, 2005; Nucci, 1997; Homiak, 2003). Secular definitions fail in their presentation of an understanding of the true nature of character and how that character is manifest in a person's life. Though secular definitions understand character as traits or attributes of a person's personality they do not specify from where these traits originate and they do not specify how these traits are formed. They also do not specify that each trait has an opposite. It is the lack of acknowledgement of the existence of both the positive and negative - or opposite character traits - and the factors that cause them which make most of the definitions of character deficient.

The attempts to understand character fail even more spectacularly when they are examined in the light of personal traits most praised by God in the Bible. The Bible only praises positive character traits. It explains the origins of both positive and negative character traits. The Bible teaches that God creates everything including the potential for both good and evil (Isaiah 45:7). It teaches that the positive traits of our character originate in the nature of God Himself.

From a psychological perspective, the accomplishment of Erickson's stages comprise the formative aspects which are necessary to create in us the character necessary for intimacy. The question then becomes how do we develop our character? In my opinion, our character is formed as we progress through each of Erickson's stages. The resultant desirable outcome of each stage is an aspect of character which must exist in us if we are to be considered persons of high character. This development of our character is a lifelong process. We never fully develop our character in this life.

Let us examine what happens in our lives if we do not develop the appropriate character for intimacy.

1. Without hope we will not pursue intimacy with another person. We will not desire relationships. Instead we will live in great fear of more brokenness and rejection in our lives.

2. Without self-individuation we tend to present ourselves as a part of another person's personality. In other words we are like Jello, conforming to whatever shape and mold we perceive our friend, family, partner, or mate desires for us to reflect. We think we are pleasing or complimenting the other person, or we are seeking acceptance by the other person. Instead we are frightening the other person because that person sees us as attempting to be an extension of his or her self.

3. Without purpose we are adrift. We have no direction and no goal. Another person will not seek to align his or her life with us because he or she cannot see where we are going.

4. Without competence we do not have the skills to form successful relationships. We end up creating confusion and havoc in our relationships with another person.
5. Without fidelity we are not capable of staying in a relationship. We flee at the earliest sign of trouble instead of fighting for the relationship to succeed. We have no friends because we are incapable of being a friend.
6. Without love, we are incapable of loving. We have nothing to give to the relationship. We consider ourselves unworthy to be loved, and we fear rejection.
7. Without care we are incapable of investing our lives in other people's lives. We will fail at being parents and at being a spouse. Our lives will become self-centered. As a result we will drive people away from us.
8. Without wisdom our lives lack meaning. We hold no value to ourselves or to anyone else. We do not understand others, and we are not understood by others. We are not even understood by ourselves.

The completion of each of these aspects of character provides us with adequate character development to thrive at each stage of our life. These character traits also provide the foundation for developing social, cognitive, physical, and other skills necessary for our success in life. It is only with the development of these aspects of character that we are adequately prepared to form the relationships necessary for social interactions, and the quality intimacy which we desire in our relationship with Jesus and with the people most important to us in life.

Relevance of Character to Intimacy

Character is comprised of two things: 1. An integration of the personality that eliminates compartmentalization and disassociation. 2. Personal holiness that integrates a person into a relationship with

God. The Bible calls this holiness (Make every effort to live in peace with everyone and to be holy; without holiness no one will see the Lord - Hebrews 12:14 NIV). This integration of our personality and of our relationships is then behaviorally displayed in various traits, which we normally refer to as character or character traits. These traits are well expressed in the fruits of the Spirit listed in Galatians 5:22-23. Many other character traits are listed in other biblical passages.

Character and holiness are closely related. As I grow as a Christian and seek to walk with God, I am gaining some new insight. I used to think holiness was just getting rid of the sin in my life in a manner that brought purity to my life. The presentations of holiness which were presented to me seemed to always be performance based: The Christian life is about living your life for God not what God can do for you. Now read this statement again carefully; in performance based Christianity holiness is based on what you do. It is not based on what you allow Jesus to do in changing your life, and it is not based on walking with Jesus each and every day of your life.

I am coming to a new appreciation of holiness. As I read the Old and New Testaments, the most critical aspect of any nation's or any person's life is permanence in their relationship with God. This permanence can only exist where there is holiness in people's relationship with God. Only in the context of permanence can intimacy grow in a relationship. This is why people date and marry. They want both intimacy and the permanence that corresponds to it in relationships. Only by growing in intimacy do we continue a context of permanence.

Getting rid of sin in our lives is important. Having purity in our lives is important. Holiness involves both of these. What many people fail to realize is that holiness can only exist in a relationship. Theoretically, a person can be perfect with regards to having no sin and being totally pure, and still not have holiness of life. Look at the model Jesus set before us. The Bible states his perfection and purity as sinlessness, but it does not emphasize these features of His life. Instead the biblical emphasis is always Jesus' relationship to God the Father. Without the relationship with the Father, Jesus' sinless perfection is virtually worthless.

I have come to the point in my life that being sinless is not important. Instead being holy is urgent to me. I define holiness in terms of my intimacy with a context of permanence in my relationship with God. I cannot stand to lose the intimacy that I crave and love in my walk with Jesus. God is welcome to remove anything in my life that blocks my intimacy with Him. Any sin that I used to find pleasurable is now just an obstacle that I want Jesus to remove so that I can have more intimacy and permanence with Him.

I have come to see holiness as integration of the whole personality of an individual and also of all relationships. Sin is a disease that destroys. It breaks permanence. It fragments our personality, our integrity as a person and fragments our relationships. When I meditate on the nature of God, I see a being who is completely integrated in each person of that being. Jesus is completely integrated within Himself. The Holy Spirit is completely integrated within Himself. The Father is completely integrated within Himself. Because each person is completely integrated within Himself, the whole being of God – Father, Son, and Holy Spirit - is completely integrated within their self. The relationship of each person with the other person is completely integrated. There is no sin in any one person because each person is fully integrated within His own personality. There is no sin in the relationship of the three persons of the Godhead because both the individual persons are integrated and the relationship of the three persons as a whole is fully integrated. In a full integrated personality there is no sin because the person is whole. There is no brokenness which through its pain leads to sin.

It is the integration of our personality and the integration of our relationships which enable us to develop intimacy. The more integrated we are the stronger our positive character traits will be. The stronger our character traits and the stronger our integration of personality and relationships, the more intimate we are capable of being in relationships.

The Bible never defines how we achieve character. It just assumes each person has character. Each person will have a mixture of good character and bad character, The Bible lists several people of positive character, even though they clearly have deficiencies in their character and have committed acts which are very displeasing to God. The Bible makes it clear that God measures our character and our life not by our failures, but by our success. Even more important to God is that we establish and maintain a relationship of intimacy with Jesus Christ.

Character is more than behavior. It includes attitudes and aspirations which you express to God, yourself, and others. It is the expression of who you really are deep inside of yourself. Character or lack thereof is what comes out of you when you are facing the most difficult trials in your life.

If you do not have intimacy with yourself, how can you have intimacy with anyone else? Intimacy starts with your own self. You must be aware of your own thoughts, feelings, behaviors and sensations, and also know why they are occurring.

If you do not know why you think a certain way, or feel the way you do, or behave in a certain manner, then you have compartmentalized yourself to the point that you are incapable of intimacy. The extremes of compartmentalization are demonstrated in many ways. Business people disassociate their personal beliefs about morals and ethics by sacrificing what is right and good in a business deal in order to make more profit. Religious leaders frequently make excuses for the behaviors of their family members, while at the same time demanding moral and ethical behavior from other people. Spouses compartmentalize their marital vows in order to have affairs. In the extreme form compartmentalization is expressed in dissociative states such as amnesia, frugg, and multiple personality disorders.

Personal holiness is that which integrates a person into a relationship with God. Sin separates us from God. It also separates us from ourselves. Each act of sin compartmentalizes our personality and disassociates us from our relationships with ourselves and with God. The shame and guilt left by sin in our lives leave us cowering and afraid to face ourselves, let alone to face God. It finally gets to the point where the amount of sin in our lives keeps us from being intimate with our own selves. This also prevents us from being intimate with God. Personal holiness builds intimacy with self, God, and other people. The holiness that is brought about in our lives when we integrate our personality and eliminate sin brings about healing to our whole person. It makes us mentally, physically, and spiritually healthy in our personality and in our relationships. Once our personality is healthy we quit trying to hide our true self from other people and we begin to enjoy all of the relationships with the various people with whom we associate in life. When we have integration of personality and personal holiness, we begin to automatically care about the people around us. We naturally enter into intimacy with them without even trying to achieve intimacy. Only through Godly character can we become intimate with ourselves and with other people. The development of an integrated personality and the forsaking of sin go hand in hand. The more you remove the practices of sin in your life, the more you integrate your personality. The more you integrate your personality, the more you desire and seek to remove sin from your life. The more these two (forsaking sin and integrating personality) are developed in your life, the more holy you become, the more positive traits of character you develop, and the more intimate you become in all of your relationships.

God's Description of Aspects of Character

Erickson describes aspects of character which are a part of our natural human development and demonstrate our ability to adequately accomplish each stage of life. In the Beatitudes God describes the moral and spiritual aspects of character which He desires to develop in us. These aspects of character can only be attained as we walk with Jesus. It is these aspects of character which distinguish those who are true followers of Jesus from those who would pretend to be followers of Jesus. These aspects of godly character take years to develop. They may not show strongly in the early years of adulthood. However, there will be enough evidence of their existence and development to enable a person to make a sound determination of a person's walk with Jesus. Only the person who demonstrates the aspects of godly character has the proper foundation for becoming the kind of mate who is truly capable of developing intimacy with both Jesus and with you.

In Matthew 5:1-12 Jesus presents the Beatitudes as a part of the Sermon on the Mount.

1. Poverty of spirit - Those who recognize that that all sustenance and especially spiritual sustenance comes only from God. They crave the knowledge of God and sacrifice life's pleasures just to spend time in prayer and fellowship with Jesus

2. Mourning - Those who grieve deeply over the sin in this world and the sin in their personal lives. They are the ones who will devote their lives to investing in the lives of sinners they seek to bring to Jesus and in keeping other Christians faithful in their relationship with Jesus.

3. Meekness - Those who rarely show outward strength, but use spiritual authority and principles of spiritual warfare to wage war against principalities and powers of darkness on behalf of their brothers and sisters in Christ. They submit totally to Jesus' Lordship.

4. Hunger and thirst for righteousness - Those who prize holiness in their lives above all sin, and seek to spend time only on pursuits that bring holiness to themselves and to others around them.

5. Merciful - Those who seek to sacrifice their lives for the good of others. They see all other persons as equals to whom they must give whatever they have to provide for others' deepest needs.

6. Pure in heart - Those who seek only to please God and to develop mastery over their own lives. Their lives are not about themselves. Their lives are about Jesus.

7. Peacemakers - Those who are at peace within themselves. Wherever they go people have a sense of the peace that these people bring into a room with them. They bring peace to the

lives of the people to whom they minister, and to situations which are volatile, because they carry the presence of the Holy Spirit with them.

8. Persecuted because of righteousness - Those who always stand for Jesus and for truth no matter what the personal cost. They will sacrifice their families and their lives to honor God and accept martyrdom as the cost of living for Jesus.

(Matthew 5:1-12)

Spiritual Aspects of Intimacy

We know we need the normal human aspects of character developed in the stages of life for building intimacy in human relationships. We also need the spiritual aspects of character for developing intimacy with God. What most people do not realize is that your human intimacy cannot exceed your capacity for spiritual intimacy and your spiritual intimacy cannot exceed your capacity for human intimacy. To understand why our spiritual and human capacity for intimacy go so closely together in our development of intimacy, we only need to look at the foundations on which our intimacy is built.

Our humanity limits our ability to experience the spiritual realm, gain knowledge of relationships and understand aspects of intimacy. These are three of the five pillars of intimacy in our relationships with ourselves and with others. Many times we have difficulty explaining our decisions, behaviors and thoughts to ourselves, let alone to anyone else. We are unable to understand why different people have such differing political, religious, and other beliefs. We wonder why other people do not see things the same way we see things. Why are our perspectives on life and society so differently? As humans we do not know and understand many things about another person. Even when we know certain details about a person's life, we often do not know how these specific details truly impact the other person.

It is the spiritual aspect of intimacy which bridges this gap. There have been multiple times when I have prayed for someone over many months during which time God has shown me things about the person's life and eventually helped me to understand what was causing the issues in the person's life.

Since 2014 God has brought the daughter of a distant old friend to my mind repeatedly. When this happens, I know that God is telling me to pray for the person whom He brings to my mind. I have never met my friend's daughter and I have only met my friend once since high school about 40 years ago. I sent a message to my friend and told her God was telling me to pray for her daughter. She told me her daughter was newly married and that the couple was fighting so intensely it was likely to destroy the marriage.

I prayed for this couple for about a year. As I prayed God slowly would show me things or bring concepts to my mind, and then He would show me how the concepts which I was thinking about fit the couple I was praying for.

Eventually after much prayer, I wrote the couple a few letters and told them what I had perceived in praying for them. Thankfully my comments were well received and my prayers were appreciated. In prayer God has built a spiritual intimacy between this couple and me. They will always be dear to me even though I have never met them.

It is through spiritual intimacy that we gain the insight and knowledge to understand the people in our lives with whom we seek to form the strongest intimacy. Many times we can gain this insight in no other manner than through prayer and the spiritual dynamics which create intimacy on both the human and the divine levels. What we cannot know or understand on a human interpersonal level can be made known to us on a spiritual level.

Aspects of Relational Intimacy

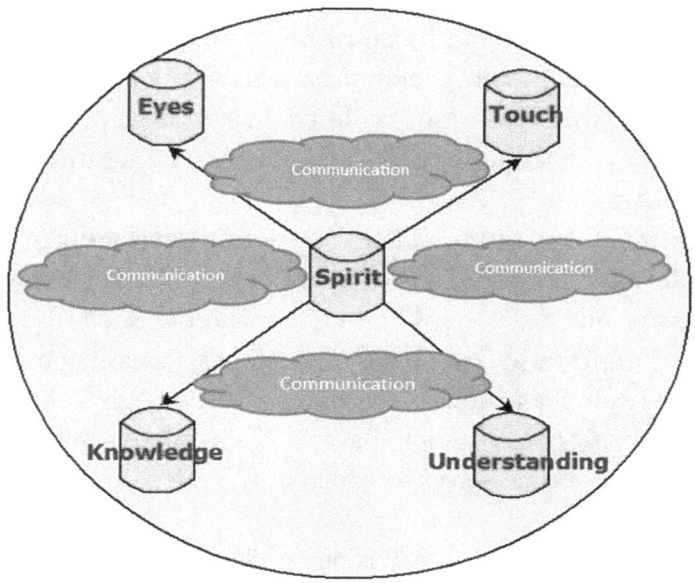

Figure 5-3

I believe there are five pillars of intimacy: Eyes, touch, knowing, understanding, and spirit. These are the forms of expressing intimacy which we use to draw close to other people. Most people would consider communication to be the first pillar of intimacy, but it is not. Communication permeates and facilitates all of the pillars. It is the ether in which intimacy lives. However, in and of itself communication is not a pillar of intimacy.

The Pillars of intimacy

The first pillar of intimacy is the eyes. The old saying that the "eyes are the window to the soul" seems to hold much wisdom when it comes to intimacy. I do not know of anything that will endear you to a stranger faster that to look them in the eyes and smile. The eyes convey intentions. A deep longing gaze, framed with a nice smile, indicates trust. The eyes are also a very strong indicator of the truth and honesty of a person's intentions.

The second pillar of intimacy is touch. Somewhere in the past, I have read that if you do not touch a person within the first hour of meeting them, you do not develop trust with that person. Traditions throughout the world have long centered on greeting a person with a hug, a kiss, a handshake, or a bow. These first greetings initiate trust between individuals.

The third pillar of intimacy is knowledge. In developing intimacy we must develop a strong knowledge of the person. This knowledge encompasses not only peripheral information such as name, occupation, and family members, but extends to having a person tell us what he or she thinks and believes about any given issue. For great intimacy to occur, people have to begin to exchange private information about themselves to which only a select few or no other individuals are party.

The fourth pillar of intimacy is our understanding. This pillar is not knowledge about the other person. It comes through developing a cognizance of the personal motivations driving the person's feelings, aspirations, beliefs, and actions. Proper understanding of another person is the ability to see the person from within that person's perspective and filters instead of your own perspective or filters. This kind of perception is related to, and dependent upon, the fifth pillar of intimacy.

The fifth pillar of intimacy is our spirit. This is not the same as the personality, even though people sometimes confuse these. I am referring to a person's spirit at the core of his or her being. I rarely hear anyone other than a Christian refer to another person's spirit. For Christians the spirit is a supernatural connection at the deepest and innermost core of a person's being. We can sense another person's spirit only with our own spirit. The more sensitive we are to the spiritual realm, the more discerning we are of other people's spirits. We make our strongest connection to another person when we interact with that person in a spiritual connection.

We talk and sing about all of these pillars of intimacy in the church. We say we want to see Jesus. We want to touch and be touched by Jesus. We want to know Jesus. We want a spiritual relationship with Jesus. However, we never talk about "I want to understand Jesus or I want to be understood by Jesus." Do you know the answer to why we do not want to understand or be understood? Why do Christians and the church want every form of relationship with Jesus except this one?

I believe we are scared to death of actually understanding Jesus and even more scared of being understood by Him! As long as we do not understand Him and He does not understand us, we feel we are safe. We have not risked a part of our selves which we cannot take back. Many people do not want to follow Jesus because they do not want to give up specific sins and behaviors which they enjoy in their lives. They believe they cannot follow Jesus until they overcome these sins and they have no desire or intention to overcome any of these behaviors. Some people will not follow Jesus because they do not want to relinquish to Him the control they have of their life. They believe they are in control and they fear to give up control. These people fail to realize the sins and behaviors they will not give up are destroying their lives, and the control they feel they possess over their own lives is more like speeding over a cliff in a car with a disconnected steering wheel.

Deep on the inside these people crave to be rescued from the brokenness and self-destruction which they are inflicting on their lives. They crave intimacy with other human beings, but it is the sins and behaviors which they refuse to relinquish to Jesus which destroy the very intimacy which they seek in their lives.

I am sorry to disappoint you, but only those people who actually force themselves to understand Jesus and to be understood by him actually have an intimate relationship with Him. Only those who allow understanding in their lives are prepared to live for Jesus and to live under His lordship. Do not ever tell me you love Jesus unless you understand Him and allow Him to understand you. He already understands you. You are just afraid to admit it.

Only a God, who completely understands me, can completely love me.

My greatest desire in life is to have a God who knows and fully understands everything about me, on every level of my existence. If I am not understood by my God, then why should I even understand myself? Our greatest fear is for our existence to be meaningless. Only a God who completely understands me can completely love me. The greatest value I have as a human being is being understood by my God and learning to understand God's perspective of my life. If I do not gain this understanding and perspective, then my life is ultimately meaningless.

The greatest value I have as a human being is being understood by my God and learning to understand God's perspective on my life. If I do not gain this understanding and perspective, then my life is ultimately meaningless.

I have learned through praying for other people that you do not have to know another person to understand that person. When you pray for someone long enough, you begin to sense his or her spirit. When you sense the person's spirit, you begin to know and understand that person. If you pray for your mate, you can develop an understanding of him or her that is not normally possible through the combination of all the other pillars of intimacy.

Intimacy Starts with Integrity

What makes for a successful relationship? What are the key ingredients that determine whether the relationships in your life are successful or not? All relationships are dependent on a good foundation. The foundation necessary for building any relationship is intimacy. It is even the key foundation for building a relationship with one's own self. The ability to be at peace when one is alone derives from an intimacy with oneself.

Intimacy derives from integrity. The completeness of integration of all aspects of your being forms your integrity and allows you to develop intimacy within yourself. Only when you have developed the capability for intimacy within your own being do you become capable of intimacy with other persons. The development of one's capacity for intimacy is a lifelong process. It can become broken and even stop should one become severely damaged in his or her personality. Normally, however, this capacity grows as we grow and develop as human beings.

The Process of Intimacy

How does a person learn to be intimate?
Intimate with self
Intimate with a friend
Intimate with the opposite sex
Intimate in a marriage

As stated previously, the number one issue in developing a capacity for intimacy is your own personal integrity. You cannot be intimate with other people until you can be comfortable in being intimate with yourself. Intimacy involves coming to understand the deepest and most private aspects of your soul. You cannot sort out your understanding of another person unless you have come to a deep understanding of yourself. At the same time, it is the practice of gaining insight into other people that often leads us to the most profound understanding of our self. The more we seek to know another person, the more we have to differentiate our own feelings, desires, and behaviors from those of the other person. This struggle, for separation of understanding of ourselves in contrast to understanding of the other person, enhances our capacity for intimacy as it sharpens our perception of the motives and desires which drive our own life.

Social Contexts for the Expression of Intimacy

There are five social contexts in which we express intimacy with other people. These social contexts are critical for our development of intimate relationships. A fully integrated person will be able to express and experience emotional and psychological intimacy with friends of both sexes in all social contexts.

As a person develops social skills, he or she will embrace friendships in a number of social spheres - family, friends, acquaintances, and mates. He or she will also be able to create spiritual relationships with him or herself, with other people, and with God. We start life with physical intimacy with our parents. We continue life with appropriate touch and appropriate interpersonal boundaries. When we share intimacy we relate to ourselves, to God, and to other people in multiple social contexts.

On the Physical level – Touch is very important in establishing and maintaining relationships. Never betray a person's trust in the manner in which you touch the person. Inappropriate touch destroys a person's ability to open him or herself to intimacy. Do not ever destroy another person with touch that is inappropriate and unwelcomed. On the other hand, freely give touch where it is welcomed. Appropriate and welcomed touch builds not only the intimacy of the relationship, but also the context of safety and security that allows the person to pursue self-development in social relationships.

On the Intellectual level – Always seek to connect with people on a high intellectual level. You will compliment them in this manner. You can always lower this, if needed, to the intellectual level of communication where they are comfortable communicating with you.

On the Emotional level – Only relationships that reach the affective aspects of a person's being bring change. You must connect with a person's emotions if you are going to assist them to bond with you and to enable them to trust you as they engage in the relationship with you.

On the Social level – You cannot be a bashful or timid wall flower if you want to have relationships with other people. You have to learn to talk freely with people you do not even know. In order to build successful relationships you must be willing to reveal successive levels of personal information about yourself. This is especially critical to building trust in relationships. However, it is also important to not reveal too much personal information at one time. Too great a revelation of personal information, provided too freely or too quickly, can drive people away from you.

On the Spiritual level – For most people talking about spiritual issues is like talking about politics. It is considered a social foible. However, as a Christian it comes as a part of your job description (Jesus' command to make disciples). Raise the subject with those to whom you would minister and see where it leads. The goal of intimacy is to be known and understood on this spiritual level. Even in marriage, it is somewhat rare to find spouses who truly understand each other spiritually. They know each other's behavior. They know what their spouse will do in a specific situation, but they do not truly know what motivates their spouse. They can predict behavior, but lack true depth of understanding of the subconscious factors that motivate behaviors. Moreover, until they have gained an understanding of their own personal subconscious motivations and feelings, they will be incapable of understanding the same kind of motivations and feelings in another person. (Emerge Ministries)

Intimacy's Love Languages

Gary Chapman developed the concept of a person having love languages. These languages demonstrate the manner in which a person both gives and receives intimacy. For each person there is a specific emotional trigger that is engaged when a person is shown love and intimacy using that person's preferred love language.

The love languages include:

> **Words of affirmation** build up another person. They create potential and self-belief in that potential. They bring about expectation, freedom, and change in a person's self-image and behavior.

Quality time can be separation time, proximity time, or interactive time. Determine what form of time your partner needs the most at any given point. We all need quality time, but the form that quality time takes can vary from day to day.

Gifts are presents which everyone likes to receive, but not everyone likes to give. The choice of the gift is as critical as the gift itself. Never give a gift that the other person does not want. Take time to determine what the person cherishes and desires and make that the target of your gift giving.

Acts of service are most beneficial when they demonstrate respect for a man or a context of love, security and provision for a woman.

Physical touch is one of the most powerful forms of intimacy we can ever give to another person. Different people like to be touched in different ways. Explore how the intimate people in your life desire to be touched.

Determining your own love language is most clearly done by listening to the words, actions, or behaviors which you use most frequently to convey love to other people. The things you desire, expect, and complain about in your intimate relationships also express the manner in which you need to receive and give love.

Responding in your spouse's love language is a primary determinant in developing intimacy with your spouse. You spouse's love language normally is different from yours. Explore the love language that gets the best response from your significant other. (Chapman, 1995).

Love languages may seem innocent and unimportant, but they speak like thunder and lightning when we use the proper love languages in our social relationships and most significant relationships. My wife likes to give and receive gifts. I express love by doing things for other people. We have to work at using the proper love language in expressing love and intimacy with each other. It does not come easily, but it makes a great difference in our lives when we force ourselves to speak our mate's language.

The Role of Culture in the Development of Intimacy

There are many psychological coping mechanisms and cultural trends which enable us to evade, hinder, or prevent intimacy. Here is a short list of the more common ones.

Culture
1. Our culture does not teach us how to be intimate with other people, especially our spouse.
2. Very few parents model intimacy for their children.
3. Many careers limit or prevent the development of intimacy, empathy, and compassion in our lives. (Gordon, 1969)

Where can you go in society to learn, to develop the ability to be intimate with another person? – TV, church, a club, parents, another couple? Who is your role model for intimacy?

Perhaps the biggest hindrance to developing intimate relationships as an adult is emotional deprivation in early childhood. Research has shown us that babies cannot live and develop without intimacy and touch. They will simply die. Any person who lacks intimacy, and the aspects of relationships associated with intimacy, will become either physically or mentally ill and usually both. Without empathy, tenderness, cuddling, caring, understanding, and compassion, along with emotional interaction and love, we become angry, depressed, and self-destructive. If people shut off their emotions and do not provide adequate intimacy for their significant others in relationships, they destroy the relationship and ultimately their own lives. The number one cause of most mental illness, and the acting out in anger or violence, is the lack of intimacy in the nurturing stages of early development.

Our culture and society frequently limit our ability to develop or express intimacy. In a world of broken relationships, there are no role models for young adults exhibiting how to develop healthy, intimate relationships. Very few people in our society are sufficiently healthy to develop strong bonds of intimacy with other people. Many marriages are little more than people living parallel lives. They may stay together, but true intimacy is lacking in the relationship.

Even our churches often fail to provide guidance in developing intimate relationships. The church's silence about intimacy is as deafening as the church's silence about sex. Not only does the church separate younger persons by sex in order to prevent immoral and inappropriate behavior. The church treats intimacy with the same cowardly disdain of being taboo. So, how do you learn to be intimate with another person? If the church will not enable and encourage people to explore appropriate intimacy with others of both sexes, while maintaining sexual purity, then why should the church complain when people turn to Hollywood for examples of appropriate intimacy in relationships?

Clues to the Capability for Intimacy

Equally important with understanding a person's preparation and ability to build and share intimacy is the understanding of the clues to a person's inability to share intimacy. The strongest clue any person reveals about his or her capability for sharing intimacy is his or her circle of friends. Who are your most intimate friends outside of your family? True friendship is measured by the level of intimacy which we share with our friends and family. A person who does not have intimate friends is very limited in his or her capacity for intimacy. If you are going to appraise a person's potential as a mate, start with the person's ability to be intimate with his or her friends. If the person has no friends, or is not capable of being intimate with his or her friends, then the person is not capable of intimacy with anyone and is not marriage material. When we begin to examine a person's friendship with those in social proximity, we begin to see strong clues about the person's capacity for intimacy. This examination soon reveals boundary issues, avoidance techniques, and emotional inhibitions.

The Perversion of Intimacy – The Hollywood Deception:

It is interesting that our culture, popular media, and Hollywood seek to portray intimacy in relationships in a manner that is the exact opposite to the intimacy that most people have experienced in their lives. If you look at the message of Hollywood about relationships and intimacy, you find the following.

The Hollywood Couple
Males and females are sexual predators.
Males and females are searching for perpetually
elusive security and satisfaction.
Relationship transgressions have no lasting negative impacts.
All relationships are new and exciting while at the same
time emotionally significant and meaningful.
Idealistic relationships have highly dysfunctional aspects.
There are no permanent and stable relationships.
All forms of sexual relationships are equal.
If you are uncomfortable with this, then you are less
than a man or a woman and a hate filled bigot.
Power, money, and sex are the real aspects of relationships.

(Johnson & Holmes, 2009).

The Hollywood perspective serves to warp people's understanding of romance and intimacy. This may lead individuals to idealize the Hollywood relationship, and to substitute the idealized relationship for true intimacy with other persons and with God. When the Hollywood perspective fails to produce the kind of intimacy a person seeks, the person may begin to see him or herself as a defective person incapable of satisfying relationships and wholesome intimacy.

The Hollywood perspective leads to a perverted view of intimacy, relationships, marriage, sex and sexuality. In this warped perspective sex is substituted for intimacy. Males and females are generally stereotyped as crippled and broken human beings. They are forever incapable of wholesome relationships with themselves or with anyone else. As a result, the crippled and broken person comes to see the opposite sex as a person to be used simply for one's selfish pleasure and gain. Relationships become what you can take from the other person instead of what you can give to them. The measure of morality is always "if it feels good do it!"

Following the Hollywood pattern leads to a relationship built on deception and lies, where the intimacy in the relationship decays instead of grows. For Hollywood, love is the poison which kills, instead of brings life to, a relationship filled with proper intimacy and trust.

In the Hollywood perspective marriage is a death trap, which is to be disposed of at the earliest sign of difficulty or the earliest cessation of pleasure. Sequential monogamous but disposable relationships are the ideal, instead of a unitary monogamous relationship of true intimacy, which is refined by struggle and lasts for a lifetime.

Broken Boundaries

Every relationship has boundaries which must not be crossed. It does not matter our age or our sex or the person with whom we hold a relationship. If we cross the lines of propriety, we destroy the relationship and whatever intimacy that once existed in the relationship.

Intimacy can only be shared to the extent that the other person is capable of granting and receiving intimacy. Each of us is restricted in our ability to experience intimacy. This restriction is a result of three factors in our lives.

1. The existence of sin in our lives.
2. The compartmentalization of our personality.
3. Any violations of our personal boundaries which we have experienced.

Each and every time we sin we compartmentalize our personality, disassociating ourselves from ourselves, from other people and from God. When we sin, we first have to be forgiven by God. The act of being forgiven of sin by God does not automatically reintegrate our personality and remove the compartmentalization we have inflicted on ourselves. This is why the Bible is very clear about forgiving other people and asking other people for forgiveness. We also have to forgive ourselves. We have to be forgiven by other people and we have to ask other people for forgiveness. Without the interaction of all of these forms of forgiveness, we do not experience the healing process which results in the reintegration of our personality. Without an integrated personality, we cannot trust ourselves, other people or God. Without trust we cannot allow ourselves to experience intimacy. Only to the extent that we have been through the forgiveness process, and experienced the healing and reintegration of our personalities, are we able to trust other people enough to allow them into our lives and to share intimacy with those people.

Intimacy that exceeds proper personal boundaries becomes predatory. It violates the lives of all the people involved. These personal intimacy boundaries are set by three guardians: 1) Biblical restrictions guarding relationships; 2) societal laws and mores guarding relationships; and 3) personal and subconscious boundaries guarding personal safety in relationships. To sum up these safeguards, the Bible is very clear that any sexual relationship outside of marriage is prohibited; society prohibits any form of touch without permission as assault; and personal boundaries seek to prevent violation of one's capability to share intimacy and, hence, destruction of trust. This predatory intimacy can also further compartmentalize a person's personality, as the person seeks to block off the pain and trauma they have experienced in the violation of the personal boundaries for intimacy.

Intimacy Avoidance

Some people, due to damaged personalities and subsequent use of psychological coping mechanisms, are very destructive to intimacy. They sabotage relationships as a way of avoiding intimacy. Let's look at some of these intimacy avoidance behaviors.

There are several behaviors that people frequently use to prevent, hinder or destroy intimacy in relationships. These are coping mechanisms they use out of fear that intimacy will ultimately result in pain, and so they seek to prevent the intimacy and the pain.

A Wall – a projection of inability for intimacy to all but a few select friends. This action is mostly used to declare the person off limits for relationships with the opposite sex.

A Mask – the presentation of a false personality as the "good me," or "socially acceptable me." This false personality enables a person to present different personalities to different people or groups. The true self is never presented socially. It is allowed to be known by very few people and possibly to no one including self.

Avoidance – purposely staying away from people who are perceived to be a threat. It is not that the people avoided actually seek to harm the person, but rather that the person using the avoidance behavior just desires to avoid certain people. The avoidance is perpetrated out of fear that they will be forced to disclose personal information which will ultimately bring pain into their lives.

Pre-rejection – rejecting other people before they can reject you. Usually this is used to seal off any possible pain from being rejected by people whom you love and care for the most.

Projection of anger – by pretending to be angry or mean, other people are warned to avoid you.

Buried emotions – The person with buried emotions is usually unaware of his or her own feelings. He or she lives only in the cognitive world. Personal emotions and the emotions of others are never considered. These people are totally oblivious to their own emotions and barely have any sensitivity to other people's emotions.

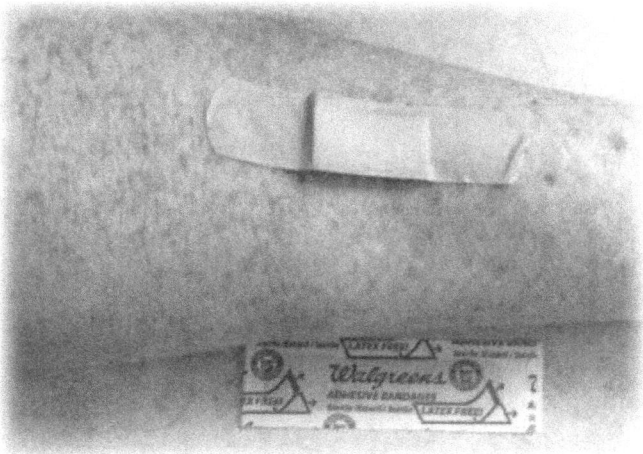

Band Aids do not heal. They only cover wounds.

Figure 8

Would you attempt to heal a person's issues about intimacy with a band aid? Putting a band aid on a person will not heal a person of cancer or any other disease. It will not heal a person's deepest psychological and emotional wounds. In the same manner, band aids cannot heal a person's issues with intimacy. The sad part is that many approaches to mental health are functionally no more significant than putting a band aid on a person's deepest psychological wounds. I am not saying that all forms of therapy are ineffective. I am saying that any form of therapy that does not involve forgiveness, at all aspects of the vertical, horizontal, and interpersonal relationship levels, will never accomplish the degree of healing necessary to free a person to live in intimacy with the people around him or her.

Forgiveness is the greatest factor in healing both the existing compartmentalization in a person's personality and in a person's relationships with other people. In summary, forgiveness involves four levels. We must be forgiven by Jesus. We must forgive ourselves. We must forgive those who have emotionally harmed us. Finally we must seek to be forgiven by those whom we have emotionally harmed. Until these four levels of forgiveness are accomplished, we will remain unable to reintegrate our personality.

Traumatic and or Abusive Events

The inability to express emotions is always an indication of abuse in childhood or the result of an extremely traumatic event in a person's life.

1. Some people cannot talk about their feelings
2. Some people conceal their thoughts, emotions, and hurts
3. Some people who cannot be intimate sow seeds of destruction

If you cannot talk about your feelings, you cannot be intimate. Many people who conceal their emotions also conceal their thoughts. They will not reveal to others what the truly think. Instead they reveal only what they think others want to hear or see in the relationship they share together. They also seal off and avoid sharing their hurts with their partners. This behavior sows seeds of destruction, both in their own lives and in their relationships. Failure to be intimate destroys not only our own selves, it also destroys the people around us. As an example, recent research has begun to show that the root of much of the crime and destruction in our world is directly related to a lack of intimacy in our lives.

A very high percentage of people in this world are ill equipped for intimacy. Many have suffered one or more forms of abuse throughout the key growth years of their life. Their ability to be intimate is either crippled or highly inhibited. The only way they can ever find a significant depth of intimacy with any other person, or with God, is to experience a great deal of healing in their lives.

The Cost of Intimacy

When you begin to look at the level of intimacy in your life, there are some important questions to ask.

What is your past costing you? Intimacy is mostly destroyed by the pain in our past. This pain robs us of the most important relationships and joys in life. The pain of our past changes a heart of love into a heart of stone.

What price are you extracting from your current partner? The pain of our past causes us to extract an emotional fee from our loved ones for every ounce of intimacy that we give to them. What is the price you charge? What do you seek to extract from your family and friends each time they ask you to be intimate with them?

What are your emotional triggers? We all have things in our lives which trigger in us anger or other emotional states. Anger in itself is a good thing when it protects us or motivates us to feel strongly about the injustices in this world. Anger that is not properly expressed and controlled can do exceedingly great harm to both our relationships and to our goals of righting injustices around us.

What do you need from your partner? What do you need your partner to do to overcome your emotional triggers? How can your partner avoid triggering your negative emotional reactions? (Gordon, 1969).

The Role of Sex in Intimacy

Sex can only function as a healthy aspect of intimacy when it occurs within the confines of marriage. The purpose of sex clearly is to boost the bonds of intimacy within the marital relationship. This is clearly demonstrated in the functioning of the human brain chemistry surrounding relationships. It is also seen as the pleasure experienced in the sexual relationship reflects and models the pleasure experienced by humans in a relationship with God.

Outside of marriage sex always brings destruction and brokenness. Sex outside of marriage damages not only the intimacy of the present relationship, but also the intimacy of future relationships. Marriage is the only relationship designed to last in deep intimacy. Some other types of relationships last but, by definition lack the extremes of intimacy which are shared and built in marital intimacy. Friendships last, family lasts, but none of them are designed for the intimacy that is shared in marriage.

Relationships (regardless of whether they last or not) which involve sexual intercourse outside of marriage automatically break the trust necessary for intimacy. They twist and pervert the brain's sexual chemistry and pleasure into brokenness long before the relationship ends.

Sex is not intimacy!

Sex is designed to apply to marriage. When you apply sex to any other relationship, you destroy its purpose. If sex is designed to work in a specific context, why do you expect it to work as designed when applied outside of that context? In our current world most work is accomplished in teams. What would happen if you went to work and had sex with all of your co-workers everyday – regardless of sexual orientations? How long do you think your healthy and successful work environment would last? What if you went to school and had sex with every person in your class every day? Would this behavior enhance or destroy your relationships with your classmates? What types of destruction and brokenness would occur from this behavior? If sex is not conducive to a healthy and productive work or school environment, why do people think it is healthy to friendships, dating, hookups and other kinds of relationships for which it was not designed? If you have sex outside of the context for which it is designed, why do you expect it to bring you happiness, peace and success? This is about the same logic as trying to row a boat across a desert and expecting to easily make it to the other side without leaving deep scars on both the boat and the desert. Sex outside of marriage is always a means to destroy your own life and future and the life and future of your sexual partner.

Sexual impurity always leads to the destruction of relationships. A common belief is that sexual impurity can only destroy a current relationship. For most people there seems to be no concept that it can and will destroy a future relationship. Sexual impurity brings a profound sense of guilt. It destroys the integrity of a person's personality, and it creates behavior patterns of self-destruction that repeatedly occur in a person's life. Most people will not discuss the destruction that has occurred in their lives through sexual immorality. The destruction is too personal and the pain is too great. They do not want to relive the excruciating devastation they have experienced. As a result, they leave themselves and other people without any warning of the consequences they will face for the uninformed choices they make, when they assume there are no future consequences for inappropriate behavior in present relationships.

Many people have no concept that impurity can destroy all possible future relationships and make it impossible for them to succeed in a marital relationship in the future because of the baggage they carry from past choices and behavior. They also have no concept of the consequences which will be paid in the life of their spouse and in the lives of their children because of their bad choices and behavior.

I do not know of any normal physically and mentally healthy person who would deliberately harm his or her own children. Yet people continue to practice forms of sexual immorality in their relationships that bring devastating consequences upon their future and/or present children, not to mention their future and/or present spouse.

It only takes a quick look at societal statistics of child and spouse abuse, sexual molestation and rape, divorce, and murder to see the devastation of broken lives that is left in the wake of choices for sexual immorality that have ruined and severely damaged millions of lives in our society (Finkelhor, 1990; Finkelhor, Hotaling, Lewis, & Smith, 1990).

Chapter 7

God's Plan for Intimacy

Biblical Patterns of intimacy

The most profound experience of intimacy that people encounter in life is experiencing the presence of God. The second most profound experience of intimacy is the love for each other which a couple shares in marriage.

The biblical pattern of intimacy presents a rich, durable, and wholesome presentation of relationships, marriage and sex. In the Bible, the greatest extent of intimacy can only be achieved when two persons bond together on the physical, psychological/emotional, and spiritual levels all at one time.

Intimacy from the Biblical perspective is the polar opposite of intimacy from the Hollywood perspective.

In biblically patterned relationships, intimacy involves a person's whole being. To truly be intimate with another person you must bond with that person. Bonding requires a relationship on all levels of the person's being – physical, emotional, and spiritual.

The Bible expresses several forms of intimacy dynamics. These dynamics include intimacy between God and man, between husband and wife, between parent and child, and between friends of either sex. We see the implication of a daily pattern of God walking in intimacy with humans in the Garden of Eden, "in the cool of the day," likely each and every day (Gen 3:8-9). This is a clear presentation of what God wants in intimacy with us. He expects to walk with us each and every day. He also expects us to walk with Him in intimacy each and every day. Intimacy is the primary pattern and factor of a relationship with God. Without intimacy a relationship with God does not exist.

The Song of Solomon is full of teaching about intimate thoughts and intimate behavior between a husband and wife. The covenant between David and Jonathan clearly expresses a deep abiding intimacy between two friends.

This type of intimacy is not limited to heterosexual relationships. Males can bond and form intimacy with males, females can bond and form intimacy with females. Same sex bonding for Christians, however, does not include homosexual relationships.

In I Samuel 18:3 we read that David bonded with Jonathan, so tightly that they formed a covenant between them. This relationship was never a homosexual relationship. The exchange of robes between the two men is a symbolic act of covenant whereby each party takes on the person and identity of the other person. (Hurt, Bruce 2013)

We need to look equally at the Bible's description of bonding in heaven and in our relationship with God. God is a spiritual being and therefore our bonding with Him on a physical level does not occur either in this world or in heaven. Bonding with Jesus on a psychological, emotional and spiritual level very clearly occurs both in this world and in heaven. From all the descriptions we have of heaven in the Bible, it is likely that bonding on a spiritual level will replace bonding on a physical level.

Need for intimacy

Our need for intimacy comes out of our being created in the image of God. Intimacy in the three persons of the godhead was part of God's own image. Please look closely at these following verses which speak of intimacy in God's creation of human beings.

26 Then God said, "Let us make mankind in our image, in our likeness, so that they may rule over the fish in the sea and the birds in the sky, over the livestock and all the wild animals, and over all the creatures that move along the ground." 27 So God created mankind in his own image, in the image of God he created them; male and female he created them. (Genesis 1:26-27)

The Lord God said, "It is not good for the man to be alone. I will make a helper suitable for him." (Genesis 2:18)

Then the man and his wife heard the sound of the Lord God as he was walking in the garden in the cool of the day, and they hid from the Lord God among the trees of the garden. 9 But the Lord God called to the man, "Where are you?" (Genesis 3:8-9)

<u>*Relationships of Intimacy in the Bible*</u>
Intimacy between man and God
Intimacy between husband and wife
Intimacy between parent and child
Intimacy between friends

The Bible expresses several forms of intimacy dynamics. These dynamics include intimacy between God and man, between husband and wife, between parent and child, and between friends of either sex. We see the implication of a daily pattern of God walking in intimacy with humans in the Garden of Eden, "in the cool of the day," likely each and every day (Gen 3:8-9). This is a clear presentation of what God wants in intimacy with us. He expects to walk with us each and every day. He also expects us to walk with Him in intimacy each and every day. Intimacy is the primary pattern and factor of a relationship with God. Without intimacy a relationship with God does not exist.

The Song of Solomon is full of teaching about intimate thoughts and intimate behavior between a husband and wife. The covenant between David and Jonathan clearly expresses a deep abiding intimacy between two friends.

God's Model of Intimacy

Blood Covenant

The Bible is very clear that God wants an intimate relationship with us. To understand the significance of this intimate relationship between us and God, we have to understand the concept of covenant in the Bible.

Blood Always Represents Life

It all begins with blood. In Genesis 9:3-6 we are informed that there is always an accounting for the shedding of life's blood. In Leviticus 17:10-12 we are told that life is in the blood. In the Bible, blood always represents life. To unite God and man in intimacy required the shedding of blood. When blood was shed in the formation of a covenant, it represented an exchange of blood between the two persons or parties forming the covenant. In this shedding of blood of the sacrificial animal there was not just a symbolic act but an actual exchange of blood creating an exchange of life. One person's life became the other person's life. The other person's life became the first person's life. The two people or parties exchanged lives with each other. In this act the two parties were forever mutually bound in a sharing of their lives and a sacrifice of their lives for each other (Trumbull, 1975).

In an old American Western movie there is a scene where an Indian and a white man become blood brothers by cutting their hands and then clasping their hands together so that the blood of one man intermingles with that of the other man. This is an example of a blood covenant.

A blood covenant brought an outside person into the other participant's family. The outsider was now considered to be so much a part of the family that a sexual relationship with any of the family members was considered to be incest. Thus, an incestuous familial relationship was not only prohibited, but a strict betrayal of the covenant relationship. This covenant resulted in the obligation to defend each other's families, to the point of fighting in each other's wars and owing each other your life. A blood covenant obligated you to sacrifice the protection of your family, your wife, and your children for the protection of the person to whom you had bound yourself in covenant. While these connotations of being made a part of the family are at best only alluded to in the Old Testament, they shed much light on the depth of meaning and significance of covenant in the biblical period. Such a covenant, once made, could never be revoked. It was a lifelong bond (Galatians 3:15-22) (Trumbull, 1975).

The very act of shedding blood in creating a covenant brought severe repercussions upon both parties who entered the covenant. In Genesis 15:1-21, God forms a covenant with Abraham. In the formation of this covenant, God butchers an animal and places the two halves of the animal on two separate altars. God then burns the halves of the carcass split on both altars, while He marches in a figure eight around and between the two altars. By this act, God is making a statement to Abraham. "May I be cut in half and burnt, just as this animal is burnt if I ever break this covenant." This declaration of commitment through covenant may not be exactly what you would call an intimate relationship, but it establishes a super bond between the two parties to form a relationship in which intimacy is safe to grow (Trumbull, 1975).

The Sacrifice of Isaac

A few chapters later in Genesis 22:1-18, with the sacrifice of Isaac we are presented with an even more formal declaration of God's desire for intimacy with us. Let me explain the customs which provide context for this gruesome act of Abraham sacrificing his son to God. In the Ancient Near East, the greatest sacrifice a person or a father could make was a sacrifice of his family and children, especially his first born son. His children represented his future in life. Without children, the father's life ends and without a son the father's name ends. In the Ancient Near East, a man would rather lose his own life than the life of his son – especially his first born son (Trumbull, 1975). Therefore, there is no greater sacrifice God could ask of Abraham than the offering of his son Isaac. Only in Abraham's willingness to offer Isaac, could Abraham be brought to understand both the severity of the blood covenant's relationship bond and the extreme love that God offers to us in a covenant relationship.

When you are willing to kill your own children to preserve your relationship with another person – that is love! Thankfully, God spares Isaac's life at the very last second. In this brutal act, Abraham is brought to understand the full measure of the price we must be willing to pay to love God and have an intimate relationship with him. Only by submitting to this excruciating test, could Abraham begin to understand that God is just as willing to sacrifice His own first born son for Abraham. We have no reason to believe that Abraham had any knowledge of Jesus Christ at this point, but we do know Abraham has been brought to experience the pain and grief necessary to understand the extreme love that is provided in a covenant relationship between us and God. We get to experience God's love for us in the death of his first born son, Jesus Christ, on the cross for us. As a result of this test of Abraham, to sacrifice Isaac, Abraham is called a Friend of God – James 2:23. This title is a technical term which represents an extreme intimacy that now exists between God and Abraham. This title, and expression of intimacy, is not given to any other person in the Bible except Abraham (Trumbull, 1975).

With this test of Abraham's allegiance to the covenant relationship we are shown the extreme of the bond allegiance which God forms with us. We are presented with the perception that God is more willing to sacrifice Himself for us than he is to sacrifice his only son for us. Just as the Near Eastern father protected his son at all costs in order to ensure his progeny and his family name, we are presented with a God who will make the ultimate sacrifice in forming a covenant with us.

Hesed

Hesed is a term that is translated as **lovingkindness**. Its full and complete meaning has no equivalent in the English language. God always expressed his loyalty and favor to the nation and people of Israel in the Old Testament by using the Hebrew term hesed. This hesed is always expressed only in a context of justice and righteousness (Glueck & Nelson, 1967, p 89). When you look at the term in the many passages in which it was used and in the context of those passages, you realize that it expresses an eternal loyalty that God had with the people of Israel. This loyalty could never and will never be broken. It also expresses God's intimacy with the nation of Israel.

God demands that we be intimate with Him, through a covenant relationship with him, and God wants us to insist upon Him being in an intimate covenant relationship with us.

"To me this is like the days of Noah, when I swore that the waters of Noah would never again cover the earth. So now I have sworn not to be angry with you, never to rebuke you again. Though the mountains be shaken and the hills be removed, yet my unfailing love for you will not be shaken nor my covenant of peace be removed," says the Lord, who has compassion on you. (Isaiah 54:10)

31 For no one is cast off by the Lord forever. 32 Though he brings grief, he will show compassion, so great is his unfailing love. (Lamentations 3:31-32, NIV)

God promises to never break His blood covenant with the nation of Israel. They will always be loved by Him. That love is so complete that it will not tolerate the breaking of the blood covenant on Israel's part. Each time Israel breaks the covenant, God calls them back into relationship with Him. He allows disaster and punishment to come upon them in order to force them back into covenant where He can bless and protect them. The covenant is an act of love given by God to the nation and people of Israel. It is His blessing upon them. By it He protects them and provides for them.

In breaking the covenant, Israel breaks God's heart. Israel's disobedience always leaves great pain in God's heart for His people. He loves them so greatly that He forms a covenant with them, so that He will always be able to protect them, love them, and bless their lives. Even though he allows them to reap the consequences of their disobedience, He still rescues them and returns them to their homes and homeland. Each and every time the people rebel against God and turn to other gods, they forcibly remove themselves from God's ability to protect and bless them. When they return to God, He is able again to resume his love, protection, and blessing of them. He is able to bring the good which he wants to lavish upon them into their lives.

As Christians, it is the same with us. God forms the New Testament covenant with us through salvation in Jesus Christ. Jesus died a cruel and tortuous death on the cross to shed his blood so that we can be forgiven of our sins and have an intimate relationship with God. When we commit our lives to Jesus Christ and ask for forgiveness of our sins, we start a process of salvation that develops and continues throughout our lives. In this process of salvation we are united in an intimate relationship with God. He gives to us the same protection, love and blessing that He gives to His people Israel. The problem is that most of us are so scared by the sin in our lives, we cannot comprehend the awesome love, favor, protection, and blessing with which God wants to enrich our lives. It takes us years to heal from the pain which our disobedience to God has left in our lives and to learn to trust God with our lives. Because each of us has experienced brokenness and compartmentalization in our souls, we also fail to allow ourselves to be fully intimate with another person. We intuitively know that every other person in this world has experienced the same forms of brokenness and compartmentalization as we have experienced.

Hesed always accompanies covenant. It is an act of loving, loyal, intimacy from God to His people. In a single word it expresses the intimacy of relationship which Jesus wants with us. When we enter into a relationship with God, we experience intimacy with a person who has no brokenness, no compartmentalization, and no sin. He is whole. There is no fragmentation of His personality. We are free to allow ourselves to experience a level of trust and love which we would never allow ourselves to experience with another person. When we do learn to trust God, the love he has for us washes over us. It is the greatest thing we can ever experience in this world. There is no greater intimacy than the intimacy we experience in our relationship with God.

Idolatry Destroys Intimacy

There is a powerful difference between intimacy and idolatry. Idolatry destroys intimacy. It is not uncommon for people to fail to achieve intimacy because they are practicing idolatry.

In the Ancient Near East, pagan religion was based on manipulating and controlling the world in which the people lived. Religious worship practices were focused on controlling the natural realm and environment, the divine realm or spiritual world, and the human realm of relationships with other people. The practice of religion used sympathetic magic, religious ritual practices, and direct forms of manipulation to control these three realms. The people of that time and culture believed that whatever they could control in one realm would also impact related things, people, gods, etc. in another realm. They based this belief on everything being related as a universal whole. Therefore controlling or manipulating a person, object, or God also resulted in controlling the aspects of intimacy in the relationship with that object, person, or god.

World View of Ancient Near Eastern Peoples

In the WORLD VIEW of Ancient Near Eastern peoples we find the following beliefs:

1. Law of Correspondence and Continuity. There is a direct correlation between events in the human life, the natural world and the spiritual world.
2. The Spiritual world is directly continuous and directly correspondent to everything else which exists. There is an open flow through all parts of the cycle. The gods become human, the humans become nature, the nature becomes gods, the humans become gods, the gods become nature, nature becomes human, and nature becomes gods. Everything in the natural world is in filled with a supernatural dynamism.

Law of Similarities

Interest was not in differences but in similarities. All things occur in a cycle. Any differences are just chance happenings. Individuals are not important; therefore, all people must seek to be similar. There is a cycle each year to bring the god back to life so that nature and all other life may be brought back to life.

These laws bring about the following Ancient Near Eastern Religious Concepts:

1. There are many gods because deities corresponding to natural forces are necessary (nature/gods).
2. There is a unity of the gods with natural forces. (In order to affect the tree god, I must strike the tree.)
3. There is a great interest in the origins of the gods.
4. There is a heavy emphasis on the sexuality of and sexual practices among the gods.
5. All of life is the result of sex.
6. All the gods are in conflict with each other.
7. The gods are subservient to magic and ritual.
8. Absolute power is beyond the deity. It is impersonal and immaterial.
9. There is a complete disinterest in history. There is no past, present, or future. All is "Now."
10. Religious truth is always expressed in the timeless realm. (Livingston, 1974; Oswalt, 1977)

In this world view, idolatry was the practice of attempting to control one's personal world in order to provide for security in the world. The strongest expression of this idolatry was in the attempt to manipulate and control God or the gods.

The Nature of Idolatry in the Ancient Near East - Sympathetic Magic is the manipulation of the gods. This concept of sympathetic magic and the control of the god is also easily seen in the Old Testament:

The golden calf - Exodus 32:1-35
The capture of the Ark of Covenant - I Samuel 4:

The nation of Israel had become accustomed to seeing the Ark of Covenant leading the progression of the people. This continued in their crossing the Jordan River to enter the Promised Land (Josh. 3:15–16; 4:7–18). The Ark also led in each battle they entered into in the process of conquering the Promised Land (Joshua 3:3,15-16; 4:7-18, 6:4-20).

As a result, they began to believe that all they had to do was to take the Ark of Covenant with them into any battle or venture. If the Ark led the people, then God would be forced to bring about results in their favor.

They came to see God as a "god in the box" (Thompson, 1979), which they could control and manipulate into granting their wishes and doing their bidding on command. This concept is very forcefully demonstrated in I Samuel chapter 4, when the Ark of Covenant is captured by the Philistines. The Israelites thought that by marching the Ark at the head of the army, as was the normal practice, they would automatically be granted victory.

The problem was, they had reduced their relationship with God to a relationship based on sympathetic magic. For them, God was to be manipulated and controlled instead of obeyed and worshiped. To them, the ark had ceased to be the functional object of God's presence in their nation and had become a magic amulet which they used to control God. Instead of allowing His people to manipulate Him, God allowed the Philistines to defeat the Israelites and to capture the ark. The very object of the presence of God in the nation was now gone.

Their intimacy with God had become Idolatry of God, copying that of other Ancient Near East pagan religions which always focused on controlling the human, divine and nature realms through ritual, magic, and manipulation in order to maintain the status quo of life.

As long as they could manipulate and control the aspects of any one of these realms, they believed that their day to day lives would go on as normal, they would be blessed, and life would be secure and good. Idolatry was the practice of controlling and manipulating the three realms, so that the gods behind these realms would be forced to protect and provide for their prosperity in all aspects of their lives. The problem for the Israelites occurred when the God of Israel would not fit into their "box." He refused to cooperate in their attempts to control and manipulate Him.

Many people approach intimacy in their relationships with other people and with God in the same manner that Israel sought to manipulate their relationship with God. However, God will not be controlled and manipulated, nor will the people around us be controlled and manipulated.

Many people at some point in their lives put God in a box. When they get into a critical situation they are desperate for God to rescue them from the situation. They want God to answer their prayers and fulfill their desires in a specific manner. When God refuses to abide by their dictates, they lose faith. They feel that God no longer loves them. They feel that they no longer can trust God with their lives. As a result, they abandon their relationship with God and destroy all the intimacy they had with God. Many people also destroy their intimacy in human relationships in the same manner. When the person they love fails to honor the manipulative requirements which they place on the relationship, the intimacy and trust between them is lost and broken.

Any time we make God or another person into an idol that we can manipulate to ensure our personal quality of life, we destroy the vibrancy and trust which provides the fertile context for intimacy in our relationships. What we find in both human and divine relationships is that when traumatic events occur, they will often damage our trust relationships, and prevent us from developing intimacy with God, or with the people around us. We must constantly ask ourselves – "Is my relationship with this person based on intimacy or on idolatry?"

Psychological Factors - The sub-conscious need for control
Are you an Idolater? In what areas of your life are you seeking to manipulate others for the purpose of maintaining the status quo of your life?

Many people have a subconscious need to control the people around them. The Bible calls this witchcraft. By biblical definition, witchcraft is the manipulation and control of God or other people for personal gain (see Deuteronomy 18:10-11 and 1 Samuel 15:2 where Samuel performs a sacrifice to manipulate God into granting favor for battle). This need for control over our lives usually derives from a time of trauma in our lives when we were unable to control a very difficult situation. Frequently, people will bargain or promise God anything in an attempt to control or manipulate God (Livingston, 1974).

The control and manipulation of God can be very subtle. It is as much precipitated by our beliefs as by our desires. It may be caused by the conviction that God is going to answer our prayers in a specific manner, or by guilt manipulation. In guilt manipulation we seek to make God feel guilty if he does not act to please us. It may also be an overt attempt for us to be more righteous than God. It is not uncommon for a person to become so disillusioned with God's behavior that the person seeks to behave in a manner which he or she would consider to be more righteous than God's own behavior. Ultimately this is nothing more than an attempt to shame God because we feel he has failed us.

Ultimately any attempt to control or manipulate others is a practice of both witchcraft and idolatry. Idolatry destroys intimacy because it causes us to use a person, or to use God, for what we can get out of the relationship instead of what we can give to the relationship. When we use God or another person, we are demonstrating our distrust of that person and destroying any hope for intimacy with that person. If we cannot trust the one who made us, how can we trust our partner or mate? If we cannot enter into relationships without endeavoring to manipulate others, how can we expect to experience intimacy with them?

The Meaning of Life

Only in intimate relationships do we find the meaning of life. We ask ourselves – what is the meaning of life? The meaning of life comes down to being understood. We need for people to not only know us, but to understand us. Without high quality intimacy in our relationships, our lives have no meaning. The greatest meaning in our lives is derived from being understood by God. We can only achieve this level of meaning if we are first capable of understanding ourselves, and also of understanding the people we love the most. If we do not give other people knowledge of what we believe, how we think, and how we feel, we will not enable anyone to know and understand us. We have to become capable of giving the deepest core aspects of ourselves away to another person before we can begin to find the meaning we desire in our lives. The quality of your intimacy in relationships with other people is what gives your life meaning. The quality of intimacy in your relationship with Jesus Christ is what gives your life its ultimate meaning!

God's covenant with us is absolute. It is sealed with the death and blood of Jesus Christ our Savior and Lord. The covenant which God forms with us draws us into intimacy with Him. The intimacy which Father, Son and Holy Spirit experience in the Godhead sets the standard for all relationship intimacy which we experience in life. This includes both our relationship with God and with other humans. Sin brings brokenness and death into our lives. It separates us from God and from each other. It destroys, disfigures and prevents true intimacy. After all, it is only the one who created us who can know us, understand us and love us in a manner that brings the greatest depth of intimacy into our lives.

PART 3

Factors in Attraction and Bonding

Time with Grandpa

Chapter 8

Attraction

N ow let's examine the factors which foster mate selection. These include attachment, dating, guidance, faith, character, brain chemistry, psychological development, and mental health issues.

The Top Factor in Mate Selection Is Character

Have you ever poured concrete or watched it being poured? Concrete may be poured in multiple stages or layers. It is only the final layer or very top section which is smoothed or finished in a specific manner. The formation of our character follows this same pattern.

Though there are many definitions of character, I consider the virtues developed at each of Erickson's stages to be the key concepts and pillars in the development of a person's character. This does not mean that a person's faith and relationship with Jesus is not critical in the development of character. Instead, I consider that seven virtues of Ericson's stages of life to be the aspects of character development which are most foundational and the faith aspects to be the finish which God applies in our character development.

Research shows that we primarily choose our mate based on a person's character. If we measure character by the virtues each person must achieve to properly develop as a human being, then young adults must develop the first six of these virtues before they possess enough character in life to maintain an intimate relationship.

Hope is the virtue of trusting other people. In the stage of young adulthood, it deals with the ability to trust another person with issues of intimacy and sharing what is personal to us. *Biblical terms – hope and trust.*

Will is the virtue of being mature enough to individuate oneself from the crowd. Only with autonomy can a person have the will to put what is good, right, and true above their own desires or the desires of others. *Biblical terms – stand, good, righteous, faithful.*

Purpose is the virtue of being able to accomplish whatever is needed to achieve and succeed in life. It is the ability to take initiative and responsibility for one's own actions. *Biblical terms – personal responsibility and corporate responsibility.*

Competence is the ability to proficiently complete the tasks necessary to live and function in this world. Competence is the ability to succeed for others and not just for oneself. *Biblical terms – crown of righteousness, perfection.*

Fidelity is the faithfulness necessary to be loyal to oneself and to another person. Only a person who is faithful and loyal can earn the trust necessary to become intimate with another person or even with oneself. Only a loyal person can be worthy of love. Only a loyal person can give love. *Biblical terms – faithful, loving kindness, covenant.*

Love is the virtue that flows out of intimacy. It can only exist in a relationship with another person. Only love can value another person more greatly than a person values him or herself. Only with love can there be intimacy with God, a mate, a family, and a friend. A person who does not love himself or herself cannot love another human being. *Biblical terms – love, loving kindness.*

Care is the desire to provide what is necessary and gives pleasure in other people's lives. It is the desire to enable other people to achieve the virtues of character which are necessary to live a full, complete, and healthy life in relationship with other people. *Biblical terms – righteousness, justice, mercy, kindness.*

Wisdom is the ability to differentiate what is important, true, and righteous in life. Wisdom values only that which will bring greatness to a person's relationships with God, self, and others. Only with wisdom can we know another person with the kind of intimacy and love with which they most desire to be known and loved. *Biblical terms – holiness, truth, justice, mercy, wisdom.* (Linn, D, Linn, M. & Fabricant, 1988)

> *Character traits provide the most important criteria in determining whom to select and whom to reject as a prospective mate. Secular Concept of Character*

Secular Concept of Character

The postmodernist concentrate strongly on the fluidity of character. (Doris, John M. 2002, p14). According to the Bible this concept of fluid character demonstrates the brokenness of sin in our lives.

What are traits of character? Though many attempts have been made to summarize and define character no one is exactly sure that character is accurately postulated. This is easily confirmed by comparing the character categories provided by Benjamin Franklin, William Bennet and the Boy Scouts of America. Research has shown that there are six traits of character that seem to be universal across all cultures.

Universal Virtues of Character
Courage
Justice
Humanity
Temperance
Transcendence
Wisdom

(Peterson, Christopher & Seigman, Martin E.P. (2004).

When we compare this list to the many other list of character traits passed down through history we have to admit that a fully functioning definition and categorization of traits eludes us.

Character in the Bible

The Bible never explicitly defines character or explains how we originally develop character. It speaks of people of character. It calls for people to have godly character. It list traits of character that are demonstrated in people's behavior. It demonstrates that both good and evil character exist in all people. It demonstrates the character of God both in the names of God and the attributes of God. It demonstrates that good character is brought forth in struggle. It is very clear that people who follow Jesus Christ have changed lives and develop a righteous character.

In 2 Peter 1:5-9 we are given a list of traits of divine character that are to be developed in our lives as we follow Jesus Christ:

Goodness is living for what is right and just without weighing the consequences. It is a wholehearted dedication to doing what is best for every person you meet in life.

Knowledge in the Bible is always coupled with understanding. It is never enough to just have knowledge. We are also expected to understand. God wants us to know Him and also to understand what holiness is and why He wants to make us holy. God always gives us only what is good for us. This does not mean that what God gives to us will always come in an easy manner. God never wants anything in our lives which will deprive us of experiencing the greatest good which He wants to bring forth in our lives. The only things He seeks to withhold from us are things that will bring evil and brokenness into our lives. Only when we understand this concept of what God wants in our lives do we really have knowledge coupled with understanding.

Self-Control is the ability to choose what is right and good over what is wrong and destructive in our responses to situations in life. It is a disciplined choice to accommodate only what is good in the decisions we make life.

Perseverance is the ability to single-mindedly continue in the path which God sets before us in life, even when that path is full of struggle and difficulty.

Godliness is much more than a strong moral character. It is coming to the point in life where we want God more than anything else. It is walking with God in each and every moment of our life. It is living and being with God regardless of the consequences.

Brotherly Kindness describes the gracious behavior we demonstrate to other Christians and other people in the world. It is acting on their behalf in order to bring good into their lives and into their relationship with God.

Love is a desire to know and understand the people around us. It is taking every opportunity to inquire about what is happening in the lives of the people we meet, as well as those we love. Love wants to know, understand and help other people, just as much as we ourselves want to be known, understood and helped in life (Christian Broadcasting Network, The Biblical Perspective on Character Development).

Godly Character

In Galatians 5:19-23 we find a contrast between the traits found in an ungodly character and the traits found in a godly character. Verses 19-21 list the evil traits: "The acts of the flesh are obvious: sexual immorality, impurity and debauchery; idolatry and witchcraft; hatred, discord, jealousy, fits of rage, selfish ambition, dissensions, factions and envy; drunkenness, orgies, and the like...." Following these are listed the Godly traits: "love, joy, peace, forbearance, kindness, goodness, faithfulness, gentleness and self-control...." This list provides a clear statement of what to look for in selecting and rejecting a prospective mate. The godly traits presented in this list should be verified early before a person even considers a relationship with another person. Any person who does not demonstrate a godly character is not marriage material.

Only through godly character can we become intimate with ourselves and with other people. What is your character? Who do you choose to be before God?

Biblical Methods of Building Character

Character is not measured in a few isolated events of our life. It is measured over the course of our lives. It is what God sees deep in our hearts. Our character may be destroyed by a few indiscretions, or it may be tempered by a few righteous decisions made in the heat of our own personal inner struggles. God measures our character not by our failures, but by our successes. This is clearly demonstrated in the list of people whom the Bible describes as having noble character – Ruth (Ruth 3:11), Hanani (Nehemiah 7:2), David (Psalm 78:72), and Job (Job 2:3). Each one of these people had failures in the quality of character they demonstrated in life, but God looks at the ultimate success of the quality of their character.

Here are some of the Bible's strongest statements about building character:

Controlling your thoughts (Philippians 4:8)
Practicing Christian virtues (2 Peter 1:5-6)
Guarding your hearts (Proverbs 4:23; Matthew 15:18-20)
Being a good example for others to follow (Titus 2:7-8)
Mastering yourself (Proverbs 16:32)
Purging yourself (2 Timothy 2:21)
("What does the Bible say,")

Character in a Mate

What are the traits of character which you desire most in a mate? Is the person marriage material? The traits of character which are required for godly character are the best determinants for evaluating a prospective mate's suitability for marriage. Here is a short list of character traits that provide a good starting point in validating a prospective mate as marriage material.

Honesty, trustworthiness and loyalty
Wisdom and knowledge

Love, compassion, mercy, and forgiveness

Integrity – presents one face at all times

There are many possible mates who are exciting and fun to be with. There are many who have strong health and beauty characteristics. There are many who indicate strong social status and ability to produce wealth, but are they marriage material? It is only when you examine a person's character that you find whether the person is mentally and spiritually acceptable as marriage material.

> "...we also rejoice in our sufferings, because we know
> that suffering produces perseverance; perseverance,
> character; and character, hope" (Romans 5:3-4).

The best marriage material comes not from the people who have had an easy life, but form those who have suffered and struggled in life. These people are rarely the wealthy or the beautiful. More frequently they are the less attractive and the poor. Many people reject the best marriage prospects while they look only for the flash of wealth and beauty. Do not overlook your prince or princess because you refuse to look at that which is less attractive

The root of our character is our integrity (which issues from a non-compartmentalized personality). The Bible is very clear that God prizes and honors people with integrity. There is no concept that encompasses godly character more than integrity. Integrity exists in God's own nature. God is one – One being in three persons (Deuteronomy 6:4).

Integrity is the term frequently used in describing people for whom God holds high praise:

1 Kings 9:4 "As for you, if you walk before me faithfully with integrity of heart and uprightness..."

1 Chronicles 29:17 "I know, my God, that you test the heart and are pleased with integrity."

Nehemiah 7:2 "I put in charge of Jerusalem my brother Hanani, along with Hananiah the commander of the citadel, because he was a man of integrity and feared God more than most people do."

Job 2:3 "Then the Lord said to Satan, 'Have you considered my servant Job? There is no one on earth like him; he is blameless and upright, a man who fears God and shuns evil. And he still maintains his integrity.'"

Job 2:9 "His wife said to him, 'Are you still maintaining your integrity?'"

Job 6:29 "Relent, do not be unjust; reconsider, for my integrity is at stake."

Job 27:5 "I will never admit you are in the right; till I die, I will not deny my integrity."

Psalm 7:8 "Let the Lord judge the peoples. Vindicate me, Lord, according to my righteousness, according to my integrity, O Most High."

Psalm 25:21 "May integrity and uprightness protect me, because my hope, Lord, is in you."

Psalm 41:12 "Because of my integrity you uphold me and set me in your presence forever."

Psalm 78:72 "And David shepherded them with integrity of heart; with skillful hands he led them."

Proverbs 10:9 "Whoever walks in integrity walks securely, but whoever takes crooked paths will be found out."

Proverbs 11:3 "The integrity of the upright guides them, but the unfaithful are destroyed by their duplicity."

Proverbs 13:6 "Righteousness guards the person of integrity, but wickedness overthrows the sinner."

Isaiah 45:23 "By myself I have sworn, my mouth has uttered in all integrity a word that will not be revoked: Before me every knee will bow; by me every tongue will swear."

Isaiah 59:4 "No one calls for justice; no one pleads a case with integrity. They rely on empty arguments, they utter lies; they conceive trouble and give birth to evil."

Matthew 22:16 and Mark 12:14 "'Teacher,'" they said, 'we know that
you are a man of integrity and that you teach the way of God in
accordance with the truth. You aren't swayed by others, because
you pay no attention to who they are.'"
2 Corinthians 1:12 "Our conscience testifies that we have conducted
ourselves in the world, and especially in our relations with you,
with integrity and godly sincerity."
Titus 2:7 "In everything set them an example by doing what is good.
In your teaching show integrity, seriousness...."
(Bible Study on Character – "Integrity")

> *God puts us into relationships to teach us to live in intimacy with other people and with Him. Ultimately he also uses relationships to make us Holy.*

Chapter 9

Guidelines for Dating

The Biblical Plan for Dating – Divine Design

G od puts us into relationships to teach us to live in intimacy with other people and with Him. Ultimately he also uses relationships to make us Holy. You should always seek to maintain purity in yourself and anyone you date. If you are a Christian, the only acceptable mate for you is another Christian, one who matches you in the value you place on your relationship with Jesus. The purity of your life especially your sexual purity should also match the purity of your prospective spouse.

Relationships are about purity and holiness. God puts us in all kinds of relationships in life – marriage, dating, friends, coworkers, fellow members of organizations, etc. In relationships, we become holy either by adopting the good traits of holiness and purity found in another person's life, or by rejecting the bad traits which we find in other people's lives. Regardless of how we become holy, God wants us to maintain purity in our lives and create purity in the lives of the people we touch. Continuing a relationship outside of marriage is positive and good only as long as we maintain our own purity and bring purity and holiness into the life of the other person with whom we have a relationship.

Over 50% of girls and over 40% of guys never date in high school. (McAllister, 1997)

The purpose of dating is to learn to develop relationships and intimacy with other people as well as to determine what character and personality traits we desire in a mate. Therefore, people are not ready to date until they are comfortable enough with intimacy and self-purity to seek to use dating as a method of listening in the life of another person. Notice, I did not say evangelism. Long term dating is to be done only between Christians.

The purpose of dating is to learn to develop relationships and intimacy with other people as well as to determine what character and personality traits we desire in a mate.

Deal Breakers

There are some very important questions you need to discuss early in a relationship. These questions determine whether the person you are dating is mate potential or a reject. By reject, I do not mean someone is a bad person. Instead, he or she is just a person whom you should avoid as a mate.

1. Do you each want to have children? Whatever the answer is, it must be a mutual agreement.
2. What is the person's attitude toward money and debt? Will it be family money or personal money? If it is not family money or family debt, it is not a proper marriage attitude towards money. Remember - You marry a person's assets and liabilities as much as you marry the person. It is important to determine not only to what extent your mate is indebted or wealthy, but to determine also if you are willing to take upon yourself those assets and liabilities should you marry that person.

3.   Does the person have a healthy attitude towards sex? The ability to politely talk about sex is a strong measure of a healthy sexual attitude.
4.   What are the in-laws like? You should know the dirt and know the good about the person's family. If there is someone that is never mentioned, find out why.
5.   What is the person's attitude toward household chores? Regardless of preference for indoor or outdoor chores, each person must be willing to do all chores in case of an emergency. Be sure you are willing to live with the person's attitude toward chores.
6.   What does the person do during free time? Will this time be spent together or apart? Are you willing to live with this person's leisure activities and attitude toward free time? Who does this person spend time with during free time?
7.   Does the person have any addictions or addictive behaviors? This is not limited to drugs and alcohol. It includes pornography, lusty novels, collectables, gambling, etc.
8.   Has this person ever physically hit another person? Why?
9.   What is this person's attitude towards faithfulness in relationships?

Dating the Wrong Person

The longer you persist in dating the wrong one, the longer you prevent God from bringing into your life the right one.
Until you are willing to have no one, you are not ready to meet the right one.
If you never give up the wrong one, you will forever wonder - who was the right one?
The only thing worse than marrying no one, is marrying the wrong one.

There may be multiple people whom God would choose as the right one for you to marry, but there is no such thing as God choosing the wrong person for you to marry. It is not uncommon for people to continue dating someone who is definitely not a proper choice for him or her as a mate. They continue dating the wrong person simply because they are afraid of having no one to date or to marry. As long as they are dating someone, they feel secure and valued.

The person who fully seeks God in his or her life will choose to be with no one before he or she will choose to be with the wrong one. Only when you choose to have no one in your life can God bring into your life a right person as your mate. If you never choose to take the risk of being without someone, there is little chance you will meet and marry the right one. As long as you know you are with the wrong person, or a person who is not fully desirable to you, you will forever wonder who would have been the right one for you to meet and marry. Do you really want to live with that kind of doubt for the rest of your life?

God wants you to love Him above all else and to put Him first in your life. Only when you take the risk of having no one in your life will God be able to bless you with a right person as a mate. The longer you persist in dating the wrong person, the longer it will be before God can bring you together with a right person as a mate. There is nothing better than marrying a right one and knowing God has brought that person into your life and put you together forever.

Dating and Marriage Needs Vary by Sex

Men and women differ in their respective relational needs. With well over 30 years of counseling experience, psychologist Willard F. Harley identified, in order of importance, the five most basic needs of a husband and wife. The husband needs sexual fulfillment, recreational companionship, attractiveness, domestic support and admiration. The wife needs affection, conversation, honesty and openness, financial support and family commitment (Harley, 1986, p 10).

Five Needs of Marital Partners

Male	Female
sexual fulfillment	Affection
recreational companionship	conversation
attractiveness	honesty and openness
domestic support	financial support
admiration	family commitment

(**Harley**, 1986, p 10)

Dating Practices Vary by Culture

Western Culture – Recreational dating
Eastern Culture –Father controlled dating

All dating and marriage patterns have both good and bad aspects. There is no perfect method for choosing a mate for dating and marriage other than through prayer. We need to look at both the present Western style of dating and mate selection and the Biblical Eastern style of dating and mate selection.

In current Western culture mate selection is much more predatory. Individuals – male and female - target a specific individual whom they find attractive and strategize ways to become acquainted with the person. Once the acquaintance is made, assuming the interest is mutual for both persons, they will go on dates together and proceed through the bonding process in pursuit of the ultimate goal of marriage. At some point in the relationship they will arrange to meet each other's parents. The parents' input is considered to be an important consultation, but it is in no way the final deciding factor in the mate selection process. The good aspects of this process are that couples tend to form relationships at a much older age and are more capable of making wise choices in mate selection. As a result of having dated multiple people, the individuals have a stronger base for sharing intimacy. They also have developed a strong understanding of personal life and career goals. In this way, they tend to choose a mate who is more compatible with their chosen direction in life. The negative parts of this methodology of mate selection are that the individuals may tend to either be sexual predators (seeking relationships without commitment) or tend to enter relationships of serial monogamy. The serial monogamous relationships may overly compound brokenness in the development of intimacy and the bonding processes. A breakup of these relationships leaves deep emotional scars in each person's life. Both the predatory and serially monogamous relationships tend to develop deep brokenness and depression in the individuals because many of the relationships do not result in marriage.

In the Eastern and biblical culture, a woman lived with her parents until she was married. The marriage for a woman was always arranged by the father or an elder brother in the family. The father (or suitable representative) of the prospective bridegroom would go to the parents of the prospective bride and arrange an agreement for marriage. A dowry price would be established, and the bride would consent to the marriage. The bridegroom would then build the house and furnish it while the bride waited at home with her parents. When the groom had everything ready, he would come and claim his bride. The wedding celebration would last for a week while the bride's parents got to know the groom, and then the couple would go and establish their marriage in their new home. The couple was expected to then come to love each other during the marriage (Edersheim, 1883).

In this way the parents were responsible for choosing an appropriate mate for both the bride and the groom. The parents were seen as the most competent people capable of selecting mates for their children. They frequently chose these mates in a manner that would form not only business and socio-political alliances for the prosperity of both families, but would also provide a mate who was the best social and psychological match for their son or daughter. The marriages normally were quite successful and filled with love. Only in a few cases involving deceptive or unscrupulous parents were these marriages arranged to the detriment of the bride and/or groom. The culture was such that children grew up as responsible adults conforming to the teaching of the Bible and societal norms of their communities. Disobedient children who were a menace to society were executed by their own parents (Deuteronomy 21:18-21).

The good aspects of this method of mate selection assured the bride and groom of a suitable mate. The parents who knew them best, and had more mature judgment than they, were the persons responsible for arranging the marriages. There was much less promiscuity because it was frowned upon and punished by the community. Also, by forming early marriages couples spent much less time facing the sexual drive issues that lead to promiscuity. As a result, children were born and raised in more stable home environments. The drawback of this method was that the individuals tended to marry very early, before reaching full maturity. They were much less likely to make wise and well-reasoned choices and decisions in life. They subsequently had children at a very early time in life, when they were not adequately prepared for this role. This method worked best when the extended family all lived in the same small community and assisted the young couples with their decisions and childcare.

In Conclusion:

As both Western and Eastern cultures have evolved, a need has developed for a blend of these two methods of dating and mate selection. I suspect that in most cultures of the world, neither of these traditional methods of mate selection is highly beneficial for the single males and females of the respective societies.

While I agree that individuals need to date several different individuals in order to assist them in determining the traits that they most desire in a mate, I do believe most of this form of dating could and should be accomplished through group or chaperoned dating. I believe individuals need to be provided a secure and pure environment in which they can learn to develop healthy forms of intimacy with people of both sexes.

Individuals also need to be provided more formal and structured guidance from their parents and other adults involving criteria and wisdom for forming lasting marital relationships. Individuals and couples need to be provided with positive methods, messages, and structure for maintaining sexual purity before and after marriage.

The Purpose of Dating

What is the role of dating in preparing for marriage? The purpose of dating is to teach you about yourself. When a person has a date with the intention of assessing a partner's potential as a mate, that person initiates a very positive process of developing his or her own criteria for mate selection. Dating is not as much about finding a potential mate as developing your ability to select a mate. When you date you learn more about yourself than you learn about your partner. You learn aspects of personality and behavior that attract you and you learn about those that repel you. You learn to sharpen your senses and perceptions of other people. You learn to discern aspects of personality in another person which indicate whether you can trust or not trust that person.

Dating is not just a means of finding the right person. It is even more effective as a means of ruling out the wrong person.

You also learn to develop the social graces and skills which will make you attractive to the opposite sex and to your friends and family. Most importantly, you learn that life is not about you. Life is about those around you and those with whom you choose to associate and to love.

Many Dates, Few Relationships

If you have ever moved to a different community or lost someone you love due to death, then you know the pain and tragedy of deep loss. You know that with the loss of the person comes, also, a loss of part of yourself. If you have ever broken off a close friendship or been betrayed by someone you trusted, you know that a tragedy has taken place that is very difficult to heal. Loss and death always leave us with a big hole in our soul, and our emotions are dumped into a swirling funnel of disruption and destruction. Marriage, engagement and dating relationships all leave us very vulnerable to this form of loss and to pain. This is a good thing. It is positive for us. With the pain of loss we show we value the person with whom we held the relationship, and we have difficulty putting our selves and our world back together. However, loss can also weaken and disorient our ability to be discerning about people who would prey on us. It even weakens our ability to trust the people who seek to help us the most.

It is for this reason I believe that many dates and few relationships is one of the best forms of preparation for marriage. Multiple dates enable us to prepare ourselves for our future mate. The loss of a couple of relationships prior to marriage enables us to gain perspective as to the value we place on the relationship and on the person. The loss of these relationships also comes with a great price. Each loss runs the risk of destroying our ability to trust and to bond with another person in the future. Loss presents to us a risk of becoming so broken that it takes us years to heal. It may even prevent us from ever entering another relationship or marriage, even with a very desirable and godly mate. For these reasons, I consider it important for us to date wisely and to enter relationships even more discerningly.

Always remember, staying in a wrong relationship too long may leave pain and scars that never heal and that prevent you from ever having the most perfect relationship and marriage God would desire for your life (White, S. & White, T.).

Relational Aspects of Dating

Personal Space

People have space boundaries (Baldassare, & Feller, Susan 2009). This is commonly referred to as proxemic behavior. They become very uncomfortable when another person invades their personal space. The amount of personal space varies by person but normally is 45 centimeters or 18 inches. The more intelligent a person is, the greater the space required for a person's comfort. The friend zone is about 1.2 meters or about 40 inches. The area of social comfort is about 3.6 meters or 157 inches. The closer the friendship you have with a person, the more the person will tolerate your invading his or her personal space. The boundaries of personal space also impact a person's tolerance for crowdedness of a room.

Highly intelligent people tend to be a little more paranoid than the average person. For this reason they are also more guarded in their acceptance of space intrusion. They also have much less tolerance for anyone approaching them from the rear. If you want to make people afraid of you and not listen to you, just try invading the person's personal space (Sol, Mateo 2016).

Flirting

Both males and females seek casual clues of reciprocal interest from those they target as a possible mate. They use flirting to both solicit cues form a potential mate and to send cues of interest to a potential mate. Flirting is the universal method of having fun with the opposite sex and of communicating degrees of interest to potential mates. Flirting is also sometimes used as a healthy approach to soliciting signals that affirm a person's attractiveness to the opposite sex.

> *Flirting Tips:*
> Flirting is communication of interest in another person
> Flirt with people of equal attractiveness
> Flirt with people who are interested in you
> Men tend to mistake friendliness for flirting
> Non-verbal flirting peaks interest without risking rejection
> (Fox, 1997-2014)

Flirting is our best form of communicating our interest in another person. The question then becomes -whom should you pursue with your flirting?

The longest lasting and best relationships are between people of equal beauty. Where there is inequality in beauty, the relationship may fail more easily. Women usually underestimate their own beauty. Men frequently overestimate their own marketability to females. If you do not take the time to flirt with those who are not interested in you, then you cannot adequately determine your own measure of desirability on the market with the opposite sex.

Also, you need to flirt with people who are truly interested in you. Continual fixation on a person who is not interested in you is a waste of time and effort. God is making you into a great person. Do not waste your efforts to find a mate on someone who cannot figure out how great you are. Some people will never be attracted to each other. No one knows why. The attraction just is not there. Move on to someone who is interested in you, so that God can bring you together.

> *Keys to Flirting:*
> The best flirts get the most attention
> It takes thirteen glances to convey interest
> Watch the feet
> Flirters flaunt their assets
> Look for the smile response
> (Kelly, 2009)

In a public setting the best flirts get the most attention. It is not necessarily the most beautiful person who is the most attractive or popular. On average, it takes thirteen glances at a person to convey your interest in him or her. Watch the person's feet. We go in the direction to which our feet point. If a person is interested in you the person's feet will point in your direction. Flirters flaunt their best assets. It does not matter what the asset is, the flirter will make sure you see that asset in its best light.

If your target is responsive to your flirting, look for the person to smile until they squint. When we squint it expresses our deepest joy.

If a person is really attracted to you, this squinting smile will express the person's level of enjoyment (Kelly & Dutton, 2009).

> *Understanding Attraction in Flirting:*
> It takes less than four minutes to decide if you are attracted to someone.
> Staring into a person's eyes is the most powerful form of flirting.
> People frequently misinterpret fear for feelings of love.
> ("The Science of Flirting," 2014).

Get rid of your pickup lines. Pickup lines are a very bad way to start a relationship. There is no better way to flirt with another person than to stare them in the eye. Young men frequently have difficulty concentrating on the eyes over other parts of a woman's anatomy. If a man is unable to stare a woman in the eye, then he is too immature to date, let alone to marry. When people are truly attracted to each other they will tend to mimic the other person's posture and movement ("The Science of Flirting," 2014).

First Impressions

When you first meet new people, their initial impression of you will be based 55% on your appearance and body-language, 38% on your style of speaking, and only 7% on what you actually say (Fox, 2016).

The Role of the Human Voice

What role does a person's voice play in mate selection? There is limited research on this issue. (Hodges-Simeon & Gaulin, & Puts 2011) I do believe that the voice of a prospective mate, at least for males, is a make or break factor in mate selection. I expect men and women have different ranges of pitch which appeal to them, and which differ from person to person. Personally, I like females with a lower pitch range and a definite softness to their voices.

Three Stages of Love

The stages of love are mostly driven by hormones in both men and women.

1. Lust is driven by estrogen and testosterone which may regulate sexual arousal and sexual interest in both males and females.
2. Attraction is believed to be driven by the chemicals in our neurotransmitters. Dopamine stimulates desire and rewards aspects of pleasure. It also results in increased attention. A drop in serotonin levels will make you obsessive/compulsive about your sweetheart. Adrenalin causes you to sweat, your heart rate to increase, and your mouth to go dry.
3. Attachment uses the hormones oxytocin and vasopressin which are both effective in causing strong bonding in relationships.(Arun, 2010)

Chapter 10

Gender Issues in Attraction

Marriage Material

" Marriage Material" is a measure of quality of goods. When a person chooses an item for purchase, the quality of goods versus the purchase price is the determinant in the final decision for purchase. It works the same way in selecting a lifelong partner for marriage. The question is always – will my partner provide me with the quality as a spouse and the durability of a relationship to justify my investment of my life in this person?

Many people will invest themselves in a person regardless of the person's value to the relationship if they altruistically believe they can help or reform the person. When it comes to investing your life in a mate, altruism should never be considered. God does not put people together for one person to rescue or reform the other person. God puts people together to bear witness to Jesus and to minister to other people around them. God wants a couple to be a team for life. Therefore, we should never marry any person with whom we cannot form a team for lifelong ministry. It is this aspect of a couple's capability for being a team that determines each partner's marriageability. A person may be marriageable for someone else, but the question to be answered is the quality of the person's marriageability for *you*.

Gender Bias in Attraction

Attraction is much more than that stupid stare where your mouth is open and your chin hangs to the ground. Real attraction looks past the facial beauty and the desirable figure. Attraction focuses on what we most desire in a prospective mate. In the following sections we will examine the factors research has shown to be most important to both men and women in the mate selection process.

In this chart we see the aspects of desirability which must be ascertained in evaluating the attraction potential of a prospective mate.

Gender Focus in Mate Attraction

Women	Men
spend time with her	have fun with
tender with her	exciting sex partner
spiritual leader	homemaker
good father to her children	mother to children
good provider	responsible partner
talk with her	respect and admire him
(Dobbins, 2011)	

What men and women seek in a mate is different but complementary. After a person passes the character and intimacy test, we start evaluating that person on the basis of what is most desirable in a mate. Surveys of large groups of women and men have revealed many of the prized qualities each gender would like to find in a spouse (Dobbins, 2011; Henry, Helm, & Cruz, 2013).

The Measure of Attraction

For men the quality of a woman's beauty has become increasingly important in mate selection. For women the importance of beauty has become twice as important in selecting a mate as it is for men. With these factors in mind it becomes much harder for beautiful people to sort through the abundance of suitors to find those who can provide the necessary aspects of character and intimacy of a suitable mate. For this reason both sexes need to learn to look past the outer façade to find the real beauty of the inner person. Once the true measure of beauty is evaluated and accepted by each party in the relationship, the emotional connection has to be examined. Without an emotional connection the relationship dies.

An emotional connection must be expressed on multiple levels for a relationship to succeed. The first level of response any person wants to see is your ability to demonstrate any emotional response. The second level any person wants to see is an emotional response toward him or her. The third level any person wants to see is an emotional response toward other people. Emotions are normally demonstrated in relationships first through casual conversation. If you cannot name and express a feeling that you have, then you are not capable of an emotional connection. As the relationship progresses, emotions will be expressed through touch and other forms of intimacy. The relationship deepens and grows only as there is a balance of emotional expression on all three of these levels ("Relationships/How Men Select Women," 2014).

Forms of Attraction

1. Social attraction – desirability on the socio-economic scale
2. Physical Attraction – looks and beauty
3. Accomplishment attraction – can we work together and get something accomplished?
(McCroskey & McCain, 1974)

Researchers have theorized there are three main determinants for measuring attraction in couples. The first of these is social attraction, which is the extent of desirability that partners attach to a person's social status. Research has shown that women never marry below their perceived socio-economic level, and men rarely will marry below their perceived social-economic level (Townsend & Roberts, 1992). All societies have their own standards for determining social position. Some researchers classify these as economic prosperity, prestige, popularity and influence, and power. Social attraction also includes economic prosperity. This includes wealth, earning potential, and the security of owning a home and/or business.

The second aspect of attraction is physical attraction. This is usually measured by looks and beauty. Physical attraction includes posture, indications of physical and mental health, an oval facial structure, youth, maturity, intelligence, verbal communication, and the ability to relate on an emotional level.

The third measure of attraction is accomplishment. This measure is based on the individual's perception of the partner's ability to be a team player for accomplishing common goals in the relationship and family. Moreover, it is not just what the partner has to offer in skills and abilities for the common good of the relationship, but also how well the two individuals can work together and pool their skills to accomplish even greater mutual goals in the relationship (McCroskey & McCain, 1974).

Marriage Material According to Women

Women also prefer mates who are highly physically attractive. However neither sex readily admits this factor (Hadjistavropoulos & Genest, 1994)

Superiority perception
Emotional stability and maturity
Relationships with children
Strong familial relationships
Lives in his own home and has a good job
Someone who entertains them
("Relationships/How Women Select Men," 2014; Demyan, 2005)

Women prefer males whom are seen as superior and dominant in society (Kenrick, D.T. & Neuberg, S.L. & Zierk, k. l. & Krones, J. M., 1994). These males will demonstrate superior health, physique, height, intelligence, social skills, athleticism and wealth. They also tend to be flashy and sexually aggressive. These males will demonstrate superior power to win, lead, and influence others. They will be men who dress well, have excellent verbal skills, and make small gestures to help the less fortunate. Perhaps the strongest draw for women is men's ability to entertain. Men who are talented and funny are much more flashy and appealing to women. Also, men with feminine facial features are considered to be the most handsome. Women prefer men who are 5'11" (180.34 cm) or taller and are on average 3.5 years older. Women who have never married place higher value on a man's looks, while previously married women value a man's character.

The age at which men and women first marry has been slowly increasing over the decades as life expectancy has increased.

In 1956, men married at 22, women at 20

In 1990, men married at 26 women at 22

In 1998, men married at 27, women at 25

Currently couples tend to practice cohabitation instead of marriage. Men cohabitate at 22 and women at 20 or 21.

("Relationships/How Women Select Men," 2014)

Couples that marry younger than 25 have dramatically higher divorce rates. This is most likely due to factors in mature brain development. Both males and females make better relationship decisions after age twenty-five.

Emotional stability and maturity is the ultimate prize valued by women selecting a mate. A man who is emotional, empathetic, and compassionate with other people is considered to be emotionally healthy and mature. Only such a man is considered capable of a long term relationship.

Women also look for men who are mature and stable. They want a man who is dependable, has stable employment and a quality occupation. They look for men who show signs of being reliable and faithful in long term relationships. The more confidence a man displays in times of stress and difficult situations, the more highly he is prized by women.

A man who has a strong relationship with his parents and siblings is considered to be more mature and stable. The better he responds to children, the more highly he is prized. If he has his own home, he is almost guaranteed consideration as proper marriage material. Women will not tolerate a man who ignores or mistreats children and those who are less fortunate ("Relationships/How Women Select Men," 2014; Demyan, 2005).

For women an emotional connection enhances the desire for sex.

For men an emotional connection enhances the desire for a long term relationship.

("Relationships/How Men Select Women," 2014)

Marriage Material According to Men

Perceptions of attitude, demographic similarity, and physical attractiveness are more important determinants of attraction for men that actual similarity or objective physical attractiveness To physical attractiveness is added the perception of fertility of the female. (Townsend &Marshall & Roberts, 1993)

How do men select women? Men prefer women who have the best capability to produce offspring and who have a high pitched, youthful voice. They also look for a woman with large eyes, lips, and smaller noses and chins. The more a woman resembles an early teenage girl the more attractive she is considered to be. Women with healthy, youthful skin and hair add to their physical attractiveness. Men also prefer women with high status jobs and advanced education.

Men's preference regarding women's body structure varies by cultural environment. People who live in metropolitan areas prefer thin women. Rural areas prefer more voluptuous women with full figures. Agricultural areas prefer women who possess more height and strength for heavy work. Overall, the average sized women are considered the most attractive.

Teenage males seek girls who are a year older. Males age 20 to 30 prefer women 1 to 2 years younger. Males age thirty to fourty prefer women five to ten years younger. Males age forty to sixty prefer women ten to twenty years younger. ("Relationships/How Men Select Women," 2014).

What are the top items that men consider in determining whether a woman is proper marriage material? The factors that determine a woman's attractiveness to a man and the factors that determine consideration of a woman as marriage material are different.

> *The primary factor for considering a woman as marriage material is whether or not she is loyal.*

The primary factor for considering a woman as marriage material is whether or not she is loyal. A woman's loyalty is not just measured in the relationship between her and the man; it is measured even more by her relationship to her family and to her friends. Any woman who is not loyal in all of these areas is so extremely damaged that she cannot be trusted as an acceptable mate. There may be some situations where exceptions are made for extenuating circumstances, but, overall, the lack of loyalty is considered the number one trait for rejection of any woman as marriage material. Other factors include caring, humor, intelligence, and faithfulness (Unknown, DivineCaroline, "Male Mind Survey Challenges Popular Attitudes").

Men's Attitudes

Most men are morally opposed to unfaithfulness in marriage or a relationship. They will not cheat, either out of respect for their partner or on moral grounds. Even though most men prefer skinny or average women, overweight issues are not a deal breaker in most cases. Many men consider cohabitation to be a good measure of compatibility. In this case they are incorrect. We will examine this issue later. Men are uncomfortable with a woman's ex-partners. They prefer women who have no ex-partners, and they do not want any ex-partners who maintain ties to the woman.

Most men want sex at least multiple times per week. Even when the sexual relationship is very good, men always prefer improvement. They may be content, but they are never satisfied. Even though at least half of men will not profess love in order to get sex, there are still fifty percent who will say anything to get sex. Most men consider a woman faking orgasm to be an insult.

Most men will never pry into your personal correspondence or email. However, exceptions may be made if a man has reason to suspect you are unfaithful ("Male Mind Survey").

> *Men's Thoughts about reatlionships*
> 70% of men choose to remain faithful
> 52% will not end a relationship over weight issues
> 63% consider cohabitation to be a reliable test for marriage compatibility
> 75% are uncomfortable with a woman's ex (spouses and dates)
> 50% consider the sexual relationship as good with room for improvement
> 76% of men want sex multiple times per week
> 50% of men will not profess love to get sex
> 80% of men are offended by a woman faking an orgasm
> ("Male Mind Survey")

In general, men consider women's behaviors to be more sexual in nature than women perceive them to be. The extent to which a man perceives a behavior to be sexual depends on his preconditioning towards sexuality in behaviors (Pierce, Tyra & Hewitt, Jay, 1993). Higher anxiety levels will also increase a man's sexual perception of a natural behavior. These factors may cause him to be inappropriate in his response to women's behaviors when perceiving them as sexual in nature. For women, anxiety decreases the sexual perception of both male and female behaviors (Kowalski, 1993).

> *Marriage Material According to Women*
> Women prize a man with the following qualities:
> Neat and healthy
> Fiscally responsible
> Able to pursue compromise
> Good interaction with children
> Bachelor life – maturity
> Trusting of other people (limited jealousy)
> Respectful toward his mother
> (Diem)

Women's Attitudes

What do women consider to be the most essential aspects of marriage material in a man?

"In this same way, husbands ought to love their wives as their own bodies. He who loves his wife loves himself." (Ephesians 5:28)

If a man does not treat a woman as well or better than he treats himself, he is not marriage material. Women want a man who can and will care about them and who will provide for them. Therefore, women want a man who demonstrates some level of neatness and organization. A man who cannot tidy up his own appearance, cannot keep his living space in some semblance of order, and cannot demonstrate an understanding of timeliness is not prepared to take care of a woman. In the same vein, a man must demonstrate the desire and ability to keep himself healthy.

The way a man responds to children determines his ability to be a father to his own children. It demonstrates his ability to relate to and respond to people of weaker strength, who can offer him nothing in return.

"Anyone who does not provide for their relatives, and especially for their own household, has denied the faith and is worse than an unbeliever." (1 Timothy 5:8)

Any woman should run from a man who is not fiscally responsible. A man does not have to be rich, but he must be capable of providing a day to day living for himself and his family. Without this the man offers no security, and no chance to raise and care for children.

"Submit to one another out of reverence for Christ." (Ephesians 5: 21)

Willingness to compromise is the main demonstration of submission. A man must be able to stand on principles and to compromise on non-essentials. Any man who must win every argument or control every situation is incapable of creating a loving environment and home life for his family.

"For this reason a man will leave his father and mother and be united to his wife, and the two will become one flesh." (Ephesians 5:31)

"That is why a man leaves his father and mother and is united to his wife, and they become one flesh." (Genesis 2:24)

The man's ability to leave behind the bachelor life and demonstrate maturity speaks of his preparedness for marriage. If he is not preparing himself in this way, then he is still a boy who has never properly matured.

"Love does not delight in evil but rejoices with the truth. It always protects, always trusts, always hopes, always perseveres." (1 Corinthians 13:6-7)

A woman wants a man she can trust and who trusts her. There has to be trust for loyalty and faithfulness to exist in the marriage. There has to be trust for how the family funds are being handled. There has to be trust before a woman can respect a man and before he can love her.

"For God said, 'Honor your father and mother' and 'Anyone who curses his father or mother must be put to death.'" (Matthew 15:4)

"When the wine was gone, Jesus' mother said to him, 'They have no more wine.'" (John 2:3-4)

The way a man treats his mother speaks volumes about the way he will treat his wife. Any man who will dishonor his mother will dishonor his wife. Even Jesus was obedient to his mother in turning water into wine to save the marriage feast and Canaan of Galilee (Diem).

Chapter 11

Social Determinants of Attraction

Characteristics which Males and Females Most Desire in a Mate

S ince 1939 research on the most desirable characteristics in a mate has been repeated approximately every decade. The results have remained fairly stable with slight changes. The male and female preferences fluctuate some in the ranking of the various characteristics.

We need to realize there is a difference between the characteristics which initially attract people and the characteristics on which to base the choice of a mate. With economic, educational and other factors delaying the maturation process (which enables a person to move out from parents and establish a home of his or her own), it is easy to see why dependable character and maturity have escalated to the top rank of characteristics for mate selection. Likewise health and domestic abilities register highly as characteristics necessary to provide a stable home life. In an age of brokenness, characteristics demonstrating stability, wholeness, and permanence become top priority.

The following table presents the top factors which we use in choosing a mate. Results of recent studies clearly demonstrate a person's character, as the key factor in mate selection. Other factors also rate very high. Most of these other high rated factors are commonly known as attractants to persons seeking a mate.

It is interesting that the highest ranking of these factors are also key in reflecting emotional, physical, and spiritual health. They are the key factors for determining a person's abilities to conceive children and sustain healthy marital relationships. While these factors are specific to the setting in which they were measured, there are some indications that they retain validity regardless of culture and country.

Categorization of Factors in Mate Selection

Physical	*Social/Psychological*	*Spiritual*
Fertility	State of Origin	Religion
Physical Health	Education	Character
Body structure	Profession	
Weight, Height, Age	Financial standing	
Dentition	Age	
Complexion	Intelligence	
	Character	
	Religion	

Figure 19

This chart lists the predominant factors in mate selection. These factors may be subdivided into three main categories: Physical, Social/Psychological, and Spiritual.

The *Physical* category carries the second largest predominance of characteristics. These characteristics indicate overall physical capacity for health, fertility, and ability to provide for a family.

The *Social/Psychological* category carries the largest predominance of characteristics. These characteristics indicate overall educational and social ability to provide for a family. Intelligence and character also indicate a person's mental health. State of origin would indicate a person's cultural background for suitability as a social match in a mate.

The *Spiritual* category only has a couple of characteristics. These characteristics indicate religious belief/affiliation to be both a social, moral, and spiritual complement as a mate. The aspect of character is a key for indicating both psychological and spiritual health in a prospective mate. It indicates a person's ability to excel in a moral society, have strong mental health, and be passionately intimate with both God and family.

In *summary*, the strength of these factors determines the overall desirability of a person as a prospective mate. They present a picture of a person as physically, mentally, socially, and spiritually healthy. It is this state of health on all levels of a person's being that makes a person suitable and desirable as a mate. Character is rated the highest in desirability of all these factors. It alone indicates a person's ability to be healthy in all other areas of life and personhood. If your character is not healthy, you will not be healthy physically, socially, psychologically, or spiritually.

In spite of the factors which are most attractive to a person in a prospective mate, many people seek much more superficial factors as initial attractants in selecting a prospective mate. Girls want glitter and flash. They also want intimacy. Glitter and flash mask a man's capacity for intimacy. Insecure girls frequently have difficulty looking past the glitter and flash in evaluating a man's capacity for intimacy. As long as a woman focuses on men who present flash and glitter, she will not find the men who are capable of sharing the greatest intimacy in a relationship.

Men want curvy figures, beauty, and flirting. They also want stability and permanence. Insecure men are blinded by curvy figures, beauty and flirting which hide a woman's capacity for independence, stability, and permanence. Frequently men mistake attention for respect and manipulation for romance. Many men find it difficult to evaluate a potential mate who is not as social as other females. The highly verbal, flirty, and social female will attract the most potential mates, but will not necessarily win the hearts of the men who possess the strongest potential as long term mates.

The Cultural Perspective on Marriage

There is no such thing as an interracial marriage or relationship. We are all one race. There is such a thing as an intercultural relationship. We all come from different cultures and the color of our skin does not matter to God or to marriage (Gal 3:28). Culture is not listed in the top factors of mate selection.

The key issue that needs to be considered in an intercultural marriage is how the couple and any offspring will be treated in society. Society in the past has had a long history of strong prohibition and rejection of all intercultural marriage. In some parts of the world tribal restrictions are as strong as societal restrictions. Much of western society places much less restriction on intercultural marriages and relationships, but individuals and families may still hold prejudices toward such relationships.

Political alliance and relationship with God, not race, are the deciding factors in any prohibition of intercultural marriage in the Bible. What the Bible considers key in intercultural relationships is that Christians do not enter into relationships which hinder, prevent, or destroy their relationship with God. The big issue here is idolatry. The God of your spouse greatly impacts your relationship with Jesus Christ.

Solomon was married to women from many foreign countries. These intercultural marriages were prohibited not because of culture, but because of relationships with other gods. In the case of Solomon, it was the political alliances for which these intercultural marriages were originated that brought God's objection. In Deuteronomy 17:17 marriage for political alliance is forbidden for the kings of Israel. In Solomon's life we see just how devastating these political marriages became (see I Kings 11:1-13). These marriages turned Solomon's heart away from God, and caused God to take the kingdom away from Solomon's descendants. In the same way, any marriage with a person who practices a religion other than following Jesus Christ is unacceptable for a follower of Jesus Christ.

Israelites were strictly admonished to marry only other Israelites to prevent their accommodation of idolatry with foreign gods. In the book of Joshua we are told of Rahab who sheltered the twelve Israelite spies. Later she is absorbed into Israelite society (Joshua 6:25). In the book of Ruth, we are presented with two brothers who move with their parents to another country during a famine and intermarry with local women. When the brothers die, one of the women comes back to Israel with her mother-in-law and again marries a Jewish husband. This marriage is never frowned upon in the Bible. Because both Rahab and Ruth become faithful followers of the one true God, they are absorbed into Israelite society and included in the genealogical line of Jesus (Matthew 1:5-6). If race/culture is not an issue in the lineage of Jesus, then it cannot be considered an issue for Christian marriage.

Secular Mate Selection Theories

> The Evolutionary Approach
> Darwin /Fisher Model
> The Direct Benefits Model
> The Model of Indirect Benefits
> ("Motivation and mate-seeking," 2010)

Much of the secular perspective of mate selection is based on animal research. Theories derived from the mate selection process practiced by animals are imposed upon human mate selection. Therefore, human mate selection is viewed through the lens of animal mate selection. The overwhelming emphasis in the secular theories is to present mate selection though the concept of Darwinian evolution. As a result of this secular perspective of conformity to evolutionary concepts, factors that do not conform to the evolutionary perspective are disregarded. This leaves secular research bereft of a solid foundation upon which to base mate selection theories and conclusions.

Psychological Research on Mate Selection

What does psychological research teach us about mate selection?

> William Schutz – focus on interpersonal needs: inclusion, affection, and control
> Mary Anne Fitzpatrick – focus on relationship styles: ideology (conventional-unconventional), interdependence-autonomy, and conflict engagement-avoidance
> John Gottman – focus on level of emotional expression and conflict management. "magic relationship ratio" – five positive behaviors to every one negative behavior = the ability to maintain positivity during interactions, and thus marital satisfaction
> (Givertz, 2011)

That which you find attractive in a partner while dating can easily become that which you find most annoying in a partner when you are married. For this reason, couples need to possess a healthy analytical detachment in examining the various emotional and relational needs in a prospective mate. For example, each person has varying levels of relationship and emotional needs for inclusion, affection and control of relationships. These needs vary both by person and by culture (Schutz, 1958). While you may enjoy a partner who demands a high degree of control of the relationship, will you be able to tolerate the same degree of control later in marriage? Will you be able to include your partner in everything you do both while dating and in marriage, or will you need some time to yourself? While the affection which your partner demands now is very pleasurable to you, will you be able to keep up that level of affection in marriage?

An unconventional person can be very attractive if you are very conventional, but will the unconventional lifestyle becomes an irritant to your conventional lifestyle in the long run? Will the person who likes a lot of autonomy and independence be attractive as a mate to a person who is dependent and clingy in relationships? Can a person who avoids conflict handle the constant emotional conflict of a person who has no fear of a good fight? (Fitzpatrick, 1988).

Gottman emphasizes that you mate needs to be a person who always finds the good in a negative situation. The person who can find at least five positive aspects of a relationship to every one negative aspect will be able to find marital bliss in spite of the partner's shortcomings (Gottman, 1994; Givertz, 2011).

Differences in the Sexes – Male and Female

Even though both males and females are equal in God's creation and in marriage, they are created to be substantially different (1 Pet. 3:7). Some of the main areas of difference are in physical development, brain development and emotional development. These differences provide each sex with distinctive roles and functional differences in their relationships with each other and even in society. The differences also provide males and females with complementary skills and abilities which enable them to be much more effective in their function as a couple than they can ever be as individuals.

In terms of body strength, men have 50% more muscles than females. Male muscles are lean and their limbs are longer. This gives them greater strength, leverage and power than women and better prepares them for physically demanding activity. Only women's stomach muscles, which are used in childbearing, have as much lean muscle as do men's muscles. Men increase in muscle mass until middle age. Women stop developing muscle in childhood. Women have greater fat storage, adding curves to their bodies which men find to be very desirable.

Men have larger hearts and lungs which enable them to further excel in physical activity. The larger heart in the males pumps his twenty percent more red blood cells. This is further supplemented by the male's two additional quarts of air found in his greater lung capacity.

Females have a smaller larynx. This is coupled with shorter vocal chords. As a result, women have a higher pitch voice with a greater range of tones, resulting in a softer and pleasing voice.

Males, from birth, focus on the objects surrounding them, while females focus on words spoken to them. This gives males an advantage in awareness of surroundings and a facility for understanding the impact of objects on those surroundings. For women, the focus on words grants them an astute awareness of interpersonal interactions and communications.

The physical senses are stronger in women (touch, taste, sight, hearing, etc.). For this reason women excel at precision and detail. They have a much greater awareness of their surroundings through their senses. This power in the physical senses, in combination with verbal skills, give to women a much stronger memory for precise details as opposed to a general perception of the whole.

Men's skin is thicker which enables them to endure harsh environments more easily than women. Women's skin is about one fourth thinner and therefore softer. This gives women's skin a sensitivity to touch which provides a medium for receiving tenderness and affection.

Men and women have equal intelligence. However, that intelligence has differences deriving from distinct brain functionality. Women have strong connectivity between the two parts of their brains. This enables them to use their brain as one functioning whole and to focus both halves of their brain on a single problem. As a result, women excel at analogy and intuition. The connection between the two halves of the brain enables women to pass information between brain parts more quickly, resulting in speedier formation of conclusions. This also enables women to associate disparate information much faster and form conclusions about the information much more quickly. The one drawback/advantage of this connected brain activity is a woman's ability to stay focused on one issue and her inability to let go of any given issue. This makes women very single minded crusaders in their approach to issues.

Men have split brains. This allows males to excel at math, geography, space and depth perception and mechanical tasks. They also excel at problem solving. With the split between men's brains they are able to focus on two or more issues at one time and problem solve much more easily without being distracted.

Men are more aggression focused and women are more emotion focused. For this reason men and women approach emotions differently. Both sexes deeply crave emotional interaction. Men tend to pursue that emotional interaction with aggression, while women approach the same interaction with understanding and compassion. In times of emotional crisis men react with the urge to fight, while women react with words, facial expressions, and movements which express defense (Dawson, 1996).

Brain Development

The brain does not fully develop until around age twenty two (Dosenbach & Nardos & Cohen & Fair & Power & Church & Nelson & Wig & Vogel & Lessov-Schlaggar & Barnes & Dubis & Feczko & Coalson & Pruett & Barch & Petersen & Schlaggar 2010).

Therefore decisions of mate selection optimally should be delayed until after the brain is fully developed and capable of making a wise decision. The exception to this decision deferment is in cases where there is strong parental guidance and agreement with the relationship. In societies where young people are required to mature much faster and take responsibility for their families at younger ages, the lack of completed brain development is offset by the young person's ability to take responsibility for other people in their lives

If auto insurers charge people higher rates for those under age twenty nine because of higher risks, what does that say about your ability to choose a mate before age twenty nine?

Over All Attractiveness

There are several factors which determine a person's social attractiveness. These include physical attractiveness, personality, physical proximity, familiarity, and similarity.

1. Physical attractiveness is the initial factor in a person deciding to pursue social attraction. You get further in a relationship with another person when you both have similar levels of beauty. Possessing equal beauty to your mate also tends to engender a longer lasting relationship
2. Personality attractiveness is frequently measured by your warmth. This includes such things as a positive outlook, your attitude towards life, and your competence in social skills and intelligence.
3. Physical Proximity when two people are attracted to each other is highly desirable. Depending on the level of attraction and the willingness to pursue the relationship, the closer the physical bodies become the better for the relationship.
4. Familiarity attractiveness is simply getting to know another person and developing a friendship. As the friendship grows the liking increases.
5. Similarity attractiveness is determined by shared attitudes values, culture, education and socioeconomic level. The more similar you are to your mate, the greater the attraction.

(Burriss, 2014)

Chapter 12

Biblical Criterion for Mate Selection

Biblical Criteria for Mate Selection

Teens View of Marriage
80% want to marry. They believe their parents have
good marriages
64% in 2006 support cohabitation.
47% want to delay getting married
Girls are not as positive about marriage as boys.
69% of boys and 56% of girls favor marriage over
singleness
39% have cohabitated when reaching adulthood
(Pfleiderer, Joanne 2008)

All mate selection should begin with one consideration. Is he or
she someone who will be mutually submissive? Only a person
who is appropriately submissive is prepared to devote his or her
life to another person. If you do not know how to submit, then you
are incapable of truly being intimate with another person. If you
are not submitted to another person, then you are not prepared to
appropriately submit to God. All relationships begin with submitting
to another person. Without submission there is not a relationship.
Without submission to an equal there is only slavery. God does not

want us to live in slavery to each other. He does want us to live in loyal submission to each other as equals.

Both males and females need to look for a mate who is an equal to them. In naming the animals, in Genesis 2:19-24, Adam came to realize that none were his equal. Only when God presented Eve to him did Adam find his equal. In verse 23, Adam's words "bone of my bone and flesh of my flesh" expressed Adam's realization that the woman was truly his equal. These words also express the greatest compliment that any man can ever give to his wife. Only an equal could walk with Adam and not be his servant or his ruler. Only an equal could walk with Adam and truly be a complement who would fulfill his need for companionship. Only his equal could teach Adam how to love. We care about our belongings, we love our pets, but only when we have someone who is equal to us do we come to understand love. Love cannot exist in one person. It has to have not only an object, but an equal object. It has to be given away freely in devotion to another person before it can be reciprocated and fulfilled. Only when Adam had an equal could he become a man who could understand how God loved him just as he, Adam, loved his wife.

The word for submission is frequently translated as obedient. It expresses the kind of loyalty with which a soldier submits to the orders of a commanding officer (Kittle & Friedrich, 1972). In the Hebrew of the Old Testament we have the word *hessed* which means loving kindness and expresses passionate loyalty. This word has no exact equivalent in English. Even though the words love and *hessed* are not equal, I do consider them to be complements which express the passion and emotion bound into the meaning of each term. Only a person who is submissively loyal can be obedient to a leader. Only a man who is passionately loyal to his wife can be the kind of leader worth following. When the Bible speaks of a husband as the head of his wife, it is describing a person who provides leadership through passionate loyalty. This is a man who sacrifices everything to creatively enhance the emotional, spiritual, and physical wellbeing of a spouse. He is a man who seeks to provide protection, to please, to love, and to provide sustenance and shelter. Only the wife who responds in submission to this kind of leadership can develop the necessary loyalty and obedience to wholeheartedly submit and cultivate the leadership that her husband offers. Leadership ability has to be cultivated and developed as much by the person who submits to the leadership as by the person who must exercise the leadership. If a man and woman cannot create a proper balance in leadership and submission, they will forever be stymied in creating a marriage which is mutually beneficial for both of them. This is why trust and intimacy are so critical in a relationship.

Biblical Criterion for Mate Selection

Ephesians 5:21 -33

Male	*Female*
An equal to me	An equal to me
A leader and head	Submissive and loyal
A creator of perfection	Whole and perfect
Loves mate as much as himself	
Leave parents, cleaves to mate	
Someone to be respected	Someone to be loved

Mutual Submission

The Biblical Plan for Marriage – Divine Design

Marriage is clearly seen to be part of God's "very good" creation. (Genesis 1:31)

"it is not good that man should be alone. I will make him a helper corresponding to him." (Genesis 2:18)

"He that finds a wife finds a good thing and obtains favor from the Lord." (Proverbs 18:22)

These teachings are reaffirmed by Jesus in Matthew 10:6 and Mark 19:4-6. The Bible is also clear that singleness is the exception rather than the rule (1Corinthians 7:7, 7:32-35).

There are several key biblical factors in seeking a mate which are strongly implied in the second chapter of Genesis. According to God's original design, Adam's mate was to be "bone of my bone and flesh of my flesh." Do not overlook the significance of this statement.

> God wants you (all adults) to be married. The fact that God and Jesus have Wives, clearly present the importance and esteem given to marriage in the Bible.
>
> God's wife is Israel (Isaiah 50.1, 54:4-6, Jeremiah 3:20)
> Jesus' wife is the church (2 Corinthians 11:2 Ephesians 5:31-32)

These words describe a mate who is perfectly equal to Adam and uniquely qualified to be his mate. These words also express three main factors which are critical in a mate for Adam and for each of us: someone who is an equal, a complement, and a mate.

Someone who is equal to me – Biblical, Sociological, Psychological

Human beings seek someone who is an equal. This can be both good and bad. The kind of person we are will influence us to seek a person who shares those qualities. This may cause us to seek a mate who is not good for us, or it may prompt us to seek a mate who is very good for us. What we are like as a person will determine what our mate is like as a person. If we are battered and broken, then we will attract broken people. If we want a mate of excellent moral character and mental health, then we need to be a person of excellent mental health and morals in order to attract that kind of mate.

The greatest compliment we give to our self is to seek someone who is like us or someone who is equal to us. We frequently find people seeking a mate who is similar– similar body build, similar facial shape and similar in beauty. We also seek a mate who has similar desires, interests, beliefs, and goals in life. We seek a mate who is similar in intelligence. For example, we always marry someone who matches us within sixteen points of our IQ.

Biblically speaking, we seek a mate who is like us in that the person is a human being. Adam rejected all the animals as a mate.

It was only another human being that was considered acceptable to be a mate.

Sociologically speaking, we know that women seek a mate whom they consider to be on the same sociological and economic levels as themselves. Males will rarely marry below their socio-economic level.

Psychologically speaking, we know from abnormal psychology that people seek friends and associates who are their equals in mental health. If the person is mentally healthy, he or she will seek coworkers, friends, associates, and mates who are equally mentally healthy. If the person has poor mental health, he or she will also seek coworkers, friends, associates, and mates who are equally mentally unhealthy. As a result of this search for mental equality, we consistently find mentally unhealthy bosses who hire mentally unhealthy workers and/or other mentally unhealthy bosses (Litchi, 1995). People in churches subconsciously seek out churches and pastors who are on the same level of mental health as they are. People who are mentally unhealthy always seek a mate who is also mentally unhealthy. They do not do this consciously. It is a subconscious act, which is fully reciprocated by friends, coworkers, acquaintances, and spouses, also on a subconscious level.

A person who is mentally healthy will seek a mate whom he or she considers to be an equal. A person who is mentally ill often seeks a mate whom he or she can dominate and rule.

Someone who is a complement to me.

A complement is someone who adds to me. It is defined as that which makes complete and perfect. A complement is someone who makes you a better person. A coach seeks to make you a better athlete. A spouse makes you a better human being. A spouse will challenge you to push yourself and to excel in ways you never thought possible. The best spouse you can have will complete you as a person, to the point that you become perfect.

When looking for a mate you want to find a person who is just enough opposite of you to complete all of the aspects of your personality which are underdeveloped. As you live together and learn from each other, you grow and develop the aspects of your personality which are the strengths of your spouse. In this way you round out your personality and become even more of a whole person.

As a part of a clergy couple, my wife and I truly complement each other. Her strengths are social graces, loyalty, interpersonal skills, and drive to accomplish new things. My skills are mechanical, persevering, analytical, and intellectual pursuits. In our early years, my wife constantly insisted that I develop the skills at which she excelled. Many of these I finally developed to a proficient level of mastery. My wife has also improved some of the skills at which I excel. She always has had a strong thirst for knowledge and excellent analytical ability. She has complemented me and made me a much better and well-rounded person.

One of our former church members summarized the relationship between my wife and me in this manner. We were co-pastors of the church, and the woman commented that she felt the church finally had a whole pastor. Our skills and abilities brought a full spectrum of pastoral and personality features to the church.

Someone who is mate to me.

A mate is someone to whom you are linked in such a manner that you fit together suitably. Mates fit together in a manner that multiplies the power and effectiveness of each other's performance. The wheels of the gears mesh together and multiply power throughout the drive train of a vehicle. A true mate is someone who will enable the marriage union to multiply the power of each person in the relationship, and in the couple as a whole.

"Do not be yoked together with unbelievers. For what do righteousness and wickedness have in common? Or what fellowship can light have with darkness?" (2 Corinthians 6:14)

First, notice the context of the passage. This verse is not dealing with marriage. It is dealing with living among people who worship false gods. This does not mean that the passage should be rejected in its application to marriage. The principle of not living among those who worship false gods applies even more profoundly to marriage than it does to your associations in society. To fully apply the principle, it would be equally valid to say that we should not have business partners and friends who are unbelievers. This does not mean we cannot go on a date or cannot associate with non-Christians. It just means that we should not form long term, binding relationships with people who do not worship Jesus Christ. This includes an engagement and marriage relationship.

In 1 Corinthians 7:25-40 we read the apostles Paul's advice to those who are unmarried. This passage should in no way be considered as a command not to marry. Paul considers remaining single as the best choice and he also considers getting married as a very good choice. His real concern is a person's focus on God. I think the passage's most important point is the need to consider which choice will enable you to best honor God in your life. Some people handle singleness well and some do not. Some people handle marriage well and some do not. Even if you choose singleness and consider it the best choice for your life, do not think that your choice should not be changed later in life if God brings someone special into your life.

What to look for in a Mate

God's Criteria for Mate Selection
Ephesians 5:21-33 Gen 1:-3: and Malachi 2:10-16
> Jesus is Lord
> Perfect and Equal
> Submissive and Loyal
> Truth and Trust
> Respect and Love
> Differentiation from Parents
> Blood Covenant

God's criteria for mate selection are much different than what most people use as selection criteria. Here is a summary of God's criteria.

First, the Bible makes it clear: The most important issue in our lives is always our relationship with God. Only by having a strong and solid relationship with God, do we become capable of having a strong and solid relationship with other people. If our relationship with God is not right, our relationship with other people cannot be right. I must also say that, if our relationship with other people is not right, then our relationship with God will not be right. When we get our relationship with God corrected, He then begins enabling us to correct our relationships with other people. When God, and God alone, is first in our lives, all other relationships begin to self-correct and become much more healthy and pure.

Second, Jesus wants us to be joined with an equal. There is the old saying that God took Eve out of Adam's side so that she would not walk before him or behind him, but beside him. While I do not endorse this as the correct interpretation of that verse, there is a lot of truth in that statement. When Adam makes the statement "bone of my bone," he is declaring that Eve is truly his equal. Eve is not inferior to Adam. She is not superior to Adam. She is his exact equal. If either the man or woman fails to recognize his or her equality to his or her spouse, then the relationship becomes that of a superior spouse treating an inferior spouse as broken and less than desirable goods. At the same time an inferior spouse may treat a superior spouse as a god or as a parent. God wants us to live together, love together, minister together, and grow together as two equal and perfect people in Christ Jesus. It is important that you consider your spouse to be perfectly and normally healthy in every way. This does not mean that neither of you have any faults. It just means that neither of you have any grounds to consider your mate as inferior or superior.

If you see your prospective mate as less than perfect, then you will treat your mate as a crippled person who is less than perfect. By the words you speak to your prospective mate you either create a perfect complement for yourself in marriage, or you create a cripple whom you will always abuse as an incomplete person. How your prospective mate treats you and speaks of you tells you everything you need to know about what life will be like in marriage to that person. Remember: The manner in which you perceive your spouse speaks volumes about how you perceive yourself.

> *Both males and females are equals. You words create either a perfect mate or a cripple. Perfect people create perfect spouses. Crippled people create crippled spouses.*

Third, God wants us to choose a spouse who is submissive and loyal to us. This submission is a mutual relationship. Both partners must be loyal. Both partners must be submissive in living out his or her dedication in love to each other.

Fourth, God wants us to choose a spouse whom we can trust and who will trust us. Relationships cannot be built on lies and deceit. Where there is not absolute trust there will be lies in the relationship. This is one of the reasons sexual purity before marriage is so important. The greater the purity in the life of each person before marriage, the greater will be the capacity for trust between the partners after marriage.

Fifth, your mate must be someone whom you will love as much as you love yourself, and who will love you as much as you love yourself. You must be people who share compassion and mercy for each other and for people around you. The kind of love you are to build and share with each other demands respect for each other. Respect must always be earned. It is not to be handed out freely, but to be radically deserved. If you do not or cannot respect and/or love each other, then you are not the proper persons for each other. The man must earn and deserve the respect of the wife and make the wife know and feel that she is the most loved and important person in his life next to God. The woman must lavish the respect on the man that he has earned and receive his love with grateful appreciation.

Sixth, you must each have differentiation from parents. If you have never left home physically, then you must have left home mentally. If during the time of your courtship, you cannot separate yourself from your parents and bond as one person mentally, then you are stuck at home and unable to adequately bond to your mate. It is this transition in courtship that declares your readiness to become married. This is probably one of the reasons in Jewish marriage customs, as portrayed in the Bible, that the bride and groom became engaged and then the groom went away to build the house for the couple to live in. In doing this, the groom created the context for both partners to make the transition of allegiance from parents to each other.

Seventh, marriage is to be with a person with whom you can form a permanent and lifelong covenant. Marriage is a covenant. From God's perspective a covenant is never to be broken. No matter what happens in the relationship, covenant demands self-sacrifice and passionate loving loyalty which always chases and woos a straying partner back into the faithfulness of the covenant relationship.

Choosing the Wrong Person

Billy Graham's wife said she would have married the wrong man four times if God had given her the person she thought was right for her. She found the right person because she wanted God's best, and He kept her from making the wrong choice. (azquotes.com)

The biblical pattern for marriage is Adam and Eve (Genesis 2:18-25). Jesus declared this pattern in Matthew 19:4-6, that is, there is one woman for one man. The woman was created for the man, not the man for the woman (1 Corinthians 11:7-9). This doesn't mean that woman is a lesser person than man, but speaks concerning the wife's role in marriage. The Adam and Eve pattern is clear: woman was created as a help meet for the man, and God said it was very good (Genesis 1:31). This woman was chosen by God for the man, presented by God to the man, and the wedding ceremony was officiated and sanctioned by God.

Amos 3:3–"Can two walk together except they be in agreement?" - Obviously, the answer is no.

("Finding the Right Mate")

A Biblical Model of Choosing - Isaac and Rebecca (Genesis 24):

> Choose someone who is similar to you in background, faith, and morals
> Pray for God's guidance and direction and do not shortcut the process
> Look for a servant's heart and strong traits of character
> Use wisdom in evaluating whether the couple is a correct and appropriate match
> Ask God for signs of direction, but don't get fleeced

In Genesis chapter 24 we have the presentation of an act of mate selection. Parents are well aware of how important similarities in background are to successful mate selection. Unless the choice of a mate illustrates a high degree of cultural and background similarity, the chances of long term marital success are highly diminished. Abraham, at Sarah's prompting, made sure the choice of a mate for Isaac was not a person from the territory in which they were living. The local Canaanites practiced the vilest forms of idolatry. Their religious practices included human sacrifice, promiscuous sex in fertility rites, and perverse forms of sexual rituals. These perverse practices were repeated with each god they worshiped.

Even though Abraham's servant knew the general area where he was to go to seek a wife, he still sought guidance from God for direction to the specific person and family which would provide an appropriate mate of Isaac. His prayer for direction also included a test that would ensure that the appropriate mate would be a person of exceptional character with a servant's heart. Watering camels, which can drink up to thirty gallons of water each, is exhausting work. I do not know of any adolescents who would be willing to draw and carry five to seven gallon jugs of water to supply thirty gallons of water to a single camel, let alone several camels. Rebecca would most likely have been in her early to middle teens at this point of the mate selection process. This simple test, which Abraham's servant witnessed as it was fulfilled, demonstrated many of the most important characteristics of a proper wife. She sought to trust and to please a complete stranger. Hospitality was a strong custom in her culture, and she was willing to go to extremes in taking responsibility to fulfill this custom. She was willing to work and work hard. She had the desire to serve other people. By the time she finishes agreeing to commit herself to this marriage, she has demonstrated a strong autonomy from her friends and family.

Think about the characteristics Rebecca demonstrates – <u>trust</u>, <u>initiative</u> (demonstrated in responsibility to fulfill the custom of hospitality to a stranger), <u>work</u>, <u>identity in servanthood</u>, <u>autonomy</u> from her peers in being willing to leave her family and friends. If you compare her character to Erickson's stages of life, you find that she has fully accomplished each and every task in the character building process respective to her age. When you appraise the character of your prospective mate, does he or she demonstrate all the aspects of character appropriate to his or her age? ("Contemporary Social Issues").

How Do You Validate your Choice?

How do you know you have chosen the right person?

With a divorce rate hovering at twenty-eight percent, for first time married couples one of the scariest thoughts is – How can I know I have chosen the correct person? (Murashko, 2014). Can I really be sure my mate will stay with me for a lifetime? There is no guarantee that you will have a forever marriage. However, there are some selection criteria which will lower the risk of your becoming a divorce statistic.

A summary of what to look for in a mate:
1. Marry someone whose life is about Jesus Christ. I am not talking about someone who claims to be a Christian. I am talking about someone who seeks to walk with God and who places Jesus Christ as the most valuable relationship in his or

her life. The easiest way to determine this is to find out if the person regularly reads the Bible and if the person has a well-developed prayer life.

2. Marry your equal. This must be someone whom you love and respect. Marry someone who complements you. This is someone who is sufficiently similar and adequately different from you. Do not marry someone who is identical to you in personality. Also marry someone who meets your needs as a person.

3. Marry someone who is developmentally mature and mentally healthy. You can only be intimate with someone who is mentally healthy.

4. Marry someone of character. You can only trust someone who has a godly character. Without character, there will be enough impurities in your relationship to destroy your marriage.

5. Marry someone who is sexually pure. Only a person who is sexually pure before marriage can be trusted to remain sexually faithful after marriage.

6. Marry someone whose parents have a strong one-time only marriage. The healthier the marriage of your mate's parents, the more positive the patterns, expectations, and object relations are for a successful marriage.

7. Marry someone who is differentiated from his or her parents. Differentiation demonstrates maturity and psychological preparedness for marriage.

8. Marry someone with whom you have not cohabitated. Living together destroys your ability to form a proper covenant of marriage. It sets a contractual pattern that can be abandoned at any time and makes both yourself and your mate as disposable as the daily garbage.

9. Marry someone who prays regularly for you. If the person does not love you enough to pray for you, then the person does not love you.

Remember that mate selection is not about finding the perfect person. It is about finding the person whom Jesus would most prefer for you to marry. The Bible gives us guidelines. Only Jesus can bring us together with the most preferable person who is capable of being just a little more compatible with us than any other person. God may take you thousands of miles from home to meet another person thousands of miles from his or her home in a different country who will be your "perfect soul mate." On the other hand, Jesus may only have to take you around the block a few streets. It does not matter the geography. If you follow Jesus He will take you to where you need to be to find the person He prefers for you.

Chapter 13

Biblical Marriage Practices

Steps to Prepare for Marriage

Become a provider
Build a house
Start bonding steps
Get married
Consummate the marriage
Continue bonding steps
(1 Timothy 5:8, Proverbs 24:27, Matthew 19:4-6, Malachi 2:14-16)

The Bible describes a definite pattern of relationship building in preparation for marriage. In the marital relationships at the time of Jesus, the normal pattern was for the groom to choose a bride. The groom's father would then approach the woman's father to arrange the marriage. The groom was also responsible for developing a trade as a means of supporting a bride and subsequently a family. The groom was required to build a house, which would become the residence of the couple at the end of the marriage celebration. This house building could take place subsequent to the engagement, but it was expected to be completed before he could take his bride away from her family. During the period of engagement, the couple would develop the necessary steps in their bonding process. From the time of the initial engagement, the couple was considered to be married as husband and wife. However, sexual intercourse was reserved for the marriage celebration. The woman was expected to be a virgin until the consummation of the marriage on the first night of the marriage celebration. At the end of the week long marriage celebration, the groom would take his new bride to their new house to begin their family life together (United Church of God, 2010-2015).

Sex in Biblical Marriage Practices

Marriage begins in Genesis 2:24. "That is why a man leaves his father and mother and is united to his wife, and they become one flesh" (NIV). Marriage is a covenant and biblical covenants are formed with blood. The seal of the covenant was not a written agreement or a religious ceremony. It was sealed by intercourse and the shedding of the woman's blood from the penetration of the hymen. Both males and females were in covenant with God by virtue of being part of the chosen people and the covenant at Mount Sinai (Ezekiel 16: and Ruth 3:9). At the consummation of the wedding ceremony, both male and female were brought into the marriage covenant with each other. There are an abundance of religious rituals for worship in the Old Testament. However, there are no rituals prescribed by God for marriage. It was not a ritual or worship service, but the shedding of blood that formed the final proof of the covenant formed between the couple in marriage. Covenant was always a lifelong commitment of two persons' lives to each other, which could never be dissolved or ruptured. It bound the couple in a loyalty to each other which superseded all other loyalties. It is generally believed that couples in the biblical period married as adolescents. Girls were rarely over fifteen and boys were rarely past twenty. The wedding was celebrated through a ceremony and a week-long feast, but the actual act and seal of the marriage, in God's eyes, was the act of intercourse. This resulted in few occurrences of rape or promiscuity before marriage.

The girl went straight from being under her father's protection and care to being married to her husband.

The girl's parents preserved the bed cloth from the wedding night as formal proof that the girl was a virgin at the time of the wedding consummation. Accusations that she was not a virgin were easily refuted, and false accusations by her husband would result in whipping, fines, and legal ramifications, whereby he was prevented from ever divorcing his wife during her lifetime. If the accusations were proven true, the woman was brought to the door of her father's house and stoned to death (Deuteronomy 22:21).

The Biblical Perspective on Marriage

What is the purpose of marriage? God created marriage, and officiated at the marriage of the very first couple in the Garden of Eden. God even specifically chose mates for some of the people recorded in the Bible. He designed our minds, bodies, souls and spirits to fit and to function together with a person of the opposite sex. God created sex to bind a couple together in a manner that provides the greatest extent of pleasure known to a human being.

> *All relationships begin with submitting to another person. Without submission there is not a relationship.*

What is God's design for marriage? Does He even want us to be married? In the Bible with very few exceptions every person is married. There are a few about whom we do not know if they were ever married. There were a few biblical personalities who were married to too many women. Even the apostle Paul must have been married at some point in his life in order to be a Pharisee. Jesus is the only major character who is never mentioned as married and traditionally is understood to have never married.

With the preponderance of evidence indicating that most biblical characters were married, we have to conclude that marriage is God's plan for our lives. When we look at the first three chapters of Genesis, it is very clear that the divine plan is for us to be married. Genesis tells us that it is not good for man to be alone. God created the first mate. He performed the first wedding. He created everything and called it good. This includes sex and marriage. Even the ideal woman of Proverbs chapter 31 is a married woman.

Genesis 2: 18-24 makes it very clear that the opposite of lonely is complete. God wants us to have a mate who is our equal and who will walk alongside of us. When we look at Genesis chapters one through three, it is clear that Adam was incomplete without Eve. None of the animals were capable of providing Adam a suitable helper or complement. Adam could only become a complete person in union with Eve.

Marriage is the model of our relationship with God, and it reflects the relationships within the three persons of the Godhead. The three persons of the Godhead are not in a marriage as we know it. The intimacy of marriage, however, reflects the intimacy of the relationships within the Godhead. Both God and Jesus are married. This pattern of marriage is woven not only into human relationships, but also into the spiritual dynamics of God's marriage to Israel (Isaiah 50.1, 54:4-6, Jeremiah 3:20) and Jesus' marriage to the church (2Corinthians 11:2 Ephesians 5:31-32). Marriage is the pre-eminent pattern which demonstrates the richness of all healthy relationships.

The Bible teaches *"He who finds a wife finds a good thing and obtains favor from the Lord." (Proverbs 18:22). "Then the Lord God said, 'It is not good that the man should be alone; I will make him a helper fit for him.'" (Genesis 2:18)* In Corinthians we read, *"But because of the temptation to sexual immorality, each man should have his own wife and each woman her own husband."(1 Corinthians 7:2)* These teachings are reaffirmed by Jesus in Matthew 10:6 and Mark 19:4-6 (Cheddie, 2008).

The Bible contains many verses extolling the virtue of a good marriage. It clearly demonstrates that God places a high value on marriage. Any marriage that is not honored by both spouses is considered by God to be an act of violence to the marriage and the couple (Malachi 2:16).

I do not believe this means that single people are broken in any way. I do believe that there is a completion that comes to us in marriage. God's design from the beginning was for us to be married. I also believe that if you are not seeking a mate, you should be. If you are not able to find a mate, then you need to take a serious look at your life and seek God about what in your life is preventing you from finding a mate. Singleness is presented as an exception to the principle of marriage and is limited to individuals who seek to remain single for the purpose of ministry (1 Corinthians 7:7, 32-35). This clear pattern of God's desire for people to be married is an indication that to remain single, in many cases, may be an act of disobedience to God. At best, the decision to remain single, for a purpose other than ministry, is a clear indication of the brokenness possible in the lives of people who are not capable of entering into or maintaining a marriage relationship.

God's Plan for Your Mate

One of the greatest questions you ever face in life concerns finding a mate. Even as little children, we each plan to marry at some point in our lives. I have never met anyone who does not desire to find a mate and live happily ever after. Even with people who do not have a heterosexual orientation, the desire and drive for marriage is still present. It is this drive and desire for a mate that brings each of us to ponder God's plan for our lives regarding a mate for life.

In answer to our pondering, I believe the biblical evidence is very clear. God wants each of us to have a mate for life. The preponderance of biblical evidence is that God intends for you to marry. If we base our lives on the biblical evidence, the abundance of marriages spoken of in the Bible indicate that not to marry is contrary to God's plan for our lives.

If God wants us to marry, and He is the person who guides our lives then the question becomes, does God tell us whom to marry? I believe the answer to that question is yes and no. In the Bible, God only told one couple and two men whom to marry – Adam and Eve, Hosea, Joseph (who became the husband of Mary). God may tell you who you are supposed to marry if you earnestly seek His guidance. However God does not choose your mate. He frequently brings good choices of a mate into your life, but He leaves the final decision up to you. I believe God purposely does not arrange our marriages. For a marriage to work it has to be our decision and no one else's decision. God never allows us to blame Him because we are too lazy to make our marriage work.

I believe Christians who truly seek God's guidance in mate selection can and will be told who God's choice is for them in selecting a mate. There are plenty of accounts where God was very specific in stating His intentions for a person's specific selection of a mate. However, each of us has a choice to remain faithful in following God. Even if God tells you whom He desires for you to marry, the prospective mate also has a choice in the selection process. For this reason, even with God's strongest guidance, humans frequently destroy God's wishes for their lives even in mate selection.

For the half-dozen or so couples who have attained a long term marriage and whom my wife and I have interrogated as to how they knew whom they were to marry, the answer frequently includes a description from the man of an encounter, providing a surreal experience of the first time he saw the woman he was to marry. From these descriptions and other accounts I have read, I believe men know whom they are to marry the first time they see the woman. I have never found women to be as direct and forthcoming in describing how they know whom they are to marry. The decision for women seems to be much more gradual in nature.

The phrase "took a wife" is used repeatedly in the Bible as basically a technical term for marriage (Genesis 26:34, Genesis 25:1, 1 Chronicles 7:15). This phrase encapsulates the necessity of deliberation and work as aspects of our process of mate selection. Mates do not just fall into our laps. We have to learn through study, trial and error, and other processes, to discern the core traits and values which will make a prospective mate acceptable to us and which will secure for us a long term successful marriage.

How to Take a Wife
Take a prisoner of war - Deuteronomy 21:11-13
Take a prostitute - Hosea 1:1-3
Leveret marriage - Ruth 4:5-10
Take a dancer - Judges 21:19-25
Trade foreskins for a wife - I Samuel 18:27
Pick one from a beauty contest - Esther 2:3
Have parents arrange marriage - Judges 14:2
Marry a widow - I Samuel 25:1-41
Check the rooftops for nude bathers - 2 Samuel 11
("How to Take a Wife")
Figure 22

The Bible provides some very interesting and unusual descriptions of how men may acquire mates. I do not necessarily recommend these methods in current society.

People who wish to enter a permanent lifelong marriage place a high emphasis on the quality of the person whom they would choose for a mate. For them the selection process is very narrow and may take a long time. They consider their choice in a mate to be worth whatever wait the selection process necessitates. The Bible contains adequate examples of poor mate selection and unhappy marital unions. Even in some of the most highly praised personalities documented in the Bible, we find less than desirable marriages and less than desirable spouses.

If you want to find a good mate you have to look in a good place. The character of a godly mate far outweighs all other factors in the choice of a mate.

Several of the marriages in the Bible are recorded as less than perfect. Job's wife suggested that he curse God and die (Job 2:9).

Abigail was married to Nabal (the Fool) (1Samuel 25:14). Proverbs gives many warnings to young men about their choices of a mate (Proverbs 12:4, 19:14, 18:22, 21:19, 27:15-16, 31:30).

Beauty fades; people with poor dispositions become cranky and obnoxious. Choosing an unbeliever will wear and tear at your soul and spirit. Choosing a mate with a godly character outweighs all other criteria and is a choice you will never regret (Deffinbaugh, 2011).

Decisions Have Consequences

Choosing a mate is the most exciting and sometimes the most painful process anyone can ever go through. What most people do not realize is that the decisions we make may have consequences which are more far reaching than just our immediate lives. Our decisions in selecting a mate affect not only our own lives and our children's lives. These decisions may affect the lives of people around us for many generations to come. Our decisions always have consequences both good and bad. These consequences reach far beyond what we are able to imagine. We humans just do not have the length in intrapersonal and historical perspective to understand the impact which our decisions force on the lives of the people with whom we intersect.

> *According to the Old Testament, mate selection decisions have equal, if not far greater, ramifications in the course of a nation's history than politics.*

Adam and Eve chose to eat of the forbidden fruit and forever unleashed sin upon this world. This not only resulted in their own banishment from the Garden of Eden and ultimate death, but also created a chain of sin and death which affects every person who lives in this world from the beginning of time till the end of time (compare Genesis 3: Romans 5:12-17).

The greatest shame for a man in the Ancient Near Eastern culture was to have no son for an heir. Abraham wanted a son and so he listened to his wife and had a son through his wife's maid named Haggar. The son born to this union was named Ishmael. This method of procuring a son for an heir was contrary to God's plan to give him a son through his wife at a later date. Because Abraham attempted to force God's plan to completion in a manner that was not of God, he set up the conflict between the Arabs (descendants of Ishmael) and the Jews (descendants of Abraham's son Isaac), which has brought about the constant contention between the nations in the Middle East which we see today (Genesis chapter 16).

Solomon was the wisest man in the world. He chose to enter into international treaties and alliances through marriage to the princesses of foreign nations. Even though God had clearly dictated that this practice of marital alliances would be very devastating, Solomon still did it. As a result, his kingdom was split in two and Solomon's sin created a chain of rebellion (through the worship of false gods). This rebellion ultimately led to the Northern ten tribes of Israel being scattered and lost throughout the known world of that time (compare Deuteronomy 17:1-17 to I Kings 11:1-13).

The consequences of our decisions can be either good or bad. Decisions which we make against God's will result in destruction of our own lives and other people's lives. These decisions can initiate a chain of events that destroy whole nations. What kind of decisions do you make? Will your choices bring blessing, or will they bring curse to those around you and the generations which follow you?

On the positive side, both Rahab the Harlot (Joshua 2) and Ruth the Moabite (Book of Ruth) decided to support God's plans and God's people and became two of the women mentioned in the genealogical line of Jesus the Messiah. (Matthew 1:5) (United Church of God, 2002).

I have seen multiple cases where women and men fall in love with a person whom God did not choose to be that person's spouse. In many of these cases, the people, who have chosen contrary to God's will, never marry. They are unable to ever get past the incorrect choice they have made. In some cases they even commit suicide. The pain of living without the person they love is too much to bear.

They continue believing in a wrong choice instead of allowing God to bring about a right choice. Their lives are forever broken simply because they refused to accept or to properly seek God's will in the selection of a mate.

I have also known of couples who simply never got around to telling each other how they felt about each other. For some reason the fear of rejection, complicated circumstances, or other issues kept the couple from fully realizing the declaration of their choice of each other. As a result, they waited too long and drifted apart never to be reunited again. Many times these individuals never marry throughout their whole life.

The only way to make the correct decisions in life is to have your life fully focused on honoring God in your life. The story of Hezekiah in the Old Testament is the strongest account I know of the importance of honoring God and focusing your life to be about God, instead of God being about your life. This story clearly amplifies the consequences of the decisions we make.

Hezekiah Did Not Want to Die

Hezekiah was one of the greatest, if not the greatest, king of Judah. He was such a great religious reformer that he would be considered a great spiritual leader on the scale of a Billy Graham. Hezekiah was famous for restoring the celebration of the Passover (2 Chronicles 29:30-31) and defeating the Philistines (2 Chronicles 28:18) and (2 Kings 18:8). He refused to acknowledge the sovereignty of Assyria (2 Kings 18:7). His history is recorded in 2 Kings 18:, 2 Chronicles 29: and Isaiah 36: -38. Yet Hezekiah, like all great spiritual and political leaders, was severely flawed. His greatest flaw was that he did not want to die.

We could easily look at Hezekiah's history of revival and restoration and ask why God would want him to die. Was not God being mean to him after all he did for God? He restored the temple as the center of the nation's worship. He forbade idolatry and tore down the high places of idol worship. He was a king who honored God with his life.

God told Hezekiah he was going to die. **Why did God want Hezekiah to die?** How many people do you know who have had God tell them when they are going to die? Hezekiah needed to die. God did not want Hezekiah to die because he was evil. Instead God wanted Hezekiah to die because he was righteous. Hezekiah's death would have been a blessing in contrast to what resulted from the continuation of his life.

When God told Hezekiah that he was going to die, God was working to prevent one of the greatest spiritual leaders in the Old Testament from becoming the dad of Manasseh who was one of the most destructive rulers in the history of any nation (2Kings 21:1–18 and II Chronicles 32:33–33:20; Jeremiah 15:4).

Instead of accepting God's decision concerning his death, Hezekiah asked God to let him live. In what appeared to be an act of great favor and reward for all of Hezekiah's faithfulness, God grants Hezekiah another fifteen years of life. Within the first two years of his expanded lifespan Hezekiah fathers a son, Manasseh (2Chronicles 33:1). Manasseh was known for restoring local shrines and polytheistic worship of Baal and Asherah (2Kings 21) in the Temple. He also sponsored the Assyrian astral cult. He even sacrificed his own sons to pagan gods (2Chronicles 33:6). This son became the most evil king in Judah's history (2Chronicles 33:2-9). How would you like to be the man most responsible for turning your nation back to God and turn around and sire a son who is the most evil and destructive in the history of the nation? Manasseh was so extremely evil that he is the culmination of the extreme wickedness for which God judged Judah with destruction and exile to Babylon.

This was such a devastating exile and destruction that the nation never really began to recover until 1948 when Israel became a nation. The people of Judah returned in 70 years, but they never held significant power within their own nation for over 2000 years. It all happened because one man was afraid to die, and that one man was among the greatest of spiritual leaders.

We have seen many spiritual leaders and even political leaders fall in our nation and world simply because their accomplishments led them to believe they were special and entitled to riches, power, and favor. They allowed sin to remain in their lives because they had accomplished so much for God that they felt God should reward them. At this point Hezekiah was choosing for God to serve him instead of his serving God. He in effect made himself his own God.

Instead of living in continued faithfulness, Israel was destroyed because one great king and spiritual leader chose to refuse God's greatest offer of favor on his life. That favor was the grace of letting him die and giving him warning and time to prepare for his death. Instead Hezekiah rejected this allowance of God's favor and begged to live.

Here is the question to ask yourself: **Is my God about my life or is my life about my God?**

If I choose to reject what appears to be very displeasing and even evil from God, then I am asking God to do things in my life which may result in great destructiveness to my own and many other people's lives. It does not matter whether I have lived a holy life and feel that I deserve blessing from God. It matters that I choose to honor what God requests of me regardless of what it costs me.

If you walk with God you can expect at some point in your life God is going to ask you to endure something in your life which is very painful and may bring great brokenness to your life. If you do not accept what God wants in your life, you cannot live as a man or woman of God! Only when you are willing to accept what appears to be pain and evil from God is your life truly about God. When you reject what God asks of you, then you are asking God to be about your life. What are you destroying in your life and other's lives because you are afraid to accept what God offers you but rather seek to force God to give you something you think is greater?

Is your life about your God or is your God about your life?

Chapter 14

Social Aspects of Guidance

There are many possibilities in mate selection. How do you begin to piece together the qualities you most desire in a mate? What factors can you look at to give you direction? What are the indicators which will point you along the correct path? Where do you even begin?

Guidance Through Prayer

> Prayer as Guidance in mate selection:
> Pray for a mate
> Do not pray with your date
> Pray with your mate after you are engaged

Before you marry, please limit your instances of praying together! Prayer binds a couple together more powerfully than anything else. Make sure you have chosen the correct mate before you bind yourselves together in prayer.

The primary form of guidance in mate selection is prayer. You must always begin with prayer. Pray for God to give you a mate. I cannot understand how some people just expect God to give them a mate without ever asking for one. They treat mate selection like a teacher assigning seats in grade school or neighbor passing out candy. Ask God to bring you into each other's lives and to open your eyes to see the person He desires for you to marry.

My wife and I met in seminary. We could not stand each other. I did not find her attractive and she did not find me attractive. She has an extremely strong personality. I had been raised in a culture where strong personalities in women were unacceptable. God brought us together after seminary and we have now been married for over thirty years. It took God to bring us together because we would not have chosen each other if we had not prayed for His guidance in our mate selection.

Pray with your mate after you are engaged. Prayer will bind you together on a spiritual level as equally as you are bound on emotional and intellectual levels. Advance to this stage in your bonding only after you have made your final decision in mate selection.

> The purpose of mate selection, like marriage, is to make you holy. Holiness does not occur without pain. If you do not endure the times of pain you are not prepared for marriage.

Even though young adults seek relationships out of a need for intimacy, the primary purpose of any relationship is to make us holy. This holiness does not occur without wear and tear and pain. Just like rocks in a tumbler polish each other and make each other smooth, so relationships chip away at our rough spots and make us smooth and holy in our lives.

Parents

Another key form of guidance in mate selection is parents. What role do you want your parents to play in your selection of a mate? Parental input can be a chief determinant of a wise and successful mate selection decision. Contrary to the beliefs of most young people seeking a mate, parental guidance in the mate selection process can be vital to both the success and vitality of this lifelong relationship. Parents have the ability to examine the choice of a mate from both a prejudiced and non-prejudiced view. They have the ability to separate their own prejudices in order to give a fairly nonbiased evaluation not only of the choice of mate, but also of the viability of the relationship in the long run.

> Does the person mirror your standards of physical and mental health, appearance, socio-economic level, character and ethics?
> Does the person mirror you in social, political, and religious beliefs and world view?
> Does the person mirror you in life goals, relationship goals, and sexual purity?

Beliefs and Values

> We marry people who are similar to us in religion.
> Most people will not marry someone of a different religion.
> (Maliki, 2009)

Before I was married I worked with a man who shared with me the greatest pain of his life. He had been married for several years and recently had become a Christian. His wife was still a non-believer. There was constant tension and fighting between them because of his commitment to Jesus Christ. When you marry someone with differing religious beliefs and values, you are introducing tension into your marriage from the start.

I also performed the marriage of a couple of radically different religious backgrounds. Neither one placed much value on their religious heritage. For the most part they were both indifferently agnostic. It only takes one person reaffirming his or her faith to bring great tension into the marriage. It only takes one person accepting Jesus as Lord and savior to result in that person being rejected by his or her mate.

Education and Occupation Level

Education level is another situation where likes marry likes. Males select mates who have equal education. They prefer mates who are equally educated but also evaluate a prospective mate on more domestic issues. Women want a mate who has equal or greater education than they do. The value of educational factors increases in proportion to the woman's education. For women, the mate's education is considered to be an indication of earnings potential. For men, educational level is not as important. (Maliki, 2009)

Women place high value on mates who have high value occupational aspirations. Women also end relationships where the mate's behaviors express a lack of strong career goals. In a modern society marrying beyond a couple of years of variation in age, disrupts similarity in background and lessens companionship and intimacy. In traditional and rigid cultures, age variance is much less of an issue. (Maliki, 2009)

Age Differences

In a modern society marrying beyond a couple of years of variation in age, disrupts similarity in background and lessens companionship and intimacy. In traditional and rigid cultures, age variance is much less of an issue. (Maliki, 2009)

Sociological studies of various age groups in our society have shown radically different social values and cultural norms between generations. These differences can have strong impacts on mate selection and marriage. Individuals frequently place strong values on selecting a mate of similar age. The ability to share a common set of experiences acquired in the formative years of life creates a foundation upon which the couple more easily establishes a common bond. In rapidly changing societies, a few years of age difference can create a dissonance of culture that is equivalent of being raised in a different country and society (Maliki, 2009).

Marriages with twelve or more years of age variance frequently result in parent/child marriages. When couples have over twelve years of age difference, they normally do not develop a healthy marital relationship. Instead the younger partner in the relationship enters into the relationship seeking a parent. These younger individuals frequently seek out older individuals who are seeking a child instead of an equal in a mating relationship. As a result, these marriages take the form of either Father/Daughter or Mother/Son relationships which are perpetuated throughout the life of the marriage (Lichi, 1995).

Counselors

Within the church, traditionally the clergy or premarital counselor is supposed to provide the final determination in guidance for a couple as to whether they should marry. The advice and guidance of these professionals can be very valuable to a relationship if it is heeded. The problem is that most premarital counseling by these professionals, especially clergy, is way too short and frequently limited to the spiritual interests of the couple. Most couples only meet with counselors or clergy if they are compelled to complete such counseling as a requirement for marriage. Even then the couples desire more complete information and wise guidance on sexuality than spirituality (Boisvert, Landouceur, Beaudry, Freeston, Turgeon, Tardif,Roussy, & Loranger, 1995).

Motives That Doom Marriages

Some people get married for the wrong reasons. Their motivation for marriage is to escape what they perceive as a bad situation in their life. Instead of dealing with the issues that are destroying their lives, they seek to escape into what they perceive to be a marriage that will rescue them from all that is destructive in their current life situation. In many of these situations, the subconscious thought is to escape the present situation through their present mate, and then to seek a better mate later in life.

Some seek to marry the first person who comes along. They believe there will be no second chances and no better options. It does not matter that their mate is a second rate choice and their relationship is so full of destructive issues that the relationship is doomed from the start. Others feel that they are advanced in age, and therefore they will have no other options. It is either marry the current prospect or be forever doomed to singleness.

Some are seeking to escape from a bad former relationship or a bad home situation with their parents. Some even marry because their parents have predetermined a bad marriage partner as the parental choice, and they want to escape to a person of their own choosing. Many have developed a pattern of sequential relationships in their lives. Therefore, when they become of marriageable age they just take the next one that comes along. Some even leave a former marriage or relationship in order to marry the next one on the rebound.

Some people are sufficiently mentally unhealthy that they just want someone whom they perceive will meet their needs. It does not matter to them that the person they choose is as mentally unhealthy as they are.

Finally, many choose to marry simply to escape issues of pregnancy or the stigma of single motherhood. They believe they are spoiled goods. They believe whatever man they marry will be sufficient to rescue them from the present situation.

The sex trap is probably the most powerful reason couples marry for the wrong reason. When a couple moves their relationship to the sexual level, they become somewhat addicted to the bonding chemistry in their brain resulting from sex. God gave us sex to bind us together in marriage. When we have sex outside of marriage, we become bound together in the relationship. This can easily become a relationship where the couple no longer seeks a mate, but where the couple just seeks sexual pleasure. Eventually they may decide to marry in order to sooth their guilty consciences and to legitimize their sexual relationship. It does not matter to them whether they have adequately bonded as a couple and prepared themselves for marriage.

It only matters that they have sexual pleasure. What happens when they become married and the pursuit of sex is replaced with marital responsibilities and raising children? The pursuit of sex prevents the completion of the proper bonding process, and these couples are left without a solid foundation on which to develop their marriage.

Risk Factors to Permanence in Marriage

When choosing a mate, it is equally as important to know what to avoid in a spouse as to know what to desire in a spouse. Recent psychological research has demonstrated eight high risk factors which indicate possible future marital problems:

> One or both partners coming from a family where your parents are divorced.
> One or both partners having cohabitated before marriage.
> One or both partners previously divorced.
> One or both partners raising children of a previous marriage.
> Both partners having dissimilar religious views and orientation.
> Marrying in the late teens or earlier.
> Entering into the marriage without knowing each other for a reasonable length of time.
> Encountering financial hardships, especially early in the marriage.
> (Markman, Stanley, & Blumberg, 2001, p 39)
> Additional issues in marital satisfaction.
> Children of divorced parents are 76% more likely to divorce (Amato & Booth, 1997).
> Virgins score higher on the marital happiness prediction inventory correlating with better sexual

adjustment in marriage (Dunn, Ryan L. & Fine, Mark A. & Kurdek, Lawrence A. 1992).

Seeds of Disaster

In a children's survey, a 10-year-old boy named Martin was asked, "What do most people do on a date?" He replied, "On the first date, they just tell each other lies, and that usually gets them interested enough to go for a second date" (Hoffman, 2004).

Your first rule in dating should be never lie and never tolerate a lie. Any relationship built on lies will ultimately be destructive.

There are at least five factors which will doom your relationship or marriage from the start. I am not saying they cannot be overcome, but they will plant such strong seeds of disaster that there is little hope for the relationship in the long term. Do not sow these seeds in your relationship.

1. Impurity, in any of its forms, always sows seeds of disaster which destroy relationships. Impurity in relationships takes four basic forms.
2. Lies and deception break the most basic levels of trust and crush the intimacy at all levels of our lives.
3. Intimacy without commitment is another term for a sexual predator.
4. A serial monogamist is a person who deeply desires intimacy, but is so broken, that he or she is incapable of a long term relationship.
5. Persistent immorality is seen in a person who is so destructive that he or she is incapable of intimacy in any form and whose behavior is totally destructive of all relationships.

The greater the purity before marriage, the greater the capacity for trust and intimacy after marriage.

PART 4

The Role of Sex

What we do not talk about in church

Chapter 15

Sex Purity Facilitates Mate Selection

I n her article "Why God's People Make the Best Lovers," Patsy Rae Dawson, references three research studies demonstrating that sexual purity before marriage highly impacts the sexual relationship in a marriage.

> According to the Hite Report men who have multiple sexual partners find sex boring and sexually liberated women do not enjoy sex. Bernie Zilbergeld, PH.D., Male Sexuality, [New York: Bantam, 1978], chapters 1-4.
> In a Redbook survey of 65,000 women found that very religious women had the most orgasms and enjoyed the best sex. Claire Safran, "65,000 Women Reveal: How Religion Affects Health, Happiness, Sex, and Politics," Redbook [April 1977],
> A Woman's Day survey of 50,000 women found that traditional women have the best and most frequent sex. Claire Safran, "Does Anybody Care About Sex Anymore?" Woman's Day [Oct. 25, 1988], pp. 70-78. (Dawson, 2011-2015)

The psychological and spiritual aspects of sexual pleasure are much more important and rewarding over the long run of the relationship than the physical pleasure in the short run. The pleasure of sex may be fantastic while it last. The pleasure of the touch of the partner's body and the intimacy of the psychological and spiritual association shared between the couple are what make the lasting memories which the couple cherishes for a lifetime. Real sex is not so much the physical pleasure, but the treasured memories of the intimacy encapsulated in the blinding pleasure of those moments shared together. Only couples who bind their relationship in intimacy will experience the real joy of sex instead of the physical pleasure that lasts only for a few minutes.

> *God thought up marriage and designed you for marriage.*
> *God created sex so that you could experience the greatest intimacy on earth which, in a small way, approximates the intimacy which God wants you to have with Him in heaven.*

The purpose of sex is to prepare us to understand the greatest pleasure in the universe that we can ever experience: the bond of a relationship with the divine God who created us. Sex teaches us about the pleasure of the intimacy which we experience in a relationship with God. In comparison to our relationship with God, procreation is just a side benefit and blessing.

Sexual Addiction

Sexual addiction is the result of impeded emotional intimacy in childhood. This impeded emotional development and lack of intimacy destroys marriages as much or more than the sexual addiction itself. Traumatic episodes, which cripple the development of emotional intimacy in childhood, may create warped and perverted concepts of intimacy. These warped concepts of intimacy may result in behaviors which are self-destructive and prevent the development of healthy relationships. For these reasons, marriage or long term relationships suffer high risks of failure for persons who live in any form of sexual addiction.

The healing of sexual addiction is a three sided process. It begins with examining and healing the limited emotional intimacy developed in childhood relationships with parental figures. This can only be accomplished by forgiving those who destroyed or inhibited emotional intimacy in childhood. It continues with deliberate work at exploring and developing intimate relationships with significant others. Finally, it must be conducted in conjunction with deliberate behavior changes to restore sexual purity in the person's life.

Marrying anyone with any form of addiction is a deal breaker. Only those who are not in bondage to the dictates of their emotions and hormones can make wise decisions in selecting a mate.

Safe Sex

What do you consider to be safe sex? Is your idea of safe sex physically, mentally, psychologically, and spiritually healthy for both you and your partner?

> *The consequences of illicit sex are so great that you do not ever want to consider bringing that kind of pain and destruction into your life or the life of your present or future marriage and family.*

With records starting in the 1940's, it is recorded that 90% of Americans have participated in premarital sex. The median age of marriage for women is 25 and men 27.

In 2002 95% of all people in the US had premarital sex.

(Chandra & Mosher & Copen & Sionean, 2011).

A family story:

Many people grow up in homes where their parents do not love each other. They live together out of necessity for the sake of their children. I grew up in one of those homes. As best as I can understand the story, the dad had been unfaithful to the mother before and possibly after the marriage, at the early point of their relationship. As a result, the most affection the children ever saw in the relationship between the parents was the routine morning kiss when dad left for work. The father's promiscuity followed him into marriage and destroyed the marital happiness and success he most desired. This destruction of the marriage resulted in the destruction of the family. Around sixth grade, a half-sister, from an illicit relationship, came to live with the family for about six years. The pseudo-normal, happy family life was turned into one of rage, hatred, and pain. Those six years were six years of great pain for the whole family. The broken trust with the dad and the hatred in the heart of the mother resulted in strong emotional and psychological damage which left gaping wounds in the psychology of the children. These wounds caused damage both to the children as individuals and to their marriages in our adult life. Please, believe me when I tell you that the seeds sown in your illicit sexual pleasures will greatly harm and possible destroy the lives of your children, not to mention the devastation it will render in your own marriage.

As a result of the pain one son had experienced, he determined at a very early age that he would not participate in illicit sexual relations either before, during, or after marriage. He chose not to ever risk repeating the same behaviors which destroyed his home life as a child. He never wants to experience that kind of pain again, and he never wants to be responsible for passing that kind of pain on to his daughter or any grandchildren that may come in the future. A few minutes of illicit pleasure are not worth the damage, destruction, and pain which result in the lives of the people you love. You may think there will never be any consequences. That family will tell you there are consequences which may not show up until many years down the road. Those consequences are so great that the children would rather be dead than to pass those consequences on to any of their wives or children.

Thankfully God has brought forgiveness towards each and every member of that family, including the half-sister. As a result of that forgiveness, the members of the family no longer have to live with the destructive consequences and pain that destroyed their lives. The pain was so great that for many years it nearly prevented some of the children from ever marrying any one.

Testimony of a friend:

"As a teen mom, I believe that it [premarital sex] doesn't destroy her life. It may make it a lot harder, but not destroyed. God turned my bad choices into something great. He used my disobedience as a way to bring me back to Him. Should I have stayed pure before marriage? Yes, but God is bigger than my sin. Would I strongly encourage boys and girls to save themselves for their spouses only? YES!

Most teenagers don't know why sex outside of marriage is wrong (other than pregnancy/STD). It isn't spoken of often, if ever. No one talks about the fact that intimacy within the confines of marriage is a wonderful thing. No one talks about how intimacy between a man and wife strengthens their relationship, and the lack of it deteriorates it. No one talks about the emotional repercussions of sex outside of marriage. No one talks about how hard, when you do marry, it is to have that pure intimacy with your spouse.

Sex does bind a woman to a man. Maybe not physically, but emotionally. It takes a lot of work and prayer to have a pure relationship with a spouse when one was intimate with another person. Maybe it's easier for men. I don't know, but for women, it's hard.

It is the responsibility for both genders to say 'no' to intimacy before marriage."

Sarah

Benefits of Marrying a Virgin

Multiple studies have confirmed that virgins have longer lasting marriages, are dramatically less likely to divorce, have better sex lives and fulfillment in marriage, and are more faithful to their spouses.

In an analysis of the 1995 National Survey of Family Growth, it is revealed that lifelong monogamous females thirty plus years of age were eighty percent more likely to live in stable relationships. One extra sexual partner drops the relationship stability percentage to fifty-four and two extra partners reduce the relationship stability to forty-four percent. From this study it is quite clear that the more sexual partners you have in life, the more dissatisfying your marital relationships will be. In addition, your potential for divorce will radically increase (Rector and Johnson, 1995; Fagan, February 15, 2007).

Studies have shown that premarital sexual intercourse is related to subsequent marital dissatisfaction and divorce (Kelly & Conley, 1987), with divorced people reporting having had more premarital sex (Janus & Janus, 1993). Premarital sex is also predictive of extramarital sex (Newcomb & Bentler, 1981). (Also see Galatians 5:19-21 and 1 Thessalonians 4:3.) These studies lead us to a question. Who determines if a couple will have sex before marriage – the male or the female? The answer to this question tends to indicate who should be the most responsible for maintaining purity in the relationship. Multiple studies have indicated that it is the male gender which is the most dominant and influential in the relationship. In areas concerning sexual relations even highly dominant females will defer to the male's lead in in decisions regarding sexual behavior. Gender trumps dominance in the sexual aspect of decision making (Gerrard & Breda & Gibbons, 1990). From this I would conclude that males are to be held much more responsible for protecting the virginity of both persons in the relationship.

Real Men and Real Women

Real men wait until marriage. All the rest are just pretend!

Real Men

Real men want purity in their relationships. They do not desire to use their partners for sex. They also do not want some other person's used leftovers as a marriage partner. Real men want a woman of purity, whom they trust to be faithful to them, as a lifelong partner.

A real man would rather have one woman who will be intimate with him and allow him to pour out his soul to her than a great night in the bedroom. A real man would rather have a woman to share his life and his hobbies with than a pretty woman to show off to his friends. A real man would rather have a woman who is intelligent and compassionate, and who will love him with her whole heart. A real man would rather have a woman who will be a great mother to his children, and a person he can trust with both his wallet and his life, than a thousand sexual playmates for a million nights of fantasy.

Only a man who trains himself to live in purity, with integrity and character, can be a real man. Many men will pursue sexual pleasure as a substitute for the true intimacy which they desire with a spouse who is a real wife. A man may tell himself these liaisons of pleasure are just a temporary interlude until he finds the one woman who will fulfill him with the intimacy which he most craves in life. He never bothers to realize that these temporary pleasure interludes are delaying and destroying all possibilities of a permanent marriage with a real woman who will not only fulfill his dreams, but whom God will use in making his life whole.

What men want and need from women, more than anything, is not sex, but respect. A woman does not respect a sexual predator or a sexual conquistador. A woman can only respect a man who truly loves her. A real man wants a woman for whom he can sacrifice his life. When he finds her, he spends his life seeking to please her in every way he can. He devotes his life to seeing that she is cared for and loved.

Only a very sick and broken man will sacrifice the woman and the life he most desires for a lifetime of destructive and unfulfilling pleasures. Only a man who keeps his own purity until the wedding night is worthy to present to himself in marriage a woman of purity and perfection.

> *Real women wait until marriage. All the rest are just pretend!*

Real Women

Real **_women_** wait until marriage! **All the rest are just pretend!** There is nothing a man prizes more highly than a woman of perfection and purity. You do not have to look far in the literature of the world to find examples of the value that is placed by most cultures on a woman's virginity. Virginity is more than just sexual abstinence. Real men desire a woman who is pure in her thinking, pure in the integrity of her relationships with people in society, and pure in her trust in the people with whom she associates. The pureness of her beauty is just an added plus.

Real women also desire a man of purity. They want a man who seeks to preserve the purity of himself, his partner, and the relationship which they share. It is normally men who determine when a couple will have sex. Women who are secure in themselves and their marital expectations will form relationships only with men whom they perceive as bringing security and purity to the relationship. They want a man who values the woman enough to maintain her purity above all other desires in the relationship. Only a man who maintains the perfection and purity of a woman until the wedding night can truly relish the realization of the prize that he presents to himself in the form of the woman he marries.

> *Personal purity is the greatest prize either partner can bring into a marriage! Only those who wait and remain pure have no regrets!!!!*
>
> *Only a relationship built on complete purity, complete trust, complete respect, and love can develop complete intimacy.*

A man who cannot maintain this level of purity in the relationship is broken, unworthy, and unprepared for a lifetime commitment of marriage. Real men and real women wait until they can fully invest themselves in one spouse and one spouse only. They seek purity in their lives, in their relationships, and in their marriage.

Real women who prize themselves will preserve their purity for the one man they choose to marry. A woman who values herself and wants to give herself as a special prize to the man she marries will reject any sexual advances prior to the wedding night. Any man who pressures a woman to sacrifice her perfection and purity prior to the wedding night is broken and damaged, and not a real man. Any woman who pressures a man for sexual pleasure before the wedding night is equally broken and unworthy of presenting to herself the prize of a real man.

When you settle for second rate relationships based on sexual pleasure outside of marriage, you lose what you most desire in a permanent relationship. Men want to be respected by their spouse. How can a man completely be respected by the woman he loves when she knows that he was incapable of being sexually pure before marriage?

How can a woman be loved and prized by a man when she was incapable of maintaining her purity before marriage? Love and respect may grow through the years between the marriage partners, but the knowledge of the brokenness and impurity which each partner brought into the marriage will always remain. The knowledge of this impurity greatly damages and limits the trust which each partner has for his or her spouse in the marriage. Even as trust grows between the marriage partners in succeeding years of marriage, there is always the nagging doubt about the partner's ability to remain faithful and pure in the marriage.

Only when perfect purity is brought into the marriage are there no regrets, no damage, no broken trust, and no worries about future unfaithfulness.

Only a relationship built on complete purity, complete trust, complete respect, and love can develop complete intimacy.

Only real men and real women seek to develop the kind of personal character and integrity which attracts mates of highest character and integrity. They seek relationships based on purity and holiness. They value trust as the foundation of all intimacy. They also put God as the head of their relationship and seek only the kind of relationships that will honor God.

Anytime you have sex outside of marriage, you lose the right to be called a real man or a real woman. If you get a woman pregnant or become pregnant outside of wedlock, you are the antithesis of everything defined by the term man or woman. If you abandon the child you have brought into this world or the child's mother or father, you are not even qualified to be called a parent. You are a disgrace to your sex and an abomination to everything for which manhood and womanhood stands.

The good news is that if you will allow God to change you, He can still make a real man or a real woman out of you.

Purity and Predators

Girls, there is something I want you to know. THE MOST PRECIOUS THING TO A BOY IS A GIRL'S PURITY! I am always amazed when another teen girl gets pregnant. I cannot help but think, "Doesn't she know that sex outside of marriage greatly damages your life?" I cannot understand why girls think that sex will enable her to keep her boyfriend and bond him to her. Why do they fear losing the sexual predator boyfriend?

Hollywood and society have done everything to convince people that the only thing that puts a couple together and keeps them together is sex. Girls, there is a secret that most boys will never tell you. Boys admire girls who keep their sexual purity! Also, they most prefer to marry a girl of purity. The problem is that they have been brainwashed into believing that the only way to prove your manhood is to have sex with as many girls as possible. They want to marry a girl of purity, but they believe the only way to do that is to destroy the purity of every girl they meet.

Boys - get a brain! You want a girl's respect more than anything else, but you go around being a sexual predator. If you want a girl's respect, then be a man who protects her purity. How do you ever expect a girl to respect a sexual predator? It is you the male that determines when you as a couple will have sex. It is your responsibility to say no! Grow up and be a man.

Girls, if a boy wants sex then dump him. Sex will not bind him to you. Sex will cause him to lose respect for you, and shortly thereafter he will end the relationship. If you want to keep your boyfriend, then keep your purity. Boys, why do you want to destroy that which you prize the most in girls? Sex outside of marriage does not make you a man. It makes you a predator.

Life Without Sex

Only those who are not in bondage to the dictates of their emotions and hormones can make wise decisions in selecting a mate.

Can you live without sex? If you have always been faithful to one partner and one partner only, then living without sex is not that difficult. Many married couples live without sex. This is not an act of choice. It is a factor of a spouse's health. If your spouse is disabled or psychologically broken to the point that he or she is incapable or undesirous of having sex, can you still live a life of faithful loyalty and sexual purity with your mate?

Many people use the lack of sex or the inability to have sex with a mate as an excuse for infidelity. Sex is not a requirement for marriage. If you have always been faithful to one partner and one partner only, then living without sex is not that difficult.

It takes women multiple sexual episodes in a committed relationship with the same man to begin to enjoy sex. Therefore, women normally enjoy more orgasms after ten or more years of marriage and even more orgasms as the length of the marriage progresses.

Most sexual dysfunction in marriage is not a physical issue. Instead sexual dysfunction derives from personal psychological issues and marital relationship issues.

Men are programmed for sex by what they see. Men remember everything they see regarding sexual arousal. Women are programmed for sex by touch. They remember every touch they experience in sexual foreplay, arousal, and intercourse. Only a couple who program themselves for sexual arousal with each other will be capable of experiencing the greatest sexual satisfaction. People who are programmed with people who are not their mates bring disruptive programming into their sexual relationship.

As a Christian you only date your sister or your brother. This means that you always treat your date as if you were with your brother or your sister. When you do this, you do not have to worry about how you should behave. You will automatically behave properly. Until you are ready to get engaged, you do not begin to think of your date as anything other than a sister or a brother (McDowell & Lewis, 1980, p. 107).

Sex is Not Intimacy

Studies of sexual intimacy have shown that sex can occur at any level of developing intimacy. Our brain chemistry creates a false euphoria of closeness when we have sex that is not bound by the highest level of intimacy. Sex early in the relationship frequently prevents progression into higher levels of intimacy. This is because the couple feels safe at the present level of intimacy. They do not want to risk destroying the sexual closeness, which has been established between them, by moving into a higher level of intimacy.

For this reason, couples tend to stay at the emotional level of intimacy at which they start having sex. This becomes a barrier to progression into deeper levels of intimacy between the couple. It is much safer to stay in the false intimacy, provided by the brain chemistry during sexual intercourse, than to risk being rejected in the pursuit of deeper levels of intimacy.

When the progression of intimacy is hindered by the chemical euphoria of sex, the couple may need to declare a sexual fast. This is done to allow the relationship to progress naturally, so that sex can be resumed at a higher level of intimacy (Wilson, 2015).

Trust

What is the level of trust between you and your prospective spouse? The rate of promiscuity before and during marriage determines the level of trust that can be held by a couple. The more promiscuity there is in prior relationships, the more promiscuity will exist in the present relationship. This promiscuity limits the level of trust that can be developed before and during marriage.

Chapter 16

The Number One Sex Manual

What the Bible Teaches About Sex:

The Bible is much more thorough in its discussion of sexual matters than most people would assume. The good part is that it shows the benefit of a proper sexual relationship and mate choices. It also shows the long term consequences of improper choices and improper behavior. Here is a small sampling of what it teaches about sex and relationships.

> Profound sexual pleasure
> Lust, sexual dysfunction, sexual perversion
> Immorality, adultery, homosexuality
> Having much sex and great sex
> Good relationships and bad relationships
> Real sexual liberation
> (Dawson, 2011-2015)

It is clear that the Bible strongly teaches there are improper sexual relations which are very destructive to sexual pleasure, destructive to the quality of people's lives, and ultimately result in the complete destruction of relationships. However, the Bible also teaches that sexual relations which are restricted to the context of marriage lead to extreme sexual pleasure, a high quality of life, and long term successful marriages. The Bible spends more time discussing sexual relations than any other subject with the exception of idolatry.

Please remember, God (and the Bible) never seek to limit your life in any manner except that which is positive and healthy for you and your relationships. Instead, the Bible and God always seek to present to you the information which will bring into your life the most blessings, peace, joy and long term success in any and all aspects of your life.

The question is, do you want to have a long term, successful marriage with a joyful and fulfilling life, or do you want to destroy (or at least limit) the potential for your marriage in exchange for a few minutes of pleasure? A few minutes that will ultimately bring more pain, embarrassment, and destruction to your life than they ever give to you in pleasure?

Sex Manual – The Bible

There is more correct and helpful information about sex, love, respect, marriage, and relationships in the Holy Bible than any other book. If you have not read this book, how do expect to be able to find an excellent mate and develop a fulfilling, lasting, and permanent marriage? It is the best *how to live* and *how not to live* book on relationships ever written. If you want a great marriage, then read this book!

The Bible describes:

The first marriage

The purpose of sex in marriage

The joy and wonder of love

The great love story of an arranged marriage

Consequences of broken families, broken relationships, and broken marriages

The pain of adultery and unfaithfulness in marriage

The brokenness of people's lives

The healing and redemption of the lives of prostitutes, murderers, the self-righteous, and all other kinds of people

If your partner slept in a bed with another man or woman, would you be able to trust him or her to be sexually pure and to maintain his or her faithfulness to you? What would your answer be to this question? How much can you trust the sexual purity and faithfulness of the person you date?

There are likely more articles about sex published every year than on any other subject. Some stress sexual purity and faithfulness to your partner. Some stress sexual pleasure and doing whatever you desire. Some stress serial monogamy, or even serial profligacy. How many of the writers of those articles are living in happy, fulfilled and loving relationships? How many of those authors can really say that what they presently have in their relationships is the best of all possible relationships? How many will say they would choose their relationships as a model for every person they know? How many would say they have no regrets about how they have lived sexually, and have all of the love, respect, and intimacy they could desire in their present marriage or ongoing relationship?

Now, recall your own sexual experiences. How many of you would recommend to your friends the kind of sexual experiences you have experienced in life? If sex outside of marriage is really the best way to live, are you recommending it to everyone you meet? How many of you would recommend to your friends a life of sexual purity outside of marriage? Or do you believe sexual purity and faithfulness bring more fulfillment and joy in all relationships before, during and after marriage?

Sex by God's Design

The pleasure in the sexual relationship between two human beings is a model and reflection of the pleasure at the peak of intimacy which we experience in a relationship with God on the spiritual level. Sex is meant to be a healthy expression of love and intimacy. It is meant to express pleasure. It is meant to reflect a holy and trust filled relationship between two individuals. The reason the Bible speaks so much of joy in the Christian life is because joy is the form of pleasure which we derive from our intimacy with God and our intimacy with each other.

When we find pleasure in things and relationships which are not godly, we damage, stifle, and destroy our relationships. We introduce a sickness and disease into our relationship with God. We stunt the growth of our intimacy with God. When we participate in a sexual relationship prior to the peak of intimacy which occurs in marriage, we stunt the growth of our relationship with our spouse. We may even be bringing a cancer into the present relationship which may destroy a future marriage.

Sex in and of itself is not intimacy. In God's design, sex is an expression of the intimacy between the male and female in a fully bonded marital relationship. Its purpose is to express the intimacy which is shared between the individuals. God created sex. He knows what He wants it to accomplish in a couple's life of marriage together. Sex is not dirty. Instead, sex is meant to be holy. It is meant to bring health and wholeness into a relationship which is properly nourished in intimacy by a couple reaping the love they have created in their relationship together.

Couples frequently jump to the same level of sexual practice in a new relationship as the level of sexual practice in which they participated in the previous relationship (Lichi, 1995). As a result, they frequently circumvent the proper steps in the bonding process which are necessary to form a fully healthy relationship. The missed steps in the bonding process result in unresolved issues. These issues frequently blindside and damage the growth of intimacy prior to and during marriage. Instead of a relationship of intimacy which grows like a ripening fruit becoming plump for harvest, they create a relationship where the fruit is rotten or insect ridden.

When sex is saved for marriage it becomes like full ripe fruit, as the intimacy is picked from the garden at the proper time. We either invest ourselves in sex which hinders and damages the growth of intimacy in the relationship, or we invest ourselves in sex which enriches and expresses the rapture of intimacy built into a marriage. When we reserve sex for marriage, we model the capstone of the pleasure we experience in a relationship with God.

> *You likely will regret having sex instead of waiting.*
> *You will never regret waiting instead of having sex.*

The reason God wants you to remain sexually pure is so that you will condition yourself to avoid the damaging sexual relationships which hinder you from becoming an adult who thoroughly enjoys the sexual pleasure of bonding in marriage. God designed you to be sexually monogamous for life! Any animal can have sex. Only lifetime monogamous relationships can form marital bonds that bring pleasure for a lifetime. Polyamory as opposed to monogamy is destructive to every aspect of society which it touches. Polyamory lives for self and monogamy lives for others (Fagan, 2010).

> *Of all the religions in the world, only Judaism, Christianity (and some cults derived from them) insist on sexual purity before and after, faithfulness during marriage.*

History of Sexual Practices and Customs

Every culture, outside of Judaism and Christianity, in the period of the Old and New Testaments, condoned sex outside of marriage. Premarital and extramarital sex are never condoned in the Bible. In the Bible, only Idolatry was more strictly forbidden than pre- and extramarital sex (Brooks).

According to Demosthenes, the Greek culture around the time of Jesus had multiple forms of sexual relationships. This included courtesans who were escorts and casual sexual partners, concubines who were frequently slave mistresses, wives who bore children and maintained the home and children, and finally male and female temple prostitutes.

The Greeks also had a long history of homosexual participants, sex orgies, and drunken debauchery. These sexually excessive relationships were considered normal and brought no shame to any participants, either male or female. Roman culture was almost on a par with Greek culture for participation in sexual excess. Some cultures, like the Phoenicians, permitted the parents to acquire wealth from prostituting their daughters prior to marriage.

In Jewish culture, sexual relationships outside of marriage were strictly forbidden. The Old and New Testaments are replete with prohibitions and exhortations to maintain sexual purity outside of marriage and sexual faithfulness in marriage. Sexual impurity and unfaithfulness were considered to have consequences, not just in creating impure persons, but also in having serious ramifications for the society as a whole (Leviticus 18:27-29). In Jewish society the blood stained sheets of the wedding consummation were kept by the family of the bride, long after the wedding night, to refute any claims of sexual impurity in the bride.

Jewish couples were considered to be married from the time of engagement through the time of the wedding celebration and thereafter. Any groom who falsely accused his virgin wife of sexual impurity was sentenced with a very steep fine and prohibited from ever divorcing the woman. Such judgments were enforced by the society as a whole (Deuteronomy 22:18-19).

The Phoenician custom of selling the daughters for service in prostitution was strictly prohibited in Israel (Leviticus 19:29). Incest, adultery, and bestiality are also strictly prohibited in the Old Testament (Leviticus chapters 18 – 20, Deuteronomy chapter 27). Adultery was punished by stoning the participants to death (Deuteronomy 22:22-27). Adultery was specifically considered to be a sin against God (Genesis 39:9).

Rape or premarital sex with a virgin resulted in a steep fine and permanent marriage without the possibility of divorce. This permanent marriage had to be agreed to by the bride and her father (Exodus 22:16-17, Deuteronomy 22:28). Premarital sex in cases other than rape was only set right by the marriage of the participants.

Sexual promiscuity was considered to have wrought folly in Israel. This term was used to designate behavior of such serious nature that it brought judgment from God on the whole Israelite society.

The Old Testament prophets persistently condemned any form of sexual promiscuity (Isaiah 57:3; Jeremiah 9:1; 23:10, 14; 24:23; Ezekiel 16:38; 18:6; 22:10, 11; 23:48; 33:26; Hosea 4:2, 13, 14 and Amos 2:7). This was especially true in cases where prostitution was conducted as a part of idol worship and apostasy (Leviticus 20:6, Amos 7:17, Proverbs 6:24-29, 32-33, Proverbs 7:19-27).

The sacredness of marriage (Ephesians 5:22 ff) and the prohibitions of promiscuity are equally sanctioned by the New Testament. See biblical instruction on the following forms of sexual immorality:

> Prostitution – 1Corinthians 6:15-16
> Adultery and any form of sexual immorality (poneria) – Matthew 5:32, Galatians 5:19
> Incest – 1Corinthians 5:1. The term poneria was also used to express homosexuality in the Greek language of the New Testament period.
> Fornication – Revelation 17:1-2, 1Corinthians 6:13 & 18, 1Corinthians 7:2 Acts 21:25
> Multiple forms of sexual impurity – lasciviousness, fornication, uncleanness, passion, evil desire, and covetousness -- Colossians 3:5, Matthew 5:32, Galatians 5:19, Jude 1:7
> (Brooks)

Sexual intercourse, regardless of the brevity of the act, always binds the persons into one flesh. Both the Bible and social/psychological research confirm the severe devastation brought to a person's life when such acts are not mutually consensual.

Cases of adultery with a married woman resulted in the stoning to death of both persons who committed the adultery (Deuteronomy 22:22, John 8:4-11). In cases where an unmarried woman accused an unmarried man of rape, they were considered to be married by the act of sexual intercourse. They were considered to have voluntarily engaged in intercourse and therefore to have become married through the act of intercourse (Deuteronomy 22:1-29). The issue of pregnancy was never a consideration in this legal binding of the two persons in marriage. The man was not allowed to refuse to marry the woman. The woman, however, could refuse to marry the man who had raped her. In such cases, the man was required to pay the woman her dowry and bear the public shame and ostracization from society (Deuteronomy 22:9). In cases where there was premarital sex between two non-married persons, they were required to become married and never divorce (Exodus 22:16).

As a result of these stipulations, we can conclude:

In God's eyes, even a one night stand makes two people one. There is a deep spiritual significance in a virgin bride shedding blood on her wedding night. As a covenant is sealed by the shedding of blood, so the blood of first intercourse is a seal of the marriage covenant.

In the New Testament the word poneria (**poneria**) is frequently translated as adultery but literally means any form of sexual immorality. At its root the word means bad, wicked, defective or in a deficient state (Gerhard, Kittle & Gerhardt, Friederich, Editors, 1968). This word includes many forms of sexual immorality which are more clearly stated in other New Testament passages. It is equally applied to any form of sexual sin, regardless of whether the person committing the sin is married or single (Matthew 19:3-6).

The Bible is equally clear that non-marital intercourse, with a prostitute or any other person, is equally as binding in uniting the two participants together as marital intercourse. Acts of sexual intercourse in God's eyes are as binding on the participants as a lifelong marriage (1 Corinthians 6:15- 18, Ephesians 5: 31).

From the biblical perspective, all sexual intercourse outside of marriage should be considered to be as repulsive and as devastating as rape itself. If the act does not constitute rape of the woman, it definitely constitutes rape of God's provisions for enabling you to live a physically healthy, psychologically integrated, morally positive, and spiritually holy life.

For those who have been sexually promiscuous or sexually violated, the New Testament is equally clear that you can be forgiven and you can also be restored to a reasonable level of wholeness. Jesus forgave the woman taken in adultery. Jesus forgave the Samaritan woman who had been sexually intimate with five men (husbands) (John 8:11) (Morris, G.).

The Double Bond

In his second book Donald Joy takes a look at the biblical understanding of sexual relationships, sexual perversions, and God's ideals for intimacy, marriage, and divorce. He makes it very clear that God never intended for human beings to develop more than one sexual bond with another person. We are designed for one mate only. To consummate another marriage after having been divorced always creates an adulterated and double bonded situation. He points out that adultery or any other form of sexual immorality which results in the termination of a marriage is not a ground for divorce from God's perspective. Instead it is a tragedy that results in a double bond when a divorced person sexually consummates a relationship with another partner (Joy, 1986, pp. 65-72). His emphasis is that sexual purity is necessary for proper attachment and bonding in a marital relationship. Only the forgiveness and the healing grace of God can return a sexually promiscuous person to a state of sexual purity in God's eyes and in the person's own eyes (Joy, 1986).

Biblical Teaching on Sexual Immorality

From these and many other verses in the Old and New Testaments, it is very clear that sexual immorality is a huge issue with God. There is little that is more devastating to a Christian's relationship with God than the addiction of sexual sin. The only thing more devastating is the coupling of sexual sin and idolatry.

3 It is God's will that you should be sanctified: that you should avoid sexual immorality; 4 that each of you should learn to control your own body in a way that is holy and honorable, 5 not in passionate lust like the pagans, who do not know God; (1 Thessalonians 4:3-5)

3 But among you there must not be even a hint of sexual immorality, or of any kind of impurity, or of greed, because these are improper for God's holy people. (Ephesians 5:3)

3 It is God's will that you should be sanctified: that you should avoid sexual immorality; 4 that each of you should learn to control your own body in a way that is holy and honorable, 5 not in passionate lust like the pagans, who do not know God; (1 Thessalonians 4:3-5)

3 But among you there must not be even a hint of sexual immorality, or of any kind of impurity, or of greed, because these are improper for God's holy people. (Ephesians 5:3)

7 Now for the matters you wrote about: "It is good for a man not to have sexual relations with a woman." 2 But since sexual immorality is occurring, each man should have sexual relations with his own wife, and each woman with her own husband. 3 The husband should fulfill his marital duty to his wife, and likewise the wife to her husband. 4 The wife does not have authority over her own body but yields it to her husband. In the same way, the husband does not have authority over his own body but yields it to his wife. 5 Do not deprive each other except perhaps by mutual consent and for a time, so that you may devote yourselves to prayer. Then come together again so that Satan will not tempt you because of your lack of self-control. 6 I say this as a concession, not as a command. 7 I wish that all of you were as I am. But each of you has your own gift from God; one has this gift, another has that. 8 Now to the unmarried and the widows I say: It is good for them to stay unmarried, as I do. 9 But if they cannot control themselves, they should marry, for it is better to marry than to burn with passion. 10 To the married I give this command (not I, but the Lord): A wife must not separate from her husband. 11 But if she does, she must remain unmarried or else be reconciled to her husband. And a husband must not divorce his wife…

25 Now about virgins: I have no command from the Lord, but I give a judgment as one who by the Lord's mercy is trustworthy. 26 Because of the present crisis, I think that it is good for a man to remain as he is. 27 Are you pledged to a woman? Do not seek to be released. Are you free from such a commitment? Do not look for a wife. 28 But if you do marry, you have not sinned; and if a virgin marries, she has not sinned. But those who marry will face many troubles in this life, and I want to spare you this...

36 If anyone is worried that he might not be acting honorably toward the virgin he is engaged to, and if his passions are too strong and he feels he ought to marry, he should do as he wants. He is not sinning. They should get married. 37 But the man who has settled the matter in his own mind, who is under no compulsion but has control over his own will, and who has made up his mind not to marry the virgin—this man also does the right thing. 38 So then, he who marries the virgin does right, but he who does not marry her does better. 39 A woman is bound to her husband as long as he lives. But if her husband dies, she is free to marry anyone she wishes, but he must belong to the Lord. 40 In my judgment, she is happier if she stays as she is—and I think that I too have the Spirit of God. (1 Corinthians 7:1-40)

4 Marriage should be honored by all, and the marriage bed kept pure, for God will judge the adulterer and all the sexually immoral. (Hebrews 13:4)

18 Flee from sexual immorality. All other sins a person commits are outside the body, but whoever sins sexually sins against their own body. (1 Corinthians 6:18)

24 That is why a man leaves his father and mother and is united to his wife, and they become one flesh. (Genesis 2:24)

3 It is God's will that you should be sanctified: that you should avoid sexual immorality; 4 that each of you should learn to control your own body in a way that is holy and honorable, 5 not in passionate lust like the pagans, who do not know God; (1 Thessalonians 4:3-5)

2 But since sexual immorality is occurring, each man should have sexual relations with his own wife, and each woman with her own husband. (1 Corinthians 7:2)

18 The Lord God said, "It is not good for the man to be alone. I will make a helper suitable for him." 19 Now the Lord God had formed out of the ground all the wild animals and all the birds in the sky. He brought them to the man to see what he would name them; and whatever the man called each living creature, that was its name. 20 So the man gave names to all the livestock, the birds in the sky and all the wild animals. But for Adam no suitable helper was found. 21 So the Lord God caused the man to fall into a deep sleep; and while he was sleeping, he took one of the man's ribs and then closed up the place with flesh. 22 Then the Lord God made a woman from the rib he had taken out of the man, and he brought her to the man... (Genesis 2:18-25)

3 But among you there must not be even a hint of sexual immorality, or of any kind of impurity, or of greed, because these are improper for God's holy people. (Ephesians 5:3)

13 If a man has sexual relations with a man as one does with a woman, both of them have done what is detestable. They are to be put to death; their blood will be on their own heads. (Leviticus 20:13)

27 So God created mankind in his own image, in the image of God he created them; male and female he created them. (Genesis 1:27)

26 Then God said, "Let us make mankind in our image, in our likeness, so that they may rule over the fish in the sea and the birds in the sky, over the livestock and all the wild animals, and over all the creatures that move along the ground." 27 So God created mankind in his own image, in the image of God he created them; male and female he created them. 28 God blessed them and said to them, "Be fruitful and increase in number; fill the earth and subdue it. Rule over the fish in the sea and the birds in the sky and over every living creature that moves on the ground." 29 Then God said, "I give you every seed-bearing plant on the face of the whole earth and every tree that has fruit with seed in it. They will be yours for food. 30 And to all the beasts of the earth and all the birds in the sky and all the creatures that move along the ground—everything that has the breath of life in it—I give every green plant for food." And it was so... (Genesis 1:26-31)

10 . . .for the sexually immoral, for those practicing homosexuality, for slave traders and liars and perjurers—and for whatever else is contrary to the sound doctrine. (1 Timothy 1:10)

14 Do not be yoked together with unbelievers. For what do righteousness and wickedness have in common? Or what fellowship can light have with darkness? (2 Corinthians 6:14)

9 Or do you not know that wrongdoers will not inherit the kingdom of God? Do not be deceived: Neither the sexually immoral nor idolaters nor adulterers nor men who have sex with men 10 nor thieves nor the greedy nor drunkards nor slanderers nor swindlers will inherit the kingdom of God. 11 And that is what some of you were. But you were washed, you were sanctified, you were justified in the name of the Lord Jesus Christ and by the Spirit of our God. (1 Corinthians 6:9-11)

39 A woman is bound to her husband as long as he lives. But if her husband dies, she is free to marry anyone she wishes, but he must belong to the Lord. (1 Corinthians 7:39)

Sexual Purity

Sexual purity is not limited to the actual act of physical sex. It includes the approach and the touch of one person by another person. Physical proximity is a part of both sexual approach and sexual purity. Distances closer than 18 inches are a violation of personal space. Violation of personal space is a request for a response of intimacy. The motives and desires presented in the violation of personal space determine whether sexual purity is being violated. There are many reasons for violating the personal space of another person which are perfectly legitimate. Only the person violating the personal space knows whether his or her motives are pure (Brooks).

Leviticus 18:6 and 19 express the approach to a woman that requests a violation of personal space and the initiation of sexual foreplay. I Corinthians 7:1 talks about touching a woman. This touching is in reference to stimulating sexual desire in the woman. This is also an expression of violation of personal space with impure intent and motive.

In making these statements, the passages speak to sexual purity. The violation of personal space always presents a situation in which the person who is approached must decipher the intent and motive of the person violating personal space. At this point, the person who is approached must make a decision to accommodate or reject the violation. This decision is based on his or her assumption of the violator's motives. Only the personal space violator who approaches with a righteous and holy motive can maintain sexual purity and integrity in his or her person.

Sex Outside of Marriage

Why are the two belief systems of the Bible – Judaism and Christianity – the only ones which prohibit any form of sex outside of marriage?

> *The biblical message is not only that illicit and promiscuous sexual relationships are forbidden, but that they will destroy your life, cripple your relationship with God, and destroy any chance you may have of enjoying a successful, prosperous, and beneficial marriage*

See: Leviticus 19:29, Leviticus 17:-20:, Deuteronomy 22: and 27: Proverbs 6:-7:, Isaiah 57:3; Jeremiah 9:1; 23:10, 14; 24:23; Ezekiel 16:38; 18:6; 22:10-11; 23:48; 33:26; Hosea 4:2, 13-14 and Amos 2:7. Matthew 5:32, 1 Corinthians 5: through 7:, Galatians 5:19, Ephesians 5:3, Colossians 3:5, 1Thessalonians 4:3, Jude 1:7, Hebrews 13:4, and Revelation 9:21 (Brooks).

The message and practice of all cultures from the beginning of time has been to advocate illicit sex and sexual promiscuity. Many religions have even elevated sex as a dynamic aspect of their worship service. In the Ancient Near East, it was believed that sex was necessary to ensure the rising of the god from the dead each year. As a part of these beliefs, every sexually mature female, both married and single, was required to become a religious prostitute for at least one day each year. This prostitution occurred as an aspect of social and religious responsibility. Males also frequently participated in this practice. As a result, there would be no virgins at the time of marriage and there would be no wives who had not committed adultery in marriage. Instead, each and every man was married to a prostitute, and many women were married to male prostitutes. Adultery was considered acceptable and normal for all males. Sexual immorality was so flagrant in the ancient world that some cultures and religions made a practice of raising money for the local temple by forcing their daughters to participate in prostitution (see Leviticus 19:29). In cultures and religions which enslave women, this practice of forcing wives and children to raise money by prostitution is still practiced today. Both the Old and New Testaments are very clear about God's demand for sexual purity. For the Old Testament, see Leviticus chapters 17:-20:, Deuteronomy chapters 22: and 27: Proverbs chapters 6:-7:, Isaiah 57:3; Jeremiah 9:1; 23:10, 14; 24:23; Ezekiel 16:38; 18:6; 22:10-11; 23:48; 33:26; Hosea 4:2, 13, 14 and Amos 2:7. For the New Testament, see Matthew 5:32, 1 Corinthians chapters 5: through 7:, Galatians 5:19, Ephesians 5:3, Colossians 3:5, 1Thessalonians 4:3, Jude 1:7, Hebrews chapter 13:4, and Revelation 9:21.

Western culture is equally filled with debauchery and promiscuity. Religion and worship are usually left out of the picture, but practices of prostitution, adultery, and all forms of sexual promiscuity are considered to be both acceptable and desirable for all males and females in society. Those who are sexually pure are ridiculed and despised. The only two belief systems which advocate sexual purity outside of marriage and sexual fidelity within marriage are Orthodox Judaism and Biblical Christianity.

Verification of Sexual Purity

The biblical culture and religion of the Jews in the Old Testament was the only Middle Eastern culture where virginity was prized and demanded in civil society. This practice carried over to Christianity and is still demanded by those who practice Biblical Christianity. Virginity and sexual purity is a concept which has become almost completely lost in Western society, even among many people who call themselves Christians. This does not abrogate God's standard. The Bible is very clear: Christians are to be sexually pure, both before and after marriage, and faithful during marriage. The emphasis on sexual purity in Christianity and Judaism separates God's people into a whole different category in this world. The Bible is abundantly clear that Christians are to be different. We are to be a holy people. We are not to be conformed to this world, but to be transformed (Romans 12:2). It is in the debauchery and impurity of the linkage of sex with idolatry that God pointedly declares His standard of morality. It is this linking of sex and worship for which God judges and destroys nations for their immoral practices. This is most clearly seen in the repeated condemnation of the sin the Israelites committed at Baal-Peor (Deuteronomy 4:3).

I am not advocating the condemnation of those who have chosen to break God's commands. Judgement is God's job. Instead, Christians are to show compassion and love to those who break God's commands, while at the same time upholding the biblical standards of sexual purity and faithfulness. God wants us as Christians to develop a culture and practice among Christian believers where the tolerance of sexual immorality is never acceptable. From God's perspective, sexual holiness and purity must be prized as the highest and most normal form of sexual conduct in life.

Erotic Sexual Practices in the Bible
   Song of Solomon:
   2:3 oral sex on male
   2:6 manual stimulation
   4:5 fondling breast
   4:12-16 oral sex on female
   (Driscoll)

From these passages, it appears that these sexual practices are condoned within the confines of marriage.

Chapter 17

Sex and Brain Chemistry

A couple's behaviors in triggering their personal brain chemistry significantly impact the influence of those chemicals upon the couple's sexual relationship. These impacts may be either positive or negative, depending on the context and motives of the behavior.

Brain chemistry in and of itself is neutral. What you do in relationships determines how your brain chemistry will affect you, your mate, and your relationship. Sexual excitement is centered in the brain. This is clearly seen in that nocturnal emissions demonstrate that it is possible to be stimulated and have emissions without any physical contact with the sexual organs.

Sexual Relationships

Why are those who are not virgins when married more likely to divorce than those who are virgins at marriage? Why are sexually active adolescents more likely to be depressed than their abstaining peers?

Why do married couples have higher levels of sexual satisfaction than unmarried persons with multiple sexual partners?" (McIlhaney & McKissic-Bush, 2008, p 20)

Frequently individuals who move from one sexual partner to another feel worse about themselves and their partners.

Sexually active girls are three times more likely to attempt suicide

than their virgin friends. Sexually active boys are seven times more likely to attempt suicide than their virgin friends.
(McIlhaney and McKissic-Bush, 2008, p 20)

> Sexual excitement is centered in the brain.
> *Four Sex Chemicals*
> Dopamine
> Oxytocin
> Vasopressin
> Pheromones
> (Miclhaney and McKissic-Bush, 2008, p. 20)

Chemicals in the Brain

There are four main chemicals related to sex that are produced in the brain.

Dopamine – Sex is a strong generator of dopamine reward. People are highly vulnerable to the addictive cycles of dopamine reward from sexual activity.

Oxytocin – oxytocin is a strong inducement to bonding and trust. In women, it is produced by intimate touching and sexual intercourse. In sexual intercourse the woman's brain if flooded with oxytocin promulgates a cycle of desire for repeated stimulation and intercourse.

Pheromones - are transmitted through the skin and provide a scent that only a female can perceive. They induce a woman to be attracted to a certain type of man. They are also associated with a woman's sexual satisfaction (McIlhaney & McKissic-Bush, 2008, pp. 35-44).

As a result of physical touch, oxytocin triggers a feeling of trust which may cause a woman to trust a male with whom she otherwise would be cautious about forming a relationship. Therefore, girls should not let guys hug or touch them unless they plan to form a trust bond with the guy. It is because of the oxytocin bond that girls experience extreme emotional pain when a relationship ends.

Vasopressin is the bonding chemical for males. It works very similarly to the oxytocin chemical in females. Vasopressin floods the male brain during sexual intercourse. It produces a partial bond between a man and every female partner with whom he has intercourse.

When people repeatedly bond and break up and bond again through multiple sexual encounters, they destroy their ability to maintain a bond. This is very similar to tape losing its stickiness. Repeated incidents of sexual intercourse with multiple partners cause a person to risk losing his or her ability to bond with any one partner. It, therefore, damages his or her ability to form a lasting committed marital relationship.

Because of the brain chemistry in bonding relationships, couples who have no prior sexual history and form lifetime monogamous relationships will create very strong bonds in marriage.

> Males will pursue being physically intimate until the girl presents a flat refusal.
> The majority of teens wish they had waited until they were older.
> 93% of teens want a strong abstinence message.
> Cognitive development is not mature until the mid-twenties.
> (Miclhaney & McKissic-Bush, 2008)

Just because sexual intercourse is not technically rape or forced, it is not necessarily consensual or appropriate. This is especially true for younger boys and girls. Without proper guidance, adolescent males often misunderstand, or choose to ignore, anything short of a flat refusal to become more physical in a relationship.

The majority of teens who have become sexually active wish they had waited until they were older to engage in sexual activity. Ninety-three percent of adolescents think that young people ought to receive a strong abstinence message. This ninety-three percent includes teens who have experienced sexual intercourse. The adolescent brain and young adult brain is far from its final, fully formed state. The brain does not reach full cognitive maturity until the mid-twenties. As a result, the brain lacks the completed brain circuits necessary to make the best behavior decisions. Therefore, the ability to make mature and responsible decisions, which assist individuals in avoiding damaging baggage from past mistakes and decisions, is hindered by the lack of full brain maturity in the teen and earlier adult years. This lack of brain maturity can easily prevent the individual from achieving his or her full potential (McIlhaney & McKissic-Bush, 2008, p. 90).

Individuals who wait to have sex until marriage have increased assurance about the success and quality of their marriage. Most of these marriages are faithful, and most sex in marriage is good; moreover, most people who don't have sex until marriage have more stability and more success in their lives as measured by education, economics and emotional stability (McIlhaney & McKissic-Bush, 2008, p. 94).

On the other hand, cohabitation relationships are not as permanent as marital relationships. Cohabitation before marriage creates a higher chance of divorcing after marriage. Cohabitation normally results in a lack of commitment to the relationship. Cohabiting couple are more likely to have violence in their relationship than married couples. Cohabitation is four times more likely to result in infidelity (Miclhaney & McKissic-Bush, 2008, pp. 96-97).

Testimonial statements included by McIlhaney and McKissic-Bush clearly evidence that young people who are engaged in short-term sexual relationships are cheating themselves out of authentic, fulfilling and meaningful sex (McIlhaney & McKissic-Bush, 2008, p. 113).

Sex Statistics

Once a young person becomes sexually active, it becomes almost compulsory to continue. The earlier a person has sexual intercourse, the higher the number of sexual partners he or she will have in life.

Here are some important statistics about sex in our society.

Sexual Bonding

For high school students:

46% of all high school students have had sexual intercourse.

Over 50% of 15 to 19 year olds have tried oral sex.

75 percent of graduating high school students have had sex.

Around 16% of high school students have had four or more sexual partners.

70% of female and 50% of male high school students who have had sex wish they had waited.

For girls younger than sixteen when experiencing their first intercourse, 58% of them will have at least five sexual partners by their late twenties.

For college students:

70.2 % of males and 70.9 percent of females have had sex with at least one partner in the past year.

17% of males and 10.9 percent of females reported three or more sexual partners in the past year.

42.5 % of males and 45.1% of females reported having oral sex one or more times in the past thirty days.

For the population in general:

People who have had sex before marriage are more likely to divorce after they marry.

People who have had sex before marriage will have difficulty adjusting to marriage and are less likely to experience happiness, satisfaction, and love.

Without a clear message about sex and family values from their parents, adolescents remain very confused about sex. They do not understand what is expected of them or what they should expect of themselves. Without a clear message about sex and values, adolescents remain very susceptible to sexual invitations, especially from friends. (McIlhaney & McKissic-Bush, 2008, pp. 101, 115).

Chemical Glue

Bonding is not just an emotional feeling. It is cemented by the chemistry produced in the body, especially the brain. As we have seen, these chemicals are like glue forcing and binding the couple together. Even though the brain's chemistry is extremely powerful, it is the parents' influence on their children's attitudes which has the strongest influence in shaping adolescent and young adults' behaviors in the sexual arena (McIlhaney & McKissic-Bush, 2008, p.112). The parents who take a positive attitude towards a healthy sexuality and sexual purity in premarital relationships provide the strongest assistance to adolescents seeking to steer themselves through the carnage of wrecked relationships and into the harbor permanence of marriage.

Chapter 18

The Sexuality of God

Sexuality of God

We do not know much about the sexuality of God. God the Father and Jesus the son are both presented as male in the Bible. The Holy Spirit is typically just presented as spirit. Yet, God created us in His own image.

"He created them male and female and blessed them. And he named them "Mankind" when they were created." Genesis 5:2.

Adam was the first Human. When God created/separated Eve from Adam, then Adam was presented as male in his sexuality and Eve was presented as female in her sexuality. If we are created in God's image and we are both male and female, then both male and female sexuality must exist in the nature of God. Therefore, I conclude that both male and female sexuality exist in the very nature of God. I must also conclude that sexuality is important to God. The question we should ask is - How is sexuality displayed in the relationships between the three persons of the Godhead? Does God have sexual relations with the other persons of the godhead? The Bible never presents God as having sexual relations with the other persons of the godhead, but I do believe sexuality and sexual expression is fully a part of those relationships. With all of the gods presented in the religious history of humans, sexual relations are a part of the interpersonal relationships of the gods. Worship of pagan gods in non-Christian religions of the

Old and New Testament periods focuses on sexual intercourse with multiple partners and partners of either sex as a preeminent aspect of worship. The one exception to worship consummated in sex acts is worship of the God of the Bible. Worship involving sex with any partner is never permissible in the worship of the God of the Bible and is a practice for which pagan societies were frequently decimated in warfare.

My wife is one of those rare people who has died and gone to heaven and subsequently returned to earth to live out the remainder of her life. She died over thirty years ago on the operating table. Jesus told her it was not her time and she would have to return. My wife tells me that the one outstanding impression of God which she received during her time in heaven was the awesome presence of light and love when she saw Jesus face to face. The Bible constantly presents God as love. It even defines Him as Love. *God is love...* I John 4:16.

My best conclusion is that the sexuality of God is presented in love. In marriage, sex is meant to be an expression of love. In our interpersonal relationships with both sexes, our sexuality is meant to be expressed in love for that person. The Bible expresses this clearly in Jesus' new commandment:

*"A new command I give you: **Love one another**. As I have loved you, so you must **love one another**. ... John 13:34*

We find the same expression of relational love as the foundation of our interpersonal relationships in many biblical passages: 1 John 4:7 & 12, Romans 13:8, 1 Thessalonians 4:9, 1 John 3:23, 1 Peter 1:22, John 15:12 & 17. Our sexuality is a part of our relationships with both the same sex and the opposite sex. The Bible makes it clear to us that our sexuality is to be expressed in love. The physical act of sex is our holiest attempt not only at procreation, but at expressing our love for one another on a physical level. The love we express in any and all relationships is the highest and holiest form of intimacy in which we give ourselves and our sexuality to another person. Sex was created to be a part of our relationships before the sin and fall of Adam and Eve.

Why do God and the Bible limit the sexual expression to the relationship of a single man and a single woman? God created sex to be an act which would enable couples to experience the highest form of pleasure known to human beings. This form of pleasure demonstrates to us humans the supreme pleasure that we will experience in our relationship with God when we join him in eternity. God gave us sexual drives as a way of compelling us into monogamous relationships with our opposite sex marital partner. These drives compel us to enter such a relationship and an act in which we share intimacy with our spouse on every level of our being.

If we have sex with multiple partners outside of a covenant marriage, we destroy the sanctity and intimacy of the relationship we have with a spouse and with our God. Our relationship with our spouse mimics the relationships of the persons of the Godhead.

God tolerates worship of only one being. That being exists in three persons - Father, Son and Holy Spirit. The closest we come to worship of any human being is in our relationship with our spouse, and God does not allow even that form of worship. Only in worship of God do we experience the greatest pleasure known to any human being. That pleasure is not sex. It is the pleasure of experiencing the presence of God as we worship.

In our broken world sex is seen as sharing intimacy with any person with whom we wish to share our love. As a result, sex itself becomes the replacement for love. Broken people seek sex because they have come to believe that sex in and of itself is love. They do not see the need to limit sex to one partner. They are unable to see that sex with multiple partners becomes a form of personal gratification, substituting physical sexual contact for the intimacy of love.

Sexuality in Worship

The dance performed by David before the Lord as the Ark was brought into Jerusalem indicates the expression of sexuality in worship. David was not naked as many have supposed. He wore the ephod, a priestly garment that fit loosely, instead of the regal royal robes of a king. David expressed his love for God and his joy by dancing. His wife did not approve because she considered it to be behavior inappropriate for royalty. Her punishment was to bear no children. This was as extreme as punishment could be for a woman without being executed or losing her life. It was the greatest shame any woman could bear. She was ashamed for her royal husband. God shamed her with barrenness because she elevated her royal position and husband in importance over God.

The pagan religions surrounding Israel always used sex as a part of worship. God went so far to protect his people from practicing sex in worship as to command the priests to be fully covered in clothing and to have them build a ramp to the sacrificial altar instead of steps. Sexual intercourse and nudity were never condoned in Israelite worship, but were consistently aspects of idolatrous religious worship.

The Expression of the Sexuality of Jesus

Sexuality is so much a part of our being that it is expressed in everything we do. The clearest presentation of the sexuality of God in human form is the life and ministry of Jesus. Two aspects of Jesus' ministry clearly sum up the sexuality which Jesus presents to us. First, Jesus ministry is always redemptive. Second, the goal of Jesus ministry is always Holiness.

If we examine how Jesus approaches people, we find that he is always seeking to restore people to a pre-broken state. He redeems their brokenness and brings them to wholeness. Each miracle is a work of restoring brokenness to wholeness. Each act of deliverance is reclamation of a stolen life from the control of demonic forces. The restoration He brings to the woman at the well (John 4; 1-42), Mary Magdalene (Matthew 27:56, 61; 28:1; Mark 15:40, 47; 16:1-19; Luke 8:2; 24:10; John 19:25; 20:1-18), and the woman taken in adultery (John 7:53-8:11) are all redemptive acts. It is amazing the extent to which these redemptive acts promote holiness in the lives of the people Jesus encounters. May Magdalene's life is changed forever. The disciples' lives are changed forever when they are called by Jesus.

Personal Sexuality

Our sexuality is an important part of our ministry here on earth. Many years ago I looked at the brokenness in my life from the relationship with my dad and mom. I never felt that my dad approved of me. My mother told me I would never marry because no woman would ever have me. I looked at the brokenness I experienced in some of my early dating relationships. I had a crush on one girl which took me two years to get over. It was very painful. As a result of this brokenness and pain I told God I wanted to be able to minister to women because I never wanted them to experience the pain I have gone through. God has answered this prayer. I have a ministry with women of all ages. It is a ministry mostly of prayer. Sometimes it goes beyond that.

For one thirty year old single woman, I prayed and pieced the facts together and then had a woman discuss with her a traumatic event that occurred at age twelve. The resulting outcome was that the young lady was finally able to quit dating flashes and marry a stable Christian man. I have reason to believe I have saved more than one woman's life in extreme cases just by praying at the appropriate time and manner for the woman when her life was in danger. Some of these instances I can confirm and others I cannot confirm. Sometimes the ministry is just in being a role model of a Godly man for a young woman forming a perspective of what she wants in a future husband. For one former co-worker I have tried to be a father figure, because her father abandoned her and her mother at an early age. We are still friends. I am her one human male who enables her to see God as a good father instead of someone who abandons her.

I have had other women hug me and just hold on for several minutes after I loosened the embrace. I did not know why these women held on; I just knew that there was something going on in their emotions that needed the reassurance of a physical touch, and I was a safe person to embrace without the hug becoming sexually inappropriate.

I am convinced that God is a sexual being who gives us sexuality. He wants us to use our sexuality in appropriate worship of Him, in ministry for redemption and holiness, in selection of a mate, and in lifelong faithfulness to a mate.

PART 5
Human Bonding

Together is always time well spent.

Chapter 19

Anthropological and Psychological Aspects of Human Bonding

Attraction and Power in the Bonding Process

O ur whole bodies are musical. Our bodies were created to play music as a part of bonding us to God. The music our bodies play also assists in bonding us to each other. Babies respond and bond much more effectively when their mothers sing to them (Edwards, 2011). Music frequently assists in bonding a couple together. They have a favorite song – "their song."

Money frequently determines power in the relationship. Whoever controls the money controls the power in the relationship (Vogler, 2008). Women will not marry below their perceived socioeconomic level. Men will seldom marry below their perceived socioeconomic level (Townsend, Marshall, & Roberts 1993). These factors not only indicate whether a bond will be formed in the relationship, but how that relationship will form and whether or not it will result in marriage. It is not unusual for a couple to stay in a relationship for a long time and never progress that relationship into marriage simply because one partner does not possess a job which provides an adequate socioeconomic advantage to be acceptable to the other partner in the relationship (Floyd & Wasner, 1994).

Sex is frequently used as a way to exercise power and control in a relationship (Townsend & Roberts, 1993). Men do not want to marry a person who has had multiple sexual relationships before marriage. A pure man does not want to marry a woman with whom other men have had sexual relations. Women do not want to be used and discarded. The more pure the person is sexually before marriage, the purer the couple and the relationship will be after marriage. The more pure the sexual behavior before marriage, the more successful the marriage is likely to be in the long term.

Anthropological Aspects

There are twelve steps in the human bonding process that should be progressed through in a set order. When steps are skipped the relationship becomes skewed. The skewing of the relationship can ultimately result in a deformed relationship. In order for the relationship to be properly realigned, the missed steps must be completed. This necessitates the couple backing up in the progress of their relationship and re-visiting the bonding step that was skipped. If the steps are never completed, the relationship remains forever deformed. (Joy, 1985) (Joy, 1986).

Desmond Morris proposed twelve steps in the human bonding process The following chart provides us a look at the steps in order as proposed by Morris.

1. Eye to body - is the first overall examination of the other person to notice that person as a proper object of interest.
2. Eye to Eye - is when you look another person in the eye and the other person looks back. If the eyes are truly the windows to the soul, then this is the first place you should look to see what a person is really like.
3. Voice to voice - is when the couple begins to speak to each other and share their verbal thoughts and communication.
4. Hand to Hand – is the request for intimacy and the request to form a relationship.

5. Hand to head – is not only an expression of intimacy; it is a sign of submission and trust.

6. Arm to shoulder - is the beginning of exclusivity in the relationship.

7. Arm to waist – is the first display of sexual interest in the relationship.

8. Face to face – is a sharing of understanding and information that takes place, as the couple begins to communicate just by looking at each other.

9. Hand to Head – not only an expression of intimacy it, is a sign of submission and trust.

10. Hand to body - is the early moves of petting and the formation of the communication of love and caring through bodily touch.

11. Mouth to breast - is the declaration of the intent for a lifelong commitment in the relationship.

12. Privates to privates - is the expression of desire to move to oneness in all aspects of the relationship. (Joy, 1986).

Of these bonding steps, hand to head is one of the most crucial. Any person who will not let you hold his or her head is not ready for intimacy in a relationship and is not marriage material. When the head cannot be held the person lacks the capability to trust anyone. This goes beyond refusing an act of submission. It is a complete inability to trust anyone.

A person who will allow you to hold his or her head in your hands not only trusts you but is also expressing submission to you in the relationship. Unless we submit to each other, there is no intimacy between partners that is strong enough for developing the kind of intimacy necessary in marriage.

Other researchers have investigated key factors in the bonding process. These bonding process factors form interpersonal meta-relationships:

Love

Trust
Commitment
Affection
Emotion
Dependence
Needs
Intimacy
(Moss & Schwebel, 1993; Fehr, 1987; Stede, Levita, McLand & Kelly, 1982)

Relationship Principles

In their book *Fighting for Your Marriage*, the authors define four areas that generally determine whether a couple will have a successful relationship or a termination of the relationship.

1. Be safe at home - conflict management, communication skills, mental health issues.
2. Open the doors to intimacy –sex in marriage, love, commitment, attraction, passion, friendship.
3. Do your part and be responsible – work as a team, do the right thing, ignore petty issues, be the best person.
4. Nurture security in your future together – teamwork, priorities, commitment, sacrifice, forgiveness.
   (Markman & Blumberg, 2001, p. 27)

The book's authors stress that marriage can and will have permanence if these four principles are properly cultivated in the marriage. These four principles apply easily to any relationship, as well as the mate selection process. The one thing which they do not stress is the effect which promiscuous sexual relationships have on durability of the marriage.

Psychological Evaluation

There are many psychological tests and other forms of evaluation which demonstrate compatibility and the likelihood of success in a marital relationship. We are not going to examine the professional aspects of each of these tests, but simply look at what these tests can tell us about relationships.

Stages of Faith – Fowler

The following section provides us a more general assessment of spiritual development from a faith/religion agnostic perspective. This section is a summary of James W. Fowler's book Stages of Faith. Fowler breaks the development of faith into seven stages.

1. Pre Faith - This is the faith of a young child who is totally self-centered. This is the faith in adults to provide for every need of the child. What little concept of God the child holds is mimicked from the child's total reliance and trust of caretaking adults. This trust enables the child to form a level of personal security, which will in turn enable him or her to evaluate the concept of a divine being throughout the rest of his or her life.

2. Intuitive-Productive faith - This preschool faith is based on imagination. God is more of a fantasy being. A relationship with God is as much a relationship to the stories about God as to a real being. The child's understanding of the ultimate questions of life, derive from the child's growing sense of self identity, separate from parents and other persons.

3. Mythic-Literal faith – This school age faith is adopted from the faith of the persons in the child's social environment. A literal approach is taken by the child in understanding religious practices, beliefs, morals, and rituals.

4. Synthetic-Conventional – This is an adolescent faith. The person conforms his or her faith to what he or she personally experiences. This faith is tied to the peer group and may easily be discarded when the person moves beyond the need

for the peer group. At this stage the person seeks a personal relationship and integration with God. In an attempt to unify experience and individuality into an understanding of ones place in the world. He or she relies on conformity to the peer group and significant others for an understanding of spiritual reality and ultimate questions about God.

5. Individual-Reflective faith - This young adult faith seeks to integrate a world view that takes personal responsibility for one's own beliefs, morals, and behaviors as part of the greater fabric of building intimacy with others and with God. (In my personal opinion, if intimacy is not developed in the relationship with God at this point of life, then God becomes mostly irrelevant and impersonal. Likewise, moral absolutes become guidelines instead principles which are to be followed in order to preserve the integrity and wholeness of the person's life.)

6. Conjunctive faith - Is a midlife attempt to integrate the faith understanding of all religious approaches into a comprehensive whole. Faith at this point is focused more on justice and equality. All faiths and practices are to be tolerated as the only just way to liberate human beings from societal norms in pursuit of a relationship with God.

7. Universalizing Faith – This faith at the later stages of life is very visionary. It may also become self-sacrificing and activism centered. It disregards al norms and constraints in an effort to transform society in a universal faith. In this stage the older adult seeks to develop a world view that is not personal, but theistic. He or she attempts to understand spirituality, morals and ethics from God's viewpoint instead of a human viewpoint. Most people will never reach this stage of development because they never develop an adequate understanding of God (Fowler, 1981, pp. 244-245)

Fowler's Stages of Faith deal more with religions as a whole as opposed to an understanding of Christianity. While his stages hold much validity in presenting how we form our faith as we grow in our own personal human development, his presentation either does not seek to explain or fails to comprehend a truly Christian world view and a personal relationship to Jesus Christ. For this reason, his schema of spiritual formation is of restricted value in evaluating the spiritual development of one's prospective mate.

Spiritual Formation and Moral Development

There is a very close relationship between moral development and spiritual development. In fact, it is easily argued that moral development is just an aspect of spiritual formation. Both spiritual formation and moral development begin with revelation and are consummated in obedience. Both find their ultimate fulfillment in holiness in our lives, our relationships, and our walk with Jesus in daily life.

All children are taught to obey their parents from birth. We do not live in a world that is child safe, let alone child friendly. Children must be protected at all times. We tell them - Do not touch hot items. Hold mommy's and daddy's hands. Look both ways before crossing the street. Stay close by. Do not go there. This is just a short list of the many commands we give our children. They are given for protection and safety. If these commands are not obeyed, the child runs a high risk of serious injury or death. Therefore, the first stage of both moral development and spiritual formation is obedience to commands and/ or laws.

All morality begins with absolutes. If you tell me, "There are no absolutes," then tell me how you know. Knowledge is an absolute. You either know something or you do not know that thing. If there are no absolutes there is no right or wrong. You moral values are as irrelevant as mine. If you tell me I am wrong, then I have just as much veracity to tell you that you are wrong. If there are no absolutes, then do not give your children commands and do not teach them to obey you. Your children have as much right to disobey you as you have a right to command them. Let them grow up however they please. If they live they live, and if they die they die. It is their choice. Do not create any societal laws, for no one has the right to enforce them and everyone has the right to disregard them. Also, do not send your children to school or try to educate them. If there are no absolutes, there is no knowledge to be learned and there is no veracity to what is taught.

God tells us that we must obey Him for the same reasons that our parents tell us that we must obey them. If there is no obedience to a God, then there can neither be spiritual formation nor moral development. Both require obedience to authority figures, whether they be human or divine.

It is this necessity for obedience to absolutes which convinces me that moral development is a profound and necessary aspect of spiritual formation. Absolutes do not just arise out of our human culture. You cannot get humans to agree on the color of paint let alone on a single absolute. Absolutes originate with God and Him alone. If there are no absolutes then there is no God. Also, there is no moral development or spiritual formation. Any form of development or formation is whatever you choose to declare to be some form of progress. However you choose to measure that progress.

Many people do not have a concept of an absolute God. They draw all of their moral understanding from the context of the home in which they were raised and the society in which they live. I am glad that every person develops some sense of moral responsibility. The sad part is that only those who dwell in a relationship with Jesus develop a moral understanding based on the absolutes of the only absolute person in the whole universe. God is the only absolute person in the universe. God is never born and never dies. By human standards that makes God absolute. If God is absolute then he is the only proper standard for morals, values, ethics, etc. He is the one absolute which has no adulteration, no impurities, and no compromise. He alone is absolute.

Spiritual Formation

The first eight chapters of Romans present God's plan for spiritual formation. With spiritual formation also comes moral development.

Romans Chapters 1-8:

Revelation - Romans 1:
1:16-20 and 26-32 Revelation of the Holy = Righteousness.

All revelation begins with a presentation of God's integrity in the relationship of the three persons of His one being. Revelation then moves to a presentation of God's relationship with human beings through the life, death, and resurrection of Jesus Christ. Without this revelation there is no understanding of relationships, morals, ethics, character, personality, absolutes, love, compassion, mercy, redemption, or anything else necessary for humans to function in society in relationship with God, with self, and with others.

Obedience and Judgement - Romans 2:
Without judgement and rewards there is no basis for either spiritual formation or moral development. Without living in a right relationship with God, we are irrelevant to a holy and perfect God. We are simply to be wiped out of existence at God's earliest convenience. Without the absolutes of faithfulness, righteousness, truth, and accountability, there is no basis for a relationship with God, with self, or with anyone else.

Justification - Romans 4:
Justification is when we ask Jesus to come into our lives, forgive us our sins, and live within us. Without justification we have no relationship with self or with God. When God justifies us He brings us into relationship with Himself (through faith in Jesus Christ). This aspect of our salvation instantly starts a process of self-reintegration (of our personality and spirituality) through which we build integrity in ourselves and in our relationships with other people as well as with God.

Justification is the process of coming into a right relationship with God through Jesus. This act of grace from God to us is enabled through two actions. The first action is forgiveness through Jesus' death on the cross. The second action is atonement through the shedding of Jesus' blood on the cross.

> Forgiveness – repentance from personal sin resulting in being forgiven because of Jesus' death on the cross for our sins.

> Atonement – Jesus' blood provides a covering for our sin through which God no longer looks at our sin.

Morality at this point in our lives is very self-focused. It is limited to the concern for getting oneself in right relationship with God. Before justification all humans are very self-centered. This does not mean we are incapable of being concerned about other people. It just means our behavior is motivated more by a concern for our good than by a concern for the wellbeing of others.

Righteousness - Romans 5:

Righteousness is focused on relationships. In this aspect of spiritual formation and moral development, the relationships with God, self and others are brought into a comprehensive focus. This comprehensive focus forces us to demand integrity in our personality. Integrity involves de-compartmentalization by reintegrating our own personality. Here the orientation is with our relationship with our own self. As we reintegrate our personality, we begin to demand fidelity and loyalty in our relationships with God, our-selves and with others.

Personality formation in the aspect of righteousness ceases to be self-centered and becomes other centered. Our measure of right relationship becomes the absolutes of God and His will for our lives. Out of our fidelity to God we also begin to orient our lives to focus on building relational loyalty to the people and society around us. We begin to seek a reintegration of each person's personality into a relationship with Jesus and with society as a whole. Only when each and every person develops personal righteousness will our world be whole, possessing a right relationship with itself, with Jesus, and between each and every individual in society.

Sanctification - Romans 6:

Sanctification is the process through which God makes us holy in all aspects of our being and in all of our relationships. A simple definition of sanctification is the point when you find it much more pleasurable to live a clean and pure life honoring God than a sick and perverted life lived for your own fun. Sanctification is a heavenly orientation versus worldly orientation in our lives. It brings holiness and purity. This holiness and purity is worked out in personality through integrity. Integrity is gained through de-compartmentalization by reintegrating the personality and through re-orientation of our lives with God

Being baptized into Jesus' death, burial, and resurrection applies the effects of His death in bringing freedom from the law and sin. It also applies the effects of a new life through His resurrection. These two aspects of spiritual reorientation of our lives enable us to gradually develop a life that is not bound by sin and which leads us to crave a life lived as children of a God who will properly parent us in his family.

Glorification - Romans 8:

Glorification is generally thought of as occurring only when we go to heaven. I believe glorification can also occur on earth (though rarely). Jesus was glorified on the Mount of Transfiguration and in His resurrection appearances. I believe Enoch and possibly Elijah were glorified when God took them from this earth. Glorification deals with that which is beauty, spiritual, transformational, restored, and perfected.

Redemption (Romans chapters 1: -8:)	
Spiritual Formation	Moral Development
Revelation	Goal of becoming Holy
Obedience	Pain avoidance

Righteousness/Justice	Relationship with others
Justification	Relationship with self
Sanctification – (Baptism – Death and Life)	Relationship with God
Resurrection Life – obedience	Reorientation of relationships
Glorification	Purity and perfection in all relationships

I do not believe spiritual formation is a series of steps through which a person progresses in order to become more Christ-like. Instead I believe spiritual formation is like pounding a series of long and large nails into a board. The one rule is that you cannot hit any single nail twice in a row. Also, the normal pattern is that each nail must be hit before a previous nail can be hit a second time. There are some exceptions to this general pattern. To me the nails of spiritual formation are Revelation, Obedience, Righteousness/Justice, Justification, Sanctification, Becoming alive to God (resurrection), and Glorification. God hits the first nail and drive it a little deeper and then the next nail and drives it a little deeper and then the next and the next. Until the previous nail is adequately deep in the board the next nail cannot be fully driven into the board. Sometimes God has to back up and hit a few previous nails again before He can hit the next nail. Only when all the nails are fully driven have we achieved complete spiritual formation.

Spiritual Formation in the Selection of a Mate

Spiritual formation in a couple is just as important as moral and ethical development. In selecting a mate, it is important to objectively measure your own level of spiritual maturity and your mate's spiritual maturity. There are many ways of measuring spiritual development. If you know the Bible, the signs of mature spirituality are obvious and the signs of impeded spiritual development are even more evident.

The aspects of spiritual development which are the most critical in any person's life are daily reading of the Bible, daily prayer, church attendance, obedience to God's Word, and the demonstration of love to other people. If your mate does not demonstrate these basic traits of Christian living, then he or she is not good marriage material.

The Bible never speaks of stages of faith and never presents faith from a perspective of development or spiritual formation. Instead it presents God as speaking to humans, being historically involved our lives, and having an ultimate plan for our world and our lives. This simple perspective is sufficient to tell us most of what we need to know about our mate's spiritual development. Does our mate have a sense of God speaking into his or her life? Does our mate demonstrate a historical relationship of experiencing God and living for Him? Does our mate have an understanding and a sense of direction from God for his or her life which provides guidance and direction for following Jesus? The answers to these simple questions provide us with a solid evaluation of our prospective mate's spiritual formation.

Moral Development

For a person who treasures his or her relationship with God, and is committed to being obedient to the teachings of the Bible, being and finding a moral and righteous mate is of critical importance. The question each of us must answer is - how do we measure and evaluate our mate's moral proclivity to biblical values? To answer this question we must look at what constitutes morality and how we measure morality.

Now let's look at the moral development studies conducted by Kohlberg and Piaget. Whereas Piaget broke moral development into Pre-conventional, Conventional, and Post-Conventional stages, Kohlberg refined his approach to moral development, breaking it down to even finer stages. In each of Piaget's levels of morality, Kohlberg found two stages. These are as follows.

Level. Pre-conventional Morality
Stage 1. Obedience and Punishment Orientation.
Adults dictate rules which are to be obeyed explicitly. This so called "pre-conventional" morality right and

wrong views morality and rules as external to one's personal self.

Stage 2. Individualism and Exchange.

Since there are multiple people handing down rules which may or may not be in agreement with each other the rule that is to be obeyed is the rule which accommodates personal self-interest.

In stage 1 punishment is that which verifies the existence of wrong or evil. In stage 2 punishment is coercive behavior which a person seeks to avoid.

Moral behavior therefore in stage 2 becomes actions which are mutually beneficial to multiple parties. It is an attempt to maintain fairness in relationships However, there is no concept of moral behavior on a societal level.

Level II. Conventional Morality
Stage 3. Good Interpersonal Relationships.

As people enter the adolescent years they begin to see the need for morality which fosters relationships which engender positive relationships within the community and among peer groups. Morality is that which engenders compliance which benefits all parties in the immediate group and in an extended manner all parties in a society. These moral behaviors must also create relational values which develop love, justice, trust and freedom in the community.

Stage 4. Maintaining the Social Order.

As adolescents transition into the early adulthood years they become more focused on morality which will benefit the whole of society. They develop a sense of duty wherein they are responsible not only to their peer group, but to the entire society in which they live. Society must be maintained for everyone.

Level III. Post-Conventional Morality
  Stage 5. Social Contract and Individual Rights.
At this stage young adults begin to examine the ingredients for creating a "good" society which is beneficial to all parties. They begin to construct the concept of a society which protects individual rights and freedoms while at the same time maintaining a governance which both is good for the society and which is good for the individual. The good of society and the good of the individual must be maintained together in balance with each other. Without this balance there is no morality for either the individual or the society.

Stage 6. Universal Principles.
People and societies which seek to settle conflict between personal rights and societal rights. There are times when the discrepant interest (society and individual) cannot be mutually balanced in a fair and just manner. Therefore Kohlberg postulates a sixth stage wherein morality can balance justice for all individual within the society with justice for the society as a whole. However, he fails to adequately present a stage six concept of universal principles or morality and justice.(Flemming, 2006; "Jean Piaget"; "Kohlberg's Moral Stages"; "Lawrence Kohlberg"; "Kohlberg's Theory," 2012).

The sad part is that most people never develop past stage four. Even seminary students are usually somewhere between stage four and stage five (Joy, 1979). Piaget and Kohlberg never even postulated stage seven. This stage comes only from God. Only in the Bible do we find a description of redemption as a part of our moral development.

In stage seven, the biblical design is always for redemption. This is not just to buy back a person from sin, but to restore an individual to living and functioning in Holiness. Holiness is achieved when a person is able to live and function according to the original purpose for which the person was created. It encompasses all aspects of the person's relationships to God, self and others.

Kohlberg's theory is sex-biased. Kohlberg's stages were derived exclusively from researching males. For males, advanced moral thought revolves around rules, rights, and abstract principles. The ideal is formal justice, in which all parties evaluate one another's claims in an impartial manner.

For women, morality centers not on rights and rules but on interpersonal relationships and the ethics of compassion and care. The ideal is not impersonal justice but more facilitative ways of living. Women's morality is more contextualized; it is tied to real, ongoing relationships rather than abstract solutions to hypothetical dilemmas.

Men and women frequently score at different stages on Kohlberg's scale. Women typically score at stage 3, with its focus on interpersonal feelings, whereas men more commonly score at stages 4 and 5, which reflect more abstract conceptions of social organization. Thus, women score lower than men. If, however, Kohlberg's scale were more sensitive to women's distinctly interpersonal orientations, it would show that women also continue to develop their thinking beyond stage 3.

The differences in the male and female moral perspective provide an excellent and important balance between each perspective. The female perspective counters the rigidity of the stages of the male perspective. The male stage rigidity counters the compassion of the female perspective. This provides a highly productive sense of justice and mercy in the couple's exercise of justice and moral development throughout their life together.

Most couples forming relationships in late adolescence or early adulthood will be at Kohlberg's stage four or even stage three of moral development. Therefore, couples entering marriage in early adulthood are more focused on doing "good" in their interpersonal relationships and fulfilling their familial and societal duties. These values are very appropriate to a young couple forming a marriage. Their emphasis is on their interpersonal relationship with each other and their duties to each other. It is this focus which more effectively enables them to complete the development of intimacy as a couple.

If there is a strong difference in the moral development stages between the partners, the likely result will be strong conflict. Even the existing differences between the male and the female approach to morality will likely produce conflict, which must be negotiated between the couple. When each partner is at the same or similar stage of development, the couple has a solid foundation on which to grow their future moral development as they age through life together. Dissimilarity in stages of moral development is more likely to induce the couple to grow apart rather than to grow together (Gilligan, 1982).

Berkowitz (2002) lists what he calls the components of the "moral anatomy." He considers current psychological understanding of morals and moral development to be inadequate. He urges the field of psychology to develop an understanding of the "complete moral person." His research distinguishes the following aspects of a moral personality:

1. Moral behavior (prosocial, sharing, donating to charity, telling the truth)
2. Moral values (belief in moral goods)
3. Moral emotion (guilt, empathy, compassion)
4. Moral reasoning (about right and wrong)
5. Moral identity (morality as an aspect self-image)
6. Moral personality (enduring tendency to act with honesty, altruism, responsibility)
7. "Metamoral" characteristics (ones which make morality possible even though they are not inherently moral)

Vessels divided moral thinking into moral knowing and moral reasoning. He concluded that the combination of "moral knowing, reasoning, feeling, and behaving" creates what is commonly referred to as conscience. Conscience is a combination of a person's view of his or past, present and future. Moral reasoning, moral conscience, and moral character are combined through our personal and social environments to create our integrity on both personal and social levels of interaction (Vessels & Boyd, 1996).

The current understanding of moral development is totally inadequate. It provides no understanding of absolutes without which morals are irrelevant. It also provides no understanding of spiritual formation, which is necessary for a cohesive and comprehensive understanding of the absolutes from which moral development derives.

The greatest indicator of moral development from a purely psychological perspective is a person's ability to be empathetic. The capacity for empathy is not fully developed until mid-adolescence. An adult who lacks empathy for others is incapable of being moral and is likely mentally unhealthy. Any person who is insufficiently empathetic to others should be strongly avoided as a possible mate (Schaefer & Drewes, 2014, pp. 195-209).

Biblical View of Moral Development

The most prevalent concept of morality in current culture may be summed up in these words. "In those days Israel had no king; everyone did as they saw fit" (Judges 21:25 (NIV)). In a postmodern society with no absolutes, each person does what he or she considers right in his or her own eyes.

As couples form their relationships together, it is important to understand the basis on which moral and ethical decisions are formed first individually, and then by them as a couple. To do this it is necessary to understand the very foundations of moral and ethical behavior themselves. Moral decisions are based on absolutes.

Absolutes are based on the character of God. Because God's character does not change, moral absolutes also do not change. Ethics are situational applications of moral absolutes.

Pillars of Moral and Ethical Behavior

A biblical view of Christian ethics will generally lead us to the following categories for a proper understanding of moral and ethical behavior.

1. Absolutes – morals which are derived from 100% pure truth. The Bible teaches that Jesus Christ is the way, the truth, and the life (John 14:6). There is no other determinant of truth than Jesus' knowledge of the truth. Each of us has our perspective of truth in any given situation. Jesus is the only person who knows all the facts and is therefore the only person who can declare what is truth. As the Bible teaches - Jesus is the truth (John 17:17).
2. Justice is the application of morals so that all parties are treated fairly and equally (Micah 6:8, Isaiah 1:17, Luke 18:1-8, Proverbs 21:3).
3. Love/Mercy results in the capacity for a consequence to be lessened, so that a person may be redeemed from receiving the full extent of justice due to that person (Zechariah 7:9, John 3:16-17, Hosea 6:6).
4. Situation is the circumstances and motive involved in a person's decisions as he or she commits behavior that is moral in nature (Matthew 7:12, Psalm 37:27-29, Psalm 24:24-25, Matthew 5:38-39, 1 Corinthians 6:9-11).
5. Obedience involves a decision/behavior based on a choice or preference in response to a moral standard. In this choice, the right or wrong of the decision must be determined in the individual's obedience to, and walk with, God. Most moral issues are determined by absolutes, but in some cases what is right for one person may be wrong for another

person depending on what God wants for that person's life (Deuteronomy 28:1-68).

6. Redemption – In biblical times redemption was the term used for purchasing the freedom of a slave. The slave held the worst position in society. No one wanted to be a slave. Slave owners abhorred the institution so greatly that they never wanted to become a slave. However, they were unable to understand that owning a slave was even more abhorrent than being one.

7. God always works toward the goal of redemption. God does not want us to destroy ourselves, and He does not want us to get to the point that it is necessary for Him to bring destructive judgement on us. God always seeks to change us in a manner that will enable us to become healthy and productive persons who bring good into each and every situation which we encounter in life. This redemptive change which God seeks to bring into our lives through an intimate relationship with Him also enables us to become redemptive influences in the lives of the people we encounter in day to day life (Ruth 3:9, Isaiah 44:6, and 24, Matthew 20:28, Mark 10:45, Acts 20:28, Romans 3:24, 1 Corinthians 1:30, Ephesians 1:7, Colossians 1:18-20,Galations 3:13 and 4:5, Titus 2:13-14, 1 Peter 1:18-19, Revelation 5:9).

8. Holiness - Even when God judges us, it is always in love. God will not let us continue to live in sin beyond this earth. God does not judge us out of hate. He judges us out of His love for us. He hates sin, but He never hates us. In His loving judgement he breaks the power of sin over our lives. He seeks to turn us back to Himself and to living in holiness.

Situation Ethics

Morals which are based solely on situational ethics are no morals at all. In situational ethics, morals are based on pleasure, not on justice. Each person does what is right in his or her own sight. Take a good look at the book of Judges and see how frequently this statement is used. The very reason God gave the Israelites judges was because they were living their lives by situational ethics. The whole nation was in disarray and they were not following God. *"In those days Israel had no king; everyone did as they saw fit" (Judges 21:25)*. What then is the moral solution to situational ethics?

Only in a life lived in a close walk with God can we adequately develop moral behavior based on God's absolute character. A daily study of morals and ethics as presented in the Bible enables us to build a strong foundation for applying morals and ethics in our own lives. This is a very important foundation on which to base our moral and ethical behavior. However, knowing what the Bible teaches in regards to moral and ethical behavior is not fully adequate for developing a powerful moral character. The Bible's presentation of morals and ethics must also be accompanied by a daily walk with God. It is only in worship of Jesus and walking with him, that we enable the biblical principles of morals and ethics to be fully integrated into our lives.

From a biblical perspective, moral development is most related to the term "holiness." Holiness by definition means to function according to original intended purpose. For example, you can use a skillet to cook food or you can use a skillet to bang someone over the head. Only when a skillet is used to cook food is it functioning according to its original intended purpose. Holiness is not an event which occurs in our lives. It is a relationship with God that is so extremely intimate and important that we prefer the intimate relationship with God over any form of pleasurable sin. Therefore, we diligently seek to protect our relationship with God and the intimacy which this relationship brings to our lives. Intimacy with God which we call holiness is a lifestyle which brings purity and integrity into our personality, our relationship with, and our knowledge and understanding of, God.

Think about it. We have difficulty understanding holiness because it does not exist in this world. As we study holiness in the Bible we come to several conclusions: 1. We cannot understand holiness. 2. We know that holiness is born and lived in a relationship with God. 3. We think of holiness as something that only exists with God in heaven, but the Bible consistently teaches that we are to live holy lives. 5. God is holy. 6. God is a multi-person being. 7. God is perfect and pure.

This understanding of holiness leads me to conclude that holiness is the purity of the integrity of the relationship of the three persons in God's one being. God is relational within Himself – Father, Son, and Holy Spirit. That relationship is so completely integral and perfect that God is completely intimate with Himself. This integrity of intimacy enables each person of God's being to be fully known and fully understood on all levels of being within each person of God's being. Therefore, the relationships of the three persons within God's being are perfect, whole, and pure. God calls each of us to be holy in our own being on all levels of our relationship with our self and with others. God wants us to have the same holiness of relationship with Him that he has within the holiness of relationship of the three persons of His own being. In other words, God wants us to have the same relationship with Him that he has within Himself.

When we live in a relationship of holiness with our self and with God, the answers to situational ethical decisions may not be easy, but they do become obvious to us. God has the answers and it is the relationship lived with Him that enables us to know His answer in these situations.

Conclusion

The biggest clue to a person's moral development is a person's belief in absolutes. Without absolutes, a person has no morality which will last. Instead the person's morality is transient. A person's understanding of right and wrong is simply what is most convenient at the present time. Couples need to be as integrated in their understanding and practice of biblical morals and ethics as they are in all other foundations of developing their intimacy as a couple. Without being equally integrated in the moral/ethical aspect of their lives, differences in moral and ethical development will gradually tear the couple apart. Morality can only be measured in reference to a person's holiness in relationship with Jesus. Without a relationship with Jesus, a prospective mate possesses insufficient morality to live compatibly in a long term relationship with a person who is morally disciplined through a relationship with Jesus.

Psychological Development
Erickson's Stages of Life – Again

Here is an overall chart of Erickson's Stages of Life. In the following section we will examine the crucial issues a person faces in each of these stages of life ("Erikson's Stages," 2015).

In relationship to mate selection, we will skip Erickson's earlier stages and focus on the adult stages in which mate selection and marriage occur. Erickson provides us with three stages of adulthood.

Stage: Young Adulthood
> Age: 19-35
> Psychosocial Crisis: Intimacy vs. Isolation
> Virtue: Love
> Significant Relationships: Partners in Friendship, Sex
> Competition, Cooperation

The sixth stage is Young Adulthood which occurs between ages 19 and 35. This stage deals with the need to develop intimacy. This is the period of seeking a lifelong mate. Now that the search for identity has been completed, there develops a desire for sharing intimacy with other people, both male and female, who will be lifelong friends and partners. Friendship partners are as important as sexual partners in having someone with whom to share intimacy. However, in friendships, intimacy is not shared as deeply with non-sexual partners. It is this development of intimacy and respecting proper boundaries in intimacy which allow a person to develop working relationships with co-workers and social relationships with friends. This stage establishes the proper concepts of boundaries and intimacy which enables the relationships which provide the ultimate meaning of a person's life. If intimacy is successfully developed, the young adult is adequately prepared for building loving relationships. Love cannot exist without intimacy, and intimacy cannot exist without love.

In the young adulthood stage of development, men are more focused on what is external and transcendent about their world and universe. For this reason men focus on their career. The career is the means to purchase what is necessary for the spouse and family to live. Men will seek someone to mentor them through their career and other aspects of life. In the late twenties and early thirties, men change their life goals. Men often change careers and frequently also change spouses and mentors.

In this stage, women are more focused on what is internal and imminent about their world and universe. Therefore, women seek to develop intimacy with their spouse, family and close friends. They may give up all other goals in their lives to ensure the success of the intimacy which they seek to develop. It is through this intimacy that they nurture their spouse and their children. It is these relationships which give meaning to their lives. Women also go through changes in life (usually a couple of years earlier than men) where they begin to focus more on developing themselves.

The only way to overcome the sense of isolation that becomes so prevalent without a life partner is to either find a life partner or to subsume that isolation in a relationship with God and/or other people.

The biggest challenge is for the young adult to find the healing for issues in his or her life, so that he or she is able to bond with a life partner. Any time a person has not succeeded in bonding with a life partner, it is likely that he or she is stuck in a prior stage of development that prevents success in the current stage of development. Because the young adult has such a strong sense of isolation, there is the constant fear of rejection by any partner. The more rejection experienced in the search for a life partner, the more a sense of rejection by God develops. After all, if no one else likes me, why should God like me?

Stage: Adulthood

Age: 35-65

Psychosocial Crisis: Generativity vs. Stagnation

Virtue: Care

Significant Relationships: Divided Labor and Shared Household

The seventh stage is adulthood which occurs between ages 35 and 65. This stage deals with the need to develop generativity. Generativity deals with a new question: What will I pass on to succeeding generations? This may be as simple as what a person desires to pass on to his or her children and grandchildren. Generativity may also encompass what a person desires to leave as a legacy to the whole human race. What a person passes on is most frequently knowledge and wisdom. A generative person wants to know that he or she has taught someone how to be successful in life in at least the ways he or she has been successful. That which is produced by a generative person is not just physical objects and relationships. It also includes skills learned, life lessons, and values that a person considers critical for future generations to master.

In this generative stage the most critical accomplishment is the ability to pass on intimacy – to one's own and other children, to grandchildren, to friends and to a mate. The even greater accomplishment is the ability to pass on one's own intimacy with God. If you want to leave a mark on the world, teach at least one other person to be intimate with God.

At this point women move from caring for their family, their spouse, and their friends, to caring for their own needs. Men, who have sacrificed family, spouse, and friends for their careers, now begin to develop the need to spend their time passing on love, care, values, skills, etc., to the other people around them. It is this focus on generativity which frequently provides the cure for the so called midlife crisis. This crisis may occur multiple times at the early stages of this life stage. During the generativity phase, women develop their masculine side and men develop their feminine side.

Failure to complete this stage will result in stagnation. This stagnation is epitomized in a sense that the person is leaving no success and no legacy in life. Failure at this stage creates the feeling that life is passing the person by. He or she is a bystander, watching as his or her own life amounts to nothing and no one cares. Stagnation ultimately results in deep depression.

The only way to overcome the sense of stagnation is to have a spouse or other partner who will push the person to mentor other people and to find some task which will enable him or her to leave behind a mark of success on this world. Because the adult has such a strong sense of stagnation, there is the constant fear that life has no meaning. As a consequence, he or she feels alone in being the only person who will never leave a positive mark on the world. Ultimately, this adult begins to feel rejected by God. This sense of rejection occurs because there is no sense of accomplishment, of anything that can be passed on to successive generations. The adult feels he or she has no worth before God.

Stage: Old Age

Age: 65+
Psychosocial Crisis: Integrity vs. Despair
Virtue: Wisdom
Significant Relationships: "Man Kind" "My Kind"

The eighth stage is old age, which occurs after age 65. This stage deals with the need to develop wisdom. Wisdom deals with the issue of understanding the meaning of life. This meaning is derived from a relational and philosophical perspective. For a Christian it is also a biblical perspective. This stage is much more than a legacy to be left behind. In this stage a person begins to teach through relationships. The insights from this stage do not come in a treatise. They come from ponderings that attempt to explain why the person's life has followed a specific path. They come from insights into the significance of why certain events, interactions, and statements occurred in the lives of all parties involved. This is the time when a person begins to understand why and how his or her life has fit into the overall plan for mankind in this world. It is an understanding of the role of the person's life in that which has passed and in that which will be in the future.

Without this integration of life there is great despair and

emptiness. There is no understanding of the role played and the meaning which the person's life has held for society as a whole.

Very few people seek a mate at this point in life. For those who do, it seems that they seek a partner to live with for the remainder of their life instead of a mate with whom to develop intimacy. I do not see this approach to marriage and mate selection as wrong. However, it seems very hollow compared to the aspirations of mate selection and marriage in early life.

Holland Scale – RIASEC

This personality evaluation provides us great insight into a person's interests, as related to the person's occupation.

People can be easily understood once you know their personality type in conjunction with their occupations. Certain personality types gravitate to certain occupations. Once you understand the personality type of the person, it helps you know what to expect in the person's behavior.

Where to begin? There are six personality types in the RIASEC model used on the Strong Campbell personality test and more commonly known as the Holland code. Start by determining the person's occupation or hobby. This will give you a big clue to their personality profile. Of course, some people do not work in occupations that fit with their personality profile. Pay attention to whether that which you observe about their personality and that which you know about their occupation fit together. A person's hobbies can also be a good indicator. Hobbies will normally always fit with a person's personality profile.

Now let's begin to examine each of our party groups more closely.

> **Realistic** - This group likes to be outdoors. They like to work with their hands. They like to work with machinery and tools. They are very competent workers. They work best alone or in small groups. They do not highly regard those in authority. They often dress casually in flannel shirts, jeans, and boots.

Investigative – This group loves to analyze data and information. They are logical and less feeling-oriented. Many of them have difficulty making decisions or reaching conclusions because they can never get enough information to make a complete analysis.

Artistic – This group may be very talented at any form of artistic expression. They are very creative, both in their thought processes and in the work they accomplish. They are also excellent in thinking out of the box. Their artistry may be expressed through writing, music, drama, decorating, painting, crafts, and many other forms of expression. They dislike deadlines and procrastinate to the last moment. They may be temperamental and they are very creative.

Social – This group's main goal in life is to help others. They frequently rescue strays (both human and animal). They thrive on being around other people. It is hard to get them to cease talking and move on to other activities or visit with other people. They focus so forcefully on the persons with whom they are interacting that they are unaware of what is taking place in their surroundings. They will frequently dominate your time. They easily view life from the other person's perspective. They love to engage in interaction with other people, even strangers. Social relationships are more important to them than any work to be done.

Enterprising – This group likes to teach and to start new things. They barely complete one project before they begin work on a new project. They look for the big picture and the means to accomplish important projects. They are social but lack sensitivity to other people's feelings. They are leaders who are very focused on goals to be accomplished. They frequently have multiple projects going at the same time. They like to sell items or ideas to others and are self-starters.

Conventional – This group is very organized. They are task oriented and readily meet deadlines. They are meticulous in their work. They thrive on mundane and repetitive tasks. They demand excellence. They cannot function in clutter or disarray. They love to keep things neat and organized. They dislike change.

(Bolles, 1995)

How many letters can a person have in their personality according to RIASEC? How many letters did Jesus have in his personality profile? Probably all of them. Almost every person has all the characteristics of the six letters in their personality profile. The extent of the dominance of each of the characteristics determines the number of letters a person has in his or her dominant personality profile.

Most people will have a personality profile comprised of three letters or three characteristics. A few rare people have profiles comprised of four letters, and some have only two letters or a single letter. If there are less than three letters, a person has not fully developed his or her personality. If there are more than three letters, it indicates that a person has an extremely high IQ or has worked hard to develop a more rounded personality.

Studies have been done to determine what personality profiles excel at what occupations. There are six basic (three letter) personality profiles. Once you understand these profiles and you know the hobbies or kind of work the person does, you will have great insight into the personality of that person. There are always a few exceptions where a person works in a job that does not match their personality profile.

Now let's look at each of the personality profiles.

RIA's - Frequently become doctors, engineers, architects, veterinarians, truck drivers and machinery operators. They do not like to be bosses over other people. They have little use for any management. They have difficulty making decisions because they never have enough information. They are very creative and may have few people skills. They may appear very introverted, and talk very little. Their sins tend toward susceptibility to various addictions.

RIC's - Frequently become accountants, engineers, lab technicians, computer programmers, or mechanics. They may have difficulty making decisions because they never have enough information. They are very conventional and dislike change. They usually have few people skills. They may appear very introverted and talk very little. They tend to be very conservative and traditional. They view the world as very black and white. Everything is either right or wrong. There are no shades of gray. Their sins may tend toward being judgmental.

REC's - Often become military officers or technical workers, supervisors, and inspectors. They want things organized and done yesterday. They have limited patience with people and red tape. They are very adept at juggling multiple projects at a time and meeting deadlines. Their sins may tend toward exploitation of other people and situations along with greed. They frequently are insensitive to other people's feelings.

SAI's - Frequently become psychologists, nurses, counselors, lawyers, librarians, etc. They love to talk and analyze problems. They are not bothered by deadlines and often fail to meet deadlines. They often think out loud by talking their way through a problem with another person. Their excessive socializing can be very annoying to those who accompany them in social situations. Their drive to bring out the best in everyone causes them see the world through rose colored glasses. Their compassion may cause them to behave in a myopic manner and become enabling when they are focused on helping another person. Their sins tend toward being gossips and being overly critical of self and others.

SEC's - Make good caseworkers, school teachers, secretaries, childcare workers, or medical office assistants, managers, educational administrators, dispatchers, user support analysts, receptionists, and clerks. They are enterprising, well organized, and love to teach and help other people. They may be susceptible to having affairs. Their sins may tend toward playing favorites.

ASE's - Often become social workers, public relations, editors, designers, art therapists, agency directors, sales people, musicians, and actors. They tend to be liberal and idealistic. They like to work with people and are very creative and self-motivated. Their sins tend toward being susceptible to having affairs.

(Bolles, 1995)

RIASEC Conclusions

Consistency is important in defining a person's personality profile. A person's three letters or personality characteristics should fall together in a group. There should be no gaps (other letters) between letters. If there are gaps in the person's profile, it may be an indication of mental health issues.

People should work in occupations that fit with their personality profile. For some people this is not possible. If a person is not working in an occupation that fits with his or her personality profile, then he or she will need to develop a hobby that provides an outlet to express his or her true personality.

People usually marry someone who overlaps them in two letters of their personality profile. This overlap forms the strongest marriages. People who are alike in their personality profile almost always divorce because they are too much alike. People who only overlap in one letter of their profiles have to work harder at their marriage.

When a couple dissolves their relationship, they usually seek a new partner who is exactly identical to them in personality profile. These rebound relationships are doomed to failure because the partners are too identical in personality.

The personality is not adequately formed to determine a profile before a person reaches the late teen years. The older you get the more you move toward your opposite personality profile (Bolles, 1995).

FIRO-B

The FIRO-B is a psychological evaluation that is frequently used in assessing a couple's potential for strong bonding in mate selection. There are no wrong answers on the assessment, and there are no bad profiles resulting from the assessment. The FIRO-B measures three areas of personality: Inclusion, Control, and Affection. It then also measures whether these traits are possessed and expressed or are wanted and desired. What you want in each category are traits that should be strongly expressed in your prospective mate. What you express in each category should be traits that are strongly desired by your prospective mate.

INCLUSION

Is about recognition, belonging, participation, contact with others, and how you relate to groups.

Read the characteristics of Inclusion and ask yourself these two questions:

1. How important are these characteristics to me in my choice of a mate?

   2. How strongly are these characteristics expressed in the character of my prospective mate?

CONTROL

Is about influence, leadership, responsibility, and decision making.

Read the characteristics of Control and ask yourself these two questions:

1. How important are these characteristics to me in my choice of a mate?
2. How strongly are these characteristics expressed in the character of my prospective mate?

AFFECTION

Is about closeness, warmth, sensitivity, openness, and how you relate to others.

Read the characteristics of Affection and ask yourself these two questions:

1. How important are these characteristics to me in my choice of a mate?
2. How strongly are these characteristics expressed in the character of my prospective mate?

EXPRESSED BEHAVIOR

Is about your actions and reactions, both conscious and subconscious, to other people.

1. How much do you prefer to initiate the behavior?
2. How do you actually behave with respect to the three fundamental interpersonal needs?
3. What is your comfort level when engaging in the behaviors associated with the three needs?

Look at each category of interpersonal characteristics and ask yourself – Am I that person? Does my behavior exhibit these characteristics to other people? Do I enjoy acting in this way with/toward friends?

WANTED BEHAVIOR
Is about the behavior you desire, both conscious and subconscious, from other people.

1. How much do you prefer others to take the initiative?
2. How much do you want to be on the receiving end of those behaviors?
3. What is your comfort level when others direct their behaviors associated with the three needs to you?

Look at each category of interpersonal needs and ask yourself – Do I want other people to express these interpersonal characteristics to me? Do I want other people to act this way around me? Do I enjoy having other people behave this way towards me? (Schutz, 1958).

Gender Communication Differences
Differences in communication styles between males and females are critical elements for proficiency in maintaining relationships and building intimacy. More intimacy is likely broken between couples by misunderstandings due to communication differences than by any other factors. The following describes general communication pattern differences between males and females. These patterns vary by individual person and should not be ascribed to a gender as a whole.

Male – Female Communication Styles Differences	
Females	*Males*
Emotional – Empathetic	Concrete – Logical
Discounted	Valued
Build relationships in order to work	Work in order to build relationships
Social	Non-Social
Inclusion – intimacy and consensus	Superiority – status and dominance
Disagreement impacts the whole relationship	Disagreement is subject based not relationship based
Relationships	Accomplishments
Verbal and collaborative problem solving	Silent and private problem solving
Non-linear thinking	Linear thinking
Emotional problem solving	Analytical problem solving
Indirect	Direct
Understanding	Fixing

Explanation:

Emotional -Empathetic

Females are emotional and empathetic. They demonstrate a general sense of compassion and protectiveness that is frequently expressed on an emotional basis.

Males are concrete and logical. They avoid most expressions of emotions. This does not mean that they are non-emotional. For men emotions are deeply held and rarely expressed, even in private. They are even more deeply hidden in public. As a result, a concrete and logical persona is projected in public.

Discounted

Females are mostly discounted in public settings. Women are frequently less valued by men and even by other women in relationship to men. Male leadership and opinions are much more valued by women.

Males are more highly valued in social settings. However, women control and manipulate men and frequently exercise great power over men. The queen bee is the power in any group of women and frequently holds more power among the women than her male counterpart.

Relationship Building

Females build relationships in order to accomplish work. This allows them to network together and accomplish projects. In these networked groups, females always have a pecking order. This order is mostly rigid, but can become very fluid when a crisis needs to be resolved.

Males work in order to build relationships. Men slowly build relationships as they work and play together. They value the relationships as much as they value the work. Male hierarchy can be more fluid depending on skills and expertise needed to accomplish tasks. Male hierarchy tends to deteriorate with age as older men value bonds of loyalty instead of perceptions of machoism.

Social

Females are perceived as very social. The difference in the development and usage of women's superior verbal skills tends to portray them as more social. This robustness of social interaction is not always as abundant when females are compared against their own sex.

Males appear to be non-social. Actually, men are very social. They just prefer to be social in smaller groups. Their social interaction is demonstrated through their participation in activities and play. Men rarely demonstrate social interaction in groups greater than five participants. Men rarely demonstrate strong social skills in mixed sex groups except when they are the only male present.

Inclusion

Females are Inclusion oriented. They value intimacy, consensus, and inclusiveness. Women prize intimacy and consensus of the group over the individual. Women compete for status in relationship to the queen bee.

Males are superiority oriented. They value status and dominance. Men prize their own status and dominance in groups of their peers, frequently competing for status and dominance in these groups. As males get older, their quest for superiority weakens. Starting in the late 40's and early 50's, the quest for generativity begins. Life goals now become seeking to pass on skills and knowledge to engender a new generation with all the wisdom and skill the generative person possesses.

Disagreement

Females seek to maintain the status quo. Disagreement impacts the whole relationship. Women abhor disagreement because it disrupts the group. When the group is disrupted they perceive that their position in the group is threatened.

Males thrive on logical disagreement. Disagreement is subject based not relationship based. Men will disagree on a subject, but their disagreement rarely impacts their relationship with their antagonist or with the group.

Relationships

Females are relationship oriented. Women prize relationships. They will sacrifice personal goals for the security of the family and group relationships.

Males are accomplishment oriented. Men will sacrifice the family and group relationships for goals and accomplishments which they perceive as critical for the greater good of the family and group security.

Collaboration

Females are verbal and collaborative problem solvers. They talk with each other in order to think through and to solve both personal and group problems.

Males are silent and private problem solvers. They silently think through problems until they arrive at a solution, and then they implement and announce that solution as necessary.

Thinking

Females are non-linear thinkers. They freely jump from one subject to another. They eventually arrive back at the original subject with no loss of clarity on the issues in the process.

Males are linear thinkers. They process one subject at a time. Subjects out of sequence are seen as frustrating interruptions to the issues at hand.

Problem Solving

Females are emotional problem solvers. They analyze the emotional impacts of possible solutions in order to solve a problem.

Males are analytical problem solvers. They analyze the non-emotional aspects of a problem and seldom consider emotional impacts of their decisions.

Indirect

Females are indirect in expressing their attitudes, perceptions, and opinions. Women expect other people to respond to the subtle hints they drop. Directness may endanger relationships.

Males are direct in expressing their attitudes, perceptions, and opinions. Men confront relationships and other people in a very direct manner in order to prevent or alleviate any threats.

Resolutions

Females value being listened to and understood. Women want understanding from the men in their lives for the problems they face. They do not want or need men to fix their problems for them. Any attempts to problem solve, or fix an issue, will undermine their status as women, wives, mothers etc.

Males value fixing problems. Men want to fix women's problems. They do not want to waste time understanding the women's issues when they can fix a problem and move on to the next issue.

Conflict and Communication Issues in Relationships

Men are not socialized to talk. They find that their peers readily exploit any perceived weakness in their emotions. This exploitation is exceedingly painful to men, and so they learn very early in life to never talk about or display their emotions. This form of gender socialization puts men at a definite and destructive disadvantage in courtship, marriage and parenting. The expression of personal emotion and feelings is crucial to men's personal development in adulthood and to the formation of intimacy in marriage and in parenting.

Men will talk various sports, their favorite autos and engines, or any of their favorite hobbies. What they fear most in talking is a discussion of feelings. Feelings are almost never discussed between men even in their closest relationships. Women seem to mostly want to discuss feelings in their relationships with other women and with men. Women, who are sensitive to feelings, will move very quickly to asking a man to discuss his feelings in a relationship. This action produces great fear in men.

Men do not like to talk because they feel it will result in conflict. Most men are very passionate about staying out of conflict with other men and, especially, with the woman they love. For this reason men avoid discussing feelings and other personal issues at all costs. Most times in a relationship women have to teach men to talk about personal issues and feelings. This works best when women pry into a man's life only after setting a context of safety in the relationship and proceeding in small baby steps of conversation about feelings.

When I was first married, my wife had to force me to talk. At first this was very painful and very risky for me. I could not understand why I had to express my emotions and deepest feelings to her. I wanted her to just leave me alone. Yet she persisted day after day in forcing me to express the words that revealed my deepest emotions and feelings. It was a very freeing but extremely risky and emotionally daunting experience for me. It took me months and even years to learn to talk to her. All of her coercion finally paid off and I became a much more complete, mature and godly man. The thoughts and feelings I learned to express through words allowed me to develop greater intimacy with my wife and eventually also with God.

Women, let me give you a piece of advice. Force your men to talk. Go easy and be gentle. Tell them why you want them to talk. Start early in the dating relationship. Do not wait until marriage to spring it upon them. The sooner you teach your man to talk to you and express his deepest emotions and feelings, the sooner you set expectations for a future together and the more quickly he will heal and grow into the man God made him to be. I also highly recommend that you delay marriage until you are adequately confident that your mate has learned to properly express feelings and intimacy in communications between both of you.

The ability of men and women to talk with each other about personal feelings and issues necessitates an understanding of and development of conflict resolution skills in the pre-marital period of the relationship.

Conflict Resolution in Relationships

The ability to talk about feelings is the primary factor
in conflict resolution in any relationship.

Early in the relationship couples must learn to resolve conflict. Below is a model that I have created and found to be most successful in conflict resolution.

1. Both men and women need to feel that they are being heard and understood.
2. The key to being heard and understood is keeping a context of neutrality in the discussion.

3. There needs to be agreement on what issues are to be discussed, and all parties must be fully and impartially heard regardless of personal feelings and issues.
4. Insist that all parties will get an equal hearing. Keep the issues impersonal and objective. Each person must be allowed to fully express his or her perspective and perception of the situation. This includes expressing his or her personal feelings and explaining why those feelings are held. Force each person to discuss his or her feelings about the situation, issues and events which have transpired. Value the feelings expressed. Let people vent if necessary, but keep it impersonal.
5. Next present possible solutions to the issues presented. Have the parties involved discuss their perceptions of the solutions presented and chosen. Force each person to discuss his or her feelings about the optional choices.
6. Make a mutual decision based equally on feelings and on thoughts.
7. Determine how the solution will be implemented. Determine each partner's role in implementing the solution.
8. Again ask each individual to present their feelings about the chosen solution and its method of implementation. Ask each person how they feel about the proposed solution and implementation.
9. Deal with any ill feelings towards the proposed solution and implementation.

A decision without the expression of feelings is a non-decision.

I once found a couple who had great difficulty making a decision about their future plans after his graduation from graduate school. They had discussed the issue multiple times, but they had never shared their feelings with each other on the possibilities and desired decision. Without discussing their personal feelings about the factors in the decision with each other, they were stuck and incapable of making this most important decision in their lives.

Again ask each individual to present their feelings about the chosen solution and its method of implementation. Ask each person how they feel about the proposed solution and implementation.

Deal with any ill feelings towards the proposed solution and implementation.

I once found a couple who had great difficulty making a decision about their future plans after his graduation from graduate school. They had discussed the issue multiple times but they had never shared their feelings with each other on the possibilities and desired decision. Without discussing their personal feelings about the factors in the decision with each other, they were stuck and incapable of making this most important decision in their lives.

How do we build relationships with another person? Most of us would say that we talk to them. That is true, but building relationships is a process that requires much more involvement than having a conversation. This process involves multiple levels of our whole being. All relationships start with our personal self-image.

Chapter 20

Relationships

The sexiest thing a woman can wear is confidence.
The sexiest thing a man can wear is confidence.
Looking a person in the eye exudes confidence.
Your self-image determines your dating patterns and
mate selection more than any other factor.

How do we build relationships with another person? Most of us would say that we talk to them. That is true, but building relationships is a process that requires much more involvement than having a conversation. This process involves multiple levels of our whole being. All relationships start with our personal self-image.

Relationships – Self Image

There is nothing more attractive than a person's self-confidence. It shines through to every person with whom they interact. It forms a glow around them that attracts other people and makes the self-confident person stand out in any crowd. Your self-confidence is a combination of your self-image and your self-worth. It is primarily derived from how you were raised by your parents. Parents' self-esteem pours onto their children and conditions the child's self-perspective.

It is very difficult, then, for that child to ever change his or her self-perspective. The parental perspective applied to the child colors and determines all aspects of a person's dating and mate selection choices and decisions.

In many cases, self-doubt, derived from the low self-esteem instilled in a person in childhood, forever precludes a person from marrying a person of high self-esteem and high self-security. Even in marriage, the self-doubts of the person with low self-esteem will foment relational insecurity and relationship destructive behavior. This personal view of one's self impairs both partners' ability to achieve the relationship satisfaction which each desire.

Even though high self-confidence may still be impaired by the self-image passed to us by our parents, it can be changed. High self-confidence is achieved by the formation of our character. If we fully achieve each of Erickson's stages of development we will develop stronger self-confidence. In fact, there is nothing that will build a greater self confidence in you than the formation of your own character.

There are three prime factors which reflect low self-confidence:

1. Lack of trust, resulting in an inability to form relationships, or an inability to form non-sexual intimacy.
2. Negative attitudes, creating rejection of other people's attempts to provide affirming interaction.
3. Destructive behavior, either through the self-medication of substance abuse, sexual addiction, one night stands, or relationships in which the person is frequently subjected to abuse.

A strong self-image is best formed when parents do not coddle their children, but set high expectations for achievement and enable their children to experience both success and failure.

Self Confidence and Humility

The greatest indicator of proper self-confidence is a person's **_humbleness_**. People who are overly self-confident are very narcissistic. They feel they are entitled to anything and everything. God wants us to be self-confident. However, God measures self-confidence by humbleness.

> *In the same way, you who are younger, submit yourselves to your elders. All of you, clothe yourselves with humility toward one another, because, "God opposes the proud but shows favor to the humble." (1 Peter 5:5)*
>
> *⁵ In your relationships with one another, have the same mindset as Christ Jesus: ⁶ Who, being in very nature God, did not consider equality with God something to be used to his own advantage; rather, he made himself nothing by taking the very nature of a servant, being made in human likeness. ⁸ And being found in appearance as a man, he humbled himself by becoming obedient to death—even death on a cross! (Philippians 2:5-8)*
>
> *For the Lord takes delight in his people; he crowns the humble with victory. (Psalms 149:4)*
>
> *When pride comes, then comes disgrace, but with humility comes wisdom. (Proverbs 11:2)*

Self-confidence and the ability to bond to a mate are determined by a child's bonding to a parent more than any other factor. The more a person's self-esteem is discombobulated, the more vulnerable a person is in the area of romantic love.

Anxiety and other factors hindering the bonding between children and their parents in very early childhood highly correlate with their inability to develop self-confidence and to facilitate stable relationships in adulthood. People tend to be either very comfortable and secure in developing close interdependent relationships with other people, or very avoiding of stable interdependent relationships. Some people who are ambivalent about interdependent relationships find themselves in the middle of these extremes.

As stated, the stronger the bond between a parent and a child, the higher the child's self-confidence will be. Children with a stronger bond to their parents develop a greater capacity to bond in marriage. The third week after birth is the most critical for children in developing strong bonds with parents (Hatfield, 1995).

Self Confidence and Humility

The greatest indicator of proper self-confidence is a person's humbleness. People who are overly self-confident are very narcissistic. They feel they are entitled to anything and everything. God wants us to be self-confident. However, God measures self-confidence by humbleness.

In the same way, you who are younger, submit yourselves to your elders. All of you, clothe yourselves with humility toward one another, because, "God opposes the proud but shows favor to the humble." 1 Peter 5:5

In your relationships with one another, have the same mindset as Christ Jesus: 6 Who, being in very nature God, did not consider equality with God something to be used to his own advantage; rather, he made himself nothing by taking the very nature of a servant, being made in human likeness. 8 And being found in appearance as a man, he humbled himself by becoming obedient to death—even death on a cross! Philippians 2:5-8 5

For the Lord takes delight in his people; he crowns the humble with victory. Psalms 149: 4

When pride comes, then comes disgrace, but with humility comes wisdom. Proverbs 11:2.

Self-confidence and the ability to bond to a mate are determined by a child's bonding to a parent more than any other factor. The more a person's self-esteem is discombobulated, the more vulnerable a person is in the area of romantic love.

Anxiety and other factors hindering the bonding between children and their parents in very early childhood highly correlate with their inability to develop self-confidence and to accommodate stable relationships in adulthood. People tend to be very comfortable and secure in developing close interdependent relationships with other people, or very avoiding of stable interdependent relationships. Some people who are ambivalent about interdependent relationships find themselves in the middle of these extremes.

As stated, the stronger the bond between a parent and a child, the higher the child's self-confidence will be. Children with a stronger bond to their parents develop a greater capacity to bond in marriage. The third week after birth is the most critical for children in developing strong bonds with parents (Hatfield, 1995).

Primary Causes of Low Self Confidence

There are multiple causes of low self-confidence or a poor self-image. These include:

1. Inadequate bonding with parents in early childhood
2. Parental anxiety and depression which hinders bonding
3. Inappropriate parental criticism of one's behavior
4. Abusive or dysfunctional parents and family
5. Traumatic events in childhood
6. Having a poor body image
(Hatfield, 1995).

Self-confidence must always be supplemented with self-reliance and the ability to achieve in a world that does not coddle or play fair. Without these abilities self-confidence is just self-deception. The greatest self-confidence is created within us when we succeed not because someone told us we are great, but because we have learned to overcome the obstacles which life puts in our way. As important as family and parents are in building our self-confidence, parents and family are even more important in modeling behaviors which allow us to work through our negative and subconscious blind spots in our object relations with the people who come into our lives. This is especially true of one whom God would choose to be our future spouse.

Chapter 21

Family Dynamics

We cannot explain why a person likes or is attracted to us, let alone explain why we are indifferent to or repulsed by that person. Even worse is trying to comprehend why someone to whom we are extremely attracted does not know that we exist in a romantic sense. Object Relations Theory may not adequately explain the mystery of attraction, but it does give us some clues.

Object Relations Theory

Understanding Interpersonal Relationships

➤ The mystery of attraction and disinterest or repulsion
➤ Understanding subconscious behaviors in interpersonal relationships
➤ Have you ever wondered why some people for whom you have no reciprocal attraction are attracted to you?

Object relations theory is a study of the differentiation processes whereby a child develops a separate self-concept from those around him or her, while at the same time developing attachments to those same people. This differentiation/attachment process carries over into adult life. The theory basically postulates that each person differentiates all other persons as objects in his or her environment.

Those other persons who are environmental objects can be valued as positive elements to which the person chooses to attach, or they can be rejected as negative influences. The theory attempts to examine the subconscious psychological processes whereby a person chooses to associate or to disassociate him or herself from the other persons in his or her environment. Thus, object relations theory is not just about external relationships, but it is also about internal relationships within the person's own psychology. As a result, object relations provide insight into the aspects of interpersonal and personal psychological interpretation whereby we ascribe value and attachment to the person and to self (Scharff, D. & Scharff, J., 1991).

What is even worse than not understanding the dynamics of attraction and rejection in relationships is not understanding our own subconscious and the self-defeating behaviors in our relationships with other people. I cannot assert that object relations theory holds the answers to our subconscious interpersonal dynamics, but I believe this theory gives great insight into why we behave the way we do, along with why we are attracted to, or disinterested in, specific people in our interpersonal relationships (Siegel, 1991).

The correlation of object relations theory to mate selection becomes relevant when we begin to understand that we accept or reject other people based on our relationship with someone similar to that person. I once found myself undermining a leader in a group therapy session not because I disliked him or did not respect him, but because I associated him with my dad and my dad's cold, detached, dictatorial behavior in my childhood. The interesting fact was that this leader's approach to me was just the opposite of my approach to him. I have known some people to deliberately and maliciously seek to destroy another person's life simply because of the negative object relations they had in the past with a sibling or another person in their life.

As a result of object relations, we frequently form opinions and decisions about prospective mates when we do not even know them. We form these preconceptions based on aspects of our object relations with other people. We are completely blind as to why we accept or reject the person. We have no explanation for why we desire one person over another person, yet there are subconscious factors which cause us to make decisions and act in ways which we cannot explain. It is important that we gain insight into our object relations with other people, so that we have a stronger capability to overcome the prejudices, positive or negative, which influence our interpersonal relationships with possible mate choices (Scharff, D. & Scharff, J., 1991).

Object Relations Theory and the Crush

On a more personal note, we have all gone through our share of crushes growing up. I can understand why we have crushes. I believe they teach us to deal with the emotional aspects of becoming intimate with another person and with God. They are very painful, but they help us grow. They also help us understand what we are looking for in a mate.

What I do not understand is why some people never get over some crushes. Many times someone has a crush on us and we never notice the person. Even if we do notice, there is no attraction on our part towards that person. The opposite is also true. We have a crush and the other person does not notice us or has no attraction to us. I can understand this taking place in adolescents, but I do not understand it in the young adulthood years. It may be attributed to immaturity, late development, mental health issues, or even our fallen sinful condition. I do not find any of these answers satisfactory. There are far too many cases where a person is absolutely convinced that the person on whom they have the crush is the person they are to marry. There are far too many persons in dating relationships who are absolutely convinced that the person they are dating is the person to marry. All of a sudden, the relationship comes to a screeching halt. One of the persons knows the relationship is not God's will. The other person is left to pick up the pieces and put his or her life back together.

In some of these cases, the person's life is never put back together, and that person may forever pine over the lost love.

My first dating relationship with a first girl was a both a wonderful and very painful experience. I did not know how to date or how to behave on a date. I was slowly feeling my way through this relationship thing. The girl I was dating was a fantastic woman and she still is. I soon developed a disturbingly strong crush on her. A mutual friend decided to find out how strongly Regina was interested in me, so she directly asked her. Regina said she did not want to continue dating me. I was deeply crushed. It took me two years to get over her. The main reason the recovery was so difficult was that even though I knew she did not want to continue dating me, I did not know if she had ever liked me. Thirty-eight years later, I talked with Regina again at the wedding of her niece. Neither one of us recognized the other. It took her a while to figure out who I was. I gave her some clues. The smile on her face when she realized who I was told me everything I ever wanted to know. I then spent time talking with her and her husband. This talk finally brought to me the closure I had needed for many years. Always seek closure when a relationship ends, especially if a crush is involved (Sorenson, Russell, Harkness & Harvey, 1993). It is okay for a person to want to end a relationship, but both persons need some disclosure regarding the feelings and questions which can plague them forever if there is no closure. Regina was not the woman I was supposed to marry, but she was very close. I still think highly of her.

Most adults will not admit that they have crushes. This is especially true for married adults. This does not mean that they are unfaithful in their marriages. Instead the faithful adults decide to remain faithful and to restrict their crush relationships to properly constrained friendships. It is very easy for a person you meet to remind you of someone you had strong romantic feelings for in the past. These forgotten feelings can easily stir romantic feelings for that person in the present. The better you can understand what triggers these feelings and crushes, the easier they are to deal with in your life. The most important implication of an adult crush especially in a married person is the indication of an unresolved issue with a former love interest. (Levinger & Snoek, 1972; Bringle, Winnick & Rydell, 2013).

Tributary Model of Relationships

The Tributary model provides an excellent description of the multiple factors which enter into our choice of a mate. Think of all the streams that feed the brook that feeds the creek, which then feeds the river. The grandparents are the springs which feed the brook. The parents and siblings are the brook that feeds the creek. The prospective mates are the creeks that feed the river. The children of the couple are the river that feeds the ocean of families in the world. This is a good model of how families impact the couples who form new families in marriage. With all of the benefits this insight brings to us about the influence of generations of family which influence the development of the couple, this model is still not adequate. It cannot account for the decisions which the couple will make to accept or reject the family patterns handed down to them in the formation of their own family. It also cannot account for God's influence in shaping and bringing the partners together and shaping their lives into a couple and subsequently into a new family.

The Tributary model is very clear in pointing out that we merge six different families into one new family when we join in marriage. We bring together our father's family, our mother's family, our parents' family, and the same family groups of our spouse. We then merge these families into a seventh new family – the family that my spouse and I create. In this merger, all of the issues which shaped our parents and our self-image come together with all the issues that shaped our spouse and his or her self-image. These issues cannot be ignored in a successful marriage. They take years to understand. In many ways, until we understand what makes our parents behave the way they do, we cannot understand why we behave the way we do. In the same vein, until we understand what makes our spouse's parents and family behave the way they do, we cannot understand what makes our spouse behave the way he or she does. (Nichols, p. 10)

Women frequently favor or reject traditional marriage based on the happiness of their mothers in traditional marriages. For those with happy mothers, traditional marriage is favored. For those with unhappy mothers, non-traditional marriage is favored (Peplau, Hill, & Rubin, 1993). It is very critical to our marital success that we begin early to understand our own family of origin. We then need to also understand the family of origin of our spouse. Neither spouse can transform the other spouse into one of his or her parents or other family members without destroying both the spouse and the marriage. Therefore, it is critical to make sure our spouse is looking for a partner who is sufficiently different from his or her parents. It is also important that we make sure we are comfortable with the family of our spouse's origin. If the spouse's behaviors and practices are not ones with which we are comfortable, we will have difficulty accepting those behaviors and practices when they are displayed by our spouse, or approved by our spouse in the behavior of our children.

Chapter 22

Healing as Preparation for Marriage

There are many issues that affect our ability to form relationships. Many of these derive from the traumas and painful memories we have in life. The traumas and painful memories constitute issues which we cannot overcome until they are healed. If they are not healed, they will impinge on our lives forever. Most people never find healing for the issues in their life. They plod along each day living in their own brokenness and frequently creating more brokenness around them. For this reason, we need a solid understanding and implementation of a plan for healing the issues of our life.

Broken people create broken marriages.
Whole people create whole marriages.
If you want to have a whole and healthy marriage, you have to become a whole and healthy person.

Effects of Abuse on Marriage

One of the most devastating factors which erodes our ability to form successful long term relationships is any form of abuse at any point prior to or during marriage. The younger the age when the abuse occurred, the more devastating it usually is on a person's future life. The devastation includes issues in social and interpersonal relationship functioning, sexual difficulties, decreased self-esteem, interpersonal problems, and suicidal ideation and attempts. Physical abuse tends to lead to marital breakdown. Those who have been abused also have a greater tendency to re-victimization concurrent with the forms of abuse which they have previously experienced. (Mullen, Martina, Anderson, Romansa, & Herbisona 1996; Follette, Polusny, Bechtel, & Naugle, 1996; Silverman, Reinherz, & Giaconia, 1996; Polusny & Follette, 1995).

Signs of Severe Abuse in Childhood

People who have been severely abused may omit drawing hands and/or feet on people when they make a drawing. Any time you have the opportunity to see a prospective mate's drawings, look for hands and feet in the drawing. If hands are feet are missing, you can be assured that the person has never been through sufficient healing to be capable of staying in a long term relationship (Malchiodi, 1998).

Abused people will frequently enter into relationships looking for a parental figure – mother or father. They will do well in the relationship for the first few years. Soon they begin to project onto their spouse the same reactions which they previously had to abuse which they experienced from their parent or other perpetrator. The longer the period of abuse lasted, the more difficult it is to recuperate, and the less likely the abused person will be able to stay in the relationship.

Forgiveness is the primary requirement for any person who has suffered abuse. Until the perpetrator is forgiven, there is no healing which can take place. For those who have been severely abused, staying in a long term relationship is likely impossible without long term psychodynamic therapy.

The traumas in your past control your present and your future!

It takes a long time to get sick, and it takes a long
time to get well!
Psychological healing is never instant.

You cannot leave the past behind unless you deal with it in the
present. If you do not deal with the past in the present, it will control
your present and destroy your future just as it destroyed your past.

Counseling Issues

The one thing which will prevent you from ever marrying
someone is the issue of a broken heart. Broken hearts do not mend
easily, and they frequently do not heal cleanly or completely. If you
are suffering from a broken heart or some other issue which will
seriously impinge your ability to freely give yourself wholeheartedly
to another person, then the broken heart must be healed.

What does it take to properly prepare yourself for marriage?
Many people suffer from deep wounds received in their struggle
for adulthood, or in broken relationships in earlier events of life.
These wounds imperil their ability to form new, close, and lasting
relationships. Most people have difficulty even telling members of
their own family about these events and issues which have wounded
and scarred their lives.

If you cannot talk about the most painful memories and issues
in life with the people you love the most, then you are not ready to
enter a new relationship and share your life with a person whom you
have known only a short while.

In preparing for marriage the place to start is always with
yourself. You must become aware of the issues in your own life which
will impact your ability to sustain a successful marriage before you
begin examining the same kinds of issues in your prospective mate.
If you are not conscious of the issues in your own life, you will not
be conscious of the issues in your mate. These issues bear seeds of
destruction for marriage.

"You hypocrite, first take the plank out of your own eye, and then you will see clearly to remove the speck from your brother's eye" (Matthew 7:5).

Sins That Destroy Our Ability to Marry

Abortion – Jeremiah 1:4-5, Job 10:2, 8-9, Exodus 20:13,21:22-24, Leviticus 7:14

Cohabitation – Genesis 2:18-25, Hebrews 13:4, 1 Timothy 4:3

Pornography – Matthew 5:27-28, 1 Corinthians. 6:18, Colossians. 3:5

Divorce - Romans 7:2-3, Malachi 2:14-15, Ephesians 5:33, Matthew 19:6, Matthew 5:31-32, Mark 10:2-12, Luke 16:18, 1 Corinthians 7:10-15, 1 Corinthians 7:39, Deuteronomy 24:1-4

Polygamy/polyandry – Matthew 19:8, Mark 10:6

Sexual immorality – Acts 15:29, 1 Corinthians 5:1–5, 1 Corinthians 5:9–11, 1 Corinthians 6:9–11, 1 Corinthians 10:8, Galatians 5:19, Ephesians 4:19, Ephesians 5:3, 1 Thessalonians 4:3–7, 1 Peter 4:1–3, Revelation 2:14–16, Revelation 2:20, Revelation 2:21–23

Any form of sin in our lives destroys our ability to have an integrated personality. The resultant fragmentation of our personality restricts our ability to be intimate as it destroys our character, our ability to bond, and our ability to love. Sexual sins more directly impact our ability to form significant long term relationships. These sins include abortion, cohabitation, pornography, divorce, polygamy/polyandry, sexual immorality, and homosexuality. The best way to prepare yourself for marriage is to deal not only with the need for forgiveness of these sins in your life, but also with healing the personality fragmentation which these sins leave behind. Some scars these sins leave behind may never be removed, but the psychological destruction which they wield in our lives can and must be healed.

Mental Health Issues

All healthy relationships mature and grow naturally. Only unhealthy relationships become sick, decay and die. Around 75% of the human population lives with mental health issues for which they need healing. We tend to marry people who are most similar to us in their level of mental health.

People who suffer from mental illness seek partners who are mentally ill. If they are in management they hire people who are mentally ill. Socially they will surround themselves with people who are mentally ill.

(Lichi, 1995)

In some subconscious manner, people will seek out a partner who has the same or similar mental health issues. When they marry, the mental health issues undermine the marriage and may easily be passed on to their offspring. In this manner mental health issues are perpetuated through the generations. This perpetuates destructive relationships, broken marriages, and crippled lives. The Bible frequently speaks of sins of the fathers being passed down to the third and fourth generation (Genesis 15:16, Exodus 20:5, Numbers 14:18, 2 Kings 14:6, Exodus 34:6-7, Deuteronomy 5:8-10). This does not mean that a child is held accountable for the parent's sin or the parent held accountable for the child's sin (Deuteronomy 24:16). Each person is held accountable for his or her own sin. However, the consequences and effects of that sin get passed through the social environment of the home in which the child is raised. A single person's mental health issues impact every person in the family. Left untreated, these issues tend to destroy the whole family and to impact the lives of everyone associated with that family. The sins of our parents which impact our mental health also impact our search for a mate and our future marriages.

Arrested Development

Broken trust traumatizes and locks a person at a specific level of psycho-social development. The person becomes stuck at the level of development at which the trauma took place. This frequently results in an inability to express emotion and to develop intimacy. When the person becomes healed of the trauma which took place in earlier years, he or she begins a rapid process of accelerated development. In this accelerated development, the age appropriate stages of development that have been insufficiently completed (between the time of the traumatic event and the time of the person's current age level) are accomplished within a few months. Maturing through missed stages of development frequently results in the person exhibiting inappropriate and awkward behaviors during this time of accelerated change. This pattern of rapid, inappropriate, and awkward behavior continues until a person becomes stabilized at the appropriate age and development level. For example, an adult person may go through a period of behavior that is more reflective of adolescence than adulthood.

When we look at ourselves or at a prospective mate and compare that person's development to Erickson's Stages of life, we find that an undeveloped stage clearly indicates frozen development and trauma at a specific stage of life. This arrested development is an issue particularly for adopted and abused children. Children who were given up for adoption frequently have basic trust issues. This broken trust in relationship with a birth mother frequently results in an inability to trust women, and an inability to trust a church. They may spend their entire life fighting to maintain their own independence in order to avoid additional pain or hurt from other people. This results in an inability to adequately submit to a spouse, boss, or other authority figure. People who have issues with a birth father frequently have difficulty trusting God and men in general. They also develop anger which they frequently stifle with some form of addiction. People who have issues with a birth mother have difficulty with church and any type of religious or other group which places demands for conformity upon their lives.

The Mask – Presenting a False Persona

The Mask is characterized by people who:

1. present a false image, much like a wearing a mask
2. build walls to protect the false persona
3. use their mask and build their walls to prevent intimacy in relationships.

Many people who have been traumatized at an early age develop the practice of putting on a false persona, much like wearing a mask. They go to great lengths to build walls to protect the false persona which they project to other people. They will go to extreme lengths to prevent other people from seeing their real self. They will let no one see behind their mask, even a spouse. They refuse to develop close friends or to permit any form of intimacy in their relationships, even with spouse, children, or other family members. The only people who can get close to them are people who see through their mask and refuse to stay outside the wall with which they protect themselves. They begin to heal when someone tears down their wall, exposes their mask, and still accepts their real self with love and understanding.

Spiritual Aspects of Mental Health - Demonization

There are six conditions where mental health becomes greatly complicated by demonization in a person's life. These include Generational Sin, Child Abuse, ABRRR (anger, bitterness, rage, rejection, and rebellion), Sexual Perversion, Curses, and Occult Practices.

1. Generational sin in which the sins of the parents have devastating consequences on the children. See the judgment on Eli in I Samuel 3:1 through 4:22.
2. Child abuse which frequently occurs through incest, pimping children, abandoning children, molestation, and Satanic Ritual Abuse. (Satanic Ritual Abuse is the worst form of abuse.)
3. ABRRR (anger, bitterness, rage, rejection, and rebellion). These are mostly reactions to extreme forms of physical, sexual, psychological, religious, and abandonment abuse. The abuse causes such extreme damage that these emotions take over and become doorways for demons to control the person's life.
4. Sexual perversion which may include rape, incest, homosexuality, adultery, pornography, and other forms of sexual perversion.
5. Curses are spoken words which produce negative and destructive effects on a person's life. See Deuteronomy chapters 27 through 31. Curses are the opposite of blessings. Also, see the story of Balaam in Numbers chapters 22 through 24.
6. Occult practices are frequently encountered through psychic activity, idolatry, magic, and some forms of music.

People who have been involved or exploited in these practices frequently become demonically oppressed and need deliverance as a necessary step in developing intimacy and successful marital relationships (Murphy, 1992, pp. 437-476; Prince, 2006, pp. 14-16).

Chapter 23

The Healing of Intimacy

I want to set the stage for understanding how God enables us to be adequately healed so that we can begin to experience the level of intimacy which God wants for our lives and relationships. Psychological healing is dependent on a few main biblical factors – intimacy and trust (without manipulation), worship, confession, and forgiveness. These factors cover cognitive, behavioral, affective, and psychodynamic aspects of our relationships with God and fellow human beings. The cognitive aspect is to be intimate with God without seeking to control or manipulate Him. The behavioral and affective aspect is to worship God, and the psychodynamic aspect is to forgive and be forgiven.

Keys to Healing in Your Life

Six Keys to Psychological Healing
Reframe events
Remove life commandment curses
Forgive the perpetrator
Be grateful
Worship
Confess

How do you receive healing from the traumatic and painful events in your life? These answers may sound very simplistic and trite, but they are actually the biblical equivalent to some of the most current and advanced psychological forms of therapy practiced by counselors and therapists today.

1. Reframe events. Examine each of the stages of your life. For any stage where you find weakness in your development, examine what traumatic events took place at that time of your life. Reframe these traumatic events by examining how God used these events to bring about positive situations in your life or to enable you to minister to other people in similar situations.

2. Remove life commandment curses. Parents and significant people in our lives frequently speak well intentioned but very negative and limiting life commandments into our lives. In my early teens my mother told me that no woman would ever love me. This became a life commandment for me. It limited every relationship with a woman whom I desired to pursue as a mate. Some life commandments are good and should be respected in our life. These are the values we live by. However, life commandments may also serve as curses upon our life, and these should be rejected. Life commandments can be removed by:
   a. Confessing them to God and asking Him to put them under the blood of Jesus
   b. Rejecting them from limiting or impacting your life in the future
   c. Forgiving the person who placed that life commandment on your life

3. Forgive the perpetrator. For whoever caused each and every tragedy or traumatic event in your life, simply forgive that person. Healing comes through forgiveness (Ephesians 4:17-24, Philippians 3:13, Romans 12:2, Matthew 6:12).

   All psychological healing requires forgiveness. I have studied, and experienced, several different forms of psychotherapy. I have also seen multiple people, including myself, greatly benefit from psychotherapy. As a result,

I know that all forms of psychotherapy boil down to one thing – forgiveness. In the end psychotherapy is simply forgiveness. The psychodynamic concept of reframing is a form of forgiveness.

Of the people who hurt us in life:

i.   Some hurt us intentionally – and some hurt us unintentionally.
ii.   Some are repentant -- and some are unrepentant.
iii. Some broken people are just evil and mean.

We call the people who hurt us perpetrators. Perpetrators sometimes hurt us intentionally, and sometimes they hurt us unintentionally. Sometimes they are sorry for hurting us, and sometimes they are not. Sometimes people hurt us because they are just evil and mean. Sometimes kind and loving people hurt us. Sometimes the people who hurt us are our parents and family members. Sometimes the people who do evil to us are strangers. I will refer to all of these people as perpetrators, regardless of who they are or what their intent or motive is.

Forgiveness frees us from control by the trauma that the perpetrator has created in our life! <u>All perpetrators who harm us need to be forgiven</u>. Perpetrators never deserve our forgiveness. Even when they repent and ask for our forgiveness, they still do not deserve to be forgiven. Perpetrators will never deserve our forgiveness. The more evil they are in their motives and intentions, the more they deserve punishment for what they have done to us.

When we have been hurt by perpetrators, we deserve to forgive them. We deserve the healing that forgiveness brings to our life. This is the important part: When we have been hurt by perpetrators, we deserve to forgive them. Forgiveness heals. It frees us from the control and the hurt the perpetrators have inflicted on our lives. We can only be free from what they have done to us when we forgive them. Please forgive the perpetrators of the evil and the harm they have inflicted on your life because you deserve the healing that forgiveness brings to your life. You see, God created forgiveness not so much for the perpetrators, but for us. Forgiving the perpetrator heals us deep on the inside where the pain is. God created forgiveness not so much for the perpetrators, but for us

4. Be grateful for what God brings into your life and thank God for it. Also make it a point to thank God for the people he uses to bring good into your life.

5. Worship God in the midst of the difficulties of your life. The greatest demonstration of trust and intimacy in a relationship is worship. Remember Paul and Silas in jail singing and worshiping God. There are many jails in our lives. These jails can range anywhere from illness to traumatic events to physical jails. There is nothing more freeing than worshiping God in and for the jails of your life. What are the jails of your life? The jails we encounter in our lives are varied:

    a. Unforgiveness
    b. Psychological trauma
    c. Physical jails
    d. Poor health
    e. Broken family relationships

Human psychology teaches us that "Until the pain of staying the same is greater than the pain of change, people prefer to stay the same!" Until the jails of your life are so painful that you cannot stand them, you will refuse to find a way out of your jails. The Bible's secret to overcoming the jails of our life consists of two actions: worship and forgiveness.

How do you overcome the jails of your life? You overcome the jails of your life by worshiping in the midst of those jails. Worshiping in jail is the most freeing experience there is in a person's life and in his or her relationship with God. Paul and

Silas worshiped in jail. Worship makes you holy! Holiness makes you healthy and well! Holiness heals brokenness!

Paul and Silas worshiped in jail (Acts 16:16-40). Think about it. If you are locked up in a jail or prison, could you worship God there? Would you worship or would you rail at God and blame Him for allowing you to be there? Only the person who can worship God in the jails and prisons of her or his life can really worship God. The points of greatest hurt and pain in our lives are our prisons. They are what capture and hold us. They are what lock us up on the inside and prevent us from developing into the wholesome, loving people God wants to make of us.

The greatest freedom and healing in life is when we go to the point of the greatest hurt in our life. This is the point where we were wounded and killed the most. When we get to the point of greatest pain and begin to worship God for what occurred in that event, God heals us and sets us free. When you can worship God for the greatest pain you have ever experienced in life, I will assure that you will be the freest, most beautiful person on the face of the earth. Forgiveness sometimes takes time and is very hard to do, but it is worth it. It took me years to be able to worship God in points of greatest pain, but it has been well worth it. Only through worshiping Jesus Christ in the jails and prisons of your life, can you be free as you live in the midst of the captivity of those prisons.

A few years ago my wife became a walking miracle for the second time in her life. The first time is when she died on the operating table at age 28. She died and went to heaven. I have the surgeon's verification that she died. She went through the tunnel of light, past the point where you take the path to hell if you do not know Jesus as your Lord and savior. She arrived in heaven and was told by God that she had to return to earth because I needed her and it was not her time to die. She came back to me. Then about twenty five years later she had surgery for stenosis. The surgeon did not believe she would survive the surgery. She came out of the surgery completely paralyzed. She was rushed back into surgery a couple of hours later. The surgeon could not find the problem causing the paralysis. He knew she would not survive, so he performed an experimental procedure. After the surgery she was one of only three people who have had their spinal canal drilled out and lived. She went through extensive rehabilitation, learning to walk and talk, keep her balance, and feed herself all over again. Instead of complaining about what she was going through, all the surgeries she had had, and the debilitating condition she was in, she just praised God and worshiped. She led another doctor to Jesus because he saw there was no way she could be alive with what she had been through. She prayed for her nurses and therapists and caretakers. She made her visitors read the Bible and pray with her. Today, except for constant pain and weariness, she leads a normal life. She still praises God and worships each day. She faced death and lived. She faced lifelong paralysis and won. She faced pain and bitterness and lives to praise and worship God. How do you face the jails of your life?

If you cannot worship in the prisons of your life, then you cannot worship. The only way out of the prisons and pain in our lives is to worship. I do not say that worship will instantly set you free. I do say that continuing to worship Jesus in the prisons of our lives will soon set us free. It will heal us from the inside. It will make it easier for us to forgive those who have harmed us. Also, it will put us in a place in our relationship with God where we know we can never be harmed again by that prison and pain. This is the point at which God sets us free. This is the point at which He makes us truly new creatures in Christ. This is the point where God brings forth the greatest beauty and joy in our lives.

Paul and Silas demonstrated this intimacy with God by worshiping God while they were in a very difficult situation in life. We are not to worship our mate, but we are to worship

God. We are to have intimacy and trust with our mate. There is no more powerful intimacy than when we join in corporate worship of God together with our mate.

6.   "Confess your sins to one another and pray for one another that you may be healed..." (James 5:16). I believe there is a strong reason that confession and healing are placed together in this verse. For both psychological and physical healing to take place in our lives, we must confess not only our personal sins, but also our forgiveness of those who sin against us.

Many people go through great traumas and emotional pain in their lives, and they never get over them. Those traumas and pains are festering wounds that never heal. We try to forget about them, but they never go away. We bury them deep in our subconscious, too ashamed and hurt to ever speak of them with another person. We hide them as our personal secrets.

From experience in my own life and in observation of others, I have found that the greatest healing comes not when we hide our trauma and pain but when we confess it openly and publicly.

How do you know when you are healed of the greatest emotional trauma in your life? When you can tell your story to both your best friends and to complete strangers, you are not only truly healed, you are also using your pain to heal other people's lives. I have personally witnessed physical healing miracles, as well as my wife coming back from the dead. However, it is in the stories of the people who share their deepest pain that I see what I consider to be the greatest miracles of my risen Savior.

Final and complete healing for the greatest pains in our lives only comes when we worship.
If you cannot worship Jesus in the jails of your life, you cannot worship!

Chapter 24

Cohabitation

Cohabitation relationships are not as permanent as marital relationships.
Cohabitation before marriage creates a higher chance of divorcing after marriage.
Cohabitation normally results in a lack of commitment to the relationship.
Cohabitating couples are more likely to have violence in their relationship than married couples.
Cohabitation is four times more likely to result in infidelity.
(McIlhaney & McKissic-Bush, 2008)

Cohabitation goes by many names: "living together," "trial marriage," "common law marriage," "consensual union," and a few others. From a biblical perspective, I believe the practice of cohabitation is grossly misunderstood. Cohabitation is not just a matter of living together. It is a matter of marriage. By biblical definition, any time a person has heterosexual sex with another person, a marital relationship is established. If this established marriage is between a couple where at least one of the parties is already married, then it is adultery. The reason it is adultery is because the couple has entered into a polygamous relationship. One or both of the partners is now married to more than one spouse.

For centuries the church considered cohabitation to be a normal model of relationships, and it was defined by the church as "marriage by consent." This was commonly due to the lack of money to have a wedding, the lack of a priest, or other circumstances which inhibited the availability of a marriage ceremony (Tissier, 1993).

Starting in the 1970's, cohabitation has been on a steady rise. Psychological research has demonstrated that cohabitation when compared to marriage creates greater dissatisfaction in the relationship. It also leads to greater violence in the relationship. It subsequently produces negative impacts on marital bonding and less stable marriages. This, in turn, creates a higher divorce rate for couples who cohabitated prior to marriage (Smiciklas, 1995). For cohabitating couples, the divorce rate is much higher than for marital couples who have not cohabitated (Noc, 1995; Axinn & Thornton, 1992; Colella & Thompson, 1992; Teachman & Polonko, 1990).

Cohabitation is supposed to fulfil the purpose of preparing a couple for marriage to each other on a trial basis. Instead, the results clearly demonstrate the outcome is an increased divorce rate and greater marital dissatisfaction than seen in the general populace (Booth & Johnson, 1988). The research literature in more recent years is still showing the same results.

I will admit that cohabitation sounds like the perfect solution. Put two people together and let them find out how to live together before marriage, so that when they get married they will have a greater potential for a successful long term marriage. The consequences of failure should be much less traumatic and painful assuming they separate before conceiving children. Why does the research indicate that cohabitation does not lead to a successful marriage?

I believe there are several causes for the failure rate of cohabitating couples. First, the primary cause of failure is that the individual enters into the cohabitation relationship with the expectation of failure with a disposable partner. Cohabitation is supposed to be a trial run; if it fails, then it is no great loss. For this reason the relationship becomes a self-fulfilling prophecy of failure. Also, the partner is always as disposable as the daily trash. If the relationship fails he or she can always be replaced by a new and shiny partner. Again, research is showing that cohabitating couples do not work as hard at the relationship and place less value on the partner (Booth & Johnson, 1988; Nock, 1995). Second, the relationship is based on a contract instead of a covenant. Contracts are considered to be breakable with few consequences. The biblical model of covenant for marriage is never breakable. Instead, it binds the couple into a lifelong, permanent, committed relationship which values the partner more highly than anything else in life except Jesus Christ. Third, I believe many cohabitating partners upon marriage fail to move from contract to covenant in their relationship. They fail to make this transition in their thinking and in their approach to marriage. Finally, many of these couples never take steps needed for proper selection of a mate. It is too easy to slide from dating into cohabitation and then into marriage. The couple never asks the hard questions about God's will in their choice of a mate. They do not ask the hard questions about the person's character, capacity for intimacy, and other issues that are critical to examine in selecting a marital partner.

Like all relationships, much good can come from cohabitation and also much damage. Some cohabitating couples form lifelong successful marital bonds. However, for most cohabitating couples, the subsequent marital divorce rate hovers well above the normal divorce rate in many Western nations. For this reason, I conclude that cohabitation does not work. It produces impermanence instead of permanence in relationships. It leaves scars and deep wounds in the lives of those who seek an easy shortcut to a marital union instead of doing the hard work of bonding and building permanence in a marriage. The damage left in the lives of the children of failed cohabitation and failed marriage is even more devastating than the brokenness left in the lives of the partners in the relationship.

Even though there are a few positive considerations about cohabitation, the negative considerations are convincingly prohibitive of permanence in a cohabitation relationship. Recent research is showing the following negative results of cohabitation.

Negative Cohabitation Factors:
Weaker bond and more volatile relationships than married couples.
Fifty percent increase in divorce rate above societal divorce rate.
More conflicted financial issues to resolve.
Less sexual satisfaction and less sexual faithfulness in the relationship.
Only about 40% of cohabitating couples eventually get married.
Children raised in cohabitating relationships do not develop as well or perform as well as children raised in marriages. They also face greater risk of abuse. ("What You Should Know," 2014)

Research Facts About Cohabitation:
Cohabitation is the precursor for over sixty percent of marriages in the US today. (Wilcox, & Cherlin. 2011).
Cohabitating couples are more likely to permanently break up regardless of when they marry.
Women cohabitating prior to marriage are 33% more likely to divorce.
Men who cohabitate frequently make less money. At retirement this is usually 78% less wealth.
Married young mothers are frequently more privileged financially.
Cohabitating couples frequently have more mental health and addiction issues. (Thomas, 2015)

With recent revisions in divorce statistics, the accuracy of the comparison statistics for divorces of cohabiting couples versus first time married couples can no longer be considered accurate. Indications are that cohabiting couples still have a 22 percent higher divorce rate than first time married couples (Foust, 2008).

PART 6
Faith Dynamics

There is no deeper bond than prayer and worship.

Chapter 25

Spiritual Dynamics
in Mate Selection

Perceptions of God

Many people hold one of two views of God. They either believe in a God for whom they must perform or a God who is totally tolerant.

P eople tend to hold one of two secular views of God. The first view is performance based.

Many years ago, I had a very performance based approach to God. I believed that if I did all the things a Christian should do, I would be more acceptable to God. Most of this attitude came from my relationship with my dad. My dad was overly critical. No matter what I did, I never had his love and acceptance. Just before he died I finally felt that he was proud of me, but he never really told me that.

Several years later, I went through psychodynamic therapy using Metaphor Therapy. As a result of this therapy, many traumatic issues in my life were healed – especially childhood traumatic events with my dad. I found my attitudes and behaviors changing. My perspective of God and relationships changed. As my perspective changed, I stopped seeking God's approval. I realized that he loved me. All He really wanted from me was that I love him. He would take care of everything else. As I developed a much greater love for God, I realized that my behavior changes were not what brought me more love from him. Instead, my behavior changes were what allowed me to love God more.

Our relationship with God is never performance based. Nothing you do will ever procure for you approval from God. God already approves of you and always has approved of you. God does not even want us to seek to please Him. Instead he just accepts us the way we are. He does not value our performance. He values our love! There are many Bible verses which state what kind of behavior is pleasing or acceptable to God. These verses do not express behavior as a way of earning God's love and approval. Instead, they emphasize the kind of behavior which allows love to flow from God to us and from us to God. Our relationship with God is not performance based, but love based.

I do not believe that God wants us to change our behavior or performance. Rather, He wants us to allow Him to change us. He wants to change our attitudes, our understanding, our perception of reality, and our relationship with Him. When God changes us then our behavior automatically changes.

The second view of God is tolerance based. In our world where tolerance reigns supreme, people come to view God as someone who will accept them regardless of their behavior and without judging them. They come to perceive God as someone who values them and will never place any consequences on their lives. In other words, they have come to believe in God as a god of Tolerance. For them there is no right and wrong. There are no absolutes. There is only acceptance. They cannot tolerate a god who does not accept them as they are or who insists on holiness in their lives. To them, the only sin is failure to be tolerant of their sins. They cannot tolerate a god who seeks to change them into followers who must love their god and live for that god. They will gladly respond to any god who accepts them until that god insists that they become disciples and forsake the sin in their lives. Their god is Tolerance and they cannot tolerate the God of the Bible. Any god who is not tolerant is disposable. Any relationship that does insist on morality, ethics, standards, and accountability is considered to be not only intolerable but also unethical and unloving.

If we do not hold people accountable in relationships, they will never learn true love. For them love will always be disposable and relationships will be disposable. If we do not require holiness as the indispensable core of all relationships, they will never know God and will never experience permanence in any relationship.

Their concept of a person to date is someone who accepts them unconditionally. Their idea of mate selection and marriage is finding someone who **tolerates** them. Only by knowing and living in relationship with the God of the Bible will people become appropriately prepared to live in a permanent relationship of marriage. Without this foundation, people only want relationships with people who tolerate them and never hold them accountable. All they see around them are broken relationships and marriages as models of life in relationships. A God who brings permanence in a relationship to their lives is unfathomable. They cannot conceive of any god who offers anything but impermanence and a disposable relationship. They crave the intimacy of permanence in relationships, but they cannot conceive of any such relationship being a reality.

For those who worship Tolerance, the God of the Bible is a myth. They may claim to worship the God of the Bible, but they expect their god to cater to their lives instead of living their lives for their God. As long as they worship tolerance, they will forever be broken people, living in broken relationships. The god **Tolerance** does not and cannot heal brokenness. Only the God of the Bible heals. Only the God of the Bible demands that people follow his commandments as the way to avoid brokenness in their lives and their relationships.

If we are going to present Jesus to the worshipers of the god of Tolerance, we must present Him as a God who brings permanence into lives and relationships. We must present Him as a God who heals brokenness and who demands to live in intimacy with us. We must present Him as the only God who can prevent brokenness in our lives and who can deliver us from the brokenness which already exists. We must present him as the God who heals not only the brokenness in our lives, but also the brokenness in our relationships. We must present Him as the only God who is capable of intimacy with us and who can give us intimacy with other people.

At the same time we must present His church as a gathering of broken people and hypocrites whom He is in the process of healing. This church of broken people and broken relationships is where people come to learn to live in the kind of fidelity which enables intimacy and establishes permanence in our relationships with each other. The healing people seek for the brokenness in their lives cannot exist in a context which has no permanence. Jesus can only bring complete healing when a context of permanence is provided, and brokenness is not tolerated in relationships. This is why God always demands holiness in our lives and in our church.

Beliefs Matter

How important is a person's faith and beliefs to marriage? To understand the role of faith in a Christian marriage we need to understand a person's relationship with Jesus Christ. We also need to understand a person's concept of God.

One of the most desired characteristics of a mate is for the mate to hold similar or even identical religious beliefs to one's own. Once the religious similarity is established, it is important to determine how closely the prospective mate adheres to his or her belief system.

The key question for a Christian to answer:
Is your God about your life? or Is your life about your God?

For Christians this can be answered in two questions. (1) Is your God about your life? (2) Is your life about your God? These two questions will determine precisely where a person is in his or her focus on God.

Let's take a look at a Christian perspective of God. I want to present the Christian view of God more from a philosophical perspective than from a biblical perspective. Too many Christians understand only pieces and parts of the Christian view of God, instead of understanding the nature of God and His plan for human beings from a holistic perspective. Here is my summary of a holistic perspective of God.

Characteristics of a Supreme Being
One and only one God
A God who cannot be manipulated or controlled
A God who is absolute, moral, and just
A God who holds me accountable
A God who loves me
A God who communicates and protects
A God to whom I must respond and who demands something from me
A God who changes everything
A God to whom I can relate
An exclusive God

In the world in which we currently live, those who oppose Jesus Christ seek to destroy any concept of God. The result is that those who are raised in the Christian church and Christian homes have very little understanding of the Christian view of God. For this reason, it is becoming increasingly difficult to ascertain whether a prospective mate is truly a worshipper of Jesus Christ or a person who worships a quack god that has no relationship to the God of the Bible. The concepts presented here will provide criteria for determining the functional validity of a person's view of God in relation to orthodox Christian teachings.

A real God is - One and only One God. Having multiple gods is a lot like having multiple wives or girlfriends. How many wives or girlfriends can you please at one time? How long until one gets mad at you? What happens when pleasing one causes you to displease another?

If it takes multiple gods to accomplish all that you would desire in a God, then your gods are only part of a real God. They are not a whole God. This is like having bits and pieces of a spouse and not a whole spouse.

Many people treat gods like doctors. Each doctor has a specialty. It often takes many doctors with many different specialties to diagnose and treat an illness. Frequently one doctor works at curing an illness and then finally ends up referring the patient to another specialist in order to secure a cure for the illness. This is the way many people treat gods. They think each god has a specialty, and they just keep going from one specialist to another. To me, a true God is a God who is the ultimate specialist in every area of healthcare and of life itself. I do not want many specialist gods. I want only one God who is supreme at doing everything.

Anything less than one supreme God is, in my opinion, a non-god. Only a deficient god needs additional gods added to be a complete God. God is either a whole being that we accept as a whole, or one whom we reject as a whole.

I do not want to create a god who is like me. I do not want to create a god at all. I want my God to be so different from me that I can become a better person by becoming like my God. I want to have a God who inspires me to become like him. The most subtle danger in looking for a God is to look for one who is just like you. If you find a god who is like you, then all you really have is you. You do not have a real God – unless you consider yourself to be a god.

A real God is one who cannot and will not be manipulated or controlled.

A real God is one who cannot be manipulated or controlled. Any god who can be manipulated or controlled is a disposable god. People who seek to manipulate and control their god either get what they want from their god or they move on to another god. They treat their relationships with people in the same manner. Do you really want a god who is just like all the other disposable people and relationships in your life? Are disposable relationships and people healthy for my life? Am I a person who will benefit and bring health to the lives of the people with whom I enter into relationships? Is it healthy for my friends and significant others when I consider all people and relationships as disposable?

The question is - could a God who is bound by the constraints of this world be capable of loving and forgiving us? Do you know of anything that is perfect in this world? I believe that any God who is capable of loving and forgiving me must be from outside of this world and therefore beyond our control. Perfect love and forgiveness do not originate in this world.

I know that if I have a God that comes from this world, he will damage me. He will not be capable of loving me and forgiving me in a manner that is pure and complete. Whatever love and forgiveness he shows to me will always be damaged and incomplete. Only a God who comes from outside of this world and who is incapable of being manipulated or controlled, by us or anything else, is worthy of being a God with whom we enter a relationship.

A real God is absolute. There are multiple factors in the world in which we live which indicate our need for a God. I believe we need a God primarily because we need absolutes. I consider knowledge to be an absolute. You either know something, or you do not know something. There is no middle ground, no grey area in knowing something. If you do not believe in absolutes, then how do you know that you do not believe in absolutes?

The main reason we need absolutes is because we need safety and justice. Safety protects us from injustice. If we do not have justice, we cannot be held accountable for the good or evil we commit in our lives. Without absolutes there is no morality; there is no right or wrong; there is no good or evil. Anyone can do anything they want to us and harm us in any way. There is no right or wrong in what they have done. We can do any good or evil we want to another person, and there is no right or wrong in what we have done. Only an absolute God can bring right and wrong into a world of good and evil.

I want a God who has the absolute power and answer to every question I could ever ask. I want a God who is so powerful and so beyond the limits of this world that he has the power to create and control everything. I want a God who has no limits upon his power except the limits he imposes upon himself. Such a God would create everything that is good and everything that is evil. A God who is absolute will also create human beings with the free will and ability to choose between good and evil.

Many people ask the question – "How can a good and loving God allow evil things to happen to good people?" Any intelligent person will also ask this question: How can a good and loving God not allow evil? Without the choice between good and evil, there can be no absolutes. There is no justice and no safety for us in this world. **How can a God who creates evil** not allow evil? How can an absolute God permit free will and not allow evil? Only when we have the possibility for evil to occur can we have an absolute God. Isaiah 45:7 - I form the light and create darkness, I bring prosperity and create disaster; I, the LORD, do all these things (NIV). The NIV translation of this passage does not properly express the Hebrew understanding of this verse. The concept of God portrayed in this passage is advanced to the point that it easily declares that God Himself creates evil. Good and evil go together. Without one you cannot have the other. The Bible clearly expresses this understanding of the existence of good and evil as well as their origin. This does not mean that God created a dualistic universe. Instead it is an emphasis on the human ability to do evil in a fallen world. It also emphasizes the fact the God created us to do good (Young, 1972).

If the people of this world evolved randomly from the chemical elements that make up this planet and/or from lower forms of life, then it is only logical that some would evolve having free will and some would not have free will. If we all had no free will, then we would all worship the same God or gods, and we would all respond to that God or gods with complete obedience. No person would be able to ever choose to follow a different God or to leave the collective. We would all be in complete unity and agreement within our society and culture.

If all people were created by a God, instead of evolving out of lower life forms, then we could reasonably expect the creator to make all people with free will or to make all people without free will. The multiplicity of gods worshiped by people in this world, as well as the capacity for people to do good or evil, convinces me that all people are both created and have free will.

If we do not have free will, can we be held accountable for what we do in life? If we do not have free will, then it is the being who gives us the orders which we must obey. That same being is the only one accountable for what we do. We cannot be held accountable for following orders if we have no free will. If, on the other hand, we have free will, then we are accountable for each and every choice we make in life. If there is no free will, then there is no good or evil in our world. If each person is not accountable for every action which we perform, then the actions we perform must be considered to be morally neutral. Events occurring in our lives and in our world cannot be measured as good or evil because there is no moral scale by which to measure them. There would be no need for justice or redemption. Our world would not be moral or immoral, but amoral.

If a person's god is capable of moral behavior and is accountable for moral behavior, then the ideal God would be a God who is completely loving, perfect, holy, and just – all at the same time. A real God will always function morally. A perfect, holy, and moral God will always rule this world with justice and love.

A real God is moral and just. Many people believe that if the amount of good done in their life outweighs the amount of evil committed in their life, they will be rewarded with a positive afterlife. Many people also believe that if the evil committed in life outweighs the good committed in life, then either the person has no afterlife or the person is punished in the afterlife, or someone else has to contribute enough good to rescue the person from punishment in the afterlife. Good acts cannot outweigh evil acts in order to restore balance in the universe. It only takes one act of evil in our entire lives to forever upset the balance of justice and preclude the ability for our good acts to outweigh our evil. We can only add good or add evil by the acts which we perform in life. Adding good does not erase evil. Unless evil can be erased, justice can never be re-established for even one act of evil committed by any person or being in the universe or this world. The goal must be to erase evil, not to balance it. The erasing of evil is the only thing in the universe that re-establishes justice. If balancing good and evil cannot re-establish justice, and the erasing of evil is the only thing that can re-establish justice, we must ask this question: What does it take to erase acts of evil?

The only way to wipe out evil in our world is to destroy every being who has or ever will commit evil in this world. God has to wipe out every last human being on earth because we have all committed evil. Only a God who supremely loves those he destroys can be a just God, whereas a God who destroys evil without loving those he destroys is an unjust God. I think most human beings who look at any form of destruction of life cannot see the difference between evil and good. A just God who is also a loving God will destroy those who commit evil, while at the same time infinitely love the one to be destroyed. The only kind of Supreme God who can be considered acceptable as a God is one who holds himself and everyone else accountable for all the evil he or she commits in this world.

If there is no justice in our world, then there is no safety, no morals, and no accountability. Only a good, perfect and holy God can be just. Only an absolute God can be a true God. Only an absolute supreme being can be perfect and holy and just.

An absolute God would not tolerate even a single act of evil in our lives that negatively impacted our own or another person's life. It would not matter whether the mistake was intentional or not. We would be immediately rejected and destroyed.

Real love sometimes has to permit self-destruction. Without allowing self-destruction, free will could not exist. I believe a truly loving God is greatly pained and grieved when he allows us to self-destruct. Allowing us to self-destruct does not mean our God does not love us. It means he will not override our free will in order to prevent our self-destruction. So how does a real God demonstrate true love and goodness to us while at the same time maintaining absolute justice, perfection, and holiness in his being and in the universe? How does a holy, just, and loving God treat a person who has free will and is designed to function morally but who chooses to behave immorally? A just God's response to immoral behavior must always require accountability and restitution in order to maintain justice. That restitution may be required immediately or at some point in the future.

God can eliminate us through death, either by killing us now or by killing us in the future. The very delay of our destruction indicates that God has an alternative means of making restitution for the evil acts which we have committed in order to absolve us of the evil. The restitution God makes for us cannot be paid by us. The commission of even a single act of evil renders our whole life and being totally bankrupt and incapable of making any form of restitution payment on our own behalf.

A real God holds all humans accountable. Any God who would not uphold justice and morality in our world would be an unjust and immoral being, one who is not worthy to be a supreme being.

Of all of the religions, belief systems, gods, etc., known to humans, do any provide a way for an unjust person to become just? To make any person just, that person must be held accountable. That person must also compensate for all evil acts he or she has committed throughout his or her life. The problem is that the just compensation which we would receive would destroy us. We would die and cease to exist.

The only possible form of restitution that can be made for our acts of evil must be some form of substitute payment. This substitute payment must be a replacement for anything we would be required to pay. What are the criteria for an adequate substitute?

1. A substitute must have sufficient value to act as a replacement for you.
2. As substitute has to be capable of committing evil, but must have never committed any evil.
3. A substitute must have a free will to choose to be a substitute.
4. A substitute must me capable of re-establishing justice in the world.
5. A substitute must love you enough to die for you.

Other human beings would be of equal value to you, but they cannot meet the criteria of having never committed any evil. If no human being can make a substitution for him or herself, and no human being can make a substation for another human being, then what are the possibilities for a substitute? The only possible substitute is that our God must die in our place if there is to be a restoration of justice in the universe, while at the same time maintaining our life and existence.

The damage we have committed is irreparable, but it is not irredeemable. The only way to redeem that which we have lost from our life is for our God to be destroyed for the evil that we have committed. Only an absolute God can rectify the evil we have committed, and the rectification can only be accomplished by our God suffering destruction for us in our place.

What kind of God, if any, can make a substitution, can die in the place of all human beings, to pay the penalty for the evil that all human beings have committed in the world, and thereby re-establish the balance of justice in the world?

To be just, moral and holy, a real God cannot let us walk away from the evil we have committed in life without being judged and paying the penalty for that evil. Therefore, only a God who loves you enough to die in your place is capable of paying the penalty for your evil while at the same time maintaining justice in this world. Only a God who loves you enough to die in your place is capable of being a personal God and having a personal relationship with you. Only when you are willing to die for another person, can you truly say you love that person. Only a God who has died for you truly loves you.

A real God loves me. Our understanding of love is modeled on human relationships. We have no basis for understanding love in any form which does not mimic the forms of love we see displayed between human beings. A God who can love me must not only be perfect; such a God must also have experienced love in a supernatural divine relationship. You cannot learn to love unless you have someone other than yourself to love. You cannot be social and relational unless you have someone outside of yourself with whom to interact. You cannot be moral except in relationship with other people. Therefore, God as a supreme being must be a multi-person being.

By definition, a Supreme God has no equals. Also by definition, a single-person Supreme God cannot be relational, social and loving. Therefore, how can a supreme God both have no equals and yet be relational? To be a social, loving, and relational God, you must either have other Gods who are supremely equal to you, or you must be a God who has multiple persons.

Can a God have multiple persons? This would require a single God entity which has multiple persons within the God's being. We as humans find this concept - of one being with multiple persons - to be very incomprehensible. We assume that no such being could exist.

Multiple persons are the only answer, and only possibility, of how and why a supreme God can be social, loving, moral, and relational. This is also the only possible way for a God to die and then come back to life.

Humans are social, relational, loving, and (at least to some extent) moral. You can only be social, moral, loving, and relational in interaction with another being who is an equal to you. If God does not have these characteristics, then God is inferior to humans, and God is not supreme. The really good part of a multi-person God is that such a God is only one supreme-being. As a single being, the persons of God are completely unified and integrated into one whole. There is no compartmentalization and no personality disorder in such a God.

If God is a single person supreme-being, then he has no relationship with us. He would have no need for a relationship with human beings. He most likely would never have created us, for he would see no need for our existence. The very fact of our existence speaks loudly of a single God in multi-persons who is social, loving, moral, and relational. Only in a multi-person God being is there a reason for our existence. We cannot and do not exist unless there is a God who is social, loving, moral, and relational, and who wants to have a relationship with us.

Without a multi-person God to create us as social, loving, moral, and relational beings, our world as we know it would not exist. With one God in three persons you have a God who is able to sacrifice his life in our place for our evils. With one God in three persons, one person of the God-being can die and the other God-person can bring the first God-person back to life. A God who is capable of loving you, dying for you, and coming back to life is a great God indeed!

A real God is one who communicates and protects. A God who is worth having is a God who communicates his love for me. A relational God would communicate, would he not?

I also want God to talk to and with me. As humans we use our voice to communicate. I expect a supreme God to be able to communicate with me verbally. I also expect a Supreme-being to use supernatural forms of communication. The existence of a "Holy Book" as a testament to God's existence seems like a reasonable form of communication. I also would expect a truly loving, compassionate, caring, and social God to use more than a book. A book is great, but I want more from my God. I do not expect God to limit himself to human forms of communication.

It seems to me that one of the ways God would most likely communicate is through thought. I would expect God to put his thoughts in my mind. The thoughts could come as regular thoughts or as dreams. If God is truly communicating with me, I want to be able to discern when the thoughts and dreams I have in my mind are God's thoughts and dreams. I want to be able to understand those thoughts, think about them, and respond to them.

A real God is one to whom I must respond and one who makes demands on my life. I want to know that a person has the kind of moral character which I can trust. I want to be able to trust them with my life and the lives of my family. People with high moral character, whom I consider to be trustworthy, are more valuable than gold.

I believe that a God with a trustworthy moral character is a God to whom I am compelled to respond. I want a relationship with this kind of God. I want to spend my life becoming like this God.

I want a God who respects me enough to not force me into a relationship with himself. I want God to give me the space to decide if I want a relationship with him. I believe I would be a complete fool to pass up a relationship with the kind of God that I have described. He is the kind of God who is so awesome that I am compelled to respond to him.

A relationship with no strings attached, by definition, is not a relationship. Relationships have requirements. They place demands on our lives. I want a God who wants to know me, wants to talk with me, and wants to hang out with me. I want a God who demands the kind of relationship where I have to put effort and commitment into the relationship. If my God is someone who just sits somewhere out on the fringe of the universe and has no commitment to me, then I can do just as good worshiping a rock or a tree, or even worshiping myself. I want a God who demands a relationship with me and expects me to demand a relationship with him. Anything less is a waste of time and effort.

A real God changes everything. A good God wants only what is good for the world and the people he created in this world. He will not seek for people to change their lives to conform to him. Instead he will seek to change us into the kind of people he desires us to be. Think about it – God does not want you to change. He wants to change you. God does not want our world to change. He wants to change our world. God does not want the people around us to change. He wants to change the people around us.

When we allow God to change us, he does it at a pace we can handle and in a manner we can accommodate. This does not mean the change will be painless. Just the opposite is true. All change is painful. But it is worth it.

A real God is one to whom I can relate. The ultimate relationship with God is much like a marriage – only better!

There is one thing I want from my God which no one else can give to me. I want to be understood. Do you have any friends with whom you share your innermost thoughts and secrets? Even if your friends and family know your innermost thoughts and secrets, do they frequently not understand them? The only person who knows me intimately enough to understand all of my experiences, thoughts, and feelings is my God. If neither God nor humans can know or understand me at my deepest innermost level, then my life is an entire waste and my very existence is useless.

I sincerely believe that the greatest value which I have as a human being is the meaning that is ascribed to my life by being completely known, completely understood, and completely loved by my God. At the same time, I want to know, understand, and love my God just as deeply and completely as he loves me.

A real God is one who rescues. There are several things from which I want my God to rescue me. I want a God who will preserve my safety and provide for my needs. I want a God who will rescue me from threats to my life in times of danger. I want God to rescue me from sickness and disease and the deterioration to my body that comes from aging. I want a God who will rescue me from my own self-centered behavior and thoughts. I want to be delivered from evil desires and evil thoughts. I want to be delivered from greed and to be satisfied with what I have. I want to be rescued from the psychological traumas and hurts that occurred in my past, especially from those traumas that still control and impact my life. I want a God who rescues and changes me in many ways. Specifically, I want a God who changes my relationship with my world, with my self, with other people, and with my God himself.

A real God is an Exclusive God! How many ways are there to God? Answer: At least one for every individual's personal belief about his or her personal relationship with God. This is the answer our world and culture gives to this question. The problem is that we have no way of knowing if this answer works. Everyone in this world can claim to have a relationship with God. There is no objective manner for us to validate each individual's claim to a relationship with God. Also, there is no objective manner for us to qualify and quantify each person's claim.

If a person's belief system about a relationship with God is logically inconsistent, then I am not going to assign any validity to that belief system. To me a belief system that is logically inconsistent is worthless. Of all the belief systems that I have evaluated, there is only one that I have found to be logically consistent and worth pursuing to see if it works. That belief system is a relationship with Jesus Christ. Because Jesus Christ claims to be the only way to God, then that belief-system should be considered to be an exclusive approach to God. You then have to make a choice: Do you want a belief system that is exclusive in its presentation of a path to a relationship to God, and demonstrates enough evidence of logical integrity to conclude that it works? Or do you want a belief system that is inclusive in its presentation of a path to a relationship with God, but demonstrates insufficient logical integrity to ensure its ability to accomplish all that it claims to offer?

Since I consider Jesus Christ to be the only God worthy of being a God, then I want to explain to you how to have a relationship with my God – Jesus Christ. Please remember, I am not presenting to you any path, method, or criterion for a relationship with God that I have invented. What I am presenting is the path, method, criterion, etc., that my God has presented in His book – the Bible. This is His chosen and specified path for having a relationship with Him. Remember – you have no right to choose the path you will take to your God. Only your God has the right to specify the path and conditions for your relationship with Him. Here is what Jesus specifies in his book as the correct and only path to a relationship with Him.

Only Jesus Christ says, "I am the way and the truth and the life. *No one comes to the Father except through me" (John 14:6).* Jesus is the only God who specifies the path necessary to meet God. Please remember that Jesus loves you. It is he who chooses to have a relationship with you. It is he who wants to change your life and to make you into the kind of person you desire to be.

The Path Specified by God:

One – Jesus says you have to ask him for forgiveness for all the evil acts you have committed in your life. He further says that you have to continue to ask him for forgiveness each and every time you commit any evil act in the future.

Two – Jesus says that you have to believe and acknowledge as true the following things.

Jesus exists and is the only true and real God.

Jesus died on the cross to pay the penalty for your evil acts.

Jesus rose from the dead to give you a new and eternal life in a relationship with him.

Three – You must confess verbally to other people that Jesus is your God and the ruler of your life.

Four – Your relationship with Jesus is not a one-time event. It is an ongoing relationship, like a marriage, it is a covenant which you must maintain and nurture.

I know that you will truly be blessed if you choose Jesus as your God. There is nothing in this world that can compare to the importance and greatness of having him in your life to love you, lead you, heal you, and guide you. Make the decision for Jesus today. It is an offer too good to pass up.

Chapter 26

How to Get Out of the Cave

I stated the following at the beginning of this book. Now I want to bring you back to these thoughts again.

What would happen if you were trapped deep underground in a maze of caves and did not know the way out? What if the person leading you is a complete stranger and you do not know if you can trust that person? The image of being lost in a maze of caves is much like mate selection.

You are trying to find a way out of the isolation of your life. You want someone to share your life. Who in your life can offer you the best guidance and direction in finding a prospective mate, forming a successful relationship, and ultimately sealing the bond between you and your mate in marriage?

Mate selection is the second most important decision we make in life. This decision determines whether our lives will be blessed and full of joy or if they will be a painful calamity. Who is the person who can best guide us through this big decision of mate selection?

Jesus is God. He knows everything. He knows the people with whom you will be most compatible as possible mates. He can arrange your opportunities to meet the best possible person to be your mate. The only person who can correctly guide you to the best possible choice you can make in selecting a mate is Jesus Christ!

Chapter 27

How Do You Make the Right Choice?

Diamond – in the rough or finished cut

My wife told me after we had been married for a few months that she chose me because she was looking for a diamond in the rough. I did not know whether to be insulted because she was comparing me to a rough, ugly rock, or to feel praised because she saw something in me which no other woman had ever seen.

She was not looking for a man who was a finished product, but for a man who had excellent potential. Many times, I have seen people miss out on fantastic mates because they were looking for a finished product instead of outstanding potential. Those who find the best mates look for potential, not a finished product. Diamonds are probably the hardest rocks known to man. Yet they are cut by using steel chisels placed precisely on the flaws and chipping away. It takes an experienced eye to find the precise flaw on which to place the chisel.

In marriage love is the chisel. When we expose the flaws in our mate, especially the deepest flaws, and then pour our love into that flaw, it chips away the brokenness of the flaw and creates a shiny person with luster and clarity. Love, demonstrated in truth and honesty, is the only chisel which can cut the diamonds of the highest quality from the rough material in our lives ("Diamond", 2015).

You either frustrate the fulfillment of God's best for your life, or you follow God into the fulfillment of His best for your life. It is not uncommon for people to stay in long term dating relationships simply because they are afraid to be alone. They cannot stand the idea of having no one to date. They may even know that the person with whom they are involved is not the best choice of a mate, but they stay in the relationship, hoping something better will come along. Women hesitate and frequently will not go on a date with a man when their close friend has a crush on that man. Women also refrain from dating a man whom a close girlfriend has already rejected. A man will not ask out a woman on whom he has a crush when another man is dating her. What happens if all of these social influence factors regulating approachability to a prospective mate converge at the same time and they block themselves from dating each other?

If you really want God to bring the right person into your life, you must be willing to end up with no one. Only when you are alone can God properly direct you in recognizing the person who is most appropriate for being your mate for life. Frequently that person is the one you would least expect. It is not uncommon for us to be unable to see a person's potential as a mate because we are looking for someone who is more mature and knows how to flatter us, instead of seeing the person who is the most stable and has the best long term potential.

Only those who persistently pray for God's guidance in choosing a mate have a reasonable expectation of making the best choice of a mate.

Many people make decisions that cause them to miss out on God's desire for their lives in the choice of a mate. They miss out on a wonderful choice of a mate by choosing to date and/or marry a certain person when God wants to bring a much better choice of a mate into the person's life. When you stay in a dating relationship long term without having strong direction from God to continue the relationship, you are creating the potential for the mate selection preferred by God to be delayed. You may also be destroying the opportunity to enter into the relationship with God's preferred mate forever. For this reason, I believe long term dating relationships should be avoided unless the couple can truly discern that their relationship is in the will of God.

Choosing Your Mate

Your choice of a mate always affects more than one person! A wrong choice may destroy or cripple multiple people's lives, and a correct choice may bless multiple people's lives. Some of the hardest decisions you will ever make deal with choosing the right mate! This is the second most critical decision you will ever make in your life. The first most critical is accepting Jesus Christ as your Lord and Savior. Getting these decisions right is critical to not just you. They are critical to several other people in your life. They are critical to your spouse, the person who should have been your spouse, your children, and possibly, to many other people. I cannot stress enough how important it is to get this decision right.

The perfect mate does not exist.

The good enough mate is the perfect mate for you.

In the Bible, God almost never reveals to people who their correct mate will be. There are only about three times in the Bible that God specified who a mate would be. These are Adam and Eve, Joseph and Mary, and Hosea and Gomer. I believe God has a specific person chosen as the person whom He would prefer as your mate. However, He always leaves the choice of a mate up to you. If you are incapable of listening to His guidance in mate selection, I believe God can and will bring into your life a person or several persons from whom you may select a suitable mate. I also believe that if you or the person who is God's preferred choice for your mate prevents God from bringing about His preferred choice in your lives, God can and will bring about an alternative choice for your mate. However, God may not bring about an alternative choice for a mate in your life unless you sincerely ask Him for an alternative.

I have also known of a few instances where God told parents whom their child was to marry. Even in these cases I believe the wise parents should not reveal to their children the mate choice which God has put forth until after the wedding. Children need to make their own choices for a mate unless they live in a culture of arranged marriages (Cunningham, 2000).

While I also believe that for each of us there are several choices of a mate who would be suitable for a long, successful, joyful and fulfilling marriage, God still has one preferable mate for each of us. If we miss God's most preferable choice, God can still provide us with other options. Some of these options are better than others. Some of the less preferable choices may still be perfectly acceptable in God's sight.

> *Only those who persistently pray for God's guidance in choosing a mate have a reasonable expectation of making the best choice of a mate.*

I believe there are three critical factors you should always consider in selecting a mate:

1. Never marry a person who is not your equal in his or her love for Jesus. God put us together to walk as equals. A person who does not follow Jesus as faithfully as you do will never make you an adequate spouse.

2. The most important thing you can do in selecting a mate is to learn to pray and to listen to God. God will guide you. He will cause you to know when you have found the one worth pursuing.

3. Never marry the person who tells you he or she loves you. Anyone can convince him or herself that he or she loves you. The person who really loves you is the person who prays for you. If you want to know if someone loves you, find out if he or she prays for you. Get specific. Find out what the person prays for you and how frequently he or she prays for you. Find out if the prayers are driven by real love and compassion for you or are just a perfunctory exercise and formality.

4. Only if you have done the work to prepare for your marriage by becoming the kind of person you want to marry, can you expect Jesus to bring a quality person into your life for you to marry.

In matters of the heart, it is not infrequent that a person agrees to take any mate God selects for them as long as they can dictate to God who that person will be. They pray for God to give them a mate and when God gives them one, they decide they cannot accept that person because they want the person God chooses to be the person they have already picked out. It is even worse when your choice differs from God's choice and He grants your choice anyway. Your choice will always be less perfect for you than the mate God would have given to you. Your choice may be good, but it will be insufficient in ways that you will always notice in your marriage.

Personal Experiences

Some of the best guidance I can give you is from my own experience. My experience at mate selection was long and painful. I frequently envy those who find their soul mate in high school or college. I dated a few girls who firmly rejected me. My final choice, many years later, was a woman with whom I initially held a mutual dis-attraction. It was a long and complex journey, but it was well worth the thirty plus years of marriage which we now celebrate. Here is a list of the most prominent memories in my search for a mate.

I had one date with a girl in college whom I would have loved to marry. I had met her once or twice and liked her very much but did not really know her well. Friends of mine set me up on a blind and double date with her. She was drop dead gorgeous. She was so beautiful she could stop traffic and heartbeats with one glance at her. She had a great personality and a strong love for God. She wanted to be an editor of Sunday school literature. She was truly a dream for a young man headed for the ministry. After the date, my friend asked me what I thought of her and if I would go out with her again. I said

I wished I could go out with her again, but I did not think I would. He asked, "Do you find her attractive?" I said, "She is gorgeous. I would love to date her." He said, "Do you like her personality?" I said she had a wonderful personality and was a great person. He said, "Since you are going into the ministry, do you think she would be a suitable wife for a pastor?" I answered, "She is majoring in Christian Education and she would be a great wife." He said, "What is the problem?" I said, "I do not know – there is just no spark between us." All my impressions were that she was more interested in him than she was in me. My head said "go, go, go," and my spirit said there was no leading from God to pursue a relationship. I still say that the man who married that woman got one fantastic wife. Even over age 60 she still looks good enough to stop traffic.

Another girl, with whom I had a few dates, broke my heart. She was the first girl I ever dated and my first real crush. She was also very worthy of pursuing as a mate. When she rejected me I thought my life was over. Eventually I got over her and was able to realize that as exceptional as she was, she was not the right match for me. Thirty eight years later, I ran into her again at a wedding. We had a very nice visit for about an hour. Later I compared her to my wife. I still think she is an exceptional person. I also think my wife is an exceptionally better mate for me.

Between college and seminary I met a young lady who was just out of high school. We only had one semi-formal date when I wanted someone to accompany me to a piano concert. We spent a lot of time together, and I was very interested in her, but she had no interest in me.

In seminary I met another beautiful woman whom I wanted to marry. She had been a missionary. She was very beautiful and intelligent. She had a fantastic love for God. I had enough dates and talks with her to be extremely attracted to her. I knew she would make a fabulous wife. I prayed about where God wanted my relationship with her to go. I finally had to admit that as fantastic as she was, I did not believe she was ultimately God's will for my life. Finally I told her one day that I would really like to date her and pursue her as a possible mate, but I did not consider it to be God's will for us to be marriage partners. A year later I went back to visit at seminary and had lunch with this woman whom I had wanted for a wife. While we were eating she introduced me to her fiancé. It was a good thing I got out of the way so that God could put her with the best choice of a husband He had for her. When I graduated seminary, I had no wife, no prospects, and no women who were mature enough in their walk with God to consider as marriage potential.

There was another woman I met in seminary whom I found to be very abrasive. I was in no way attracted to her. We both went into the ministry and became pastors. Since we were both in the same state and same denomination, I kept running into her at meetings. We did canoe training together and a couple of canoe camps together. Gradually my opinion of her changed. We ended up getting married and we have been together for over thirty years. I believe that any of the other women would have made a great wife. I believe I would have been very happy with any of them. However, I would not trade my wife Linda for any of them. She completes me and she walks with God. She has more spunk and intelligence than any woman I have ever met. I do not know if I made the correct choice of a spouse. Only God can answer that question. However, I do know that I made a very good choice and I would do it again.

Let God guide you, and prayerfully trust him to lead you to the best choice of a mate you can make.

What if You Fail?

What If You Choose the Wrong Person?

Choosing the wrong mate may not destroy your opportunity for a long and successful marriage, even though such destruction is always a possibility. Some couples are able to overcome a less than perfect choice and yet succeed in developing a long and successful marriage. Some couples succeed for an extended period of time until the slow creep of the damage in their relationship finally destroys the marriage. Some even go for years thinking everything is blissful, until they psychologically heal sufficiently to find they are living in a relationship which is very uncomfortable.

Even a wrong choice can be overcome. For a couple that will seek proper help and allow God to work in their marriage, a disastrous choice can be changed into a great blessing. God can take brokenness and turn it into joy and blessing.

I have known of a few people who married the wrong person. I have seen cases where girls married the first male who came along in order to escape from a bad family situation. I have seen others who married for security. A couple we know went to live in another country; their daughter had just graduated from high school and stayed in the U.S. to go to college. Very soon after starting college she married a young man because she needed security in her life with her parents living in another country. The marriage lasted for many years but was always full of great struggle. Work injuries caused the man to become addicted to painkillers and then drugs. He spent many years without work. He was not a bad person; he just never was able to get his life together. Finally the girl had to divorce him.

In another case, I knew a girl who had very good parents and family, but she was always in rebellion and self-destructive. The parents tried everything they could to help her. Nothing they tried worked. When she was in eighth grade, the brother of one of the players on her team came up after a game and introduced himself to her mother. When he introduced himself, God told the mother that he was the man to marry her daughter. When the girl went to high school, she and the boy became very good friends. This friendship lasted until she made some remarks which greatly injured the young man. The young man was still friends with her, but the progression towards dating was ended at that time. At some point in the high school years, the young man's father had a dream that his son was supposed to marry this girl. The young man's sister told the girl about what her dad had said to his son about his dream. As the girl neared the end of high school, she started dating a different young man and a few years later married him. Her parents always knew before, during, and after the marriage that she married the wrong man. The man she married was a good choice for a husband. He treated her well and was a good worker. He just was not the man whom God had wanted for her mate. Both the girl and the man God had chosen refused to follow God. They refused to allow God to lead them in the choice of a mate. They are still friends, but only their parents know that they both, in their rebellion, failed to marry the person God had chosen for them to marry.

What If You Abort God's Plan for Your life?

Sometimes even God is not able to bring about his plans for a couple's life. I knew a person who felt that God wanted Him to marry a specific young lady. She was an excellent choice of a spouse until she revealed that she did not know Jesus as Savior and Lord. As a result the young man did not tell her how he felt about her and did not marry her. She spent her life in a short failed marriage and many years of singleness. Only in her later years did she accept Jesus as her Savior and Lord.

I have known a few friends who never married. In some of those cases, the lack of marriage was due to abuse, great trauma at a tender age, or a case of molestation. For a few friends, whose love life I have learned about, I have found that God brought who was probably the right person into the friend's life. In these cases, for whatever reason, the two people failed to ever date or form anything other than a close friendship. I have come to the conclusion that for many older singles the proper mate may very well lie somewhere in his or her past. The proper mate was a close friend that he or she was unable to acknowledge and pursue as a mate. Perhaps the best thing for those singles is to return to the previous friends if they are still single and see if there is any remaining romantic interest on which to build a relationship. A former roommate once told me of a close female college friend who visited with him for a week. They never became a couple. Several years after he told me about the girl and the visit, I was praying for him about a mate. While I prayed God kept pointing to that girl as the one he was supposed to have married. The last time

I talked with him, I asked him if he had ever married. He told me no, that he never met the right one. I said, "Yes, you did." His answer was "maybe." I still believe he missed the one God put right in front of his face. He has dated a sufficient number of girls and never felt he found the right one. He is an outstanding Christian man and would have made any woman a good husband.

We have choices. The decisions we make determine whether God can bring into our lives that which He plans for us. Because of our choices and the choices of our prospective mate, we either bless or destroy multiple lives. When your choices abort God's plan for your life, you also abort God's plan for the person who would have been your mate. The plans which you abort also impact the possibility for children and grandchildren, not to mention all of the other people your lives would have impacted if God had been allowed to implement his plan.

The good part is that even if we abort God's plan for our life, or someone else aborts that plan for us, God is still able to salvage our lives with a very successful marriage which proves to be a great blessing for us. Sometimes God's plan B is even better that God's plan A. God's plan A person will always be very compatible for us and a solidly good choice. That person will help us to develop as a person in a manner that is very good and enjoyable for us, and bring about a very wonderful marriage. God's plan B person does the same thing. It is just that the plan B person brings a whole set of different dynamics to the marriage; still the marriage is just as wonderful. One or the other of the possible mates may have fit us in a manner that would have been very good for us in some ways, while the other mate fits us in a totally different manner that is just as exceptional.

The key to an exceptional marriage is always being faithful to God. God can never enact plan B if you force Jesus out of your life. If you walk away from God, there is no plan B until you come back to God.

How to Marry the Right One

Only if your heart is wholly submitted to God and you are seeking his will in your life, will He be able to bring into your life the mate He chooses for you. The question is – does God actually choose a mate for you? The answer is yes and no. If you whole heartedly submit to God's will for your life in choosing a mate He will make known to you His preferred choice of whom you should marry, but God never chooses a mate for you. There are several people you can marry and have a successful and joyful life, He expects you to make the final choice. I expect of all the choices of a possible mate, there are pros and cons to each choice. One may actually be a better fit or a better choice. However, God insists that we be the person to make the final decision. Ultimately, you need to look at all the criteria presented for selecting a good mate. You need to measure your selection in the light of the criteria you place on a selection of a mate. You also need to make a decision based soul searching prayer as you seek God's guidance.

Finally, I would recommend that you make your decision based on this question: *Is your God about your life or is your life about your God?* Your answer to this question cuts two ways. You should only select a mate whose life is about his or her God, equal to the extent you are willing to have your life be about your God. If you are not willing to wholeheartedly live in complete dedication to God, do not ruin another person's life by causing him or her to marry you. If he or she is willing to live for God in a manner in which you are not willing to live for God, allow God to provide a different mate for that person. Also do not waste your life in marrying someone who is not willing to live for God to the extent that you are willing to live for God.

The answer you give, and the answer your selected mate gives to the question of mate selection, determine more than any other criterion whether you are suitable for each other as mates and ready for marriage. If you both can truly say that your life is about your God and you both worship the same God – Jesus Christ -- then you have fulfilled the primary criteria for selecting a mate. If you choose any other answer or qualify this answer in any way, then you are not suitable as mates and are not ready for marriage. *Is your life about your God or is your God about your life?*

Making the Final Choice

I do not believe in love at first sight, but I do believe in introduction at first sight. For many couples who have lasting marriages, they knew who they would choose as a mate the first time they saw that person. They may not have even spoken to their intended mate the first time they saw each other, but they chose at that specific point to pursue that person as the one they would marry. See Samson's reaction to the woman who became his Philistine wife in Judges 14:1-7. The first time he saw this woman he knew that she was the one for him.

When a man first sees the woman he is supposed to marry it is a very surreal experience. Time almost stands still. He cannot take his eyes off of her. He just keeps staring. He does not know why he is staring, but he stares, He is driven with a strong desire to know her name and to become friends with her. The few women who have been able to give me the woman's perspective on this issue say much the same thing. This is God's way of introducing us to His preference for our mate.

For this reason I believe it is critically important for people who have experienced God's introduction to their mate to carefully and fully pursue that person as a mate. If the two people do not pursue forming a relationship with each other they run a high risk of marrying the wrong person.

Bret's and Nicole's Testimony:

When We Met Our Helpmates

<u>Bret's Story</u>

As I grew and developed my desire for a wife increased accordingly, however that desire was heavily molded by my mother and her idea of a perfect wife for me. In my estimation, that is most of the reason why I overlooked Nicole as a potential mate when I first met her.

In 2010, I was attending a large and healthy church in Dublin, Ohio. This church was known at the time for broadway quality productions during the Easter season. No expense was spared and no detail was overlooked. This included a live donkey that would serve to carry Jesus onto the stage.

While on some down time between rehearsal and show time, I snuck outside to see what animals were there and maybe pet the donkey. Upon reaching the enclosure for the beast of burden, I met Nicole, who was in charge of leading the donkey that night. We struck up a conversation and the more I spoke with her, the more entranced I became. She was a cowgirl extraordinaire and very intelligent, both qualities that I found attractive.

We secured the donkey and I began to flirt ever so slightly. There was an instant comfort that I felt with Nicole that I couldn't express or justify at that time. Toward the end of the conversation I asked her out to dinner. She blushed and politely declined stating that she was engaged to be married. Upon hearing those words, I instantly felt the urge to tell her not to marry the man she had chosen, that he was bad for her and that she should marry me instead.

This of course was neither socially nor ethically appropriate at the time, yet I could not help but feel that way. I settled for her phone number and a new friend. I wrote off my feelings and moved on with my life. I did this so freely for three reasons. 1) Nicole was engaged. 2) I had been raised to want blonde hair and blue eyed women. Nicole is hazel-eyed and a brunette. 3) Though I felt a connection, I was about to enlist in the army for special forces and I did desire a wife only for the fact that I could be deployed to extremely high risk missions. Nicole and I remained in contact from that night.

Soon we were texting or following each other on Facebook on a regular basis. I made sure to keep tabs on her posts and offer my help when they turned negative. Though she was not going to the same church, we usually saw each other at the church we met at during special events. A pattern developed and I realized that Nicole was in a toxic marriage, though she would never admit that openly. I made myself available as a confidant and offered help where it was appropriate.

Just before her birthday. She and I exchanged some basic text messages and I offered some advice. A week or so later she texted me when she was drunk and it was clear to me that something was desperately wrong. I gave her the advice that hurts. She was none-too-happy about that but the next day when she apologized she told me that her husband had walked out on her and her 20 month old daughter.

As we texted it became clear to me that Nicole needed a spiritual head-of-household that her now ex-husband had woefully neglected. I told her that I would place her and her daughter under my Patriarchal covering and that I would pray for her and her daughter as a Husband and father until she could find stability in her life.

The following Sunday I drove from my home in Kentucky to visit her and her daughter. When I arrived Nicole greeted me warmly and her daughter, Isabella, was quick to climb onto my lap and asked me to read her a story. Nicole and I chatted about ministries we are passionate about and the life we wanted to raise our children in. We discussed how hard she worked and her desire to become a stay-at-home-mom.

It is important to note at this juncture that I was not considering Nicole as a viable mate. She was a dear friend and nothing more. However, in 2009 when I had been saved from the jaws of spiritual death, I knew that the desire to be a husband and father had been placed in my heart by God for the purpose of fulfilling such roles. As a result, I put God on the spot and I made a vow. I would marry the first woman that fulfilled the following three criteria in a row.

1) She must be of a Christian background and have a genuine desire to promote the Kingdom of God. 2) She must have a servant's heart and exemplify the type of woman described in Proverbs 31. 3) She must give me a genuine therapeutic massage (appropriate and without deviant desires or motives), without prompt or request and ask nothing in return.

As we finished supper I sat on the couch. Nicole asked very humbly if she could sit next to me and if I would hold her. I gladly obliged her request. As we sat there the extra pressure from Nicole's weight aggravated a few old injuries. I squirmed in discomfort and Nicole inquired as to why. When I divulged my pain, she demanded that I sit in the floor in front of the couch and she proceeded to massage my shoulders and my upper back thus releasing the tension and relieving the pain. This was the third and final fleece I had given to God. It was at this point that I knew that I held the woman God had chosen for me.

Later that night, she continued to tell me about her situation. At one point during her confiding Nicole asked me why her marriage was so toxic. Without realizing that it came out of my mouth I blurted out, "You married the wrong man. You should have married me". It was then that I told her about first meeting her and why I said nothing

She said that she was going to come visit me at my home in Kentucky. I had my most sincere doubts that she would indeed make the two and a half hour drive. I got a call early Sunday from her saying she was on her way.

Nicole was the first to articulate that she was extremely nervous about going back home and that the very thought created a pit in her stomach. Strangely I agreed and added that I did not feel that we should be separate at that moment. She vehemently confirmed such feelings. We then prayed and asked God for guidance. At this point we were both wholly terrified and unsure why we felt so unsafe. We continued to pray and felt that indeed, going back to my home in Kentucky was the best option. As we headed south to Kentucky the feelings of dread and terror faded incrementally. We both noted that as soon as we crossed the bridge on the Ohio River, the feelings of dread were entirely dissipated.

We reached my home and due to Nicole's tendency to over-pack, she was well prepared for her and Bella to remain for a few days. Nicole and I then went to see our pastor. Lynn, a grandmother and already my spiritual mentor and surrogate mother greeted us with open arms and a warm meal. We inquired as to advice for our situation. It was at this point that Lynn spoke to each of us privately and then as a couple. We had both indicated that we knew we were chosen for each other by God and that our intention was to marry soon after Nicole's legal marriage was dissolved. We were married in the eyes of man in December

We realize now that we were not ready to be married to each other at the time that we met. However without the long correspondence and watching each other become broken in our own ways we would not have the depth of love and connection that we do. God played a chess game with our lives, allowing us to get the disobedience out of our spirits and thus making us receptive to the gifts that he made for us in each other.

Nicole put it best when she said, "If I had blonde hair and blue eyes and the figure that you prefer, you would forever ask yourself where the catch is. I would be too good to be true. But God knew this so he gave you your second choice so you could relax and know that I am not perfect, but I am perfect for you." She was absolutely right. I didn't marry the woman that I wanted to marry. Instead I married the woman God wanted me to marry, and that has made all the difference.

Nicole's Story

I met Bret in the spring of 2010. At the time, I was engaged to someone else, who I went on to marry later that year. We first met while we were both participating in an Easter production put on by our church. I was responsible for handling a donkey that was involved in the production. I was struggling to get the donkey to cooperate. Bret, having plenty of animal experience, stepped in and quickly figured out the problem (we had a blind donkey). I was immediately drawn to Bret but, as I was already engaged, I thought nothing of it beyond a friendship.

But there was an undeniable spark and attraction. He quickly became a very close friend; I almost immediately felt a level of comfort with him that I felt with very few people. He became the friend that I could always turn to, including confiding in him about problems in my relationship with my fiancée.

Over the span of the next 6 years, we remained in contact only sporadically; but the level of comfort I felt with him never changed. We could go months without talking, yet when I really needed a friend to talk to, I knew I could always count on him to be there. At one point he was moving from our home state to North Dakota. I didn't understand why but when I heard this I was devastated; I feared I would never see him again. And then, I remember being elated when he moved back to Ohio. Even though we never saw one another, I liked having him close by again

About 6 years after Bret and I met, I found myself at the lowest point of my life. My husband had unexpectedly walked out on me and left me alone in raising my 2 year old daughter. I was in a dark place and did not know how to handle it. Desperately in need of a friend, I reached out to Bret. I shared with him things that no one knew, shared details of 6 years of an unhappy and unhealthy marriage. He listened, offered advice where needed, and prayed with me. The praying with me was what had the biggest impact. This affected me so much because in the 6 years of my marriage, I had greatly lacked the spiritual leader that I desperately needed.

Shortly after this, Bret came to visit me at my home in Powell, Ohio. I was floored that he would travel nearly 2 hours just to come see me. I had no expectations of his visit, yet found myself both nervous and excited for his arrival. He arrived and I was immediately drawn to him and felt a spark, although I did not know what to make of it at that moment. We spent the afternoon and evening just talking and spending time with my daughter. When I put my daughter to bed, Bret was waiting in the hall for me. He wrapped his arms around me in what was probably the best hug I have ever had. I melted into him and felt so safe. It was at that moment I realized the truth, I was in love with him. He was my soul mate. I never wanted to let go.

Over the next several days we stayed in close contact. We had a kind of connection that I had never experienced before; he seemed to know exactly what I was thinking or feeling even when I couldn't or wouldn't verbalize it. The day finally came for me to visit him. I was as nervous as a schoolgirl on her first date. I woke up early that morning to make to 2 hour trip to ensure I would have as much time as possible to spend with him

We meet in southern Ohio, at his family farm. Everything just felt wrong. It seemed as though we were being delayed from leaving. Neither of us felt good about my leaving but neither verbalized it. We decided to sit on the porch for a bit before we left. We both very quickly began to feel very uneasy, like something was very wrong. We finally discussed what we were feeling and decided that we both felt better about staying together.

We initially started driving north, unsure exactly where we were going but just knowing we needed to be moving. Yet the feeling of dread almost seemed worse. At almost the same time, we expressed the feeling that we needed to turn around. As we traveled south, we slowly began to feel better. The decision was made that I would stay in Kentucky that night. As soon as we crossed the river into Kentucky, we felt immediate relief. The plan was for me to head home the next morning. We awoke and still did not feel good about me leaving. We talked and prayed and both came to the same conclusion. It was unsafe for me to return to Ohio at that time and I was to stay there.

They say hindsight is 20/20 and this is most certainly true. I know now that Bret was the mate that God intended for me. My former marriage was not sanctioned by Him and was not the relationship I was supposed to have. While I wish I could have avoided that heartache, I know that it helped prepare me for the person God had for me. At the time of our meeting, neither of us were ready for one another. I am far happier and much more at peace married to the person God intended for me, instead of the person of my own choosing. In looking back at how our relationship fell into place, there is no doubt that God orchestrated it all.

The Decision that Chooses a Mate

I truly believe love starts at that point when one makes the decision to choose that person and to pursue that person as the intended mate. The dating period for such couples is then a period of confirming the decision they have already made. The smart individuals of these couples take their time to study their prospective mate and to confirm, in their hearts, the love that started at first sight. When they get to the point that they can confirm the decision they have already made, it is time for them to marry. Marriages that begin in this manner are some of the strongest and most enduring marriages in existence.

However, not all marriages start in this manner. Some marriages are arranged and the couples have to learn to love each other. Some marriages start in a very peculiar manner, with the two individuals not even attracted to each other. Yet, God somehow brings them together in His purpose for their lives. Even in these peculiar marriages, the individuals gradually come to the point where they choose to love each other and to form strong marriages.

It is not as important for a person to know that his or her mate is the right one, as it is for the individual to make the decision, and then love and stay forever faithful to the one he or she marries. The question then becomes - When do you have enough information to make the decision? Any relationship shorter than two years is insufficient to create a full and proper perspective of your prospective mate's capability to bond to you as a lifelong mate (Grover, 1985). Many times insufficient premarital bonding length fails to surface critical issues in personality and behavior which will seriously impact the capacity for permanence in an established marriage.

Praying Together

There is nothing that will bind a couple together as much as prayer. Prayer together bonds two people at the deepest level of intimacy. It bonds them on the spiritual level. The people I prize the most in life are the ones with whom I have spent time together praying. When a couple prays together for a lifetime, the intimacy of prayer builds permanence in their intimacy together. This prayer intimacy is not matched by any other form of intimacy in the relationship. Prayer is the superglue of our intimacy with Jesus and with each other. Because of the intimacy of prayer, it is better for couples to be certain of their commitment to each other by forming an engagement before they begin to bind themselves together in the intimacy of praying together.

A Word of Caution: Spiritual Bonds and Binds

Spiritual bonds are the healthy relationships we form with other Christians.
Spiritual binds are handcuffs in our relationships with other people.

Every Christian should have spiritual bonds with other Christians. Some of our bonds are much stronger than other bonds. Bonds are made out of mutual interest, friendship, and Christian love. They are positive factors in our lives. They create strong, solid relationships between us that last for lifetimes, but they do not chain us together with other people.

I have several Christian friends with whom I have spiritual bonds. These bonds connect me to those persons through our relationship with Jesus Christ. The bonds are sufficiently strong that God will tell me when I need to pray for them and specifically what I need to pray for him or her.

In Matthew 16:19 Jesus teaches the principle of binding and loosing. Spiritual binds are chains which bind us with other people. They can be both positive and negative chains. These chains are created when we voluntarily choose to commit ourselves to another person in a binding relationship. Some binding chains can be as simple as making a commitment to pray for another person. Marriage should always form a spiritual bind between us and our spouse. However, some chains formed in love relationships can destroy our lives.

It is not uncommon for one to become totally in love with one person and have the relationship fail or never even get off to a start. If they then pray earnestly for that person to be their mate, they form chains which can forever bind them to that person, even if they never see that person again in life. The chains that they formed in their prayers can bind them on a spiritual level so that they are never able to let go of the person. The chains of love will bind them in their subconscious so that they are never able to properly search for another mate, or the chains may bind them so that they are never able to properly love whoever becomes their mate at a later point in life.

Even worse is the damage they may do to the person with whom they are in love. Their prayers and the spiritual chains with which they bind the relationship may seriously impede the person they love from ever marrying another person in the future. They can actually destroy another person's life through the spiritual chains with which they have bound to themselves the person whom they love. It all occurs on spiritual and subconscious levels and may never come to the light of consciousness, even with the most powerful forms of therapy.

Any time you love another person, make sure you either never bind yourself to that person before marriage or that you expressly pray to "loose" that person from any binds you may have put on that person's life if and when the relationship ends. Always loose the person to marry whomever God chooses to bring into that person's life.

The End Is a New Beginning

The end of the search in mate selection is a new beginning with your spouse. This new beginning demands a whole new set of tools for maintaining a successful relationship. The good part is that if you have followed God's plan in your search for a mate, you have already developed the critical foundation necessary for your marriage. You have already developed at least half of the tools necessary for a long and stable relationship, and you are well prepared to use the new tools you will need to develop in maintaining a marriage.

The number one tool you must master as a couple is daily prayer and Bible study. I know of nothing which will bond a couple more permanently together than daily prayer as a couple before God. This practice of prayer with each other and with God builds a foundation of intimacy which can weather any storm life throws at you as a couple. Without this foundation of prayer your potential for permanence withers radically.

PART 7

Marriage

Announcing the Bride

Chapter 28

Marriage Ritual and Definition

The Biblical Ritual of Marriage:

I n Genesis 2:18, 21-24, the marriage ceremony was performed by God for Adam and Eve in the Garden of Eden. It occurred before the consummation of the marriage. Yet there is no description given in the Bible of the details and the form of practice for this wedding ceremony. The Bible gives very detailed descriptions of all forms of religious rituals for God's people to practice, but the wedding ceremony is not one of them (Leviticus 23). In God's eyes, the real act of marriage is the consummation of the union of the two individuals in the act of sexual intercourse.

The custom of the marriage ceremony is clearly seen in the stories of Isaac's marriage to Rebecca (Genesis 24:) and Jacob's marriage to Leah and Rachel (Genesis 29). The custom follows a basic pattern shown here.

The groom signs a contract frequently referred to as a marriage bond. This constitutes formal marriage. From this point on the couple are considered to be legally married but do not have intercourse until after the marital celebration The groom goes away for a couple of years and builds a house with its accoutrements for the couple to live in together.

The groom prepares the home and raises the money for the bride price (Genesis 29:15-30, Exodus 22:16–17, Deuteronomy 22:28–29,

Judges 1:11-15, 1 Samuel 18:25-27) which was payment to the bride's parents as proof that the groom was financially capable of providing for the welfare of their daughter after marriage. The woman would bring her dowry (1 Kings 9:16) to the marriage which was her portion of the family inheritance to be used as seed money for the new family or passed down to her children in the future (Staples, 2010). The bride price and dowry protected the woman as they established a fund (livestock, land, money) which would provide her with resources should she become a widow (Fletcher, 2006)

The groom contacts the bride's father, and a date is set for the formal ceremony. Then the groom journeys to the bride's home to take the bride to their new home.

The bride is attended by her maiden (virgin) friends and the groom is attended by his friends. During the wedding ceremony the bride and groom enter a private room in the bride's home and consummate their marriage. The groom cries in joy as the bride is found to be a virgin. The proof of her virginity is found in the blood stained cloth which was placed under the bride for the consummation of the marriage. If there is no blood on the cloth, the bride faces death by stoning for not being a virgin. This cloth is then passed by the groom out of the room to witnesses chosen by the bride's parents as proof that the bride is a virgin. Later this cloth may be given to the bride or her parents for safe keeping.

After the consummation the bride and groom and all of the parents and guests journey to the couple's new home for a wedding feast. People along the route of travel are compelled by custom to join the procession and follow the couple to their new home.

At the end of the feast the guests depart, and the bride and groom begin their new life together. The ritual of the marriage celebration is now complete. (Rudd, Steve. The Three Stage Ritual of Bible Marriages) (Edersheim Alfred E. 1883).)

Biblical Definition of Marriage

> All sexual intercourse is marriage!
> Rape constitutes marriage
> Marriage is a covenant which can never be revoked.
> (Brooks)

The Bible tells us that the act of consummation of marriage is completed any time you have sex with a person (1Corinthians 6:15). The problem is that this act can occur in multiple ways which are not part of God's plan for marriage. Therefore, we need a more thorough and appropriate definition of marriage. To understand God's perspective we need to begin with the marriage customs presented to us in the Bible.

There is no such thing as a sexual encounter which does not bind you in marriage with your sexual partner. It does not matter if your sexual partner is a prostitute, someone you love, or someone whom you do not even know. In the act of sexual intercourse, you become married and you are as much one flesh as any legally married couple. The only problem is that you may also be immorally married. If you have intercourse without first having a marital ceremony, the Bible clearly describes the nature of your marriage as immoral.

Even immoral marriage is considered binding both in God's eyes and in the community's understanding of the relationship. This is clearly demonstrated when an unmarried man rapes an unmarried girl and is required by law to marry her and never get a divorce. Fortunately, the girl has the right to refuse to live as his wife (Deuteronomy 22:23-29).

Malachi clearly describes marriage as a covenant (Malachi 2:14). Covenants are not an agreement written on a piece of paper or a contract which can be nullified for non-compliance. Covenants with God are sealed in blood. Marriage is a covenant which is sealed in blood with the rupture of the hymen. In Genesis 17:4, God's covenant with Abraham was sealed with the splitting of an animal into halves. The animal was then placed on two altars. God walked in a figure eight between the two altars, with the two halves of the animal being burnt upon them. By this act, God was declaring that the same butchery and destruction which was enacted upon this animal was to be enacted upon Him if He broke the covenant with Abraham.

The shedding of blood to seal a covenant represents the commitment of oneself to death. This is clearly displayed in God's formation of a covenant with Abraham (Genesis 15:9-21). The covenant when sealed by the death and blood of an animal represents a commitment of oneself to death if the covenant is broken. Consistently in the Bible blood is associated with the sealing of the covenant between God and His people (Genesis 17:10, Exodus 24:1-8, Matthew 26:27-28).

If the marriage which is sealed by a sexual union is broken, then the covenant of marriage is broken by any sexual union outside of that marriage. So what constitutes a biblical marriage? We are presented with several answers: 1. intercourse (whether moral or immoral in nature), 2. a ceremony (witnessed by friends, family, and a blood stained cloth), or 3. a covenant. Perhaps the best answer is all three combined.

The marriage starts with the betrothal which is considered to be as legally binding as a legal marriage. It continues to a ceremony attended by witnesses and sealed as a blood covenant. It then continues as a relationship in which the couple lives faithfully together in a covenant with each other.

Chapter 29

Wrinkle-Proof Relationships

Main Biblical Passages Dealing with Marriage
Genesis chapters 1:-3:
Malachi chapter 3:
Ephesians 5:18 -6:2

Introduction

> *You do not marry to change your spouse.*
> *You marry to enable God through your spouse to change you!*

D o you know what it is like to have to iron your pants every time you want to wear them? Many years ago, my wife bought me several pairs of light colored summer pants which I could wear only once. As soon as they were washed they would come out so wrinkled that not even ironing could make them look good again. They would look great on the rack, but once washed they would become so wrinkled you could never get the wrinkles out. Recently, my wife did something wonderful.

She went out and bought "Wrinkle Proof" pants. She bought me two pairs. I do not have to iron them and they look great. Don't you wish our marriages were like that? "Wrinkle Proof." No ironing, just wash and dry and everything is fine.

Mutual Submission

There is a passage in Ephesians 5:21-33 that tells us how to have wrinkle-proof marriages and relationships. When you look at the passage, you will see almost all of the English translations start the section with the 22ⁿᵈ verse. If you read the context, however, that does not make much sense. Verse 21 should be the start of this whole passage. This verse says one thing that is of key importance to understanding this whole passage. It says, "Submit to one another out of reverence for Christ." Now, who does the submitting? Both the husband and the wife are to submit. It is not just the wife, but the husband and the wife. They are to submit to each other out of reverence for Christ.

We really need to take a serious look at what the word "submit" means. In the Greek language "submit" is the word "eupotoso." It is a word used to express the relationship a group of people have to their sovereign ruler. It is a word that also, quite literally, means to come under the influence of another person. When you begin looking at the meaning of the word, there is not so much a concept of obedience as a concept of allegiance. I believe a more correct understanding of the word "submit" is based on the concept of allegiance. The twenty-second verse in effect says, "Wives - be in allegiance," or "Align yourselves to your husband as to the Lord." "Give to your husbands the same kind of allegiance that you give to Jesus Christ." That is a pretty strong sense of allegiance and a pretty strong sense of submission.

When we go down to the twenty-fourth verse, we read, "Now as the church submits to Christ so also wives should submit to their husbands in everything." In other words, wives should be in allegiance to their husbands in everything. This kind of allegiance stands by the husband in the good times and the bad times. It survives in the most difficult times. It is allegiance that is given to a husband with the same level of commitment as it is given to Jesus Christ. If husbands could live up to what Jesus Christ lives up to, the whole idea of submission and allegiance for wives would not be much of an issue.

I tend to think this is the reason the entire remainder of the passage speaks to the husbands.

Headship

The twenty-second verse says that "the husband is the head of the wife as Christ is the head of the church, his body of which he is the Savior." The husband is the head of the wife! I have a relative who told my dad years ago, "That means the husband is supposed to rule over the wife." Well, back around 1863 or 1865 there was a President of the United States who issued something called "The Emancipation Proclamation." He set the slaves free. It is illegal for a husband to rule over his wife in the United States of America. Ruling over a spouse constitutes slavery, which is both unbiblical and illegal.

In the Bible, when we look at how the word for witchcraft is defined, we see it basically means controlling another person's life. If we are really ruling over our wives, then we should be treated the same way witches were treated in the Old Testament. Witches were stoned to death. There is only one place that I can find in the Bible that says husbands are to rule over their wives. It is in Genesis 3: 16: "To the woman He said, 'I will greatly increase your pains in childbearing, with pain you will give birth to children, your desire will be for your husband and he will rule over you.'" If you notice the context of that passage, it comes after the fall when Adam and Eve sinned. Please notice that it is the serpent who is cursed and it is the ground which is cursed, but there is no curse pronounced on Adam and Eve. It does say that as a consequence of the fall, the husband would rule over the wife. What I want you to notice is that this is a fallen condition. It occurs only after the fall. Before the fall, Adam did not rule over Eve. The whole point of Jesus' resurrection is that we Christians are not supposed to live in a fallen state. We are redeemed by the blood of Jesus Christ. We are to live not in a fallen condition, where husbands rule over their wives, but in a pre-fallen condition. We are to live in the same marital equality as Adam and Eve lived in before the fall. Through the redemption of Jesus Christ, God restores to us the potential to live our lives and marriages as un-fallen people.

The Apostle Paul states that the husband is to be the head of the wife. The passage very specifically states that the husband is not to be the ruler. When you look at the Greek language, the word head is the Greek word "kepholey." It is a word which describes a person of superior rank or authority. Its contextual use indicates an understanding of a husband as a "leader." The Greek of the New Testament very easily could have used the word "archeous" to express ruler if it intended for a husband to be understood as a ruler. Instead, it specifically uses the term "kepholey."

When we look at the example of Jesus, we must concede he is indeed our ruler. What we also must concede is his leadership style. Jesus never sets himself up as a dictator or tyrant. He always presents himself as one who is to be followed, but never as one who enforces allegiance. If husbands are truly to be leaders of their wives, their leadership role must be modeled after the leadership role of Jesus. Husbands are not dictators. They are leaders.

We need to ask ourselves as husbands, "How is Jesus Christ the Head (leader) of the church?" When we can answer this question properly, we will understand how we husbands should be heads and leaders for our wives. Jesus demonstrates his headship and leadership of the church in three primary ways.

One, He gives the church its very existence. He gives the church its theology. He gives the church everything it needs to exist and to function in living out its calling to serve Jesus Christ. He is the ultimate provider. As husbands we need to be providers who see to our wives' physical needs, spiritual needs, emotional needs, etc. By this, I am in no way saying a woman should not work outside the home or be equally responsible for providing for the family. We need to be husbands who will set as our primary task (after God) the care of every need of our spouse.

Two, Jesus Christ is our leader in that He is our Savior. He not only saves us from sin, but rescues us from living in sin. He enables us to be people who are no longer alienated in our relationships. He brings healing for our relationships with other people, for our relationship with ourselves and for our relationship with God. His very role as our savior is to reconcile us to other people, to ourselves, and to God. He sets us free to live in relationships which are wholesome and full of love, instead of destructive attempts to misuse other people. Jesus is the one who leads us to wholeness in all of our relationships including marriage. If we are to be leaders of our wives, one of our goals will be to foster wholesome relationships in our own lives and in our spouse's life.

Three, in the next few verses, the passage begins to say even more to us about how Jesus Christ is our leader and what Jesus Christ does for the church when it says, "Husbands, love your wives, just as Christ loved the church and gave himself up for her to make her holy, cleansing her by the washing with water through the word, and to present her to himself as a radiant church, without stain or wrinkle or any other blemish, but holy and blameless."

Love

This next section starts with one command, one very simple command: "Husbands love your wives." Husbands, do not ever tell me that there is no love in your marriage because it is your responsibility to put it there. This passage gives a command which is very fundamental to a healthy marriage. That command is very simple: "Husbands love your wives." You are commanded to love your wives. Love your wives "just as Christ loved the church." How did Jesus Christ love the church? He gave himself up for her. Jesus Christ died on the cross for the church. I usually ask young couples in premarital counseling, "Do you love your mate enough to die for her or him?" I also tell them, "Don't answer that too quickly, because none of us really knows until we get into that situation."

Husbands, do you love your wife enough to die for her? If you can't honestly and truthfully say, "Yes, I really believe I love my wife enough to die for her," then there is something seriously wrong in your marriage. If you cannot say yes, then you are not living the way that Jesus Christ commands you to live in a marriage relationship. This is also a fair question for the wives. Wives, do you love your husband enough to die for him?

Sometimes dying for our spouse is really easy compared to living for our spouse. Jesus Christ not only died for the church, but Jesus Christ also arose from the dead and sits at the right hand of God the Father to intercede for us. Basically, Jesus Christ lives for the church. We need to ask ourselves, "Husbands, do you love your wife enough to live for her?" "Wives, do you love your husband enough to live for him?" Living for your husband or wife can be a whole lot harder than dying for him or her. Some of you know this to be true. Some of you have sat and watched your spouse day after day in a nursing home totally incapacitated and unable talk to you. If you have, you know how hard it is to live for your spouse. When your spouse has an Illness that has totally debilitated that spouse's body, do you love your spouse enough to live for him or her?

There is something else that Jesus Christ did for the church, seen in a little passage in Philippians 2:8. I had to study it in seminary because it is a very special passage. It uses the Greek word "kenosis." This word means that Jesus Christ emptied himself. Jesus emptied himself. Think about that for a moment. How did Jesus Christ empty himself? He became a human being. He lived among us. Now if you were God, do you think you would want to come down here and live among us humans? Sometimes we have enough trouble getting along with each other. If you were sitting up in Heaven, would you want to take that step? Not only did he empty himself to come down here and live among us, Jesus Christ basically set aside much of His divine right and power in order to live among us. You talk about a real major step in humility. It was a tremendous amount that Jesus Christ gave up in order to live here in this world among us. We need to ask ourselves, "Do we love our wives and love our husbands enough to empty ourselves? Are we willing to put away what we think are our rights and privileges and to live in a proper relationship with each other in marriage? Do we love our spouses enough to empty ourselves for him or her?"

Washing the Bride

This passage goes on to give us some different imagery that, while it is confusing to biblical scholars, also shows us some real gems of truth about marital relationships. We begin looking at a section here that deals with either baptism or taking a bath. The biblical scholars haven't figured out which is the correct understanding of the passage. Regardless of the correct translation, the passage deals with making our wife clean as Jesus Christ made the church clean. We are to love our spouses and give ourselves up for our spouses so that we can make them holy. We are to do this by cleansing them "by the washing with water through the Word." Now, the biblical scholars haven't quite figured out whether we are supposed to baptize our wives or give them a bath. However, when you realize that we are going to make our wives holy, you quickly realize it is a pretty big task which Jesus gives us to fulfill in marriage for our spouses. To make our wives holy means we are going to set our wives apart to function according to their originally intended purpose as a wife. The word holy means to set something aside to function according to its originally intended purpose. I frequently ask couples, "When your wife uses a skillet to fry you an egg for breakfast, is that skillet holy?" The correct answer is yes. "When your wife uses a skillet to bang you over the head to get your attention, is that skillet holy?" The correct answer is no. A skillet that is being used to fry an egg is being used for its originally intended purpose. A skillet that is used to hit someone over the head is not being used for its originally intended purpose. We are to make our spouses holy! We are going to do this by washing and cleansing them. We are going to wash and cleanse them "with water through the Word." Now in the Greek language of this passage, when it says "through the Word" it means the spoken word (Barth, 1968).

Numbers 22:-24: is the story of Balaam. Do you remember

the story of Balaam? Well, I'm going to give you the Tim Swick interpretation of this story. There was this pagan magician, at least we think of him as pagan. The really weird thing about this pagan magician was that he actually claimed to talk to the one real and true God. The magician's name was Balaam. Imagine if down the road (maybe five to ten miles away from the town in which you live) there are two and one half million strangers. They are people you have never heard of, or they are people about whom you have only heard rumors. The rumors are that these people have a very bad reputation. They have a different religion; they dress differently; they have different customs. They have no respect for you or for anyone who believes and behaves the way you do. They kill people. They kill whole groups of people who disagree with them. They wiped out a whole army that was chasing them one time. They want to invade and take over the neighboring city (or country) and to run those people out of their homes. They may decide they want your home and want to destroy your family. Are you scared yet? So, if you are living here in your town and you have two and a half million of these strangers camped out at the next nearest town, how do you feel? You drive by one day and you look around. That's a lot of tents and trailers and everything else down there. They do not even live in buildings. Are you nervous yet? Wonder what's going to happen? How soon are they coming to your town?

Now the King of Moab has two and a half million Israelites camped in his country. He has heard the stories about the plagues on Egypt. He has heard how the Egyptian army got wiped out in the Red Sea. He knows the Israelites whipped the Amalekites just south of his territory (Exodus 7-11, 15, 17:8-16). He knows that these Israelites have just wiped out two nations north of him. These Israelites are camped in his country and are using it for a base of operations. He knows they are strong enough to conquer his whole country any time they want it. He is sitting there and he is feeling very nervous. His country has already been invaded; it just hasn't yet been attacked. What is going to happen?

So the King of Moab sends for this pagan magician, Balaam. And the messenger says, "Balaam, the King of Moab wants you to come over and put a curse on these Israelites because we are really afraid of what they may do to us." Balaam prays and talks to God. God says, "NO." Balaam says to the messenger, "Sorry, God says I can't go; bye!" King Moab sends another messenger and the messenger says, "Please, Balaam you have to come. The king is desperate." Balaam says, "Sorry, God says 'No.' Can't go, maybe next time!"

The third time a messenger comes and Balaam says, "O.K., I'll go ask God again." And basically the Bible says that God says "Go." I really think what this means, if you study the context of the passage, is that God said, "Balaam, if you are so stupid that you are not going to listen to me, then just get out of here, go on. If you are not going to listen to me, then just go!" So Balaam says to the messenger, "O.K., God says I can go!"

Then Balaam goes. He is on his way, riding his trusty donkey. His donkey is as good as any new model automobile you've got. This donkey drives consistently well, rides well, and provides very reliable transportation. Balaam is on his donkey and he is going down the road. All of a sudden this donkey runs off the road. How would you like your car to run off the road? He goes out through the field and comes back on the road, and Balaam doesn't know why. So he goes on. Balaam did not know there was an Angel standing in the road ready to kill him, and the donkey was the only one who could see it. So the donkey ran off the road to save Balaam's life

On down the road there is a big wall. The people usually stacked up stones and built high fences to keep animals from getting into the crops or getting in and killing livestock. Often you would have two really high walls with a narrow road in between. Balaam is going down the road and when he gets to one of these walls, an angel is there again. At this point, the donkey starts having a little driving problem again and scrapes Balaam's foot up against the stone wall. Now you can imagine what Balaam is thinking about this time.

He is ready to have a few choice words with the donkey, and I don't mean in normal everyday polite vernacular. He goes on. The next time there are still high walls and no place for that donkey to go. The Angel is there ready to strike Balaam dead. Therefore, the donkey sits down in the middle of the road. You know what it's like when your car stops working. This time Balaam gets off the donkey, starts to beat the donkey, and I am sure he is using some very colorful, colloquial language.

The donkey talks to him. How would you like it if your car talked to you? I know that some of your cars do talk to you, but they only give polite reminders and warnings, like "turn off your lights." They don't hold complete conversations. This donkey not only gets Balaam's attention but converses in the kind of complete sentences that are a little frightening. In other words the donkey gives Balaam a full scale wake-up call. Balaam says, "Okay, what's going on here?" The donkey says, "Haven't I always been a good, faithful donkey to you?" and at that point God opens Balaam's eyes so that Balaam can see the Angel.

Now, I don't know about you, but I am sure that if I were in Balaam's shoes, I'd do exactly what Balaam did. Basically he did a real quick repentance act. "Please, God, tell me I don't have to go. Please, let me go back." And God said, "Balaam, you go, but you only say what I tell you to say." I'm sure I would be saying to God, "God, you better believe I'm only going to say what you tell me to say." And so Balaam gets down to the country of Moab. When he arrives, the King of Moab takes Balaam up on this big high mountain where he can see all two and a half million of these Israelites camped out in the field. The King says, "Okay, Balaam, do your stuff; curse them." So Balaam says what God tells him to say, and it all comes out as blessing instead of a curse.

The second time the King figures, "Well, two and a half million, that's a little intimidating; we'll get him where he cannot see all of them." Then the same thing happens. Now this same blessing is given by Balaam about 4 or 5 times. Balaam is seeing fewer and fewer of the people each time, but he keeps blessing them instead of cursing them.

I believe God is really all powerful. So if somebody is going to curse God's people, what difference would it make? Let the person curse the people; God can stop the curse, can't He? Well, that's the whole point. God could stop the curse. However, that's not the way God works and not the way God created this world. God goes to all the trouble of dealing with Balaam because he did not want his people cursed. He wanted them blessed.

Husbands, there are several passages in the Old and the New Testaments that talk about the creative power of speech and we have only looked at two of them. There is a creative power of speech that either sets God free to act in our lives or sets the enemy free to act in our lives. You are going to make your wives holy by the words that you speak to them. The power of speech is one of the most awesome powers we husbands can exercise in our marriages. It is a power that either blesses or curses. As a curse, one of the most devastating things a husband can ever do is to cut down his wife in public. You completely devastate your spouse when you say a cutting remark. Or you completely bless your spouse when you say a positive remark. You create the spouse that you want to live with by what you say to her. You may create a kind and loving woman with whom you really want to spend the rest of your life. Or you may create a woman that is so awful to live with that you would rather crawl up under a leaky roof and listen to it drip. You will create one or the other by the way you speak to your spouse in marriage. We create our spouse by what we say. We wash her and we make her holy.

Presenting the Bride

The next section begins by presenting the imagery of a Jewish husband on his wedding night. Not only do we wash and make our wives holy, we present our wife to ourselves just as the Jewish bridegroom goes to present his bride to himself on the wedding day. This passage says that we are supposed to present her without stain or wrinkle or any other blemish, but holy and blameless. These are the words that are used to describe a sacrificial animal in the Old Testament. Without stain or blemish! That means she can't be handicapped or defective in any way. God always required the best of the flock to be presented to him for sacrifice. In other words our wife is to be the best of all the women we will ever meet. To put it in plain English: "What a Babe!" God wants us to have the best wife possible!

A sacrificial animal could not in any way be handicapped or deformed, sick, injured or anything like that. It had to be a perfectly normal and healthy animal. Husbands, are your wives perfectly, normally healthy in every way? Or is your wife deformed, sick, crippled, maimed, or somehow just a little less than you are?

You know what Adam said to Eve the first time Eve was presented to him? He had just named all the animals and decided that they were not fit as companions. They were unacceptable. They were something less than he was. And Adam looked at Eve and he said, "Bone of my bone and flesh of my flesh." In other words, Adam said, "This Eve babe is a person exactly, perfectly equal to me."

You cannot present your spouse to yourself as anything inferior to whom you perceive yourself to be. If you present her as anything less than perfect and completely equal to you, you will treat your spouse as less than perfect and less than a complete equal. You will treat your spouse as deformed or sick or abnormal. If you perceive your wife as inferior, that is exactly the kind of marriage in which you will live. When we come together in marriage, God wants us to be equals. Perfectly equal to each other and treating each other as perfect equals, not as deformed, not as sick, not as something less than we are. Wives are not an appendage. God wants us to be equals in marriage.

Carved Wooden Chain by Bill Solgerius
Marriage is the chain that holds together the bond of permanence
Figure 34

Walter Trobisch tells us that in Liberia they have a custom that when a young couple gets married someone in the village carves a chain out of one solid piece of wood, and that chain at one end has a male head and at the other end a female head. There are no breaks and no joints in that chain. It is solid. When a young couple gets married, they give them this chain. The chain is to remind them that they are husband and wife and that they have been joined together permanently like a chain without joints (Trobisch, 1971). In the second half of this passage on marriage, we look at some of the ways God speaks to us about the way we are to be joined together as husband and wife.

How to Love

It is very interesting how this next section starts. "In this same way husbands ought to love their wives as their own bodies. He who loves his wife loves himself. After all no one ever hated his own body, but he feeds and cares for it just as Christ does the church - for we are members of His body." Ephesians (5:28). I want to ask you husbands - Do you take a bath at least once a month? Do you feed yourself? Do you get down at least one good meal a day? When you get sick, do you go to the doctor? You do take care of your bodies, don't you? When you get cut, you put on a band-aid and a little medicine? That's the way the Apostle Paul says that we should treat our wives. We should take care of our wives in the same way that we take care of our bodies. We should love our wives as much as we love our own bodies.

There is a really interesting statement in this short section of verses 28 through 30. It is a statement that speaks volumes about your self-image. It says, "He who loves his wife, loves himself." Think about that. The man who loves his wife loves himself. I expect the corollary of that is also true. If you don't love your wife, there is no way you are ever going to love yourself. Think about that. I really believe the only way a husband can ever love himself is to really love his wife, and if he does not love his wife, he will never love himself. It is interesting what happens to us when God puts us together. We become so united that we really cannot love ourselves unless we love our wives.

There is an interesting little dynamic that young couples experience early in their marriage. I think it really illustrates this idea of a husband loving his wife as he loves himself. This behavior is a little thing that absolutely drives couples nuts in that first year of marriage. They can't figure it out. Generally speaking, men feel loved the most when they have been to the bedroom with their wives. To be wanted by a woman sexually strokes the male ego in a manner that nothing else can match. It makes a man feel that he is most deeply loved when he makes love with his spouse. A woman, on the other hand, feels the most loved when a context of security is built around her. There is something about a woman's nature that she feels the most loved when she is sitting on the couch, has her husband sitting beside her, with their arms around each other, and they are just sitting there talking. Now, how many of you men understand that? We just can't figure it out. We know our wives are like that, but it doesn't make any sense to us. Wives seem to want to talk. They want to sit on the couch. They want to be cuddled and just to share time and intimacy together. Young couples get married, and the husband wants to go to the bedroom and the wife wants to sit on the couch. They cannot see that both actions go together. You see, when the young couple goes to the bedroom, then the husband feels a whole lot more like sitting on the couch. When the husband sits on the couch, the wife feels a whole lot more like going to the bedroom. You create a nice cycle, a nice pattern that just perpetuates itself. It builds love in the marriage. Do we love our wives as we love our own bodies? Do we love our wives enough to sit on the couch?

If we men let something come into our relationship that disrupts that context of peace and security for our wives, then we have a real problem in our marriage and our wives are going to let us know it. We need to build that context. When we build the context of love and peace and security around our wives, it is just the same as building a context of love and health in taking care of our own bodies. Build the context. Sit on the couch. Spend time talking. It is the way God has created us. If we really love our wives as we love our own bodies, then we will take the time to build that context of love, peace and security around our wives.

In studying this passage, my wife and I have tried to arrive at something that would summarize it in modern day terms. The best illustration we have been able to come up with is that of a coach. You know, a coach doesn't coach because he or she wants to rule over the other players. A coach wants to draw forth from the players their absolute best potential and performance. A coach wants to make his players able to perform greater in the athletic contest than they believe they are humanly capable of performing. A good coach will draw out a player's Olympic performance. That's what husbands should be doing for their wives as the head of the wife. Men are to make their wives' performance greater than that which they believe they are capable of. Draw out their best and bring it forth.

But you know the players have to follow the coach's instructions and give the coach their allegiance. When the player really gives the coach allegiance, the coach is motivated to be a good coach, to work that much harder at being a coach. God's invitation in marriage is very simple. Go and be a team. Go and be equals. One must function in the role of the coach, and one must function in the role of the player. Bring forth the very best marriage that God ever intended for you to have. May God bless you in that marriage and multiply all the joy that you will share together.

Back to the Beginning

The next section of this passage is a direct quote from Genesis: *"For this reason a man will leave his father and mother and be united to his wife and the two will become one flesh."* (Genesis 2:24-25). I want you to think for a moment. In our society when we talk about someone leaving home, who do we think of as leaving home? You ask young couples and 90 times out of 100 they will say that the wife is the one to leave home. The female leaves? That is not what this passage says. This passage says that the man is supposed to leave home. He is supposed to leave his mother and father. I think that is a very insightful statement on the part of the Bible. It is our responsibility as men to leave home.

When we talk about leaving home, what does that mean? Physically moving out? Yes, very definitely. If you do not physically move out from your parents, it is going to be very difficult to establish a good, proper marriage. Leaving home is more than just moving out physically. It is also cutting the apron strings. I have noticed children have a lot of difficulty breaking apron strings, and mothers are worse. They don't like to cut apron strings. They don't like to cut the attachments between parent and child and between child and parent. One of the best things mothers and dads can do for their children when they get married is cut the apron strings and leave them alone.

When my wife and I were first married, we lived six hours from my mother. Every time my mom would come to visit us, she would try to reassert those apron strings in our marriage. She would try to influence our marriage by setting expectations for how we should relate to her in our marriage. A couple of years later we moved to within about an hour of my mother. We were driving someplace and my daughter was in the back seat with mom. Linda and I were in the front seat, and we got to talking about some people we knew. It was a couple who had been married for over 20 years. They are a fine Christian couple. They have one of the best marriages for which anyone could ask. However, from the very first day of their marriage, their number one problem had been apron strings. Anything his mother wanted done always had to come first. If they were going out to eat supper together as a couple, and his mom called and said, "I need you to come up and water the flowers before you go," he had to go water the flowers. As we were driving, we began talking about this apron string problem. My wife said, "There is no way I would ever live like that," and I said, "I would not live that way either." About that time, my Mom spoke from the back seat, "Well, I guess that lets me know where I stand." I looked over my shoulder at my Mom, and I said, "Mom, yes that lets you know where you stand." I said, "We love you. We will always do everything we can to respect you and to help you in any way, but that lets you know where you stand." Ever since that conversation we have had a better relationship with my mother and a better marriage.

Sometimes in your marriage you honestly need to say to your parents, "I love you, but this is where you stand and this is where the apron strings get cut." If you do not cut the apron strings, they will hinder your marriage your entire life. Apron strings are kind of like weeds. If you don't cut them, they strangle living plants and living marriages. If you do cut them, all the foliage has a chance to live and the yard looks a whole lot better. I ask young couples when they come for marriage, "Have you moved out? Have you left home? Have you cut the apron strings?"

In the next section of this passage (remember, it is a quote from Genesis), it speaks about the bond between a husband and wife - "… and be united to his wife, and the two will become one flesh." In the Hebrew language of the Old Testament when you talk about this word "united," there is an image that goes with it. It is the image of having two piles of mud. Let's say you have a pile of gray mud and a pile of brown mud. Now when you get married you take those two mud piles and you mix them together. You stir up the mud very well. Can you ever separate the gray mud and the brown mud back out into their original piles? It is impossible. That is how united we become in marriage and that is exactly why divorce is so painful. We have been mixed like mud and we cannot be separated back out to the original way we were. When we become united as "one flesh," the other person becomes a part of us, a part of us that can never be removed. We carry that other person with us at least until death and maybe through eternity.

God wants us to be mixed, to be mixed like mud, and if we haven't been mixed like mud, then we are really not united properly. There was a young couple that Dr. Donald Joy speaks about in some of his lectures on bonding. This young couple came to him for premarital counseling, and as they sat in his office he asked them a question. He said all they did was look at each other, they never spoke, and it was like a whole volume of Encyclopedia Britannica passed from one to the other and back. You know you have been mixed when you become so united in the bonding process, and you carry the other person so deeply in your life, that you can communicate without even talking. You know how the other person thinks. You know how the other person feels. Your two piles of mud become mixed and your personal mud cannot be separated back out into the original pile.

Covenant

In the book of Malachi (2:14) marriage is called a covenant. Not a contract, not some agreement that a couple arrives at, but a covenant. A covenant is what God forms with us. A covenant in the Bible is always so binding that even when one person breaks it, both people are still required to keep it. In the Old Testament the nation of Israel broke its covenant with God time after time. Finally it came to the point that God had to punish them. Even at the end of that punishment, God said to the nation of Israel, "I still love you: get yourself back over here and get back in this covenant with me." You can't get out of it; you are never let go from this covenant. When we become united in marriage, we become united in a covenant that never ends. A marriage covenant is binding forever (Trumbull, 1975).

In combination with that covenant (according to the Old Testament) is what is called "hesed love." This very special kind of love always goes with covenant. It is a love that never stops loving no matter how often the covenant is broken, and no matter what the other person does. "Hesed" love still loves. It is incapable of stopping. When we enter into covenant with God by becoming Christians, God gives to us His "hesed" love. No matter what sin we commit God still loves us. In the same way, when we enter into the covenant of marriage, we are to love our spouses with "hesed" love. In the vows we take in the marriage covenant, we say to our spouse, "Even when you break the covenant, get back over here! Get back in this relationship with me! Let's live this marriage out! I still love you in spite of what has taken place between us!"

Gender Keys to Marriage

The husband and wife portion of this passage concludes with these words: "This is a profound mystery but I am talking about Christ and the church. However, each one of you also must love his wife as he loves himself, and the wife must respect her husband." Remember, this statement about a husband loving his wife has been the theme of this whole passage. It starts with mutual submission between husband and wives. Then the husband is commanded to love the wife; the husband is commanded to love the wife as himself. If a husband really loves his wife, then the whole idea of submission or allegiance is not that big of an issue, and the whole idea of a husband's leadership or headship is not that big of an issue. Here, at the conclusion, it says something a little different. It says the wife must respect her husband. Respect comes as a response to the role of love that the husband lives out. Respect is not something that somebody gives to you; it is something you have to earn. Husbands, if you want your wives to respect you, then earn it. Earn it by your love.

You look at what respect normally means in the Bible. An equal translation of that word is "fear," but it is a fear in the sense of awe. It is an awe of an outstanding love that someone has given to us. We fear God because he can destroy us. Even more, we fear God because we are overwhelmed and awed by the extreme power and strength of the love with which he loves us. God loves us so much we can't understand it. And our response to that love is a kind of love and fear. God's love is so strong that it actually scares us. When this passage talks about a wife respecting her husband, the respect should be a response of awe and fright. Our love toward our wives should be so immense it is scary. If we really love our wives, then we should have the same kind of love that we feel for our newborn baby. Do you remember the love you felt when you held your child in your hands for the first time just after it was born? The baby hadn't earned that love, but you looked at that little wrinkly, toothless, maybe half ugly thing, and your heart melted. We husbands should look at our wives the same way. We should look at our wives and our hearts should melt in love for them. When we have that kind of love for our wives, then it is no wonder our wives look up to us in respect and awe.

There is something else that goes with respect. As I have looked at marriages over the years and read about marriage counseling, one of the things which has been said again and again is that the number one cause of divorce in our country is lack of communication. I really don't believe that. I believe the number one cause of divorce in all marriages is the lack of respect. When a couple gets to the point that they stop respecting each other, the marriage falls apart. Communication is a big factor in maintaining a marriage, but I really believe it finally comes down to respect.

When couples come to me because they have problems in their marriage, I say, "Whatever you do, stand up to your spouse." It doesn't matter whether it is the woman or the husband. Stand up to your spouse and let them know what you want, because if you don't they will never respect you. Frequently, women think because they are Christians they have to bow down and do whatever the husband says and not complain. However, usually I have seen that when a woman bows down, the husband loses respect for his wife. The two are no longer equal in marriage as God intended them to be. When they are no longer equal partners, it is a very short time until the woman loses respect for herself and the husband loses respect for his wife, or vice versa. A wife cannot respect a husband who does not take into consideration her feelings. A husband cannot respect a wife who does not take into consideration his feelings. Both spouses need to make their feelings known and expect their spouse to acknowledge those feelings.

I had a young man in my church a few years ago whose wife had borne another man's child before they were married. The husband had come back from the Navy, married her, adopted the first child, and they had a second baby. They were a nice young couple. They had been living together as husband and wife since his return from the Navy. About a year later the wife started behaving very peculiarly. He had handed her the checkbook, but she wasn't paying the bills. She was doing other things with the money. One day she said, "I want a divorce." I heard something about the problem through his parents and cornered him after a church picnic one day. I asked him what was happening in his marriage. He was really feeling helpless like there was nothing he could do about the marriage. My wife and I looked at him and said, "Stand up to her. They are your children as much as they are hers. Tell her you want custody. Tell her you don't want a divorce. Tell her you want to keep this marriage together." The last I heard the couple was still together. If he had never stood up to his wife and let her know his position, I wonder where they would be and what would have happened.

Jesus and the Three Stranded Rope

Ecclesiastes (4:12) talks about the strength of a three stranded rope. Have you ever watched people make rope? They twist multiple strands of cord together. The more strands they use, the stronger the rope gets. Marriage is like a multi-stranded rope. It takes at least two strands to make a rope. When you add a third strand, the strength of the rope radically increases. The idea of a multi-stranded rope shows us how much we need Jesus Christ in our marriage if we are to have a successful and strong marriage.

This passage in Ephesians does not talk about Jesus Christ in the marriage. There is a reason for that. It is because you are supposed to have Jesus Christ in your life before you are married. Then, when you come together as a couple, you automatically bring Jesus Christ to your marriage. When you become married with Jesus Christ at the center of your marriage, you are like three braids of rope twisted together. When you have three, and God is the third person in the relationship, you have a very stable foundation on which to build a marriage and a family. If there are only two braids, the marriage will work, but it is weak and easily broken. It is God who makes you a whole lot stronger than you are as just two people. If you really want the best marriage you could ever have, you need Jesus Christ at the center of your marriage. You will never achieve the full potential that is possible for your life until you have Jesus Christ not only at the center of your life, but at the center of your marriage.

I would like to give you an invitation for your marriage. Read this passage in Ephesians about marriage often and put it into practice. Even more importantly, make Jesus Christ the center of your life and make Jesus Christ the center of your marriage. You may have a good marriage, but you will never have the best marriage possible until Jesus Christ is the center of your lives and the center of your marriage.

CONCLUSIONS

Most writing and research focuses on how to maintain a good and lasting marriage. As a result there is little to no research or writing concerning the kind of person you are or the kind of person you choose for a mate. The kind of person you make yourself into before marriage and the kind of person you choose for a mate in my opinion are far more important factors for marital success than what you do to maintain the marriage after the wedding.

What is permanence and why is it important? The only highly functioning pattern we have for couple relationships is traditional marriage. The basic alternatives to traditional marriage are polygamy, stayover marriages, cohabitation and open marriages. None of these forms of so called marriage have found long term popular acceptance in society. Traditional marriage has been the most accepted and most successful form of marriage since Adam and Eve. Why does traditional marriage work? Why is it universally accepted as the most appropriate form of relationship for couples all over the world? I believe the popularity and success of traditional marriage can be summed up in one word – PERMANENCE!

Cohabitation has a low success rate. The politics of the harem have cast a dark shadow on any advantages to polygamy. Open marriages and sleepovers are desired by very few people and have their own share of difficulties. Serial monogamous relationships reduce lasting intimacy to a series of sexual conquests. Marriage is about permanency in a relationship. The purpose of marriage is to develop your ability to live in a permanent intimate relationship with God. Without a relationship with Jesus, your ability for strong intimacy is severely restricted. Without intimacy in human relationships and marriage, your ability to live in intimacy with Jesus is severely restricted. Without holiness you destroy your ability to live in intimacy with both God and your mate.

So, what makes a relationship permanent? I believe permanence is brought about by these factors.

1. You marry your equal. This should be true in terms of personality traits, IQ, interests, socioeconomic level, morals, religious beliefs, etc. The issues and strengths which you bring to a marriage are very similar to or a blend of those in your parents' marriage. You do not need to perpetuate the brokenness of your parents' lives, but you most likely will marry someone who is a blend of your parents' personality traits and character. Because you marry someone who is similar to you, you should never marry a person who possesses a different set of religious beliefs, morals, etc. If you are a Christian, only by marrying another Christian do you optimize your potential for marital permanence. If you seek to become the kind of person you most desire to marry, then you will marry that kind of mate. In other words, you have to become the kind of person you want to marry.

2. The degree of brokenness and self-destructive behavior you sow in your life will determine the success or failure of your marriage and your children's marriage. Those who sow seeds of self-destruction destroy both their future marriages and their children's marriages. As the Bible says, the destruction follows to the fourth and fifth generations. Those who seek after purity sow self-beneficial behavior, and they reap long lasting marriages for themselves and their children - to the fourth and fifth generation.

3. All people want to marry and God wants all people to marry. The only exception is the few who remain unmarried for the purpose of ministry. Even people who practice rampant

sexual immorality desire to marry. Your sexual purity before marriage is the biggest determinant of the quality of intimacy which you will have with God, your spouse, your children, and your friends.

4. Your ability to live in intimacy with other people and with God is the biggest determinant of the success of your marriage. Sex is not intimacy. Sex may enhance and express intimacy, but in and of itself, it is not intimacy. God insists upon sexual purity, before, during, and after marriage because it is the only way you can maintain intimacy and successfully live in a permanent marital relationship.

    Your ability to live in intimacy is determined by your character. Your character is formed by two factors. The first is the adequate and successful completion of each of Erickson's stages of life throughout your lifelong development as a person. The second is your mastery of yourself in living a holy life in relationship with God, self and others. Sin destroys your character and brings brokenness into your life. The foundation of your character starts with trust. If you cannot be trusted, then you have no character and you are not capable of intimacy.

5. The most destructive thing which you can ever bring into your marriage, other than severe mental health issues, is a history of sexual immorality. Any sexual relationship outside of marriage will sow profound seeds of destruction in your marriage and in the lives of your children. You will likely never see how these seeds affect your marriage and your children. However, you will see the destruction which they bring into your marriage and into the lives of your children. This is why God is most clear in prohibiting sex outside of marriage. Only in marriage does sex enhance the intimacy of the relationship in a beneficial manner. Outside of marriage sex sows seeds of destruction in all the lives that it touches. God is not a prude. He invented sex. You can either use sex in the proper context to enhance your marriage, or you can

damage and maybe destroy your future (or present) marriage by having sex outside of marriage. Before you ever have sex outside of marriage, you need to decide if you want your marriage to be permanent and intimate, or if you want your marriage to be destructive and bring brokenness to yourself and all those around you - including your spouse and your children.

6. God speaks to everyone constantly. He may not speak every moment, but He repeatedly and regularly gives us guidance throughout life. If your God does not speak to you and you do not expect your God to speak to you, then either your God is a quack or your relationship with your God is quackery. God speaks to us and gives us guidance, love, fellowship, and intimacy. The guidance God gives includes direction for dating relationships, mate selection, and marriage. If you do not learn to hear God's voice and receive His guidance, you have no right to expect to get through life, the mate selection process, and marriage without deep wounds, disfiguring scars, and broken lives.

7. God does not choose your mate. You choose your mate. You can never hold God responsible if your marriage does not work out. On the other hand, God frequently will tell people who the person is that He desires for them to marry. You may not get to marry the person you believe God prefers for you to marry, because he or she also has a choice in the matter. The problem is most people do not know how to listen to God's voice. The more you learn to pray and hear God speak to you, the more he will be able to guide you through the painful process of becoming capable of intimacy and maturing as a person. It is allowing God to guide us that prevents many of the most painful experiences of broken hearts and broken lives in the mate selection process.

APPENDIX A

Recommended Textbooks

Erber, Ralph & Maureen Wang Erber. (2011). Intimate Relationships, Issues, Theories, and Research. Boston, MA: Pearson Education Inc.

Anderson, Neil T. (1993). The Bondage Breaker. Eugene, OR: Harvest House Publishers.

Eyrich, Howard A. (1978). Three to Get Ready: A Christian Premarital Counseling Manual. Grand Rapid s, MI: Baker Bookhouse.
*(The Premarital Counseling Questionnaire
on pp. 111-114 is excellent.)*

Feldhahn, Shaunti. (2004). For Women Only: What you need to know about the inner lives of men. Sisters, OR: Multnomah Publishers.

Feldhahn, Shaunti. (2006). For Men Only: A straightforward guide to the inner lives of women. Sisters, OR: Multnomah Publishers.

Larson, Jeffery. (2000). Should We Stay Together. San Francisco, CA: Jossey-Bass A Wiley Company.

McIlhaney Joe S., MD & McKissic-Bush, Freda MD. (2008). Hooked: New Science on How Casual Sex is Affecting Our Children. Chicago, IL: Norfield Publishing.

Parrott, Les & Parrott, Leslie. (1995). Saving Your Marriage Before it Starts. Grand Rapids, MI: Zondervan.

Smedes, Lewis B. (1994). Sex for Christians. Grand Rapids, MI: William B. Eerdmans Publishing Company.

Van Epp, John. (2006). How to Avoid Marrying a Jerk: The Foolproof Way to Follow Your Heart Without Losing Your Mind. Columbus, OH: McGraw-Hill Companies.

Warren, Neil. (1992). Finding the love of your life. Colorado Springs, CO: Focus on the Family.

APPENDIX B

Intimacy Exercises

1. **Same Sex Touch**

   The Rationale: You need to be able to experience intimacy with persons of the same sex as comfortably as you experience intimacy with members of the opposite sex. The more comfortable you are in experiencing and sharing intimacy, the more fluent you will be in sharing intimacy with a prospective mate.

   The Assignment: Sit and hold hands with a member of the same sex for at least three minutes. Do not say anything; just hold hands. Notice the emotions and thoughts that you experience during this time. Share what you experienced during this time with at least one other person, or record it in a diary which you will share with at least one other person.

2. **Opposite Sex Touch**

   The Rationale: You need to be able to comfortably experience intimacy with persons of the opposite sex comfortably. The more comfortable you are in experiencing and sharing intimacy, the more fluent you will be in sharing intimacy with a prospective mate.

   The Assignment: Sit and hold hands with a member of the opposite sex for at least five minutes. Do not say anything; just hold hands. Notice the emotions and thoughts that you experience during this time. Share what you experienced during this time with at least one other person, or record it in a diary which you will share with at least one other person.

3. **Opposite Sex Touch and Eye Stare**

The Rationale: You need to be able to experience intimacy comfortably with persons of the opposite sex. The more comfortable you are in experiencing and sharing intimacy, the more fluent you will be in sharing intimacy with a prospective mate.

The Assignment: Sit and hold both hands with a member of the opposite sex and stare into the eyes of that person for at least three minutes. Do not say anything; just hold hands and stare into the eyes. Notice the emotions and thoughts that you experience during this time. Thank the person for participating in the exercise with you. Share what you experienced during this time with at least one other person, or record it in a diary which you will share with at least one other person.

4. **The Questionnaire**

The Rationale: Many young adults are very uncomfortable talking with members of the opposite sex whom they do not know. They do not know how to get to know members of the opposite sex or how to open up their own person to discussing intimate issues.

The Assignment: Each week for at least 7 weeks, sit with a group of at least three members of the opposite sex and no members of the same sex for at least thirty minutes. Write down their answers to the following questions.

What are your goals for the future?

What is your occupation or your occupational goals?

What are your marriage and family goals for the future?

What quality do you most desire in a mate? Why?

How does it make you feel that I asked you these questions?

5. **Beginning Relationship Questions**

The Rationale: As a couple begins to move from dating to a relationship, there is a need to probe each other's desires, dreams, and hopes for the future.

The Assignment: Explore these questions together:

What do you find attractive about your partner excluding looks?

What are your feelings about your partner?

What would be your hopes and dreams for your partner's life in the distant future?

6. **My Family Picture**

The Rationale: Understanding your family picture can provide strong insight into your Object Relations subconscious reactions to people around you.

The Assignment: Please perform the following exercise.

Draw a picture of your family during the early years of your life. What are the traumas your family experienced during the early years of your life? What are the joys your family experienced during the early years of your life? What family dynamics and relationships still impact your life today?

Share your family picture with your mate and dialogue about your feelings related to your relationships with your family. Discuss how each person in your family impacts your relationship with your mate.

Where is God in this picture? What would God's reaction be to the dynamics of your family structure? Where would God see damage in your family dynamics?

7. **Story Telling** (Do not engage in this exercise more frequently that once per month. The subconscious needs time to process.)

The Rationale: As a couple in a long term relationship begins to bond to each other, there is a need to start understanding each other on a subconscious level as well as a conscious level.

The Assignment: Story (Warning: This exercise will reveal what is occurring in the subconscious of the story teller.)

Have your partner tell three stories. It is better if these stories are imaginary and highly embellished.

Listen to the stories and after the three stories are told,

determine the common theme of all three stories. Then discuss this theme with each other. The theme of the three stories reveals what is at focus in the story teller's subconscious mind.

Take turns telling the three stories.

8.   **Present Yourself**

The Rationale: Many young adults have difficulty talking when in the presence of someone to whom they are highly attracted. They have a great need to become comfortable in directing and participating in conversations which will promote attraction and intimacy.

The Assignment: Ask someone to whom you are strongly attracted to listen as you present your thoughts and feelings about a specific set of issues on which you choose to express your opinion.

Possible issues for discussion:

Your faith and relationship with Jesus. Your testimony of how you came to know Jesus.

Your favorite activities and proudest accomplishments and failures in those activities.

Your relationship with your parents and siblings.

Your goals, plans, and dreams for your future. Describe the people who will be most significant in the completion of those dreams and the role each will play in bringing your dreams to fruition.

9.   **Relationship Feelings**

The Rationale: One of the most important discussions you can ever have is an honest expression of feelings. Many men and some women have difficulty discussing feelings. The expression of feelings is critical to the intimacy and stability of our relationships.

The Assignment: Take turns answering the following questions with each other.

Parents: Name the five most positive aspects of your parent's or parental caregiver's relationship with each other. How does each of these individual aspects make you feel?

Name the five most negative aspects of your parent's or parental caregiver's relationship. How does each of these individual aspects make you feel?

Relationships in general:

Name the five most positive aspects which you see in relationships in general. How does each of these individual aspects make you feel?

Name the five most negative aspects which you see in relationships in general. How does each of these individual aspects make you feel?

Present Relationship

Name the five most positive aspects of your present relationship. How does each of these individual aspects make you feel?

Name the five most negative aspects of your present relationship. How does each of these individual aspects make you feel?

APPENDIX C

How to Listen to God

My Experience:

I came to know Jesus at the end of my eighth grade year. I was at a church service and responded to an altar call. I went forward and asked Jesus to forgive me of my sins, to come into my life, and to take over my life. That same night, as I lay in bed, God asked me if I would give him all of my life, not just part of my life. After tossing and turning for about an hour I finally said yes. God was pretty determined that I was not going to sleep until I answered that question. Then my Sunday school teacher (the man who led me to Jesus), asked me to start reading the Bible. I read the Bible each day of my life from high school through seminary and most days thereafter. The same man also encouraged me to pray each day. When I went to college I decided I would spend and an hour a day in the Bible and an hour and a half in prayer. Believe me, this time with God each day is of much more value to me today than all the education I ever received in life.

As I spent time with God each day while in college, I found God was speaking to me. God was giving me thoughts that were true about people, and I realized I could know these things only by God telling them to me. There would be a thought come into my mind that I would never have conceived on my own. Sometimes I would know something and know that it was true, but not know how I knew it was true. I would find myself perceiving something about another person and be absolutely convinced it was true even when I did not know the person. Sometimes the thoughts and pictures which God speaks to me come very clearly and sometimes they come so softly I am not sure I heard God correctly. Sometimes they come as pictures, and sometimes they are just thoughts. Sometimes they are both thoughts and pictures. Many times in prayer I will see pictures while I am praying about someone or something. The pictures give me understanding of what God is trying to tell me in regards to what I am praying about. Almost never do I have visions or dreams. There have been a few exceptions. I know for some people, dreams and visions are the primary form in which God speaks to them.

When I was in my college years and just learning to pray, I asked God to tell me something. It was a question for which I very much wanted a direct answer. After I asked God to tell me the information which I was requesting, I thought, "How is God going to speak to me to answer my prayer?" I did not want to be presumptuous with God, but I was only willing to accept an answer directly from Him. So when I prayed I asked God to speak directly to me. I was not sure how He would do that, but that is what I specifically requested of God. I was expecting God to speak to me in an audible voice. I also knew audible voices seemed to be reserved for special people in the Bible. When God answered my prayer I was stunned. He literally spoke to me. There were other people standing around me talking, and I could hear their voices. The voice I heard was not one of their voices. It was not even an audible voice. Yet the voice was so clear that it was unmistakable. It was a voice I heard in my head, but it was not my voice and it was not anyone else's voice. It was just a clear voice speaking a very clear message of four words in English. The words were the answer to my prayer. From then on I knew God could and would speak to me. He has never used that clear voice in my head in the same manner as He spoke to me that day, but He has consistently spoken to me, sometimes even when I was not listening.

If you are like me, you think people will think you are crazy if you start telling them what God speaks to you and shows you. For many years I never told anyone anything. After a few years enough things God had told me were confirmed to be true that I could begin to have confidence to tell people what God was telling me. I mostly started with Christian friends whom I could trust not to condemn me or reject me. Gradually as I began to tell other people what God said, they would look at me suspiciously, but no one ever told me I was crazy. Now I have spoken out so many times that I fear being disobedient to God more than I fear the rejection and mockery of other people.

One time when I was about twenty three, God gave me a vision. He used the sky as a movie screen while I was driving down the road. In this movie-like vision, He showed me a number of things I had believed and had been doing that were wrong in my life. He did not show me this to condemn me. Instead He used the vision to clear up a lot of deception which had come into my life. On a couple of occasions in recent years, I had dreams in which God showed me answers to issues about which I had been praying. On multiple occasions I have been praying with another person, and God has either shown me pictures or spoken through thoughts in my head about issues in that person's life. In one case, I know God specifically hid something He did not want me to see about another person's life.

I have not always understood correctly the things God has shown me. As a result I have interpreted some things incorrectly. As a result, I have made statements to other people which were not fully correct. It takes much practice to learn to interpret what God tells us in a precise manner. Sometimes God has shown me things in prayer, but the pictures came so fast that I could not get a proper full interpretation. Other times, thoughts or pictures have come so fast and so faintly, that I could not be sure if it was what God was telling me or something I just thought up. I have had to learn to tell other people things that I am not positively sure are correct. I may tell someone whom I spiritually trust that I thought God told me something, but I could not be sure. I know not to tell the other person whose life is directly impacted by what God is saying unless I am positive that the message is both from God and that I correctly understood the message.

Over the years I have learned that when God gives me a picture or puts a thought in my head, if I will focus on that thought or picture and ask God to tell me what He is talking about, it will lead to another thought, picture, vision, dream, or whatever. The additional information gives me more understanding. Frequently I will wait a couple of days and start praying about what God told me through His multiple forms of communication. He then will either confirm something about which I am not sure or give me additional information about that issue.

God speaks to us all the time. I mean regularly. As you practice praying and begin to receive messages from God, you begin to know when God is speaking. It takes a lot of time and practice to correctly hear what God is saying. Do not be afraid to practice. Do not be afraid to get something wrong. Do not be afraid to say to another person that you are not sure but you think God told you such and such. It is only through the mistakes that you learn to hear God more clearly and to know when you are not sure of what God was saying. I once told a woman at church who was unable to get pregnant that she might be having twins. All that I could say for sure is that I saw two children of hers. A short time later she had a baby, and then about a year later she had another baby. God had indeed healed her womb and blessed her with children. I was wrong about her having twins, but I was correct about her having two children.

Pay attention to the pictures, strange thoughts, things you know and do not know how you know them, visions, and dreams you have when you pray. Through them God will teach you to hear His voice. Remember that He speaks to you all the time. However, you will not know that he is talking unless you learn to listen.

The Greatest Doctrine in the Bible:

The most important and foundational doctrine in the whole Bible is that God speaks to us. This doctrine is presented time and again throughout the Bible but is treated by Christians today as if it did not exist. Christians are taught to pray but they are not taught to expect that God will speak to them. God speaks to us consistently. I believe the neglect of this doctrine has done more to cripple the followers of

Jesus Christ and to destroy people's lives than all of the heresies ever taught from the beginning of time. This doctrine is found from one end of the Bible to the other end. It forms most of the foundational verses of the first chapter of Genesis.

Of all the biblical teachings, the only doctrines more profound than God speaking to us are the concept of the Godhead and the doctrine of salvation. Constantly the Bible teaches that God speaks to human beings. God's voice is not reserved for prophets or special spiritual people. God has never stopped speaking to people. He speaks to us constantly. I believe that God speaks to all Christians multiple times a day. Sometime what He has to say is very significant. Sometimes, what He has to say to you is key to changing or even saving someone's life. Because we have neglected this doctrine, we no longer expect God to speak to us. We ignore him when He does speak. We treat him worse than someone we totally dislike because we treat Him like we do not know Him and do not want Him to talk to us. How do you react when your friends do not want to talk to you? What would happen to your life and relationship with God if you had been taught to expect God to speak to you each day, just as frequently and forthrightly as your parents and friends speak to you?

Please tell me at least one person in the Bible who is presented as a having a relationship with God to whom God did not speak. I am sure there is at least one. The accounts of some of these people are presented very briefly in scripture. There is at least one person in the Bible who is presented very prominently and to whom I cannot recall God speaking. That person is Jesus. God the Father spoke to other people about Jesus (Matthew 3:17 and 17:5), but I do not recall any place in the Bible that God the Father actually is recorded as speaking to Jesus. We know that Jesus in multiple instances presents divine foreknowledge (Judas' betrayal, Peter's betrayal). However, we are not told that God actually spoke to Jesus. We are also told multiple times in the gospels that Jesus separated himself from all others so that He could pray. In my opinion, there is no question but that Jesus prayed to God. Just because the Bible does not speak of God talking to Jesus does not mean it did not happen. The Bible and Jesus himself speak very openly about the relationship between God the Father and Jesus. "I and the Father are one" (John 10:30). I believe God did speak to Jesus, even though I cannot prove it. I also believe that Jesus did not need a lot of communication from God the Father since the oneness between them was sufficient to enable Jesus to know God's will in all matters.

What concerns me is that every other person in the Bible who is presented as having a strong relationship with God is a person to whom God spoke! As Christians we claim to have a strong relationship with God, but how many Christians actually hear God speak to them? If God spoke to so very many of the people who had a strong relationship with Him in biblical times, then why does God not speak to Christians today? Personally I believe that if you are a Christian and God does not speak to you, then you are actually not a Christian. The biblical pattern is acutely clear – God speaks to all people who have a strong relationship with Him and even to some who worship pagan gods. By this statement, I do not mean that God sends a prophet or another human being to speak to Christians. I mean God Himself speaks directly to Christians.

Do Christians not hear God speak to them or are they just afraid to tell anyone? Are they so afraid of being ridiculed by their friends and society that they will not admit to other people that God has spoken to them? Personally, I believe most people who call themselves Christians are either too afraid of God to develop the intimacy in their relationship with God where they hear Him speak to them, or they are afraid to tell anyone that God has spoken to them.

I am absolutely convinced that God is constantly speaking to Christians! I also am absolutely convinced that Christians are constantly refusing to listen to what God is saying to them. How in the world can a Christian claim to believe in the resurrection of Jesus and not believe that God is constantly speaking to him or her? The biblical evidence for God speaking to the people who follow Him is much stronger and far outweighs the biblical evidence for the resurrection of Jesus Christ. In other words, if you tell me that you believe in the resurrection but do not believe that God speaks to you,

I am going to tell you that you espousing a very unbiblical position. Just look at the evidence. How many times does the Bible say that "God said" such and such to a human being? How many times does the Bible say a man had a dream (for example, Daniel, Joseph). How many times does the Bible say "the Angel of the Lord spoke" to so and so? How many times does the Bible speak of a man saying "I saw" in reference to a vision from God? There is absolutely no passage in the Bible where it says that God has stopped speaking to his people. If you do not believe in God speaking to you, then why do you pray?

What I Want You to Understand:

I would dare say that you would not be able to pick out the voice of someone you just met in a crowd, but you would be able to pick out your parent's voice. It is the same way with God. You have to learn to pick him out in the crowd. The only way is to speak with Him often so that you know what His voice sounds like.

What I want Christians to understand is that God is constantly speaking to you. I do not mean every second of everyday, but frequently enough that you need to listen to His voice. The more time you spend in prayer and true worship, the more you will be able to discern what He is speaking to you. God communicates mostly by thoughts, pictures we see in our minds, visions and dreams. We have to learn to discern which thoughts are the products of our own minds and which are the product of God's communication to us.

Most of the time, God speaks to me when I am praying. Other times God speaks to me when I am engaged in some form of work and my mind is not focused on Him at all. God tells me to pray for people whom I have not thought of in years. He tells me things about the people for whom I have been praying. He also tells me to pray for specific people and then tells me what the specific needs are in their lives. When God has spoken to me, He has told me things that saved several people's lives and sometimes saved their lives multiple times. He has told me things that healed marriages and set people free of demonic control and influence. A few times He has even told me the entire future picture about the kind of person someone would grow to be. God speaks, but we have to learn to listen.

Most of the time, I cannot prove that God told me anything at all. I believe that most people to whom I say, "God told me this or God showed me that" believe I am deluded. I cannot blame them for thinking that of me. Most of what God tells us as Christians is unprovable. Yet when we act upon that information, it makes immeasurable differences in our lives and the lives of people with whom we interact.

We have to learn to expect that God is speaking to us and quit letting the church and other Christians shame us into feeling that if God speaks to us we are mentally ill. In my life most of the things God has told me are not future prophetic events but real time events. They are occurring in people's lives at that exact moment, and He is telling us to pray. God is not limited by whether or not we pray, but for some reason He chooses to act only when we pray. He wants us to pray so that He can protect the people we pray for and bring healing, protection, and deliverance to their lives.

If you are not willing to believe and expect God to speak to you, then you are being an instrument of destruction (through neglect) in the lives of those for whom God would ask you to pray. However, you can only learn to hear God's voice speaking to you if you spend abundant God-focused time in worshiping and praying to Him. Prayer is something that is not a once a day event. We must learn to pray while we work, while we drive, and while we do each and everything we do. This time of constant prayer throughout the day must be coupled with a more structured prayer time in which we meet with and listen to God each day. Learn to live in prayer and God will use your prayers as the instrument through which He saves people's physical and spiritual lives, heals, delivers, performs miracles and allows you to witness the greatest blessings to ever occur in your lives. Will you be a person who teaches people to expect to hear God speak, or will you be a person who perpetuates the silence about the most important aspect of God's relationship with those who know Him, walk with Him, and pray to Him?

The Gold and the Glory

Shane Warren made a statement a few years ago about the relationship between the gold and God's glory. They always go together. If you study the construction of the Temple and the items housed therein, you always see a close association between gold covering the items and rooms where God's glory was most prominent. The only thing which can bear the power of God's glory is gold. This includes our lives.

Gold has to be refined to get the purity necessary to contain God's glory. Our lives have to be refined to gain the purity to contain God's glory. The refinement of our lives only comes through pain and suffering. Without sufficient pain and suffering to purify our lives we will never experience the glory of God.

Many people do not believe they can ever experience God's glory, so they demand no purity in their lives or their walk with Jesus. Those who fully seek to experience God's glory in their lives may not want the pain necessary to purify their lives sufficiently to experience God's glory, but they are willing to endure it and even welcome it as a necessary part of becoming a person who is capable of experiencing God's divine presence in their lives.

All of us experience pain in our lives which can serve to purify our lives. I do not know of anyone who has not experienced painful events in their lives. Many people hide this pain and never share their experiences with anyone. The purification process, which is derived from our pain, only works if we share what we have experienced with other people. If you keep these experiences to yourself, the purification God wants to produce in you is wasted. The more you hide and bury the pain in your life, the longer you are going to live and suffer with it.

Emotional pain is usually what God uses to purify our lives. Most emotional pain young adults encounter comes through the crash of crushes and sometimes the rejection of true love. These painful events are very prominent while searching for a mate. The issue of purification comes into our lives from our decisions about how to handle the brokenness of relationships and our personal perceptions about those relationships in our lives.

Regrettably many people only allow the pain in their lives to separate and drive them away from God. In these instances they allow pain to destroy their lives and prevent them from ever receiving the blessing of the proper spouse which God would bring into their lives. In these instances the pain they experience is fully wasted. Instead of using the pain to prepare their lives for the person God most desires for them as a mate, they allow the pain to destroy them. As a result, they are never prepared to receive the proper person as a mate. Only by embracing, working through, and sharing the story of their pain can they enable God to purify and heal their lives so that the pain becomes a blessing which builds their lives to make them ready to receive their eventual mate. Those who reject God because of the pain never marry God's preferred spouse. Instead they end up in broken marriages, with broken lives that never reap the blessings which God wants to give them to fill their lives.

The saddest people I know are not those who have never experienced God's glory. The saddest people are those who have never allowed their pain to draw them closer to Jesus and to purify their lives.

APPENDIX D

The Discussion

All couples seeking to marry need to discuss the following issues thoroughly and repeatedly prior to marriage and occasionally thereafter.

Family
Immediate and Extended Family
Family history involving social mores, culture, celebration practices, work, previous places of residence
Family history involving in-laws
Family religious history
Family divorce and abuse history
Family acceptance and approval of your mate
Family history involving ethics, morals, legal issues.
Family history involving child rearing, patterns and practices of discipline
Family life commandments
Family secrets

Social activities
Food preferences

Home
Where to live

Children
Pregnancy prevention
Discipline

Secrets and keeping them
Anniversary dates- birthday, anniversary, etc.
Careers
Work or stay home
Career Priorities for both spouses

Conflict management

Religion
Relationship with Jesus
Prayer life
Bible study
Parents' religion
Born again, Spirit filled, spiritual gifts, prayer life
Family devotions
Church attendance and denomination selection

Relationship history
Dating history
Previous engagements
Ex's in dating, cohabitation, marriage, divorce

Abuse history
Sexual
Mental
Physical
Neglect
Abandonment

Finances
Budget

Autos
Insurance
Investments
Loans
Credit cards
Taxes
Home

Personal Expenses
Entertainment Expenses
Childcare and provision expenses
Tithes
Expense priorities
Family accountant duties - paying bills and keeping records, doing taxes

Sex
Cohabitation and other relationship history
Sexual history
Sex education
Importance of sex
Expectations regarding sex, including normal and abnormal or unusual sexual practices in the marriage

APPENDIX E

Listening and Learning Skills

Psychologically speaking listening should have at least one of three goals. It should change a person's feelings, change a person's behavior, or change a person's beliefs and attitudes. Any time you change one of these basic aspects of person, you impact the other two aspects of a person's psychology. If you change two of these aspects of a person's psychology, the third aspect will also change.

Affect is a person's feelings and emotions.
Behavior is how a person acts and reacts to situations he or she encounters in life.
Cognition is a person's beliefs and attitudes.

People do not just become convinced of truth because they hear it presented. They become convinced of truth when they feel it in their emotions and in their lives. People do not change their behavior until both their understanding and their emotions change. Listening is about changing lives. Therefore, those who seek to impact others in relationships must speak to the emotions as well as to the understanding.

The first skill in listening is learning to be relational. God has designed us as tripartite beings. We need to be conscious of how our listening impacts each part of a person's being.

Our speech produces sound waves that impact our body. Science has discovered that our bodies create sound waves. Our bodies were created to produce musical sounds as a form of worship to God. We speak and produce sound. Does our speech bring worship to our hearers?

All of counseling psychology is an attempt to heal. Through our listening we also seek to heal. We present God's counsel of forgiveness as the greatest means of psychodynamic healing to the deepest recesses of a person's soul. People come to church not because they want to have their ears tickled or because they want to find hope for their lives. They come to seeking healing for their souls. That healing comes through forgiving and being forgiven.

It is only the touch from God upon our spirits that communicates His forgiveness to us and heals our souls. People want to be assured that God exists. They question God's reality and His existence until they sense God's presence and hear God speak to them with that still small voice in their spirits.

Listening that changes lives touches the emotions. Most people in the workplace live in a world of thinking and doing. When people enter into a listening situation, they want to have their emotions touched. I once read that people who do not physically touch each other within an hour of the time they first meet never develop trust for each other. If we want people to have their lives changed by our listening, we have to develop trust. To develop trust, we have to touch the person physically and emotionally. It is when a person is opened up to God by a physical touch and an emotional touch that they are most receptive to a spiritual touch from God.

The Bible frequently talks about emotions. It usually presents emotions in a negative light in speaking of non-Christians. For Christians, the Bible frequently commands us to have specific positive emotions. The Bible is clear – emotions are a key aspect of our relationships with God, with the people around us and with our own self. Touching people's emotions grants them permission to trust you and to trust God. It enables them to develop community and relationships within the body of Christ.

The advent of the social networking sites on the internet clearly demonstrates the interest in social interaction and connectedness. The proliferation of social groups within the church also clearly demonstrates this demand. How does listening facilitate the demand for social connectedness in the church? Jesus and the twelve disciples were clearly a social group with a mission of discipleship. In listening we are to be a social group with a mission of discipleship. Touching people's emotions grants to them permission to develop community and relationships within the body of Christ.

If the person performing listening does not demonstrate a comfort with relationships and emotions in his or her interactions with people, then permission is not granted to people to be relational. If the person performing listening does not demonstrate openness to emotions and relationships, then he or she displays God as non-feeling, non-caring, and non-relational. Permission for a relationship with God must be demonstrated and granted by the person performing listening.

What is the greatest skill any potential mate can ever develop? The ability to LISTEN! You do not earn the right to speak until you have demonstrated the capacity to listen!

What about prayer? The ability to pray is critical to mate selection, but the ability to listen to God is even more critical. Can you really pray if you cannot listen to God? The ability to listen to the people around us is the most important skill we can ever develop for building relationships, demonstrating the love of God, and earning the right to present the Gospel. It is also the most important skill you must possess before you ever tell a potential mate that you love him or her. You have not earned the right to say "I love you" until you have listened to your mate.

SOLER
S – Face the person Squarely
O – Adopt an Open posture
L – Lean toward the person
E – Make Eye contact
R – Be Relaxed

SOLER is the most basic form of listening for which we need to develop skills. There is nothing that expresses love and compassion to a person more than the feeling they have been listened to. Practice this skill with someone and see how you feel. Do not take any shortcuts. Be careful to do this exercise correctly! If you want to improve your marriage or your relationship with someone important to you, use SOLER and just listen to them. If you want an opening to witness to a person, use SOLER and listen to them. Using SOLER will make more difference in any relationship that almost anything else you can do. (Egan, 1994).

There are several forms of listening that people use to avoid relationships. In and of themselves these forms of listening may be good. However, when they are uses for selfish purposes they become negative forms of listening or psuedo-listening. God commands you to love other people. If you use any of these forms of pseudo-listening, then you are not loving the other person enough to listen to him or her.

> passive/inattentive listening – pretending to listen while you pay attention to something else.

> pretend - also called 'responsive listening' - using stock nods and smiles and "uh hum," "yes," "of course," etc.

> biased/projective – "selective listening " and intentionally disregarding/dismissing the other person's views.

> misunderstood - unconsciously overlaying your own interpretations and making things fit when they don't fit.

> attentive - fact gathering and analysis often while attempting manipulation of the other person.

> active - understanding feelings and gathering facts for largely selfish purposes.

> empathic - understanding and checking facts and feelings, usually in relation to listener's personal agenda.

facilitative - understanding fully, and helping with the other person's needs for our own agenda.

Non Verbals

Body behavior - posture, movement, gestures

Facial expressions - smiles, frowns, biting lips

Voice related behavior – tone, pitch, intensity, intonation, rate, emphasis, pauses, fluency, silence

Observable autonomic physiological responses - breathing, rash, blushing, paleness, pupil dilation

Physical characteristics - fitness, height, weight, complexion

General appearance - grooming, dress

Listening involves both verbal and non-verbal communication. Non-verbal communication passes along much more information than verbal communication. Pay attention to the non-verbal clues which you present in communication.

Skills from LEAD LAB

1. Paraphrase – What I hear you saying is… Say the message they are conveying without parroting them.
2. Perception check – I think you are saying this… I perceive that you are feeling this…
3. Behavior description – Your words are saying this…but your behavior is saying this…

    > One of the most non-judgmental ways to communicate a behavior description is to phrase your communication in this manner.
    > When you - describe the behavior,
    > I feel - name the feeling,
    > Because - explain why their behavior makes you feel that way.

4. Creative questions – When the person you are interacting with makes a statement, start asking questions about the information they have provided in that statement.

5. Story Listening - This is perhaps the greatest of all skills because it works on the psychodynamic level of the subconscious. As you talk with a person, listen to the free information they provide. Listen to the stories they tell you, no matter how brief those stories are. A story can be as brief as a single sentence. When a person has told you three stories, determine the common denominator in the three stories. It does not matter how unrelated the stories are, they will have a common denominator. I was teaching this skill one time and asked a woman in the class to tell me three stories. She gave me three one sentence stories. The first story was about her children. The second story was about her garden. The third story was about her aloneness. There was no common denominator. I realized that she had told me two stories about what gives her great joy. The third story was about her loneliness, and yet there was a lot of joy for God's divine grace in the loneliness. The stories express what is transpiring in the person's subconscious. If you listen the common denominator of the stories will provide you with the area of greatest need for which the person desires healing in his or her life.

6. Direct expression of feeling – When, seek to determine the emotion that the person is expressing in their words. They may even directly name that emotion. Also freely express and name your own feelings in communicating back to the person.

7. Neuro-Linguistics – Match the person's speech patterns - tone, cadence, vocabulary. Also match the person's non-verbals, body language, sitting position, etc. in responding to the person. In other words mimic the person.

8. Fogging – This is a mechanism for getting around the resistance and obstructions a person raises when you seek to minister to him or her. In fogging you agree with the part of a person's statement which you consider to be true and ignore that which may be blatantly false. For example: If the person starts complaining about fat people, just tell the

person, "Some people think I am fat. I agree that I weigh more than I desire. I can see where you might even think that I am fat." Then change the subject and discuss what you want to discuss.

9. Negative inquiry – If a person criticizes you, or another person, or some event, ask the person to explicitly describe and express what they dislike about the person or thing they are criticizing.

10. Polarities – listen for contradictions and opposites in a person's discourse. Do they talk about being lonely and then change the subject to a new relationship with a new friend? Do they tell you the world is round and then tell you the world is flat?

11. Life commandments – listen for the moral values and ethics which guide a person's life. Life commandments are mostly handed down from parents. My parents taught me to treat every person the same, no matter how young or old, pretty or ugly, rich or poor, educated or ignorant, talented or un-talented. You can learn something from everyone. Take advantage of what each person can teach you. I once led a youth group of four kids. Some of the kids had genius IQ's, while the pastor's daughter had an extremely low IQ. The pastor told me his daughter had taught his family to love and love unconditionally. Within a few months I knew that in spite of the daughter's limitation, she was indeed a person who spread and taught love. She had a real God given gift of love.

Practice listening to another person. Use these forms of communication in your practice. Learn to use these communication skills so effectively that they become innate behavior for you when you listen to other people (LEAD Lab pp. 92-99).

Practice! Practice! Practice! It makes all the difference.
You will not learn to listen unless you practice.

Types of Difficult People

There are three main types of difficult people which we will encounter in our relationships.

Turtles hide in their shell when you try to talk with them. You must pry these people out of their shell. They frequently hide and do the "poor me" routine. They will reject you in order to end the relationship with you before they get hurt. Counter their perception of themselves with your perception of them. Show them your view of the reality in which they live. Do not accept what they present to you as their view of reality. Whatever you do, do not let them drive you away and destroy the relationship you have with them.

Skunks spray all over you when you try to talk with them. They will try to drive you away by sabotaging the relationship between you. The will be spiteful, hateful, and mean. They will also reject you in order to end the relationship with you before they get hurt. Whatever you do, do not let them drive you away and destroy the relationship you have with them. Ignore the spray and enjoy the stink.

Posers wear a mask of a persona which they wish to project. They will not take off the mask for anyone including themselves. They will not let you inside of their defenses. It is not uncommon for them to put up a pseudo wall that holds you at arm's length and prevents you from entering their world. All they give you is a fake persona, and they never let you see the real person.

To minister to these people you must ignore the fake persona and walk through their wall. Call them out and tell them you want to see the real person. Do not accept the fake person that they present to you (LEAD Lab pp. 92-99).

Learning Styles

Before you can communicate with people it is important to understand how they learn. Now we will begin to look at how different learning styles provide you challenges and opportunities for more effective relationships.

There are a variety of learning styles. Most people use a blend of styles. One style may be more dominant within the blend used by each person. The more learning styles you develop proficiency in using, the better you become at learning. Because of the differences in learning styles, we need to learn to perceive the dominant learning style of the person to whom we are ministering and work with that person in his or her dominant learning style.

Sensory Based Learning Styles

Much of our learning ability is based on an orientation to our senses. Whichever of our senses is strongest determines what our learning style is. These senses may also blend together to form our unique learning style.

1. Visual learners - these learners remember pictures and graphical representations of data and information.
2. Auditory learners – remember what they hear. They remember sounds and conversations.
3. Kinesthetic learners – deals with bodily movement. They remember what they touch and manipulate. They need to form or trace objects with their hands.
4. They learn best through interaction with their physical world.
5. They are very sensitive to movement.
6. They readily pick up on non-verbal gestures.
7. Olfactory Learners – need to smell. They remember fragrances and aromas.

Each of us has a different learning style. It is important to know what our learning style is. It is also important to learn about all of the other learning styles. We each will have a strong tendency to minister in our own personal learning style. This frequently leads us to ignore the dominant learning styles of the person to whom we are seeking to teach or to minister. This results in some of our attempts at listening being misunderstood or rejected. This is not because our person did not listen. It is because we minister in a learning style from which the other person has difficulty learning.

I once had a boss who was an auditory learner. He had the ability to recall entire verbal conversations from years ago. He would frequently give long verbal sets of instructions about troubleshooting very complex problems. He would give the instructions so fast there was no way to remember them, or to write them down. All of the people he supervised were visual or kinesthetic learners. It was almost impossible to complete his instructions. At best we would remember three of four things he said and try to complete them. Then we would go back and ask what else he wanted done. If he would have explained things in our personal learning style, he would have had much happier employees. We would have been more productive. He would not have needed to teach us the same things over and over again.

The best learning can occur when we attempt to appeal to the different sensory levels of learning. One of the reasons Louis L'amour was such a great western writer was his descriptions of his characters' surroundings. He described the dirt, flowers, trees, train, geography, mountains, streams, horses, and towns. When he gave a description you could see it, hear it, touch it, smell it, and taste it.

We should do the same in our discussions. Describe the places, events, characters and ideas in the Bible; make people see, hear, taste, touch, and smell all the aspects about which you teach.

Whole Learners – These are those who must understand the whole picture before they know how all the parts fit together. It is critical that they be given a framework from which to explore the parts that are presented.

How would you like to be a person who is a whole learner trying to understand the Bible for the very first time? The Bible has a lot of books and a lot of chapters. It has a lot of different accounts of different people's lives. It has historical accounts of events in the epochs of human history. How do you fit them all together? How do you understand them as a whole?

In teaching you only give bits and pieces of the Bible at a time. You will need to present to your audience that the Bible may be many books, but it is only one message. It may give many stories, but those stories are accounts of human lives and human history that fit somewhere on the timeline from the beginning to the end of the account of mankind upon this earth.

To really help whole learners you need to present to them the whole picture. Demonstrate to them that the Bible encompasses the whole timeline of human history. It starts with the creation of the world before the existence of mankind. It climaxes with the crucifixion and resurrection of Jesus Christ as the sacrifice for our sins. It ends with the return of Christ to rule the earth in the millennial kingdom and with God creating the new heavens and the new earth. The Bible not only fits on the timeline of history; each of its books fits into different segments of that timeline. Also the Bible may be sub-sectioned into units. The Pentateuch, historical books, poetry, wisdom and prophets comprise the Old Testament. The gospels, acts, epistles, and apocryphal revelation comprise the New Testament. Help your whole learners to understand that what you preach is a part of the whole message of salvation. For global learners you will also need to explain why the Bible is structured the way it is. Help them to understand that the book of Genesis is about God selecting one man and wife from who to develop his chosen people as a nation. Help them to see that the book of Leviticus is about health. It covers physical, social, relational, and spiritual health. It teaches that if you let God make you holy, He will give you health in all aspects of your life. Help them to see that the reason Jesus died on the cross was part of a plan so that you could have a relationship with God and live a holy life. Show them that God has a plan for the end of this world. In that plan God is never defeated and God is clearly victorious in the end. As a part of that plan God protects his people the church, and he brings his people the Jews to recognize their Messiah.

If you cannot explain the whys of the Bible, you can never expect your audience to understand the Bible as a whole.

Whole or Global learners are also referred to as Macro learners. To determine whether a person is a Macro learner or a Micro learner, ask this question. When they put a puzzle together do they assemble the border first or the inner pieces first? If they assemble the border first, they are seeking a structure to understand the whole. They are Macro Learners. If they put the pieces together first, they are micro learners. They will understand the whole when everything is completed.

Types of Learners:
1. Sensory Learners: If you rely too much on sensing, you can tend to prefer what is familiar, and concentrate on facts you know instead of being innovative and adapting to new situations. Seek out opportunities to learn theoretical information, and then bring in facts to support or negate these theories.
2. Intuitive Learners: If you rely too much on intuition, you risk missing important details which can lead to poor decision-making and problem solving. Force yourself to learn facts or memorize data that will help you defend or criticize a theory or procedure you are working with. You may need to slow down and look at detail you would otherwise typically skim.
3. Visual Learners: If you concentrate more on pictorial or graphical information than on words, you put yourself at a distinct disadvantage because verbal and written information is still the main preferred choice for delivery of information. Practice your note taking and seek out opportunities to explain information to others using words.
4. Verbal Learners: When information is presented in diagrams, sketches, flow charts, and so on, it is designed to be understood quickly. If you can develop your skills in this area, you can significantly reduce time spent learning and absorbing information. Look for opportunities to learn through audio-visual presentations (such as CD-ROM and Webcasts). When making notes, group information according to concepts and then create visual links with arrows going to and from them. Take every opportunity you can to create charts, tables, and diagrams.
5. Active Learners: If you act before you think, you are apt to make hasty and potentially ill-informed judgments. You need

to concentrate on summarizing situations, and take time to sit by yourself to digest information you have been given before jumping in and discussing it with others.

6. Reflective Learners: If you think too much you risk doing nothing. Ever. There comes a time when a decision has to be made or an action taken. Involve yourself in group decision-making whenever possible and try to apply the information you have in as practical a manner as possible.

7. Sequential Learners: When you break things down into small components, you are often able to dive right into problem solving. This seems to be advantageous but can often be unproductive. Force yourself to slow down and understand why you are doing something and how it is connected to the overall purpose or objective. Ask yourself how your actions are going to help you in the long run. If you can't think of a practical application for what you are doing, then stop and do some more "big picture" thinking.

8. Global Learners: If grasping the big picture is easy for you, then you can be at risk of wanting to run before you can walk. You see what is needed but may not take the time to learn how best to accomplish it. Take the time to ask for explanations, and force yourself to complete all problem-solving steps before coming to a conclusion or making a decision. If you can't explain what you have done and why, then you may have missed critical details.

Teaching

As a part of relationships we also seek to teach our prospective mate about ourselves. We do this both by listening and teaching. Most listening and teaching today focuses on the cognitive and behavioral levels. Teaching by nature is cognitive. It seeks to bring about changes in people's lives by teaching people new concepts or reinforcing old concepts. Cognitive teaching is good. People have to understand that there is something better for their lives before they can aspire to change their lives. If the cognitive approach by itself was sufficient, reading the Bible or a self-help book would be sufficient to bring about great changes in people's lives.

Some teaching may also be behavioral in nature. Behavior is teaching by presenting "ought to's with how to's." In other words this form of teaching tells people of the changes they need to make in their lives and also tells them how to make those changes. In the psychological world, behavior therapy is known to get excellent short term results. Long lasting results, however, are much less substantiated. As soon as people face another traumatic time in their life, they may lose all of the gains they have achieved through behavior therapy. I consider this to be equally true of behavior teaching.

Affective teaching deals with people's emotions and attitudes. This level of teaching is also ineffective in and of itself. Affective teaching, however, is the gateway to the psychodynamic aspects of the human soul. It is when people are healed on the psychodynamic level that long term results are truly achieved in therapy. I believe this is also true of teaching. I believe this is why Jesus taught in parables. The parables formed metaphors which touched people on a psychodynamic level.

It is when we begin to put all three levels of teaching together in our presentation of ourselves to our prospective mate we are able to present the clearest expression of who we are.

APPENDIX F

Conflict Resolution

1. Bring all parties together at a neutral location and a neutral time.
2. Summarize why the parties are gathered and the goal of the meeting.
3. Insist that all parties will get an equal hearing.
4. Talk about the situation without applying people's names to events. Keep the issues impersonal and objective.
5. Talk individually to each person about their perspective and perception of the situation.
6. Force each person individually to discuss their feelings about the situation, issues and events which have transpired.
7. Value the feelings expressed. Let people vent if necessary, but keep it impersonal.
8. Seek to gather all the options for resolution of the conflict and present them to the parties involved.
9. Bring the parties to choose the three best solutions to resolve the conflict.
10. Have the parties involved discuss their perceptions of the solutions presented and chosen. Force each person in the gathering to discuss their feelings about the choices.
11. Ask all the parties involved to choose the single best solution to resolve the conflict. Determine how the solution will be implemented. Determine each party's role in implementing the solution.

12. Again ask each individual to present their feelings about the chosen solution and its method of implementation.
13. Ask each person how they feel about and like the proposed solution and implementation.
14. Deal with any ill feelings towards the proposed solution and implementation.
15. A decision without the expression of feelings is a non-decision.
16. *(Swick, Tim. Unpublished)*

Perhaps the most important aspect of healing relationships is Conflict Resolution.

There are only three possible solutions to any conflict.
Lose – Lose
Win – Lose
Win - Win
Even a truce is a lose- lose resolution.

When performing conflict resolution, always address the issue directly. Avoiding the issue only builds a bigger bomb. It allows wounds to fester and grow.

Conflict is always a response to a perceived threat. It is not about the issues. It is about the perceptions a person holds. Conflict resolution requires strong objectivity. It requires a strong check on your emotions. It also provides opportunities for growth.

BIBLIOGRAPHY

Amato, P. & Booth, A. (1997). *A Generation At Risk. Growing Up in an Era of Family Upheaval.* Cambridge, MA: Harvard University Press. http://www.azquotes.com/quote/1264746

Axinn, W.G. & Thornton, A. (1992). The relationship between cohabitation and divorce:

Selectivity or casual influence? *Demography, 29,* 357-374.

Baker, Maureen & Elizabethe, Vivienne. (2013).Tying the Knot: The impact of formalization after long-term cohabitation, Department of Sociology, *Journal of Family Studies 19*(3), 254–266.,University of Auckland, Auckland, New Zealand.

Baldassare, Mark & Feller, Susan. (2009). *Cultural variation in Personal Space: Theories, Methods, and Evidence, Ethos,* 481-503.

Barna Group. (2009). New Marriage and Divorce Statistics Released. Retrieved from https://www.barna.org/barna-update/article/15-familykids/42-new-marriage-and-divorce-statistics-released#. VRf-QuFRK5R.

Barth, Markus. (1960). *Commentary on Ephesians 4-6.* Garden City, NY: Doubleday and Company, Inc.
ISBN 0-385-0837-9

BBC, Science: Human body & Mind, The Science of Flirting. (2014, September 17). Retrieved from http://www.bbc.co.uk/science/hottopics/love/flirting.shtm.

Boisvert, Jean Marie, Landouceur, Robert, Beaudry, Madeline, Freeston, Mark H., Turgeon, Lyse, Tardif, Chantal, Roussy, Alain, & Loranger, Michael. (1995). Perception of marital problems and their prevention by Qubeck young adults. *Journal of Genetic Psychology* (156)1, 33-44.

Bringle, Robert G., Winnick, Terri, & Rydell, Robert J. (2013, April-June). The Prevalence and Nature of Unrequited Love. SAGE Open, 1–15.

Berkowitz, M. (2002). The science of character education. In W. Damon (Ed.), *Bringing in a new era in character education*, 43-63. Stanford, CA: Hoover Institute Press.

Bible Study on Character – Integrity. Retrieved from http://www.swapmeetdave.com/Bible/Integrity.htm.

Bible Study, Finding the Right Mate. Retrieved from http://kentcrockett.com/biblestudies/rightmate.htm.

The Biblical Perspective on Character Development. Retrieved from http://my.cbn.com/livingbythebook/display.php?topicid=1062&id=56&val=296.

Brooks, Carol. (2002). The Bible and Premarital Sex. Retrieved from http://www.inplainsite.org/html/premarital_sex_and_the_bible.html#PreMar-13.

Burriss, Robert. (2014, July 24). Human Mate Choice as the Psychologists See It. Retrieved from http://www.lascap.de/Downloads/Human%20mate%20choice%20as%20the%20psychologist%20views%20it.pdf.

Browne, Angela & Finkelhor, David. (1986). Impact of child sexual abuse: A review of the research. *Psychological Bulletin*, (99)1, 66, American Psychological Association.

Chandra, Anjani, Mosher, William D., Copen, Casey & Sionean, Catlainn. (2011, March 3). Sexual Behavior, Sexual Attraction, and Sexual Identity in the United States: Data From the 2006–2008 National Survey of Family Growth National Health Statistics Report, 36.

Chapman, Alan. (2006-2013). Erikson's psychosocial development theory. Retrieved from http://www.businessballs.com/erik_erikson_psychosocial_theory.htm

Chapman, Gary. (1995). *The Five Love Languages: How to Express Heartfelt Commitment to Your Mate.* Chicago, IL: Northfield Publishing. ISBN 1-881273-15-6

Cheddie, Denver. (2008). Does God have a spouse prepared for everyone? Retrieved from http://www.bibleissues.org/spouse1.html.

Clancy, Tom. (1988). *The Cardinal in the Kremlin*, Berkley, CA.: G.P. Putnam's Sons.

Cunningham, William R. (1999). The Christian Marriage Part 1: The Definition. Retrieved from http://www.pursuingthetruth.org/studies/files/marriage2.htm.

Cunningham, William R. (2000, March). The Christian Marriage Series Part 2: Finding Your Mate, Revision 1. Retrieved from http://www.pursuingthetruth.org/studies/files/marriage2.htm.

Diamond. (2015, February 7). Retrieved from https://en.wikipedia.org/wiki/Diamond.

Dobbins, Richard, D. (2011). Winning The Battle For Your Marriage. Retrieved from http://www.drdobbins.com/guidelines-for-great-living/articles/winning-the-battle-for-your-marriage/.

Dawson, Patsy Rae. (1996). Male and Female: God's Genius! Retrieved from http://patsyraedawson.com/?page_id=231.

Dawson, Patsy Rae. (1997). Safe Sex: What They Don't Tell You. Retrieved from http://patsyraedawson.com/?page_id=962.

Dawson, Patsy Rae. (2011-2015). Why God's People Make the Best Lovers. Retrieved from http://patsyraedawson.com/?page_id=997.

Deffinbaugh, Bob. (2009, February 2). The Way of the Wise: Studies in the Book of Proverbs: The Qualities of a Godly Mate: Retrieved from http://bible.org/seriespage/qualities-godly-mate.

Demyan, Amy L. (2005). Gender, Gender Role Adherence, and Self Esteem in Long Term Mate Selection Preferences Among College Students, 7-29. College of Arts and Sciences of Ohio University.

Diem, Melissa. (n.d.). 7 Ways to Know He is Marriage Material. Retrieved from http://love.allwomenstalk.com/ways-to-know-he-is-marriage-material/.

Dobbins, Richard D. (2011). Winning the Battle for Your Marriage. Retrieved from http://www.drdobbins.com/guidelines-for-great-living/articles/winning-the-battle-for-your-marriage/.

Doris, John M. (2002). Lack of Character: Personality and Moral Behavior, Cambridge University Press Cambridge, UK.

Driscoll, Mark. (n.d.). Sex, a Study of the Good Bits from Song of Solomon. Retrieved from http://www.cerm.info/documents/mark_driscoll_sex_sermon.html.

Dunn, Ryan L., Fine, Mark A. & Kurdek, Lawrence A. (1992). Premarital Relationships Adjustment and Its Relations to Religiosity and Sexual Involvement. *Journal of Psychology and Theology*, (20)4, 356-366.

Edersheim, Alfred E. (1883). Life and times of Jesus the Messiah: New Updated Edition (1893). Hendrickson Pub.

Edwards, Jane, (2011). *Music Therapy and Parent-Infant Bonding*. Oxford University Press, Inc., NY.

Egan, Gerard. (2006). Egan, Gerard (1994). *The Skilled Helper: A Problem Management approach to Helping: 7ᵗʰ edition*. Brooks/Cole Publishing Company. Pacific Grove, California.

Emerge Ministries. (n.d.). *Foundations of Marital Therapy*, 10.

Erber, Ralph & Erber, Maureen Wang. (2011). *Intimate Relationships, Issues, Theories, and Research*. Boston,

Pearson Education Inc.

Erikson's Stages of Psychosocial Development. (2015, February 5). Retrieved from http://en.wikipedia.org/wiki/Erikson%27s_stages_of_psychosocial_development.

Eyrich, Howard A. (1978). *Three to Get Ready: A Premarital Counseling Manual*. Grand Rapids, Michigan: Baker Book House Company.

Fagan, Patrick. (2010). The culture of monogamy vs the culture of polyamory. Retrieved from http://www.cpportal.org/k/news/view/434397/383320/the-culture-of-monogamy-vs-the-culture-of-polyamory.html.

Fagan, Patrick F. (2007). Virgins Make the Best Valentines. Retrieved from http://www.heritage.org/research/commentary/2007/02/virgins-make-the-best-valentines

Fehr, Beverly. (1987). In Moss, B.F. & Schwebel, A.I. (1993). Defining Intimacy in Romantic Relationships, *Family Relations, 42*, 31-37.

Feldhahn, Shaunti. (2004). *For Women Only*. Sisters, Oregon: Multnomah Publishers INC.

Feldhahn, Shaunti. (2006). *For Men Only*. Sisters, Oregon: Multnomah Publishers INC.

Finkelhor, David. (1990). Early and long-term effects of child sexual abuse: An update. *Professional Psychology: Research and Practice, 21*(5), 325, American Psychological Association.

Finkelhor, David, Hotaling, Gerald, Lewis, I.A., & Smith, Christine. (1990). Child abuse & neglect: Sexual abuse in a national survey of adult men and women: Prevalence, characteristics, and risk factors. *Child Abuse & Neglect, 14*(1), 19-28.

First Things First, What You Should Know About Living Together. (2014, August). Retrieved from http://firstthings.org/what-you-should-know-about-living-together.

Firo-B Progfile Diagram. (2008, April 17). Retrieved from http://www.mdshongkong.com/documents/FIRO-B_Profile.pdf.

Fitzpatrick, Mary Ann. (1988). *Between husbands and wives*. Newbury Park: Sage.

Flemming, J.S. (2006). Piaget, Kohlberg, Gilligan, and Others on Moral Development. Retrieved from http://swppr.org/Textbook/Ch%207%20Morality.pdf

Fletcher, Elizabeth (2006). Money and Marriage in the Bible. Reterieved from http://www.womeninthebible.net/money_marriage.htm

Floyd, Frank J. & Wasner, Guenter H. (1994). Social Exchange, Equity, and Commitment: Structural Equation Modeling of Dating Relationships, *Journal of Family Psychology 8*(1), 55-73.

Follette, Victoria M., Polusny, Melissa, Bechtel, Anne E., & Naugle, Amy E. (1996). Cumulative Trauma: The Impact of Child Sexual Abuse, Adult Sexual Assault, and Spouse Abuse, *Journal of Traumatic Stress, 9*(1).

Foust, Michael. (2008, March 26). "Living together" before marriage a statistical risk, retrieved from http://www.bpnews.net/27699.

Fowler, James W. (1981). *Stages of Faith*. New York, New York: Harper Collins Publishers.

Fox, Kate. (2016). Social Issues Research Centre Guide to Flirting: What social science can tell you about flirting and how to do it. Retrieved from http://www.sirc.org/publik/flirt.pdf.

Gerrard, Meg, Breda, Cheri, & Gibbons, Frederick X. (1990). Gender Effects in Couples' Sexual Decision Making and Contraceptive Use, *Journal of Applied Psychology, 20*(6), 449-464.

Gilligan, Carol. (1982). *In a Different Voice: Psychological Theory and Women's Development.* Cambridge, MA: Harvard University Press.

Givertz, Michelle. (2011, June 22). The Secret to Finding Your "Perfect" Mate, Know Thyself, The Interpersonal Explorer. Retrieved from http://www.psychologytoday.com/blog/the-interpersonal-explorer/201106/the-secret-finding-your-perfect-mate.

Glueck, Nelson. (1967). *Hesed in the Bible.* Cincinnati, OH: Hebrew Union College Press.

Gordon, Lori H. (1969). Intimacy: The Art of Relationships: How relationships are sabotaged by hidden Expectations. Retrieved from http://psychologytoday.com/articles/199309/intimacy-the-art-relationships? page=3.

Gottman, John M. (1994). What predicts divorce? The relationship between marital processes and marital outcomes. Hillsdale, NJ: Lawrence Erlbaum.

Grover, K.J., Russell, C.S., Schumm, W.R., & Paff-Bergen, L.A. (1985). Mate Selection Processes and Marital Satisfaction. Family Relations, 34, 383-386.

Hadjistavropoulos & Genest. (1994).The underestimation of the role of physical attractiveness in dating preferences: Ignorance or taboo? *Canadian Journal of Behavioral Science, (26)*2, 298-318.

Harley, Willard F., Jr. (1986). *His Needs, Her Needs: Building an Affair-Proof Marriage.* Old Tappan, NJ: Fleming H. Revell.

Hatfield, E. (1995). Self-esteem and passionate love relationships. In G. G. Brannigan & M. R. Merrens (Eds.),
The social psychologists: Research and adventures, 129-144. New York: McGraw-Hill.

Henry, Jermaine, Helm Jr., Herbert W. & Cruz, Natasha. (2013). Mate Selection: Gender and Generational Differences, *North American Journal of Psychology, 15,* No. 1, pp. 63-70.

Hodges-Simeon, Carolyn R., Gaulin, Steven J.C., & Puts David A. (2011). Voice Correlates of Mating Success in Men: Examining "Contests" versus "Mate Choice" Modes of Sexual Selection. *Archive of Sexual Behavior, 40,* 551-557.

Hoffman, Terry. (May 2004). Dating Disasters and Faulty Mate Selection: There Is a Better Way!
Retrieved from http://www.ucg.org/relationships/dating-disasters-and-faulty-mate-selection-there-better-way/.

Homiak, Marcia. (2003). Moral Character. Stanford Encyclopedia of Philosophy. Retrieved from http://philosophy.csusb.edu/~tmoody/Moral%20Character.htm.

Hurt, Bruce. (2013). The Covenant Between Jonathan and David. Retrieved from http://preceptaustin.org/covenant_the_exchanging_of_robes.htm.

Intimate Relationship. (2015). Retrieved from http://en.wikipedia.org/wiki/Intimate_relationship.

Janus, S. S. & Janus, C.C. (1993). *The Janus Report on Human Sexuality.* New York: Wiley Publishers.

Jean Piaget. (2015, February 13). Retrieved from https://en.wikipedia.org/wiki/Jean_Piaget.

Joy, Donald M. (1985). *Bonding: Relationships in the Image of God.* Nappanee, IN: Evangel Publishing House.

Joy, Donald M. (1986). *Re-Bonding: Preventing and Restoring Damaged Relationships.* Dallas, TX: Word Publishing.

Joy, Donald M., Ed. (1983). *Moral Development Foundations: Judeo-Christian Alternatives to Piaget/Kohlberg.* Nashville, TN: Abingdon Press.

Kelly, E.L. & Conley, J.J. (1987). Personality and compatibility: A perspective analysis of marital stability and marital satisfaction. *Journal of Personality and Social Psychology, 58,* 27-40.

Kelly, Maura & Dutton, Judy. (2009, July 14). Four Flirting Fun Facts--With Research to Back Them Up!

Retrieved from http://www.marieclaire.com/sex-love/a3349/science-flirting-sex-body-language/.

Kenrick, D.T., Neuberg, S.L., Zierk, K. l., & Krones, J. M. (1994). Evolution and social cognition: Contrast effects as a function of sex, dominance and physical attractiveness. *Personality and Social Psychology, (20)*2, 210-217.

Kittle, Gerhard & Friedrich, Gerhard. (1972). *Theological Dictionary of the New Testament, 8*, 39-46. Grand Rapids, MI: William B. Eerdmans Publishing Company.

Kittle, Gerhard & Friedrich, Gerhard. (1972). *Theological Dictionary of the New Testament, 6*, 562-566. Grand Rapids, MI: William B. Eerdmans Publishing Company.

Kurdek, I.A. (1993). Predicting Marital Dissolution: A 5-Year Prospective Longitudinal study of Newlywed Couples. *Journal of Personality and Social Psychology, 64*, 221-242.

Kohlberg's Moral Stages. Retrieved from http://www.haverford.edu/psych/ddavis/p109g/kohlberg.stages.html.

Kohlberg's Theory of Moral Development. (2012, January 20). Retrieved from http://www.psychologynoteshq.com/kohlbergstheory/.

Kowalski, Robin M. (1993). Interpreting behaviors in mixed gender encounters: Effects of social anxiety and gender. *Journal of Social and Clinical Psychology, (12)*3, 239-247.

Larson, A.S. & Olson, D.H. (1989). Prediction Marital Satisfaction using PREPARE: A replication study. *Journal of Marital and Family Therapy, 15*(3), 311-322.

Lawrence Kohlberg. Retrieved from https://en.wikipedia.org/wiki/Lawrence_Kohlberg.

Levinger, G., & Snoek, D. (1972). *Attraction in relationship: A new look at interpersonal attraction.* Morristown, NJ: General Learning Press.

Lichi, Donald. (1995). Emerge Ministries, Ashland Theological Seminary, class lectures.

Livingston, G. Herbert. (1974). *The Pentateuch in its Cultural Environment.* Grand Rapids, MI: Baker Bookhouse.

Malchiodi, Cathy A. (1998). *Understanding Children's Drawings,* 132-160. NY, NY: The Gilford Press.

Male Mind Survey Challenges Popular Attitudes, AskMen. Retrieved from http://www.divinecaroline.com/22078/79206-male-mind-survey-challenges-popular.

Maliki, Agnes Ebi. (2009). Determinants of Mate Selection Choice among University Students in South-South Zone of Nigeria. *EDO Journal of Counseling, 2(2).* Retrieved from http://www.ajol.info/index.php/ejc/article/viewFile/60856/49066/

Markman, Howard J., Stanley, Scott M. & Blumberg, Susan L. (2001). *Fighting for Your Marriage.* San Jose, CA: Josey-Bass: A Wiley Imprint.

Maslow's Hierarchy of Needs. (2014, December 24). Retrieved from http://en.wikipedia.org/wiki/Maslow's_hierarchy_of_needs.

McAllister, Dawson. (1997). What are the Biblical guidelines for dating relationships? Retrieved from www.christiananswers.net/q-dml/dml-y006.html.

McCahill, T., Meyer, L.C., & Fischman, A. (1979). The Aftermath of Rape, Lexington Books.

McIlhaney Joe S., M.D. & McKissic-Bush, Freda MD. (2008). Hooked: New Science on How Casual Sex is Affecting Our Children. Chicago, IL: Norfield Publishing.

Miller, Jean Baker. (1976). Toward a Psychology of Women. 2nd Ed. Boston, MA: Beacon Press.

McCroskey, James C. & McCain, Thomas A. (1974). The measurement of interpersonal attraction.

Speech Monographs, 41(3), 261-266. Retrieved from http://www.jamescmccroskey.com/publications/57.htm.

McDowell, Josh & Lewis, Paul. (1980). Givers, Takers, and Other Kinds of Lovers. Wheaton, IL: Tyndale House Publishers.

Monsour, Michael. (2013). Journal of social and personal relationships: Meanings of Intimacy in Cross- and Same-Sex Friendships. Retrieved from http://spr.sagepub.com/content/9/2/277.short).

Moral Development. Retrieved from http://swppr.org/Textbook/Ch%207%20Morality.pdf.

Morris, Desmond. (1967). The Naked Ape; A Zoologist's Study of the Human Animal. New York, NY: McGraw-Hill.

Morris, Grantley. (n.d.). When is Sex Before Marriage Acceptable? Premarital Sex Re-examined. Retrieved from http://www.net-burst.net/singles/premarital.htm.

Moss, B.F. & Schwebel, A.I. (1993). Defining Intimacy in Romantic Relationships, *Family Relations, 42*, 31-37.

Motivation and mate-seeking. (2010, December 14). Retrieved from http://en.wikiversity.org/wiki/Motivation_and_emotion/ Textbook/Motivation/Mate-seeking_behaviour. These concepts are part of the Motivation and Emotion textbook.

Murashko, Alex. (2014, May 16). Author Debunks Myths About Divorce Rates, Including of Churchgoers (Shaunti Feldhahn: The Good News About Marriage), retrieved from http://www. christianpost.com/news/author-debunks-myths-about-divorce-rates-including-of-churchgoers-119843/.

Murphy, Ed. (2003). *The Handbook on Spiritual Warfare.* Nashville, TN: Thomas Nelson.

Mullen, P.E., Martina, J.L., Anderson, J.C., Romansa, S.E., & Herbisona, G.P. (1996). *Child Abuse & Neglect. (20)*1, 7–21

Newcomb, M.D. & Bentler, P.M. (1981). Marital breakdown. In S. Duck & R. Gilmour (Eds.). *Personal Relationships: Vol. 3. Personal Relationships in Disorder,* 57-94. New York: Academic Press.

Nichols, William C. (1988). *Marital Therapy: An Integrative Approach.* New York, NY: The Gilford Press.

Nock, S.L. (1995). A Comparison of Marriage and Cohabiting Relationships, *Journal of Family Issues, 16*, 53-76.

Nucci, Larry. (1997). Moral Development and Character Formation. In Walberg, H. J. & Haertel, G. D. (1997). *Psychology and educational practice*, 127-157. Berkeley: MacCarchan. Retrieved from http:// tigger.uic.edu/~lnucci/MoralEd/articles/nuccimoraldev.html.

Oswalt, John. (1977). History of Israel, Asbury Theological Seminary Lecture.

Pankau, Lisa. (2010, October 2). Beyond Seduction: Loving without Limits. Retrieved from http://beyondseductionbook.com/content/science-love-arthur-arun.

Penner, Clifford L & Penner, Joyce J. (1981). *A Guide to Sexual Fulfillment: The Gift of Sex.* Dallas, TX: Word Publishing.

Penner, Clifford L & Penner, Joyce J. (1994). *Getting your Sex Life Off to a Great Start.* Dallas, TX: Word Publishing.

Peterson, Christopher & Seigman, Martin E.P. (2004). Character strengths and Virtues: A Handbook and Classification, Oxford University Press, N.Y., N.Y.

Peplau, Letitia Anne, Hill Charles T., & Rubin, Zick. (1993). Sex role attitudes in dating and marriage: A 15 year follow-up of the Boston couples study. *Journal of Social Issues, 49*(3), 31-52.

Pfleiderer, Joanne. (2008).Teens Have Positive But Changing Views of Marriage. Retrieved from http://www.mathematica-mpr.com/Press%20Releases/teensviewsmarriage11-08.asp.

Pierce, Tyra & Hewitt, Jay. (1993). Gender differences in sexualized perceptions of others. Perceptual and Motor Skills, 78, 1168-1170.

Polusny, Melissa A. & Follette, Victoria M. (1995). Long-term correlates of child sexual abuse: Theory and review of the empirical literature. *Applied and Preventive Psychology* (4)3, 143–166.

Prince, Derek. (2006). How to Expel Demons, Break Curses and Release Blessings. Bloomington, MN: Chosen Books.

RBC Ministries. Choosing a Marriage Partner. Section 13B, Contemporary Social Issues. Retrieved from http://www.inplainsite.org/html/choosing_a_marriage_partner.

Rudd, Steve. The Three Stage Ritual of Bible Marriages retrieved from http://www.bible.ca/marriage/ancient-jewish-three-stage-weddings-and-marriage-customs-ceremony-in-the-bible.htm.

Schaefer, Charles E. & Drews, Athena A. (2014). *The Therapeutic Powers of Play.* Hoboken, NJ: John Wiley and Sons, Inc.

Scharff, David E. & Scharff, Jill Savege. (1991). *Object Relations Couple Therapy.* Northvale, NJ: Jason Aronson Inc.

Scherer, Cynthia & Kemp, Athina. (2015). The Core Issue: Intimacy. Retrieved from http://www.desert-alchemy.com/txt/intimacy. html.

Schutz, William C. (1958). *FIRO: A Three Dimensional Theory of Interpersonal Behavior.* New York, NY: Holt, Rinehart, & Winston.

Science, flirting, sex, body language. (2009, July 14). Retrieved from http://www.marieclaire.com/sex-love/dating-blog/science-flirting-sex-body-language.

Segal, Jeanne & Smith, Melinda. (2010). Playful Communication Skills: Using Laughter and Play in Relationships. Retrieved from http://www.helpguide.org/mental/eq8_conflict_resolution.htm.

Shaver, Phillip R. & Hazan, Cindy. (1988). A Biased Overview of the study of Love. *Journal of Social and Personal Relationships, 5,* 473-501.

Siegel, Judith. (1991). Analysis of Projective Identification: an Object Relations approach to Marital Treatment. *Clinical Social Work Journal, 19(1)*, 71-81.

Silverman, Amy B., Reinherz, Helen Z., & Giaconia, Rose M. (1996, August). The long-term sequelae of child and adolescent abuse: A longitudinal community study. *Child Abuse & Neglect, 20(8)*, 709–723.

Smicklas, Monica. (1995). Cohabitation. Unpublished paper for the Master of Arts in Pastoral Counseling at Ashland Theological Seminary.

Sol, Mateo. (2016). (Loner Wolf) Body Language: Personal Space retrieved from http://lonerwolf.com/body-language-personal-space/ Last updated 2016

Sorenson, Kelly A., Russell, Shauna M., Harkness, Daniel J., & Harvey, John H. (1993). Account-Making, Confiding, and Coping with the Ending of a Close Relationship. *Journal of Social Behavior and Personality, 8(1)*, 73-86.

Sprecher, Susan & Duck, Steve. (1994). Sweet Talk: The importance of perceived communication for romantic and friendship attraction experienced during a get acquainted date. *Personality and Social Psychology Bulletin, 20(4)*, 391-400.

Staples, Jason A. (2010, May 5). Dowry and Bride Price Are Not the Same Thing. Ethics, Sexuality & Family Sociology retrieved from http://www.jasonstaples.com/sociology/dowry-and-bride-price-are-not-the-same-thing.

Stapleton, Jean & Bright, Richard. (1976). *Equal Marriage*. Nashville, TN: Abingdon Press.

Steed, Levita & McLand, Kelly. (1982). In Moss, B.F. & Schwebel, A.I. (1993). Defining Intimacy in Romantic Relationships. *Family Relations, 42*, 31-37.

Stenberg, R.J. (1986). A Triangular Theory of Love, *Psychological Review, 93*, 119-135.

Thomas, Caitlin. (2015, February 13). Society Commentary, 5 Facts About Cohabitation You May Not Know. Retrieved from http://dailysignal.com/2015/02/13/5-facts-cohabitation-may-not-know/?utm_source=facebook&utm_medium=social&utm_campaign=thf02132015.

Tissier, L.L. (1993). The Pastoral Relationship Between Church and Co-habitees. *Theology, 96*, 468-476.

Thomas, Kenneth & Kilmann, Ralph. (1978). Comparison of Four Instruments Measuring Conflict Behavior. *Psychological Reports, 42*, 1139-1142.

Thompson, David. (1979). God in the Box. Sermon at Asbury Theological Seminary.

Thomson, E. & Colella, U. (1992). Cohabitation and Marital Stability: Quality or Commitment? *Journal of Marriage and the Family, 54*, 259-267.

Townsend, John Marshall & Roberts, Lawrence W. (1992). Gender Differences in Mate Preference Among Law Students: Divergence and Convergence of Criteria. *The Journal of Psychology, 127*(5), 507-528.

Trobish, Walter. (1971). *I Married You*. San Francisco, CA: Harper and Row Publishers.

Trumbull, Henry Clay. (1975). *The Blood Covenant*. Kirkwood, MO: Impact Books.

United Church of God. (2010-2015). Bible Study Guides: Lesson: Preparing for Marriage: Before You Say "I Do." Retrieved from http://www.freebiblestudyguides.org/bible-answers/preparing-for-marriage-before-you-say-i-do.htm.

United Church of God. (2002, December 7). Choosing a Mate. Retrieved from http://www.ucg.org/sermon/choosing-mate/.

Unknown, Loner Wolf.

Unknown. (2014, September 17). BBC, Science: Human Body & Mind, The Science of Flirting. Retrieved from http://www.bbc.co.uk/science/hottopics/love/flirting.shtml.

Unknown, Bible Study on Character – Integrity. Retrieved from http://www.swapmeetdave.com/Bible/Integrity.htm.

United Church of God. (2010-2015). Bible Study Guides: Lesson: Preparing for Marriage: Before You Say "I Do." Retrieved from http://www.freebiblestudyguides.org/bible-answers/preparing-for-marriage-before-you-say-i-do.htm.

Unknown. DivineCaroline. Male Mind Survey Challenges Popular Attitudes, AskMen. Retrieved from http://www.divinecaroline.com/22078/79206-male-mind-survey-challenges-popular.

Vessels, G., & Huitt, W. (2010, March 8). Moral and Character Development. Presented at the National Youth at Risk Conference, Savannah, GA. Retrieved from http://chiron.valdosta.edu/whuitt/brilstar/chapters/chardev.doc.

Vessels, G. (1998). *Character and community development: A school planning and teacher training handbook*. Westport, CT: Praeger Publishers.

Vessels, G., & Boyd, S. (1996). Public and constitutional support for character education. *NASSP Bulletin, 80*(579), 55-63.

Vogler, Carolyn. (1998). Money in the household: some underlying issues of power. The Sociological Review, 46(4), 687–713.

Waite, L. & Gallagher, M. (2000). *The Case for Marriage: Why Married People Are Happier, Healthier, and Better Off Financially.* New York: Doubleday.

Wheat, Ed & Wheat, Gaye. (1977). *Intended for Pleasure: Sex Technique and Sex Fulfillment in Christian Marriage.* Old Tappan, NJ: Fleming H. Revel Company.

Wikibooks, Relationships/How Men Select Women. (2014, June 24). Retrieved from http://en.wikibooks.org/wiki/Relationships/How_Men_Select_Women.

Wikibooks, Relationships/How Women Select Men. (2014, September 30). Retrieved from http://en.wikibooks.org/wiki/Relationships/How_Women_Select_Men.

Wilcox, W. Bradford & Cherlin, Andrew J. (2011). "The Marginalization of Marriage in Middle America." Center on Children and Families at Brookings Brief #46. Retrieved from http://www.brookings.edu/~/media/research/files/papers/2011/8/10%20strengthen%20marriage%20wilcox%20cherlin/0810_strengthen_marriage_wilcox_cherlin.pdf.

Wilcox, W. Bradford, Cherlin, Andrew J., Uecker, Jeremy E., & Messel, Matthew. (2011). "No Money, No Honey, No Church: The Deinstitutionalization of Religious Life Among the White Working Class"
Working Paper, Forthcoming in *Research in the Sociology of Work.* Retrieved from http://www.virginia.edu/sociology/publications/Wilcox_Religion_WorkingPaper.pdf.

Wilson, Barbara. (2015). The Five Levels of Intimacy. Retrieved from http://powertochange.com/familylife/articles/sex-romance/the-five-levels-of-intimacy.

Wright, N. T. (2010). *After You Believe: Why Christian Character Matters.* HarperCollins Publishers.

White, Steve & White, Terri. Koinonia. Lesson Nineteen: Finding Your Mate Retrieved from www.koinonia-all.org/finding-your-mate.html.

Whitehead, Evelyn Eaton & Whitehead, James D. (1992). *Christian Life Patterns: The Psychological Challenges and Religious Invitations of Adult Life.* New York, NY: The Crossroad Publishing Company.

Wynne, L.C. & Wynne, A. R. (1986). The quest for intimacy. *Journal of Marital and Family Therapy, 12*(4), 383-394.

Young, Edward J. (1972). The Book of Isaiah, 3 (pp. 199-201). Grand Rapids, MI: William B. Eerdmans, Grand Rapids, MI.

Amato, P. & Booth, A. (1997). A Generation At Risk. Growing Up in an Era of Family Upheaval. Cambridge, MA: Harvard University Press

Axinn, W.G. & Thornton, A. (1992). The relationship between cohabitation and divorce: Selectivity or casual influence? Demography, 29, 357-374.

Baker, Maureen & Elizabethe, Vivienne. (2013).Tying the Knot: The impact of formalization after long-term cohabitation, Department of Sociology, Journal of Family Studies 19(3): 254–266.,University of Auckland, Auckland, New Zealand

Baldassare, Mark & Feller, Susan (2009). Cultural variation in Personal Space: Theories, Methods, and Evidence, Ethos pp. 481-503.

Barna Group. (2009). New Marriage and Divorce Statistics Released. Retrieved from https://www.barna.org/barna-update/article/15-familykids/42-new-marriage-and-divorce-statistics-released#.VRf-QuFRK5R.

Barth, Markus. (1960). Commentary on Ephesians 4-6. Garden City, NY: Doubleday and Company, Inc.
ISBN 0-385-0837-9

BBC, Science: Human body & Mind, The Science of Flirting. (2014, September 17). Retrieved from http://www.bbc.co.uk/science/hottopics/love/flirting.shtm.

Boisvert, Jean Marie & Landouceur, Robert & Beaudry, Madeline & Freeston, Mark H. & Turgeon, Lyse & Tardif, Chantal & Roussy, Alain & Loranger, Michael, (1995). Perceoption of marital problems and their prevention by Qubeck young adults. Journal of Genetic Psychology (156)1, pp33-44.

Bringle, Robert G. & Winnick, Terri, & Rydell, Robert J. (2013) The Prevalence and Nature of Unrequited Love SAGE Open April-June 2013: 1–15.

Berkowitz, M. (2002). The science of character education. In W. Damon (Ed.), Bringing in a new era in character education (43-63). Stanford, CA: Hoover Institute Press.

Bible Study on Character – Integrity. Retrieved from http://www. swapmeetdave.com/Bible/Integrity.htm.

Bible Study, Finding the Right Mate. Retrieved from http:// kentcrockett.com/biblestudies/rightmate.htm.

The Biblical Perspective on Character Development. Retrieved from http://my.cbn.com/livingbythebook/display.php?topicid=1062& id=56&val=296.

Brooks, Carol. (2002) The Bible and Premarital Sex. Retrieved from http://www.inplainsite.org/html/premarital_sex_and_the_bible. html#PreMar-13.

Burriss, Robert. (2014, July 24). Human Mate Choice as the Psychologists See It. Retrieved from http://www.lascap.de/Downloads/Human%20mate%20 choice%20as%20the%20psychologist%20views%20it.pdf.

Browne, Angela & Finkelhor, David (1986). Impact of child sexual abuse: A review of the research. Psychological bulletin, (99)1, p 66, American Psychological Association.

Chandra, Anjani & Mosher, William D. & Copen, Casey & Sionean, Catlainn. (2011) Sexual Behavior, Sexual Attraction, and Sexual Identity in the United States: Data From the 2006–2008 National Survey of Family Growth National Health Statistics Report Number 36, March 3, 2011

Chapman, Alan. (2006-2013). Erikson's psychosocial development theory. Retrieved from http://www.businessballs.com/erik_ erikson_psychosocial_theory.htm

Chapman, Gary. (1995). The Five Love Languages: How to Express Heartfelt Commitment to Your Mate.
Chicago, IL: Northfield Publishing. ISBN 1-881273-15-6

Cheddie, Denver. (2008). Does God have a spouse prepared for everyone? Retrieved from http://www.bibleissues.org/spouse1. html.

Clancy, Tom. (1988). The Cardinal in the Kremlin, Berkley, CA: G.P. Putnam's Sons.

Cunningham, William R. (1999). The Christian Marriage Part 1: The Definition. Retrieved from http://www.pursuingthetruth. org/studies/files/marriage2.htm.

Cunningham, William R. (2000, March). The Christian Marriage Series Part 2: Finding Your Mate, Revision 1. Retrieved from http://www.pursuingthetruth.org/studies/files/marriage2.htm.

Diamond. (2015, February 7). Retrieved from https://en.wikipedia. org/wiki/Diamond.

Dobbins, Richard, D. (2011). Winning The Battle For Your Marriage. Retrieved from http://www.drdobbins.com/ guidelines-for-great-living/articles/winning-the-battle-for-your-marriage/.

Dawson, Patsy Rae. (1996). Male and Female: God's Genius! Retrieved from http://patsyraedawson.com/?page_id=231.

Dawson, Patsy Rae. (1997). Safe Sex: What They Don't Tell You. Retrieved from http://patsyraedawson.com/?page_id=962.

Dawson, Patsy Rae. (2011-2015). Why God's People Make the Best Lovers. Retrieved from http://patsyraedawson.com/?page_id=997.

Deffinbaugh, Bob. (2009, February 2). The Way of the Wise: Studies in the Book of Proverbs: The Qualities of a Godly Mate: Retrieved from http://bible.org/seriespage/qualities-godly-mate.

Demyan, Amy L. (2005). Gender, Gender Role Adherence, and Self Esteem in Long Term Mate Selection Preferences Among College Students (pp. 7-29). College of Arts and Sciences of Ohio University.

Diem, Melissa. (n.d.). 7 Ways to Know He is Marriage Material. Retrieved from http://love.allwomenstalk.com/ways-to-know-he-is-marriage-material/.

Dobbins, Richard D. (2011). Winning the Battle for Your Marriage. Retrieved from http://www.drdobbins.com/ guidelines-for-great-living/articles/winning-the-battle-for-your-marriage/.

Doris, John M. (2002). Lack of Character: Personality and Moral Behavior, Cambridge University Press Cambridge, UK.

Driscoll, Mark. (n.d.). Sex, a Study of the Good Bits from Song of Solomon. Retrieved from http://www.cerm.info/documents/mark_driscoll_sex_sermon.html.

Dunn, Ryan L. & Fine, Mark A. & Kurdek, Lawrence A. (1992). Premarital Relationshipsadjustment and its relations to religiosity and sexual involvement. Journal of Psychology and Theology, (20)4, 356-366.

Edersheim, Alfred E. (1883). Life and times of Jesus the Messiah: New Updated Edition (1893). Hendrickson Pub.

Edwards, Jane, (2011). Music Therapy and Parent-Infant Bonding. Oxford University Press INC, NY.

Egan, Gerard. (2006). Egan, Gerard (1994). The Skilled Helper: A Problem Management approach to Helping: 7th edition. Brooks/Cole Publishing Company. Pacific Grove California.

Emerge Ministries. (n.d.). Foundations of Marital Therapy, p. 10.

Erber, Ralph & Erber, Maureen Wang. (2011). Intimate Relationships, Issues, Theories, and Research. Boston, Pearson Education Inc.

Erikson's Stages of Psychosocial Development. (2015, February 5). Retrieved from http://en.wikipedia.org/wiki/Erikson%27s_stages_of_psychosocial_development.

Eyrich, Howard A. (1978). Three to Get Ready: A Premarital Counseling Manual. Grand Rapids, Michigan: Baker Book House Company.

Fagan, Patrick. (2010). The culture of monogamy vs the culture of polyamory. Retrieved from http://www.cpportal.org/k/news/view/434397/383320/the-culture-of-monogamy-vs-the-culture-of-polyamory.html.

Fagan, Patrick F. (2007). Virgins Make the Best Valentines. Retrieved from http://www.heritage.org/research/commentary/2007/02/virgins-make-the-best-valentines

Fehr, Beverly (1987). In Moss, B.F. & Schwebel, A.I. (1993). Defining Intimacy in Romantic Relationships, Family Relations, 42, 31-37.

Feldhahn, Shaunti (2004). For Women Only. Sisters, Oregon: Multnomah Publishers INC.

Feldhahn, Shaunti (2006). For Men Only. Sisters, Oregon: Multnomah Publishers INC.

Finkelhor, David (1990). Early and long-term effects of child sexual abuse: An update. Professional Psychology: Research and Practice, Volume 21 Issue 5 Pages 325 American Psychological Association.

Finkelhor, David & Hotaling, Gerald & Lewis, I.A & Smith, Christine (1990). Child abuse & neglect: Sexual abuse in a national survey of adult men and women: Prevalence, characteristics, and risk factors. Child Abuse & Neglect, Volume 14, Issue 1, Pages 19-28

First Things First, What You Should Know About Living Together. (2014, August). Retrieved from http://firstthings.org/what-you-should-know-about-living-together.

Firo-B Progfile Diagram. (2008, April 17). Retrieved from http://www.mdshongkong.com/documents/FIRO-B_Profile.pdf.

Fitzpatrick, Mary Ann. (1988). Between husbands and wives. Newbury Park: Sage.

Flemming, J.S. (2006). Piaget, Kohlberg, Gilligan, and Others on Moral Development. Retrieved from http://swppr.org/Textbook/Ch%207%20Morality.pdf

Fletcher, Elizabeth (2006). Money and Marriage in the Bible. Reterieved from http://www.womeninthebible.net/money_marriage.htm

Floyd, Frank J. & Wasner, Guenter H. (1994). Social Exchange, Equity, and Commitment: structural equation Modeling of Dating Relationships, Journal of Family Psychology 8(1): 55-73.

Follette, Victoria M. & Polusny, Melissa & Bechtel, Anne E. & Naugle, Amy E. (1996). Cumlative Trauma: The Impact of Child Sexual Abuse, Adult Sexual Assault, and Spouse Abuse, Journal of Traumatic Stress, 9(1).

Foust, Michael (2008) 'Living together' before marriage a statistical risk, retrieved from http://www.bpnews.net/27699, March 26, 2008

Fowler, James W. (1981). Stages of Faith, New York, New York: Harper Collins Publishers.

Fox, Kate. (2016). Social Issues Research Centre Guide to Flirting: What social science can tell you about flirting and how to do it. Retrieved from http://www.sirc.org/publik/flirt.pdf.

Gerrard, Meg & Breda, Cheri & Gibbons, Frederick X. (1990). Gender effects in Couples Sexual Decision Makin and Contraceptive Use, Journal of Applied Psychology 20(6): 449-464.

Gilligan, Carol. (1982). In a Different Voice: Psychological Theory and Women's Development. Cambridge, MA: Harvard University Press.

Givertz, Michelle. (2011, June 22). The Secret to Finding Your "Perfect" Mate, Know Thyself, The Interpersonal Explorer. Retrieved from http://www.psychologytoday.com/blog/the-interpersonal-explorer/201106/the-secret-finding-your-perfect-mate.

Glueck, Nelson. (1967). Hesed in the Bible. Cincinnati, OH: Hebrew Union College Press.

Gordon, Lori H. (1969). Intimacy: The Art of Relationships: How relationships are sabotaged by hidden Expectations. Retrieved from http://psychologytoday.com/articles/199309/intimacy-the-art-relationships? page=3.

Gottman, John M. (1994). What predicts divorce?: The relationship between marital processes and marital outcomes. Hillsdale, NJ: Lawrence Erlbaum.

Grover, K.J., Russell, C.S., Schumm, W.R., & Paff-Bergen, L.A. (1985). Mate Selection Processes and Marital Satisfaction. Family Relations, 34, 383-386.

Hadjistavropoulos & Genest. (1994).The underestimation of the role of physical attractiveness in dating preferences: Ignorance or taboo? Canadian Journal of Behavioral Science, (26)2 pp298-318.

Harley, Willard F., Jr. (1986). His Needs, Her Needs: Building an Affair-Proof Marriage. Old Tappan, NJ: Fleming H. Revell.

Hatfield, E. (1995). Self-esteem and passionate love relationships. In G. G. Brannigan & M. R. Merrens (Eds.), The social psychologists: Research and adventures (pp. 129-144). New York: McGraw-Hill.

Henry, Jermaine, Helm Jr., Herbert W. & Cruz, Natasha. (2013). Mate Selection: Gender and Generational Differences, North American Journal of Psychology, 15, No. 1, pp. 63-70.

Hodges-Simeon, Carolyn R. & Gaulin, Steven J.C. & Puts David A. (2011). Voice Correlates of Mating Success in Men: Examining "Contests" versus "Mate Choice" Modes of Sexual Selection. Archive of Sexual Behavior (40) pp 551-557.

Hoffman, Terry. (May 2004). Dating Disasters and Faulty Mate Selection: There Is a Better Way!
Retrieved from http://www.ucg.org/relationships/dating-disasters-and-faulty-mate-selection-there-better-way/.

Homiak, Marcia. (2003). Moral Character. Stanford Encyclopedia of Philosophy. Retrieved from http://philosophy.csusb.edu/~tmoody/Moral%20Character.htm.

Hurt, Bruce. (2013). The Covenant Between Jonathan and David. Retrieved from http://preceptaustin.org/covenant_the_exchanging_of_robes.htm.

Intimate Relationship. (2015). Retrieved from http://en.wikipedia.org/wiki/Intimate_relationship.

Janus, S. S. & Janus, C.C. (1993). The Janus Report on Human Sexuality. New York: Wiley Publishers.

Jean Piaget, (2015, February 13). Retrieved from https://en.wikipedia.org/wiki/Jean_Piaget.

Joy, Donald M. (1985). Bonding: Relationships in the Image of God. Nappanee, IN: Evangel Publishing House.

Joy, Donald M. (1986). Re-Bonding: Preventing and Restoring Damaged Relationships. Dallas, TX: Word Publishing.

Joy, Donald M., Ed. (1983). Moral Development Foundations: Judeo-Christian Alternatives to Piaget/Kohlberg. Nashville, TN: Abingdon Press.

Kelly, E.L. & Conley, J.J. (1987). Personality and compatibility: A perspective analysis of marital stability and marital satisfaction. Journal of Personality and Social Psychology, 58, 27-40.

Kelly, Maura & Dutton, Judy. (2009, July 14). Four Flirting Fun Facts--With Research to Back Them Up!
Retrieved from http://www.marieclaire.com/sex-love/a3349/science-flirting-sex-body-language/.

Kenrick, D.T. & Neuberg, S.L. & Zierk, k. l. & Krone s, J. M., (1994). Evolution and social cognition: Contrast effects as a function of sex, dominance and physical attractiveness. Personality and Social Psychology, (20)2, pp 210-217.

Kittle, Gerhard & Friedrich, Gerhard. (1972). Theological Dictionary of the New Testament, Vol 8, 39-46. Grand Rapids, MI: William B. Eerdmans Publishing Company.

Kittle, Gerhard & Friedrich, Gerhard. (1972). Theological Dictionary of the New Testament Vol 6, 562-566. Grand Rapids, MI: William B. Eerdmans Publishing Company.

Kurdek, I.A. (1993). Predicting Marital Dissolution: A 5-year Prospective Longitudinal study of Newlywed Couples. Journal of Personality and Social Psychology, 64, 221-242.

Kohlberg's Moral Stages. Retrieved from http://www.haverford.edu/psych/ddavis/p109g/kohlberg.stages.html.

Kohlberg's Theory of Moral Development. (2012, January 20). Retrieved from http://www.psychologynoteshq.com/kohlbergs theory/.

Kowalski, Robin M. (1993). Interpreting behaviors in mixed gender encounters: Effects of social anxiety and gender. Journal of Social and Clinical Psychology, (12)3, 239-247.

Larson, A.S. & Olson, D.H. (1989). Prediction Marital Satisfaction using PREPARE: A replication study. Journal of Marital and Family Therapy, 15, 3, 311-322.

Lawrence Kohlberg. Retrieved from https://en.wikipedia.org/wiki/Lawrence_Kohlberg.

Levinger, G., & Snoek, D. (1972). Attraction in relationship: A new look at interpersonal attraction. Morristown, NJ: General Learning Press.

Lichi, Donald. (1995). Emerge Ministries, Ashland Theological Seminary Class lectures.

Livingston, G. Herbert. (1974). The Pentateuch in its Cultural Environment. Grand Rapids, MI: Baker Bookhouse.

Malchiodi, Cathy A. (1998). Understanding Children's Drawings (pp. 132-160). NY, NY: The Gilford Press.

Male Mind Survey Challenges Popular Attitudes, AskMen. Retrieved from http://www.divinecaroline.com/22078/79206-male-mind-survey-challenges-popular.

Maliki, Agnes Ebi, (2009). Determinants of Mate Selection Choice among University Students in South-South Zone of Nigeria. EDO Journal of Counseling, 2, No. 2. Retrieved from http://www.ajol.info/index.php/ejc/article/viewFile/60856/49066/

Markman, Howard J., Stanley, Scott M. & Blumberg, Susan L. (2001). Fighting for Your Marriage. San Jose, CA: Josey-Bass: A Wiley Imprint.

Maslow's Hierarchy of Needs. (2014, December 24). Retrieved from http://en.wikipedia.org/wiki/Maslow's_hierarchy_of_needs

McAllister, Dawson. (1997). What are the Biblical guidelines for dating relationships? Retrieved from www.christiananswers.net/q-dml/dml-y006.html.

McCahill, T & Meyer, L.C. & Fischman, A. (1979) The Aftermath of Rape, Lexington Books.

McIlhaney Joe S., MD & McKissic-Bush, Freda MD. (2008). Hooked: New Science on How Casual Sex is Affecting Our Children. Chicago, IL: Norfield Publishing.

Miller, Jean Baker. (1976). Toward a Psychology of Women. 2nd Ed. Boston, MA: Beacon Press.

McCroskey, James C. & McCain, Thomas A. (1974). The measurement of interpersonal attraction.

Speech Monographs, 41(3), 261-266. Retrieved from http://www.jamescmccroskey.com/publications/57.htm.

McDowell, Josh & Lewis, Paul. (1980). Givers, Takers, and Other Kinds of Lovers. Wheaton, IL: Tyndale House Publishers.

Monsour, Michael. (2013). Journal of social and personal relationships: Meanings of Intimacy in Cross- and Same-Sex Friendships. Retrieved from http://spr.sagepub.com/content/9/2/277.short).

Moral Development. Retrieved from http://swppr.org/Textbook/Ch%207%20Morality.pdf.

Morris, Desmond. (1967). The Naked Ape; A Zoologist's Study of the Human Animal. New York, NY: McGraw-Hill.

Morris, Grantley. (n.d.). When is Sex Before Marriage Acceptable? Premarital Sex Re-examined. Retrieved from http://www.net-burst.net/singles/premarital.htm.

Moss, B.F. & Schwebel, A.I. (1993). Defining Intimacy in Romantic Relationships, Family Relations, 42, 31-37.

Motivation and mate-seeking. (2010, December 14). Retrieved from http://en.wikiversity.org/wiki/Motivation_and_emotion/Textbook/Motivation/Mate-seeking_behaviour. These concepts are part of the Motivation and emotion textbook.

Murashko, Alex. (2014, May 16). Author Debunks Myths About Divorce Rates, Including of Churchgoers

Shaunti Feldhahn: The Good News About Marriage, retrieved from http://www.christianpost.com/news/author-debunks-myths-about-divorce-rates-including-of-churchgoers-119843/.

Murphy, Ed. (2003). The Handbook on Spiritual Warfare. Nashville, TN: Thomas Nelson.

Mullen, P.E. & Martina, J.L. & Andersona, J.C. & Romansa, S.E. & Herbisona, G.P. (1996). Child Abuse & Neglect. (20)1,Pp 7–21

Newcomb, M.D. & Bentler, P.M. (1981). Marital breakdown. In S. Duck & R. Gilmour (Eds.). Personal Relationships: vol. 3. Personal Relationships in Disorder (pp. 57-94). New York: Academic Press.

Nichols, William C. (1988). Marital Therapy: An Integrative Approach. New York, NY: The Gilford Press.

Nock, S.L. (1995). A Comparison of Marriage and Cohabiting Relationships. Journal of Family Issues, 16, 53-76.

Nucci, Larry. (1997). Moral Development and Character Formation. In Walberg, H. J. & Haertel, G. D. (1997). Psychology and educational practice (pp. 127-157). Berkeley: MacCarchan. Retrieved from http://tigger.uic.edu/~lnucci/MoralEd/articles/nuccimoraldev.html.

Oswalt, John. (1977). History of Israel, Asbury Theological Seminary Lecture.

Pankau, Lisa. (2010, October 2). Beyond Seduction: Loving without Limits. Retrieved from http://beyondseductionbook.com/content/science-love-arthur-arun.

Penner, Clifford L & Penner, Joyce J. (1981). A Guide to Sexual Fulfillment: The Gift of Sex. Dallas, TX: Word Publishing.

Penner, Clifford L & Penner, Joyce J. (1994). Getting your Sex Life Off to a Great Start. Dallas, TX: Word Publishing.

Peterson, Christopher & Seigman, Martin E.P. (2004). Character strengths and Virtues: A Handbook and Classification, Oxford University Press, N.Y., N.Y.

Peplau, Letitia Anne & Hill Charles T. & Rubin, Zick 1993. Sex role attitudes in dating and marriage: A 15 year follow-up of the Boston couples study. Journal of Social Issues, 49)3, pp31-52.

Pfleiderer, Joanne (2008).Teens Have Positive But Changing Views of Marriage. Retrieved from http://www.mathematica-mpr.com/Press%20Releases/teensviewsmarriage11-08.asp

Pierce, Tyra & Hewitt, Jay, (1993). Gender differences in sexualized perceptions of others. Perceptual and Motor Skills, (78) pp 1168-1170.

Poluany, Melissa A. & Follette, Victoria M. (1995). Long-term correlates of child sexual abuse: Theory and review of the empirical literature. Applied and Preventive Psychology (4)3. Pp 143–166.

Prince, Derek (2006). How to Expel Demons, Break Curses and Release Blessings Bloomington, MN: Chosen Books.

RBC Ministries. Choosing a Marriage Partner. Section 13B, Contemporary Social Issues. Retrieved from http://www.inplainsite.org/html/choosing_a_marriage_partner

Rudd, Steve. The Three Stage ritual of Bible Marriages retrieved from http://www.bible.ca/marriage/ancient-jewish-three-stage-weddings-and-marriage-customs-ceremony-in-the-bible.htm

Schaefer, Charles E. & Drews, Athena A. (2014). The Therapeutic Powers of Play. Hoboken, NJ: John Wiley and Sons, Inc.

Scharff, David E. & Scharff, Jill Savege. (1991). Object Relations Couple Therapy. Northvale, NJ: Jason Aronson Inc.

Scherer, Cynthia Athina Kemp. (2015). The Core Issue: Intimacy. Retrieved from http://www.desert-alchemy.com/txt/intimacy.html.

Schutz, William C. (1958). FIRO: A Three Dimensional Theory of Interpersonal Behavior. New York, NY: Holt, Rinehart, & Winston.

Science, flirting, sex, body language. (2009, July 14). Retrieved from http://www.marieclaire.com/sex-love/dating-blog/science-flirting-sex-body-language.

Segal, Jeanne & Smith, Melinda, (2010). Playful Communication Skills: Using Laughter and Play in Relationships. Retrieved from http://www.helpguide.org/mental/eq8_conflict_resolution.htm

Shaver, Phillip R. & Hazan, Cindy (1988) A Biased Overview of the study of Love. Journal of Social and Personal Relationships. (5) pp 473-501.

Siegel, Judith (1991). Analysis of Projective Identification: an Object Relations approach to Marital Treatment. Clinicla Social Work Journal (19)1, pp71-81.

Silverman, Amy B. & Rheinherz, Helen Z. & Giaconia, Rose M. (1996). The long-term sequelae of child and adolescent abuse: A longitudinal community study. Child Abuse & Neglect (20)8. August 1996, Pages 709–723

Smicklas, Monica. (1995). Cohabitation. Unpublished paper for the Master of Arts in Pastoral Counseling at Ashland Theological Seminary.

Sol, Mateo (2016).(Loner Wolf) Body Language: Personal Space retrieved from http://lonerwolf.com/body-language-personal-space/ Last updated 2016

Sorenson, Kelly A. & Russell, Shauna M. & Harkness, Daniel J. & Harvey, John H. (1993). Account-Making, Confiding, and Coping with the Ending of a Close Relationship. Journal of Social Behavior and Personality, (8)1 pp73-86.

Sprecher, Susan, & Duck, Steve, (1994). Sweet Talk: The importance of perceived communication for romantic and friendship attraction experienced during a get acquainted date. Personality and Social Psychology Buletin, (20)4, pp 391-400.

Staples, Jason A. (2010). Dowry and Bride Price Are Not the Same Thing. 05 May Ethics, Sexuality & Family, Sociology retrieved from http://www.jasonstaples.com/sociology/dowry-and-bride-price-are-not-the-same-thing.

Stapleton, Jean & Bright, Richard. (1976). Equal Marriage. Nashville, TN: Abingdon Press.

Steed, Levita & McLand, Kelly. (1982). In Moss, B.F. & Schwebel, A.I. (1993). Defining Intimacy in Romantic Relationships. Family Relations, 42, 31-37.

Stenberg, R.J. (1986). A Triangular Theory of Love, Psychological Review, 93, 119-135.

Thomas, Caitlin. (2015, February 13). Society Commentary, 5 Facts About Cohabitation You May Not Know. Retrieved from http://dailysignal.com/2015/02/13/5-facts-cohabitation-may-not-know/?utm_source=facebook&utm_medium=social&utm_campaign=thf02132015.

Tissier, L.L. (1993). The Pastoral Relationship Between Church and Co-habitees. Theology, 96, 468-476.

Thomas, Kenneth and Kilmann, Ralph (1978). Comparison of Four Instruments Measuring Conflict Behavior. Psychological Reports.(42) pp 1139-1142.

Thompson, David. (1979). God in the Box. Sermon at Asbury Theological Seminary.

Thomson, E. & Colella, U. (1992). Cohabitation and Marital Stability: Quality or Commitment? Journal of Marriage and the Family, 54, 259-267.

Townsend, John Marshall & Roberts, Lawrence W. (1992). Gender Differences in Mate Preference Among Law Students: Divergence and Convergence of Criteria. The Journal of Psychology, 127(5), 507-528.

Trobish, Walter. (1971). I Married You. San Francisco, CA: Harper and Row Publishers.

Trumbull, Henry Clay. (1975). The Blood Covenant. Kirkwood, MO: Impact Books.

Townsend, John Marshall & Roberts, Lawrence W. (1993). Gender differences in mate preference among law students: Divergence and convergence of criteria. Journal of Psychology, (127)5, pp507-528.

United Church of God. (2010-2015). Bible Study Guides: Lesson: Preparing for Marriage: Before You Say "I Do." Retrieved from http://www.freebiblestudyguides.org/bible-answers/preparing-for-marriage-before-you-say-i-do.htm.

United Church of God. (2002, December 7). Choosing a Mate. Retrieved from http://www.ucg.org/sermon/choosing-mate/.

Unknown, (2014, September 17). BBC, Science: Human body & Mind, The Science of Flirting. Retrieved from http://www.bbc.co.uk/science/hottopics/love/flirting.shtml

Unknown, Bible Study on Character – Integrity. Retrieved from http://www.swapmeetdave.com/Bible/Integrity.htm

United Church of God, (2010-2015). Bible Study Guides: Lesson: Preparing for Marriage: Before You Say "I Do". Retrieved from http://www.freebiblestudyguides.org/bible-answers/preparing-for-marriage-before-you-say-i-do.htm

Unknown, DivineCaroline, Male Mind Survery Challenges Popular Attitudes, AskMen. Retrieved from http://www.divinecaroline.com/22078/79206-male-mind-survey-challenges-popular

Vessels, G., & Huitt, W. (2010, March 8). Moral and Character Development. Presented at the National Youth at Risk Conference, Savannah, GA. Retrieved [date]. Retrieved from http://chiron.valdosta.edu/whuitt/brilstar/chapters/chardev.doc

Vessels, G. (1998). Character and community development: A school planning and teacher training handbook. Westport, CT: Praeger Publishers.

Vessels, G., & Boyd, S. (1996). Public and constitutional support for character education. NASSP Bulletin, 80(579), 55-63.

Vogler, Carolyn. 1998) Money in the household: some underlying issues of power. The Sociological Review (46)4, pp. 687–713.

Waite, L. & Gallagher, M. (2000). The Case for Marriage: Why Married People Are Happier, Healthier, and Better Off Financially. New York: Doubleday.

Wheat, Ed & Wheat, Gaye. (1977). Intended for Pleasure: Sex Technique and Sex Fulfillment in Christian Marriage. Old Tappan, NJ: Fleming H. Revel Company.

Wikibooks, Relationships/How Men Select Women. (2014, June 24). Retrieved from http://en.wikibooks.org/wiki/Relationships/How_Men_Select_Women.

Wikibooks, Relationships/How Women Select Men. (2014, September 30). Retrieved from http://en.wikibooks.org/wiki/Relationships/How_Women_Select_Men.

Wilcox, W. Bradford and Andrew J. Cherlin. 2011. "The Marginalization of Marriage in Middle America". Center on Children and Families at Brookings Brief #46. Retrieved from http://www.brookings.edu/~/media/research/files/papers/2011/8/10%20strengthen%20marriage%20wilcox%20cherlin/0810_strengthen_marriage_wilcox_cherlin.pdf

Wilcox, W. Bradford, Andrew J. Cherlin, Jeremy E. Uecker, Matthew Messel. 2011. "No Money, No Honey, No Church: The Deinstitutionalization of Religious Life Among the White Working Class"
Working Paper, Forthcoming in Research in the Sociology of Work. Retrieved from http://www.virginia.edu/sociology/publications/Wilcox_Religion_WorkingPaper.pdf

Wilson, Barbara. (2015). The Five Levels of Intimacy. Retrieved from http://powertochange.com/familylife/articles/sex-romance/the-five-levels-of-intimacy

Wright, N. T. (2010). After You Believe: Why Christian Character Matters. HarperCollins Publishers.

White, Steve & White, Terri, Koinonia. Lesson Nineteen: Finding Your Mate Retrieved from www.koinonia-all.org/finding-your-mate.html.

Whitehead, Evelyn Eaton & Whitehead, James D. (1992). Christian Life Patterns: The Psychological Challenges and Religious Invitations of Adult Life. New York, NY: The Crossroad Publishing Company.

Wynne, L.C. & Wynne, A. R. (1986) The quest for intimacy. Journal of Marital and Family Therapy, (12)4, pp383-394.

Young, Edward J. (1972). The Book of Isaiah vol 3 William B. Eerdmans, Grand Rapids, MI. pp199-201

CPSIA information can be obtained
at www.ICGtesting.com
Printed in the USA
LVHW080838260122
709348LV00003B/176